Emotional Intelligence at Work

Emotional intelligence has been a very popular concept since it was made known to the general public in 1995. However, it was under severe criticism among scientific researchers, and a lot of them did not believe that it should be accepted by scientists as true knowledge.

The author of this book, who is one of the pioneers in this topic, spent 18 years studying this concept. Together with other researchers, they gradually changed the conclusions of early researchers. Using rigorous scientific standards, this research team demonstrated that emotional intelligence is an intelligence dimension that has a significant impact on various life outcomes such as life satisfaction and job performance. They developed a testable theoretical framework for emotional intelligence in the workplace and attempted to show that the trainability of emotional intelligence is greater than that of the traditional intelligence concept.

The book looks at not only the scientific reports but also all of the stories behind some of the rigorous scientific studies in the author's 18-year journey. The choice of research designs and the way the designs are suited to provide scientific evidence to demonstrate the validity of emotional intelligence are also described. Through this book, the process of scientific inquiry and important issues concerning the concept of emotional intelligence are revealed in detail by vivid stories and rigorous scientific reports.

Chi-Sum WONG is a professor in the Department of Management of the Chinese University of Hong Kong. He received his PhD from the University of Purdue. His major research areas include emotional intelligence, career guidance, localization of human resources in China, Chinese management concepts, and research methodology.

Emotional Intelligence at Work

18-year journey of a researcher

Chi-Sum WONG

Routledge
Taylor & Francis Group

LONDON AND NEW YORK

First published 2016
by Routledge

2 Park Square, Milton Park, Abingdon, Oxfordshire OX14 4RN

52 Vanderbilt Avenue, New York, NY 10017

*Routledge is an imprint of the Taylor & Francis Group,
an informa business*

First issued in paperback 2019

British Library Cataloguing in Publication Data
A catalogue record for this book is available from the
British Library

Library of Congress Cataloging-in-Publication Data
Wong, Chi-sum.
Emotional intelligence at work : 18-year journey of a researcher /
  Chi-sum Wong.
    pages cm
  1. Psychology, Industrial.   2. Emotional intelligence.   I. Title.
  HF5548.8.W63 2015
  158.7—dc23
  2015014030

ISBN: 978-0-415-66151-5 (hbk)
ISBN: 978-0-367-35038-3 (pbk)

Typeset in Galliard
by Apex CoVantage, LLC

Contents

Figures

Tables

Preface

This book is a record of my personal experiences and the research studies that resulted from my investigation of the emotional intelligence (EI) construct in the past 18 years since 1996. At the beginning, I did not expect I would spend so much time and effort on this line of research. I intended to conduct only one or two studies to demonstrate the effect of EI on job outcomes. It turned out, however, that I did quite a number of studies, and the research papers were published in management, education, and psychology journals and in books with the specific theme of emotions and Chinese organizational behavior.

EI is a very appealing concept to ordinary people. We all have emotions, and it is almost common sense to believe that there are advantages in our lives if we can handle emotional issues well. However, common sense is only a necessary condition for social science. Rigorous scientific research requires clear definitions of concepts and systematic empirical evidence collected and analyzed using state-of-the-art methodology. My journey of studying EI is quite special because EI had gained a lot of attention in the media before rigorous scientific discussion and evidence had accumulated. I hope this book will make readers, especially those who are interested in the EI concept, know that while the concept is appealing, we should not exaggerate our understanding of EI and the role of EI in our lives.

On top of introducing the scientific research studies on EI that I and my co-authors conducted in the past 18 years, another objective of this book is to uncover the rationale and process behind each research study. Scientific research methods and techniques can be trained systematically, and this is an important part of the content of graduate programs. However, a lot of elements in scientific research, such as discovery of topics, difficulties and unexpected issues during data collection, journal submission and review processes, and preparation for rejections, are usually learned in informal ways. Although my experiences shared in this book are certainly not comprehensive, I hope they can have some value to graduate students and junior faculty who would like to contribute to the body of scientific knowledge. For those who are also interested in the EI concept, I hope they can make a greater contribution in this line of investigation in the future. For those who may not want to build a career in scientific discovery, I hope they will know more about the work of social scientists.

From the materials reported in this book, I also hope readers will realize that most of our scientific discoveries progress slowly and step by step. I and my co-authors have moved toward more understanding of the EI concept after 18 years of investigation. However, the advancement is by no means a very big step. This is normal in building up scientific knowledge. A responsible scientist would draw conclusions only with sufficient evidence based on the state-of-the-art research methodology and techniques. In social science, opportunities to conduct studies for some research questions may not happen so easily. A lot of preparations have to be made, and there is no guarantee that the research setting can fulfill all our requirements. We seldom have shortcuts. All we can do is to try again and again with patience. I hope readers can have a greater appreciation for the knowledge that is accumulated through the hard work of scientists.

For readers with formal training in research methodology in management, psychology, education, or related areas, the technical parts of the studies reported should be straightforward. For readers in other areas or readers who have little training in scientific research, I hope Chapter 1 provides the necessary background to somehow master the technical parts of the studies. Although it is impossible to understand all the details, I think conscientious readers can probably comprehend the meanings of the technical analyses. From Chapter 2 to the Appendix, the chapters represent various research questions that we have attempted to gather empirical evidence to answer. I hope readers, regardless of their previous training, will realize how scientific studies are conducted in my area of expertise. To be a little bit greedy, I hope all readers could also take some interest in the material.

Finally, I want to thank my co-authors of the research studies reprinted in this book and the publishers who granted us the reprint permission. Without them, I would not have conducted those studies, and I would not be able to reprint them here. I particularly want to thank Ms. Yongling Lam, associate editor at Routledge (in economics, finance, and business management). Without her invitation, I would not have imagined publishing this book.

Chi-Sum WONG
March 14, 2015

1 Basic concepts of scientific research

This book is mainly a collection of research studies on emotional intelligence that I and my colleagues have conducted in the past. In conducting the research projects, we followed the scientific standards in our research area – organizational behavior and human resource management. To facilitate the reading of the research papers, some understanding of the scientific approach and related methods is necessary. I am not trying to make this chapter a comprehensive introduction to the scientific approach and methods in this area. In fact, it is out of the scope of one chapter, and some ideas introduced in this chapter may still be debatable among scientists. What I want to introduce are some basic concepts in science and quantitative research that are used and reported in the papers. I will present some of my understandings of science and the scientific method that have been very useful to me. I regard these understandings as basic, and whenever I have doubts, I can go back to the basics and make sure that I am on the right track in conducting the studies. I believe they should have some reference value for people who do not need to conduct scientific research projects as well.

Science and its assumptions

The first important understanding is about the nature of science, especially for social science. What is science? There may be a lot of answers to this question. Similar to other academic disciplines, we can regard science as a particular type of knowledge generated by some kind of predetermined methods. Many people think that science is about rational thinking and knowledge generated from systematic methods such as mathematical proofs and experiments. Some even think that science is the only type of knowledge that is objective and systematic and thus is the most important type of knowledge. All other types of knowledge, such as theology, literature, and history, have a certain amount of subjectivity and are thus not as good as scientific knowledge. Although my training is in social science, I think there is no need to overstate the role of science and the scientific method. To me, science is similar to other types of knowledge, but it specializes in describing the reality in a particular way.

What makes science different from other academic disciplines is the method it uses to describe phenomena that human beings encounter. The particular method that science uses to describe phenomena is related to its assumptions and purpose, which are not the same as for other academic disciplines. When I was a doctoral student, I needed to take several research methodology courses. Interestingly, even though we covered the topic of philosophy of science, very little discussion was about the assumptions of science. This created some difficulties when I tried to discuss with people from other academic disciplines. I gradually realized that in order to clarify the differences between science and other academic disciplines, at least two important assumptions of science have to be noted.

The first important assumption of science is that the phenomena encountered by human beings are real and objectively exist. While individuals may have different perceptions and understandings of the phenomena, we have to assume that the phenomena themselves are real and objective. This makes science different from some academic disciplines such as arts and literature. Arts and literature are about the expression of people's subjective thinking and feelings, and there is no need to assume the existence of real and objective phenomena.

The second assumption of science is that there are underlying rules or principles behind the phenomena that human beings encounter. For examples, there are principles governing how materials are attracted to each other in the physical world, and these principles are applicable to different types of materials; there are common reasons for why some employees are happier in their jobs, and these reasons are applicable to different types of companies. In academic disciplines such as theology or even history, there is no need to make this assumption.

Recognizing the two assumptions of science can make us understand why science is different from other academic disciplines. As other academic disciplines do not need to make these two assumptions, we should not compare the knowledge generated by them with science. We can also realize the scope and limitation of science. We will no longer believe science can provide answers to all questions, such as whether God exists or not. This is not a scientific question because before science can study a particular phenomenon, we have to assume the objective existence of that phenomenon first. So, whether God exists is an assumption instead of a scientific question. Similarly, a famous ancient Chinese philosopher once said that he had a dream, and in the dream he was a butterfly. After waking up, he wondered whether he was a man having a dream of being butterfly or was in fact a butterfly having a dream of being a man. Science definitely cannot provide an answer to this question because it is not in the scope of science.

With the above two assumptions, we can get an idea of what science and scientific knowledge are about. Science is the attempt to discover the underlying rules or principles behind the "real and objective" phenomena that human beings encounter. In other words, we are trying to describe the underlying rules or principles of the phenomena using languages that can be understood by human beings. The purpose of this description is to explain and predict the phenomena. Once we have a description of a particular phenomenon, we could systematically collect data from the "real and objective" phenomenon and see whether the data confirm our description. If the data do not confirm our description, we may need to revise our description because it is not an accurate representation of the reality. The advantage of scientific knowledge is that we can examine whether it is correct or not from the data collected from the "real and objective" phenomenon. In other words, there is a standard to check the validity of scientific knowledge, which is unique when compared to knowledge from other academic disciplines.

Scientific theories

In order to describe the underlying rules and principles of the phenomena, we have to work on variables. My scientific training is in the organizational behavior and human resource area, and so I will use this as an example. In my area of scientific knowledge, we are trying to discover the underlying rules and principles that can explain and predict the attitudes and behaviors of individual employees and work teams in the workplace. Variables refer to some characteristics of the objects (i.e., individual employees or work teams in my area) that differ among them. For example, age is a variable that differs among individual employees, and it may be one of the factors contributing to their differences in attitudes and behaviors in the workplace. Age is objective and easy to measure. As long as the employees are not telling lies, we can ask them directly, and the responses should accurately reflect their differences in this variable.

By specifying the relationships among variables, such as the impact of employees' age on their attitudes and behaviors, we can describe and explain phenomena such as why employees have different attitudes and behaviors. However, some variables are not as simply and directly measurable as age. For example, how can we describe differences in employee attitudes? Attitudes are too broad, and thus we need to make this variable more specific and focused. "Job satisfaction" is an example of such an attempt to make a variable clear and focused. In its simplest sense, it refers to the extent to which an employee is happy with his/her job. It certainly will vary among employees: some will be happier, and some will be less happy. It is an attitudinal variable but not directly observable or measurable. This variable needs some abstract thinking to define and conceptualize. It is created to help us to understand the phenomena, and so it is labeled as a concept or a construct.

To make it simple, science is using relationships among variables to describe phenomena so that we can explain and predict the phenomena. As explained above, some variables need abstract thinking to define and conceptualize. A more comprehensive system to describe the phenomena using relationships among variables is called a "scientific theory." This system includes at least (1) basic assumptions about the reality (e.g., the human nature of seeking happiness and avoiding pain), (2) clear definitions of variables (including abstract constructs such as job satisfaction), (3) relationships among variables and the reasons those relationships exist, and (4) situations where these assumptions and relationships will be valid. This definition of "theory" may be subject to debate because some scholars may include some other requirements for a scientific theory. However, most scholars will agree that the development and refinement of theory so that they can more accurately describe phenomena is the work of scientists.

Qualitative and quantitative research

In order to develop and refine scientific theories, we need to conduct empirical studies to test whether the theory accurately describes reality. Most of my training is about conducting empirical studies in the area of organizational behavior and human resource management. There are two important parts of conducting empirical studies. The first part is the development of testable hypotheses in terms of relationships among variables derived from existing theories, logical deduction, and direct observation of the phenomena. The second part is the systematic collection of data from the real world and testing of whether the expected relationships among variables exist or not.

In collecting data, there are two major approaches. The first approach usually involves very in-depth observations and understandings of the objects under investigation. Usually, it does not involve direct measurement of the variables, and so differences among objects are not represented by numbers, and the relationships among the variables are not tested with mathematical methods. Instead, through detailed understanding of the objects, it can be judged whether they are consistent with the principles prescribed by the theory. As this approach does not require tests by mathematical methods, we refer to this approach as "qualitative research."

The second approach is to systematically study a relatively large sample of objects. For each object, we measure the variables and represent them with numbers. After measuring the variables for all objects, we can examine the relationships among the variables by mathematical methods. We refer to this approach as "quantitative research." My training is mostly in the quantitative approach, and so most of the studies reported in this book utilize this approach. The most common way I used to collect data was by surveys. That is, I contacted the participants of the study and measured variables with questionnaires. Then I examined the expected relationships among the variables using various statistical techniques.

Reliability and validity of measurement

In conducting quantitative research, the first important issue concerns the accuracy of our measurement of variables. We need to have evidence showing that our measurement is reliable and valid, that is, that we are actually measuring what we want to measure, especially for those abstract constructs. For example, if we use several questions to measure job satisfaction and come up with a number representing the job satisfaction level of a particular employee by the average response to the questions, we need to show that the employee's responses are related to his/her actual job satisfaction level. That is, employees who get a high mean score should have a high job satisfaction level, and vice versa. In most of the research papers in my area, we need to report evidence of reliability, which represents the stability of responses to those questions. This is the minimum requirement. If the responses are not stable, we will not be sure what the final number represents.

One common indicator of reliability is internal consistency reliability (or coefficient alpha). It means that if we use several questions to ask about the same construct, the responses to these questions from the same employee should be similar. There is a specific mathematical formula to calculate this reliability coefficient, which ranges from 0 to 1; the closer to 1, the higher the estimated reliability. Other ways of showing reliability may be to ask the same questions again after a short period of time. For example, we might ask the same set of questions concerning job satisfaction again one week later. If the responses have changed greatly, it means the measurement may not be valid. This indicator is labeled as "test–retest reliability." Another possibility is to have multiple judges. For example, we can ask both the employees and at least one of their colleagues. If the two scores are measuring the same thing, they should be consistent. We call this reliability indicator "inter-rater reliability."

Reliability only means stability, but it does not guarantee that we are measuring what we intended to. Thus, reliability is only the minimum requirement for accuracy. The concept of validity refers directly to accuracy. Unfortunately, unlike reliability, we do not have one single indicator for validity. We usually need to examine the relationship between the scores that resulted from our measurement scale for a particular construct and other variables in order to gather evidence that the measurement is valid. For example, salary should be related to job satisfaction. If our measurement scale of job satisfaction cannot come up with scores that are related to salary, then the measurement may not be valid. Salary here is referred to as the "criterion variable." When we have multiple criterion variables and their relationships with our measurement scores are in the expected directions, we can be more confident that our measurement scores are in fact representing the variable we want to measure.

In demonstrating the validity of a measurement scale for a particular construct, we usually use various forms of criterion validity. The most rigorous way is the multi-trait multi-method approach. That is, for multiple constructs, we use more than one method to measure them. Scores from different methods but for the same construct should be highly related. This demonstrates convergent validity. Scores from the same method for different constructs should not be highly related. This demonstrates discriminant validity.

Studies using questionnaire surveys to collect data usually will ask several questions in order to measure one construct. As mentioned, if the questions are set adequately, questions intended to measure the same construct should have consistent answers. One standard statistical tool used to test the consistency of the questions on the same construct is factor analysis. In factor analysis, questions that have similar answers will form the same factor. Technically, we refer this as "loading on" the same factor by different items. Mathematically, loadings can range from –1 to +1. If the loading of a particular measurement item is 0, it means that this item has nothing to do with the factor. If the loading is closer to –1 or +1 that means that particular item is reflecting the underlying factor.

Thus, if we are measuring more than one construct, and each with multiple questions, we can test whether the questions are set adequately by means of factor analysis. That is, multiple factors should be formed, and each factor should consist mainly of the corresponding questions. Mathematically, this means the loadings of those questions are high on the same factor and low on other factors. If this is not the case, then something may be wrong. This is a common statistical tool used to show reliability and validity of the survey questionnaire items. It is also applied to analyze data collected by the multi-trait multi-method approach.

Descriptive and inferential statistics

After demonstrating the accuracy of measurement, the next step is to show the relationships among variables. Here, we need the help of statistics. The most common statistical concept to show the relationship between two variables is the correlation coefficient. It ranges from –1 to +1. When it is 0, it means the two variables are unrelated to each other. The closer it is to –1 or +1, the stronger the relationship. The sign of positive and negative indicates whether the relationship is in the same or the opposite direction. In statistical terms, we usually use the amount of variance explained to describe the closeness of the relationship. If the correlation coefficient equals 1 (or –1), it means the variation of one variable can be fully explained by the variation of the other variable. If it is not 0 but less than 1 (or –1), this means that only part of the variation of the variable can be explained by the variation of the other variable.

There is one problem in showing whether the relationships among variables actually exist when we have only a sample of objects under investigation. We can never be sure that the correlation coefficient calculated from this sample is the same as for the whole population which includes all objects of interest. Thus, we try to infer whether the relationship exists or not in the population by the data we collected from the sample. We call the reporting of the sample data descriptive statistics. In inferring the population relationships, we refer to it as inferential statistics, which involves statistical tests or hypothesis testing.

We cannot be sure about the situation of the population because we have data only from the sample. However, we can calculate the probability that the population correlation coefficient is not zero based on the sample data. In social science research, we want to be conservative. Thus, only when the probability is less than 5% will we conclude that the relationship between two variables actually exists in the population. In statistical terms, we will say our evidence from the sample is significant enough for us to make this conclusion. As a common standard, the symbol * or $p < .05$ is used to represent statistical significance at this predetermined probability of 5%. Otherwise, we will say the evidence from the sample is not significant, and we cannot conclude that our expected relationship between the two variables really exists. We probably need more evidence in order to draw such a conclusion.

Regression analysis and cross-level predictors

It is common that attitudes and behaviors will not be affected by only one factor. Therefore, our hypotheses about the relationships among variables usually will not be limited to only one predictor (usually labeled *independent*) variable and one criterion (usually labeled *dependent*) variable. If we have several independent variables to explain the variation of one dependent variable, we can use the statistical technique of regression. Basically, it will produce a statistic called R^2, ranging from 0 to 1. The meaning of R^2 is similar to that of the correlation coefficient, but it means the proportion of the variation of the dependent variable that can be explained by all the independent variables. Of course, after testing the significance of the population R^2 from the data of the sample, we can also test whether each independent variable has an effect on the dependent variable. The statistic is called the beta-weight. A significant beta means that particular independent variable is related to the dependent variable in the population, and the probability that this conclusion is wrong is less than 5%.

In many workplace phenomena, employee attitudes and behaviors may be affected by factors at different levels. For example, employees' performance may be affected by their own abilities and company compensation policies. For employee performance and abilities, they are at the same level because each employee will have a particular level of abilities. However, the company compensation policy is at a higher level because the policy will be the same for all employees working for the same company. When our hypotheses involve both types of independent variables, we call this cross-level analysis, and the data are nested data. While it is more complicated than when all independent variables are at the same level, the rationale for inferring the population situation from the sample data is the same. Similar to using regression to test the effects of a group of independent variables on the dependent variable, we can test the overall effects of independent variables from different levels on the dependent variable. Afterwards, we can test the effect of each independent variable on the dependent variable. The statistical technique usually adopted to tackle cross-level analysis is called Hierarchical Linear Modeling.

Mediating and moderating variables

Sometimes we know that the independent and dependent variables are related, but we cannot explain clearly why they are related. Perhaps it is because in reality the effect of the independent variable on the dependent variable is through a mediating variable. That is, the independent variable affects the mediating variable, which in turn affects the dependent variable. If this is the case, then the test will involve testing the indirect effect instead of a simple correlation or beta-weight in regression. While calculating the effect becomes more complicated, the rationale of inferring from a sample to the population is the same. That is, we try to calculate the probability that the indirect effect is not zero in the population based on the sample data. If the probability is less than 5%, we will say that the evidence is significant enough for us to conclude that there is an indirect effect in the population. Otherwise, we will say that we do not have significant evidence to draw such a conclusion.

The other common possibility about the relationship between an independent and dependent variable is that the relationship may change as a result of another variable. For example, analytical skills may be related to job performance. However, this positive relationship is stronger for high-level jobs, the incumbents of which often need to handle complicated problems. For simple and repetitive jobs, the relationship between analytical skills and job performance is smaller. In other words, the effect of analytical skills on job performance depends on job complexity. We call job complexity the moderating variable in this relationship. In statistical terms, we will also say that the independent variable (i.e., analytical skills) and the dependent variable (i.e., job complexity) have an interaction effect on the dependent variable (i.e., job performance).

To test the interaction effect, we will create an interaction term from the independent variable and the moderator and test the significance of the interaction term. Testing this interaction term is more complicated, but the rationale for inferring from a sample to the population is the same. That is, we try to calculate the probability that the interaction effect is not zero in the population from the sample data. If the probability is less than 5%, we will say that the evidence is significant enough for us to conclude that there is a moderating effect.

Multiple dependent variables

In the above discussion, we focus on one dependent variable. It is quite clear that for some phenomena there may be multiple dependent variables that we want to explain simultaneously. In this case, we will build up a model with multiple independent and dependent variables. Adding even more complication, the model may involve some mediating and moderating variables as well. In constructing such a model to represent reality, one important principle is that we try to be parsimonious. That is, we will try our best to use the simplest model to describe the reality. If two models have the same explanatory power for the dependent variables, we will adopt the simpler one.

Testing an overall model with multiple dependent variables is quite complicated, but the rationale for inferring from a sample to the population is similar. After testing whether the overall model is acceptable to be used to describe the reality, we can test the relationship between any two variables independently. The statistical technique adopted to tackle testing of a model is called structural equation modeling.

Another type of complicated models will involve not only mediating and/or moderating variables but independent variables across levels. Fortunately, statistical methods have been developed to analyze such complicated model types. Although these models are quite complicated, the rationale of hypothesis testing to estimate the relationships among variables in the population is similar. That is, we will determine the existence of a particular relationship if the sample data provide significant evidence that the probability of not having such a relationship is less than 5%. Otherwise, we will say we do not have significant or sufficient evidence to draw such a conclusion.

Norms for the reporting format for an empirical study

After completing an empirical study, we need to write up a report as a research paper. Although not totally rigid, the format of reporting is quite standard. In the first part of the paper, conceptual arguments and the specific hypotheses to be tested will be described and explained in the Introduction section. The sample, procedure, and measurement instruments used to collect data will be described in the Method section. The Results section will usually report the mean scores and the extent of variation (standard deviation is the indicator of variation) of each variable, as well as the correlation coefficients among all variables. These descriptive statistics are usually reported in the first table of the paper. Afterward, statistical results concerning all the hypothesis testing will be reported. The last section of the paper is Discussion, which includes at least a summary of important findings, limitations of the study, and implications for the existing literature and future research.

In the above discussion, I try to provide a brief description of the basic concepts and procedures of conducting and reporting quantitative research in my area. The information is not a comprehensive introduction to science and scientific research methods. However, the information may be necessary for us to comprehend what a research paper is about. With these basic understandings, I will describe my research papers about the emotional intelligence construct in the coming chapters.

2 Beginning of the journey
Is emotional intelligence a worthwhile construct?

Searching for topics to investigate is usually the first step in scientific research. This is a common headache for graduate students, who are starting to learn how to conduct research by themselves. When I was a doctoral student in the late 1980s, the usual practice in American graduate schools was to let doctoral students find and decide on the topics they wanted to work on. My professors at Purdue University regarded this as an important part of training. Seldom would professors assign dissertation topics to their students. Students might be involved in research projects that the professors were working on in order to develop their skills in data collection and analysis and the writing of papers. However, students were usually encouraged or even required to find their own topics for their dissertations. The reason for doing this is to ensure students will be able to conduct independent research after their graduation.

After I started working at the Chinese University of Hong Kong, I found out that the American way of training doctoral students was not universal. Up to the early 1990s, the Chinese University of Hong Kong followed mostly the British system. The doctoral program was not structured and basically was tailor-made for the individual student. The supervisor would decide what courses the particular student needed to take. For the graduate thesis, the student usually would follow the topics the supervisor was working on. In fact, the research that the supervisor was working on was the major reason the particular student applied for the program. The student's intention was to follow in the footsteps of the supervisor on that particular line of research.

Starting from the middle of 1990s, I got many chances to collaborate with researchers in Taiwan and mainland China and gradually helped offer some research-methods seminars to their graduate students. In Taiwan and mainland China, supervisors usually assign dissertation topics to their students. This is still the case for most of the graduate programs there. The advantage of this system is that it lowers the anxiety and stress levels of the graduate students. However, the disadvantage is that students may not have sufficient research experience to start their own research projects after they graduate.

Regardless of which system we adopt, finding a research topic is a real challenge for graduate students and junior faculty working in universities. Unfortunately, there is no systematic way that we can train students to discover meaningful research topics. In most of the cases, "meaningfulness" itself may be very subjective. From my own experiences, there may be several possibilities for finding good research topics. The first one is to follow the literature, especially for recent studies. In my early training, my professors asked me to read the papers published in several important journals in my field at least for the last five years. This helped me to have a sense of what topics were being studied. Of course, it is important to have a critical mind in reading past studies. On one hand, we should respect and appreciate how other scientists articulate their thoughts and present their evidence. On the other hand, we need to keep a critical attitude in evaluating the rationale and evidence the authors present. A similar way to find research topics is to discuss with colleagues in the field, such as by attending conferences and discussing with professors and schoolmates who are working on various projects.

The third way is to pay attention to the problems that management practitioners are concerned with or are actually facing. Some of these problems may be reported or discussed in the popular media, although they may not be well articulated. As social scientists, we should keep an eye on the real world instead of looking only at academic studies. If possible, it is useful to talk to friends working in business organizations and discuss issues that are bothering them. Helping our master of business administration students by providing advice for their work from time to time may also enrich our understanding of issues that concern practitioners in the business world.

With regard to my experiences in working on the topic of emotional intelligence, I initially developed my interests through reading a popular book. Later, I paid attention to people in the workplace and tried to figure out why this concept made sense in helping us to understand some phenomena in the workplace. The following are some of the lessons that I summarized from my beginning journey.

Lesson 1: are you really interested in the research topic?

I have been working on the concept of emotional intelligence (EI) from the management perspective since 1996. Unlike other scientific constructs, the EI concept became very popular with and was well received by the general public before sufficient and rigorous scientific evidence was accumulated. This is probably due to the book written by Daniel Goleman in 1995. The book was a best seller for quite a period of time. In that book, Goleman described the EI concept as if it had been studied rigorously by the scientific community and had been demonstrated to be related to a lot of aspects in human life. The media had followed up with the concept and publicized it widely via various radio and television programs.

I read Goleman's book in 1996. At that time, I had been working as an assistant professor (in the British system, the job title is "lecturer") for six years at the Chinese University of Hong Kong. I got tenure and was entitled to one year of sabbatical leave from August 1996 to July 1997. I went to Taiwan and worked with two teams of researchers on projects funded by the Taiwanese National Science Council. As I was away from my hometown and able to escape from administrative duties and other daily matters, I could run my daily life as if I was still a doctoral student. That is, my biggest obligation was to learn more and engage in self-development. Apart from this, I could ignore everything. How enjoyable it was!!! Thus, on top of working on the research projects, I made use of the chance to read a lot of materials that appeared to be interesting. Whenever I had time, I went to bookstores in Taichung city and read as much as I could. Goleman's book was one of the many books that I found worth reading.

Similar to most of the readers at that time, I took great interest in the EI concept. The concept itself is very appealing and makes a lot of sense. We all have emotions. In our daily life, we need to handle those emotions so that we can function effectively. We definitely have encountered people with different levels of ability in handling their emotions. Some of them can handle their emotions nicely and will not be blinded by emotions. These people are those whom we feel comfortable interacting with. They probably are polite, good-tempered, and considerate. We do not need to worry that we will upset them unintentionally and that they will blame or even hate us. Some other people are really bad in understanding and handling their emotions. These people are probably ill-tempered, self-centered, nasty, and difficult to reason with when they get emotional. Needless to say, we do not want to be around this type of person.

Lesson 1: Regardless of where we get the research idea, I think it is important for social scientists to really feel interested in the research topic (maybe a construct, a theory, or some phenomena).

Lesson 2: is the research topic relevant to your area?

However, when I read Goleman's book in detail, I began to have doubts about his claims. As a popular book, Goleman's writing style is quite affirmative. In places, he makes claims that are quite definitive. That is, those claims look as if they have a lot of scientific evidence. I was not able to judge most of the claims because I was not familiar with some of the studies he cited. However, I was pretty sure that up to 1995 no management studies had been reported that provided direct evidence about the relationship between people's EI and their job performance and career success. Furthermore, on top of traditional intelligence (i.e., general mental abilities or intelligence quotient [IQ]), there are non-intelligence factors that contribute to people's career success. For example, the match between people's personality, career interests, and the nature of the job is definitely important. Thus, while I tended to agree that EI should be one of the important factors that may affect people's performance and career success, I could not agree with the claim that about 20% of people's success was due to IQ while the remaining 80% could be attributed to EI.

Despite my doubts about the evidence for EI, I still liked the concept and believed that it was worthwhile to study it further. My initial thought was that as a management researcher, I could conduct a study to test the impact of EI on people's job outcomes, such as job satisfaction and performance, and, if possible, the role of EI in people's long-term career. By reading Goleman's book, I had the impression that EI had been studied in areas other than management and that acceptable measures would have been developed. That is, people's EI level could be assessed with scientifically acceptable standards. Without such measures, it would not be possible for Goleman to conclude the importance of EI. Thus, I was confident that I could conduct studies that were up to the scientific standards required in my area. In my area, the survey is a common research methodology. All I needed to do was to choose good samples of employees and measure their EI levels and job outcomes. Then I could evaluate the relationships between people's EI and their job outcomes.

Lesson 2: As there are so many disciplines in social science, we need to see the relevance of the topic in our major field of interest. There are a lot of topics that may be worth our investigation. We should choose those that have relevance to our own expertise.

Lesson 3: are you willing to take the risk?

Unfortunately, I was wrong. After carefully searching the literature in psychology and reading the references cited in Goleman's book, I was not able to find a ready-to-use measurement instrument that fit my original purpose, i.e., to show the association between EI and employee work outcomes such as job performance and job satisfaction. Without a ready-to-use measurement instrument, I faced a dilemma. On one hand, as a social scientist, I was trained to be curious and to try to understand a phenomenon that is of interest to me. However, on the other hand, pursuing this line of research might require putting in a lot of effort, and the payoff would be very risky. There were at least two reasons pursuing this line of research would be very risky. First, we had to start from ground zero to develop a new measurement scale. This would involve a lot of effort. Second, the general public believed that EI had been well studied, but as scientists we in fact did not have much evidence to offer yet. At least some editors and reviewers of scientific journals would be more critical than usual to make sure that studies on this construct were scientifically rigorous.

My dilemma at that time was: Is it still worth my effort to study something that is of interest to me but very risky, or should I find some other topics that have a higher chance to offering more payoff with less effort?

This is a dilemma that researchers have to face. When I was still a doctoral student, we usually would ask senior faculty members whether we should concentrate on lines of research that were "hot" topics in the field or work on something that relatively few people might be working on. The majority of the senior faculty members I met would say that for junior faculty members it was not wise to work on something that was risky and may not yield publications within a relatively short period of time. If we did not produce good publications within a certain period of time, we would not get tenure. The tenure system was a common practice around the world at that time. Assistant professors would be evaluated within six years. If they did not meet the publication and other requirements within these six years, they would lose their jobs. After they got the tenure, they would have a life-time contract.

I believe the tenure system is designed to protect academic freedom. After getting tenure, scholars earn the freedom to work on something that is of interest to them and do not need to worry about getting results within a particular period of time. They can also express their opinions and comments that may not be the majority view of the academic or general community, and so they can play the role of the conscience of the society. The disadvantage is that before getting tenure, most researchers are under great pressure to produce "outputs" in order to survive. Actually, even after getting tenure, producing "outputs" is still important for getting rewards from their employer (usually a university or research institute). If scholars are eager to get rewards such as pay raises and promotions, they will still be under pressure. Of course, the pressure is not as great as the "publish or perish" situation of assistant professors. Thus, it is individual social scientists' choice whether they are willing to take the risk of working on something that may require them to put in more effort but that offers a lower chance of getting more outputs.

When I encountered the relatively new concept of EI, I had just passed my initial stage of assistant professor. I got the protection of tenure, but I was still junior faculty and far from being established. However, I stood by my understanding of the design of the tenure system. As I already had my long-term contract at the Chinese University of Hong Kong and intended to stay there for my career, I decided to work on the EI concept, beginning with the development of a practical measurement instrument for EI.

Lesson 3: Science makes risky predictions. We have to assess the risk that we may not get any expected results in some of our investigations. While it certainly will be frustrating to get no results and no publications at the end, we have to live with it from time to time. We should not take unexpected results as a failure. This is one of the essential ways to learn something new.

First published paper in a mainstream management journal

This was the beginning of the journey. I knew that it would be risky and difficult to predict the results. However, I decided to work on the topic and realized the necessity to develop a practical measurement instrument. Fortunately, one of my former teaching assistants worked for a private tertiary institution and wanted to teach her students some basic skills related to surveys. She approached me, and I told her about Goleman's book. We developed some survey items based on Goleman's description and collected data from some Hong Kong student samples. It appeared that students had no problems in responding to items asking them about their EI level. We later reported these data in a local education journal (Wong, Wong, & Chau, 2001).

With this very initial trial, I started the journey more rigorously based on my training related to the development of a measurement instrument. I was fortunate enough to be able to persuade Professor Kenneth Law to work with me on this project. With patience, we carefully generated survey items, selected the most appropriate items via student samples, and cross-validated the selected items with multiple criterion variables based on both student and employee samples. We even used multi-trait multi-method analysis in our final employee sample. Although this method is regarded as one of the best ways to provide both discriminant and convergent validity for a newly developed measurement scale, it is seldom employed in the field of management. Thus, it took us about two and a half years to collect data from six independent samples and finish our analyses of the data. We then drafted our first paper and submitted it to the Academy of Management conference in December 1999. The paper was accepted in March 2000 for presentation at the August 2000 meeting (Wong & Law, 2000).

After we got acceptance notification from the conference organizer, we received a letter from a senior editor of the *Leadership Quarterly*. He said the *Leadership Quarterly* would be interested in our paper and invited us to submit the paper to the journal. We were very happy and believed that we might have been successful in our first step. Originally, we thought little revision of our conference paper would be needed and that we could get it published in a short period of time. We were wrong. From spring 2000, it took us three revisions and additional results from two more independent samples before the paper was finally accepted and published in 2002. As far as we know, this is the first paper investigating the EI construct published in a mainstream management journal. The following are the major contents of this first paper.

Wong, C. S., & Law, K. S. (2002). The effects of leader and follower emotional intelligence on performance and attitude: An exploratory study. *Leadership Quarterly*, 13, 243–274; these contents are reprinted with permission.

Abstract. Recently, increasing numbers of scholars have argued that emotional intelligence (EI) is a core variable that affects the performance of leaders. In this study, we develop a psychometrically sound and practically short EI measure that can be used in leadership and management studies. We also provide exploratory evidence for the relationships between the EI of leaders and followers and job outcomes. Applying Gross' emotion regulation model, we argue that the EI of leaders and followers should be positively related to job performance and attitudes. We also propose that the emotional labor of the job moderates the EI–job outcome relationship. Our results show that the EI of followers affects job performance and job satisfaction, while the EI of leaders affects their satisfaction and extra-role behavior. For followers, the proposed moderation of emotional labor on the EI–job outcome relationship is also supported.

Emotional intelligence (EI) is an emerging topic for psychological, educational, and management researchers and consultants (see, e.g., Shapiro, 1997; Weisinger, 1998). Many organizations have sent their employees to various EI training courses offered by management consultants. Proponents of the EI concept argue that EI affects one's physical and mental health as well as one's career achievements (e.g., Goleman, 1995). Some emerging leadership theories also imply that emotional and social intelligence is even more important for leaders and managers because cognitive and behavioral complexity and flexibility are important characteristics of competent leaders (Boal & Whitehead, 1992). However, there is little empirical evidence in the literature about the relationship between the EI of both leaders and followers and their job outcomes. One of the reasons for this gap may be the lack of a psychologically sound yet practically short measure of EI that can be used in leadership and management studies. The project reported in this paper was designed to develop such a measure and provide exploratory evidence concerning the relationship between the EI of both leaders and followers and job outcomes.

The purpose of this multi-sample, multi-study project is threefold. First, the core concepts of EI and emotional labor are discussed, and hypotheses are developed concerning their role in leadership and management research. EI is referred to as a set of interrelated abilities possessed by individuals to deal with emotions, while emotional labor is referred to as emotion-related job requirements imposed by organizations. Thus, EI is a particular set of an individual's abilities, while emotional labor represents a particular type of job demand.

Second, we develop a short but psychologically sound measure of EI for research on leadership and management in our first empirical study. Finally, in the second and third studies, we test the relationships between the EI of followers and leaders and their job outcomes, and the proposed moderating effects of emotional labor on the EI–job outcome relationship of followers.

This paper is organized as follows. We first discuss the importance of EI for leaders, as suggested in the leadership literature, and review the constructs of EI and emotional labor. Then, the potential moderating effect of emotional labor on the EI–job outcome relationship is discussed within the framework of the emotion regulation model. After proposing our hypotheses, we report Study 2.1, in which a 16-item EI scale is developed. In Study 2.2, this EI scale is applied to 149 supervisor–subordinate dyads, and the follower EI–job outcome relationship and the moderating effects of emotional labor are tested. In Study 2.3, the EI scale is applied to another supervisor–subordinate dyad to examine the relationship between leader EI and follower job outcomes. The paper concludes with a discussion of the general contribution of this study to the management and leadership literature on EI.

EI as a leadership quality

Leadership concerns the interaction of leaders with other individuals. Once social interactions are involved, emotional awareness and emotional regulation become important factors affecting the quality of the interactions. As R. J. House and Aditya (1997) summarized, "contemporary research on intelligence offers renewed potential for leadership trait research. The notion of multiple intelligence and Sternberg's theory of triarchic intelligence have implications for managerial roles. Leadership is embedded in a social context, and the idea of social intelligence as a required leadership trait is a powerful one" (p. 418). Sternberg (1997) echoed House and Aditya's viewpoint by providing vivid examples to illustrate why social intelligence may be even more important in affecting the job success of managers and leaders than traditional general mental intelligence. Many leadership researchers have also argued that effective leadership behavior fundamentally depends on the leader's ability to solve complex social problems that arise in organizations (e.g., Mumford, Zaccaro, Harding, Jacobs, & Fleishman, 2000; Zaccaro, Mumford, Connelly, Marks, & Gilbert, 2000).

By integrating EI into modern theories of leadership, Hooijberg, Hunt, and Dodge (1997) presented a framework of the cognitive, social, and behavioral complexities of leadership. They argued that the social aspect of a leader's capacity consisted of two components – social differentiation and social integration. Social differentiation was defined as "the ability of a managerial leader to discriminate and recognize the various facets, aspects, and significances of a given social situation over time. Social differentiation is a function of the leader's ability to discern existing and potential patterns of social relationships; the leader's ability to regulate emotions within self and recognize emotions in others; the number and degree of independence of a leader's value preferences; and the leader's level of self-complexity" (p. 382). In other words, good leaders need to have a good understanding of their own emotions as well as those of others, and are able to regulate their own emotions when interacting with others.

This idea is reinforced by Boal and Hooijberg (2000), who highlighted the argument that behavioral complexity is a core element of leader effectiveness. Leaders needed to play different roles at different times, and, more importantly, good leaders had the ability to select the right roles for the situation. Boal and Hooijberg argued that social intelligence was the underlying ability which governed the behavioral complexity of leaders.

Day (2000) also reinforced the importance of EI in leader effectiveness. While discussing the training and development of leaders in organizations, Day emphasized that "specific examples of the type of intrapersonal competence associated with leader development initiatives include self-awareness (e.g., emotional awareness, self confidence), self-regulation (e.g., self-control, trustworthiness, adaptability), and self-motivation (e.g., commitment, initiative, optimism)" (p. 584). As we will explain in the next section, emotional awareness, emotional control, and self-motivation are the basic dimensions of the EI construct. Based on the above discussion, it can be seen that EI is viewed in the leadership literature as a core variable that affects leader effectiveness. Before we actually test the relationship between the EI of leaders and the performance of followers and their attitudes, it is necessary to introduce the definition of EI used in this project.

The definition and domain of EI

EI has its roots in the concept of "social intelligence" that was first identified by Thorndike in 1920. Thorndike defined social intelligence as "the ability to understand and manage men and women, boys and girls – to act wisely in human relations" (p. 228). Following Thorndike, Gardner (1993) included social intelligence as one of the seven intelligence domains in his theory of multiple intelligences. According to Gardner, social intelligence is comprised of a person's interpersonal and intrapersonal intelligences. Intrapersonal intelligence relates to one's intelligence in dealing with oneself and is the ability to perceive and organize complicated and highly differentiated sets of feelings. In contrast, interpersonal intelligence relates to one's intelligence in dealing with others and is the ability to "notice and make distinctions among other individuals and, in particular, among their moods, temperaments, motivations and intentions" (p. 239).

Salovey and Mayer (1990) were among the earliest to propose the name "emotional intelligence" to represent the ability of people to deal with their emotions. They defined EI as "the subset of social intelligence that involves the ability to monitor one's own and others' feelings and emotions, to discriminate among them and to use this information to guide one's thinking and actions" (p. 189). Recently, Goleman (1995) adopted Salovey and Mayer's definition and proposed that EI involves abilities that can be categorized as being self-aware, managing emotions, motivating oneself, being empathetic, and handling relationships.

In this study, we have used the Mayer and Salovey (1997) definition of EI as a set of interrelated skills concerning "the ability to perceive accurately, appraise, and express emotion; the ability to access and/or generate feelings when they facilitate thought; the ability to understand emotion and emotional knowledge; and the ability to regulate emotions to promote emotional and intellectual growth" (p. 10). Salovey and Mayer (1990) and Mayer and Salovey (1997) conceptualized EI as composed of four distinct dimensions:

1. *Appraisal and expression of emotion in the self (self emotional appraisal, SEA)*

    This relates to the individual's ability to understand their deep emotions and be able to express these emotions naturally. People who have great ability in this area will sense and acknowledge their emotions well before most people.

2. *Appraisal and recognition of emotion in others (other's emotional appraisal, OEA)*

    This relates to the individual's ability to perceive and understand the emotions of the people around them. People who are high in this ability will be much more sensitive to the feelings and emotions of others as well as reading their minds.

3. *Regulation of emotion in the self (regulation of emotion, ROE)*

    This relates to the ability of a person to regulate their emotions, which will enable a more rapid recovery from psychological distress. A person with great ability in this area maintains positive emotions most of the time. As a result, this dimension is sometimes referred to as "self-motivation," or the ability of a person to be self-encouraging and be positive toward life stresses.

4. *Use of emotion to facilitate performance (use of emotion, UOE)*

    This relates to the ability of a person to make use of their emotions by directing them toward constructive activities and personal performance. A person who has high ability in this aspect is able to keep their behavior under control when they have extreme moods. The person will also make the very best use of their emotions to facilitate job performance in the workplace.

The conceptual and theoretical basis of EI

While there has been much theoretical discussion about, and empirical evidence for, the interaction of the cognitive and non-cognitive neural systems in the human brain, as well as how that affects emotions (see, e.g., Fischer, Shaver, & Carnochan, 1990; Izard, 1992, 1993), there is no theory that specifically discusses the role of EI and how it is related to work outcomes. To understand the relationship between EI and organizational outcomes, we borrow from Gross' model of emotion regulation (Gross, 1998a, 1998b) and develop possible hypotheses to be tested in our study.

Gross defines emotions as "adaptive behavioral and physiological response tendencies that are called forth directly by evolutionarily significant situations" (1988b, p. 272). As emotions are response tendencies and can be modulated, they can be regulated and managed. Emotion regulation refers to "the processes by which individuals influence which emotions they have, when they have them, and how they experience and express these emotions" (p. 275).

Gross' definition of emotion regulation matches our definition of EI. Before one can regulate their emotions, one should have a good understanding of these emotions (SEA). As many of our emotional responses are stimulated by the emotions of other individuals, our understanding of our own emotions is related to our ability to understand the emotions of others (OEA). Gross' emotion regulation model prescribes that one can modulate how one experiences these emotions (ROE) as well as how one expresses them (UOE). Therefore, according to the definitions of EI and emotional regulation, persons with high EI should be more able to modulate their response tendencies and have more effective emotion regulation processes. As a result, Gross' model of emotional regulation appears to be a reasonable theoretical basis for our investigation of the role of EI in the workplace.

According to Gross (1988a, p. 225), emotional response tendencies can be regulated either by manipulating "the input to the system" (*antecedent-focused emotion regulation*) or by manipulating "its output" (*response-focused emotion regulation*). Antecedent-focused emotion regulation is accomplished by four steps: *situation selection*, in which one approaches or avoids certain people or situations on the basis of their likely emotional impact; *situation modification*, in which one modifies an environment so as to alter its emotional impact; *attention deployment*, in which one turns attention toward or away from something in order to influence one's emotions; and *cognitive change*, in which one re-evaluates either the situation one is in or one's capacity to manage the situation so as to alter one's emotions. Similarly, response-focused emotion regulation also includes multiple steps. One may *intensify*, *diminish*, *prolong*, or *curtail* ongoing emotional experiences for specific purposes.

When this model is applied to EI in the organizational setting, employees will be able to modulate their perception of the work environment, which affects their emotions, through *antecedent-focused emotion regulation* by being selective about the people they interact with, modifying the work environment, focusing on specific aspects of their work environment, or changing their evaluation of the work environment. These employees can also modulate the impact of emotional stimuli from the work environment after the fact through *response-focused emotion regulation* by intensifying, diminishing, prolonging, or curtailing certain emotions. People with high levels of EI can make use of this emotion regulation mechanism effectively to create positive emotions as well as to promote emotional and intellectual growth. In contrast, people with low levels of EI are not able to use antecedent- and response-focused emotion regulation effectively, and they have slower emotional growth.

The relationships between EI and work outcomes in the workplace

Organizations are settings that require interpersonal interaction. Most of these interactions are related to the performance of job duties, for example, serving customers, receiving instructions and reporting to supervisors, or co-operating and co-ordinating with colleagues. Employees with high levels of EI are those who can make use of antecedent- and response-focused emotional regulation effectively and master their interactions with others in a more effective manner. Ashkanasy and Hooper (1999) made use of the proposition that affective commitment toward other people is a necessary component of social interaction and argued that the showing of positive emotions is associated with a high likelihood of success at work. Abraham (1999), based on her own earlier observation that optimistic insurance salesmen would perform better than pessimistic salesmen, proposed that EI is directly related to performance. These studies, together with the Goleman (1998) observation that EI is related to job performance, lead to our first hypothesis:

Hypothesis 2.1: EI is positively related to job performance.

EI should also be related to other affective job outcomes such as job satisfaction, organizational commitment, and turnover intention. The ability to apply antecedent- and response-focused emotion regulation should enable employees to have better relationships with co-workers and supervisors, as well as greater satisfaction in their jobs. The continual presence of positive emotional states among the employees will also lead to positive affection toward the work environment and the organization. As a result, the positive experience on the job and positive affective emotions should also make employees more committed to the organization and less likely to leave their jobs. Therefore, following the arguments of Goleman (1998), Ashkanasy and Hooper (1999), and Abraham (1999), we hypothesize:

Hypothesis 2.2: EI is positively related to job satisfaction.

Hypothesis 2.3: EI is positively related to organizational commitment.

Hypothesis 2.4: EI is negatively related to turnover intention.

The EI–job outcome relationships of followers as moderated by emotional labor

While the above arguments about the relationship between EI and job outcomes may be reasonable, it is difficult to argue that their relationship will be the same across job categories. There are many jobs that require extensive interaction with customers (e.g., in service industries) or co-workers (e.g., team-oriented jobs). In contrast, job incumbents in other occupations may undertake minimal interaction with others (e.g., production-line workers). We borrow the idea of "emotional labor" to represent the extent to which the job requires the management of emotions to achieve positive job outcomes and study the moderating effects of emotional labor on the EI–job outcome relationships.

Many scholars view emotions in the workplace as a commodity provided by the employees in exchange for individual rewards (e.g., Hochschild, 1983; Morris & Feldman, 1996, 1997; Sutton, 1991; Sutton & Rafaeli, 1988; Turner, 1986; Van Maanen & Kunda, 1989; Wharton & Erickson, 1995). According to these scholars, there are at least three types of "labor" to be offered to the organization in exchange for rewards. "Mental labor" refers to the cognitive skills and knowledge as well as the expertise of employees. "Physical labor" refers to the physical efforts of employees to achieve organizational goals. "Emotional labor" refers to the extent to which an employee is required to present an appropriate emotion in order to perform the job in an efficient and effective manner. Examples of jobs requiring a high level of emotional labor are flight attendants, who are required to be friendly to the customers even when they are in a bad mood, and bill collectors, who have to be tough with debtors despite their inclination to sympathize with them.

Scholars have argued that the extent of emotional labor required may vary across occupations. Hochschild (1983, Appendix C) identified a set of 44 census occupations that involve significant amounts of emotional labor. However, this view of emotional labor is not universally accepted. For example, Grandey (2000) defines emotional labor as "the process of regulating both feelings and expressions for the organizational goals" (p. 97). We do not use this definition of emotional labor for two reasons. First, it is distinct from the original definition as proposed by Hochschild (1983). Second, this process definition of emotional labor intertwines it with EI. Therefore, we follow Hochschild and use the concept of emotional labor to distinguish those jobs that require employees to manage their emotions for job performance. The above discussion leads to our fifth hypothesis:

Hypothesis 2.5: The EI–job performance relationship is moderated by the extent of emotional labor required by the job. Specifically, the relationship is stronger for jobs that require high emotional labor.

Hypothesis 2.5 concerns the EI–job performance relationship. Based on our earlier discussion, the job satisfaction of incumbents, their organizational commitment, and their turnover intention are all directly related to their ability to effectively regulate antecedent- and response-focused emotion. If that is the case, the EI of job incumbents in jobs that require them to manage their emotions frequently and extensively will have stronger relationships with their job satisfaction, commitment, and turnover intention than for incumbents performing low emotional labor jobs. For example, social workers (whose jobs require great emotional labor) would hardly be satisfied with their jobs should they have low levels of EI, because they would have less chance of doing their jobs well. As a result, organizational commitment and turnover intention would be affected. In contrast, auto mechanics (whose jobs involve little emotional labor) could still be reasonably satisfied with their job despite a low level of EI. We therefore propose the following hypotheses:

Hypothesis 2.6: The EI–job satisfaction relationship is moderated by the extent of emotional labor required by the job. This relationship will be stronger for jobs that require a high level of emotional labor.

Hypothesis 2.7: The EI–organizational commitment relationship is moderated by the extent of emotional labor required by the job. This relationship will be stronger for jobs that require a high level of emotional labor.

Hypothesis 2.8: The EI–turnover intention relationship is moderated by the extent of emotional labor required by the job. This relationship will be stronger for jobs that require a high level of emotional labor.

These eight hypotheses are summarized diagrammatically in Figure 2.1.

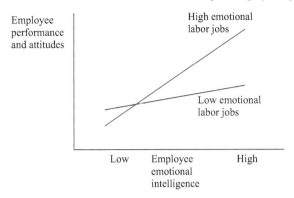

Figure 2.1 The proposed moderating effect of emotional labor on the relationship between emotional intelligence and job outcomes

Relationship between the EI of leaders and the job outcomes of followers

As already discussed, the literature indicates that the EI of leaders will influence their effectiveness. In addition, there is evidence (Fisher & Edwards, 1988) that the supportive behavior of leaders has a positive effect on the job satisfaction, and probably performance, of followers. Applying the social exchange theory to the area of leadership, some scholars have argued that followers will have stronger commitment and satisfaction should leaders treat them with psychological benefits such as approval, respect, esteem, and affection (e.g., Hollander, 1980; Jacobs, 1970). Dansereau et al. (1995) have shown that leaders are able to affect the performance of their subordinates by supporting their feelings of self-worth. Furthermore, some leadership studies have shown that the emotional maturity of leaders is associated with their managerial effectiveness (Bass, 1990). From our definition of EI, supervisors with high EI and emotional maturity are more likely to use supportive behavior and treat their followers with psychological benefits, as they are more sensitive to the feelings and emotions of themselves and their followers. This should be positively related to the job outcomes of their followers. Thus, we hypothesize:

> Hypothesis 2.9: The EI of supervisors is positively related to the in-role behaviors (i.e., job performance) of their subordinates.

> Hypothesis 2.10: The EI of supervisors is positively related to the job satisfaction of their subordinates.

> Hypothesis 2.11: The EI of supervisors is positively related to the extra-role behavior (i.e., organizational citizenship behavior) of their subordinates.

Study 2.1: development of measurement items for EI

Development of an EI measure for research purposes

There are some existing measures of EI, but they are not suitable for research on the workplace. For example, Carson, Carson, and Philips (1997) developed a 14-item measure of EI, and Carson and Carson (1998) used this measure to examine the relationship between EI and career commitment in a sample of 75 nurses. However, the authors only reported the coefficient alpha of all 14 items as .79, without mentioning any other psychometric properties of the measure. Salovey, Mayer, Goldman, Turvey, and Palfai (1995) developed a 30-item Trait-Meta-Mood Scale to measure EI. Martinez-Pons (1997) used this measure on 108 parents, teachers, and administrators in two public elementary schools. Unfortunately, the measure was designed to capture three components: attention to one's moods and emotions, emotional clarity (one's tendency to discriminate among one's emotions and moods), and emotional repair (one's tendency to regulate one's feelings). These three components do not capture all of the EI dimensions as defined in our project.

Bar-On (1997) introduced the Bar-On's Emotional Quotient Inventory (EQ-i), which contains 133 items. However, there is only validation evidence provided by the developer. Bar-On's definition of EI is also slightly different from our own, which seems to be the current view of the EI construct, and the scale includes a number of dimensions that may not relate to EI directly (e.g., problem solving, social responsibility, etc.). Goleman developed a 10-item measure of EI without any validation evidence. Similarly, Weisinger (1998) developed a short EI instrument without any validation evidence. Mayer, Salovey, and Caruso (1997) developed the Multifactor Emotional Intelligence Scale, which requires responses to more than 400 items and takes one to two hours to complete. Moreover, the psychometric properties of this measure have not been reported. The scale is also scored by a norm-referenced method. Respondents are considered high in EI when a majority of the subjects in the norm samples choose the same answer. The developer highlighted that the expert-referenced scoring method did not work as well as the norm-referenced method for this scale. Sosik and Megerian (1999) did not develop a EI measure but considered various measures which appeared to capture some dimensions of EI. However, it is not clear whether these dimensions (e.g., self-monitoring and personal efficacy) can actually capture the dimensions summarized in our discussion. Although there are some measures of EI in the literature, it appears necessary for us to develop a simple, practical, and psychometrically sound measure of EI for organizational research purposes.

To develop a reasonable EI measure, we used three groups of independent samples to develop the items and test their psychometric properties. In the first group, one sample (n = 120) generated items, while quantitative evidence was gathered in the other sample (n = 189) to select the appropriate items. In the second group, two cross-validated samples (n = 72 and n = 146) provided quantitative evidence to confirm the factorial structure of the four EI dimensions and their relationships with the external criterion variables. In the third group, another two samples (n = 110 and n = 116) were used to test the convergent, discriminant, and incremental validity of the measure by examining its relationships with existing EI and personality measures and the criterion variable.

Samples for item generation and selection

Samples and sampling procedures

We started the process of developing our own EI instrument by asking managers and students to generate items to capture the construct. Three groups of part-time master of business administration and undergraduate students (n = 120) in a large Hong Kong university were first introduced to the four dimensions of EI defined in this study. They were then asked to generate self-reported items on each dimension that would describe a person with a high level of EI. Three types of items were deleted from the item pool based on the judgment of the two authors. They were (1) overlapping or similar items suggested by different respondents, (2) items with unclear meaning, and (3) items that did not match the definition of EI as a result of the students' misunderstandings. We finally extracted nine items for each of the four EI dimensions, which resulted in a 36-item preliminary measure of EI.

These 36 items were then tested on a sample of 189 undergraduate students in Hong Kong by using a 7-point Likert-type scale ranging from strongly agree to strongly disagree. These students were second- and third-year business majors who were required to participate in an experiment to fulfill the basic requirement of a course on organizational behavior. On top of the 36 EI items, we also collected data on two groups of variables as external evidence of the validity of our EI measure. As indicated before, proponents of the EI construct have argued that one's EI level should have little relationship with one's general mental intelligence. Empirically, Ciarrochi, Chan, and Caputi (2000) and Pellitteri (1999) found a very low correlation between EI and IQ in their college student samples. We used a test developed by Eysenck (1990) to measure IQ.

We also examined the correlation between our EI measure and two constructs that are, conceptually, highly related to EI. These constructs are life satisfaction and feeling of powerlessness. Proponents of EI have argued that life satisfaction should be positively related to EI. Several empirical studies have provided evidence of this positive relationship (e.g., Ciarrochi et al., 2000; Martinez-Pons, 1997). We also argue that EI should be negatively related to a feeling of powerlessness. As described by Pearlin and Schooler (1978), powerlessness is the extent to which one regards one's life chances as being fatalistically ruled in contrast to being under one's own control. Theoretically, people with high EI will enjoy better relationships with others, have better control over their own lives, and be able to control negative emotions. Although no empirical study has investigated this relationship, it has been shown that a feeling of powerlessness is related to negative emotions such as sadness and fear (e.g., Roseman, Dhawan, Rettek, & Naidu, 1995). Thus, any EI measure developed should have a negligible relationship with IQ, a positive relationship with life satisfaction, and a negative relationship with powerlessness.

Measures

Life satisfaction was measured with the nine items constructed by A. Campbell, Converse, and Rodgers (1976). The first eight items of this scale are pairs of opposite adjectives (e.g., *interesting* versus *boring*, *enjoyable* versus *miserable*) with a 7-point Likert-type scale of numbers between them. Respondents were requested to circle the number that best described their feelings toward their lives. The last item was a direct question asking about the level of satisfaction in life, namely: "How satisfied or dissatisfied are you with your life as a whole?" Internal consistency reliability (i.e., the coefficient alpha) was .91 for this sample. Powerlessness in life mastery was measured with the seven items constructed by Pearlin and Schooler (1978). The response format was a 7-point Likert-type scale ranging from strongly disagree to strongly agree. Examples of these items include "I have little control over the things that happen to me" and "There is really no way I can solve some of the problems I have." The internal consistency reliability was .67 for this sample.

IQ was measured by the fourth test devised by Eysenck (1990). This test consisted of 40 items. Respondents were required to finish the test within 30 minutes. A correct response to an item scored 1 point, and so the maximum possible score for the test was 40. The minimum score in our sample of 189 students was 6, and the maximum was 26. The average score was 15.3, and the standard deviation was 4.12.

Results of item selection and factorial structure

The major purpose of this first study was to develop a psychometrically sound self-reported EI scale. As a result, our first job was to test the factorial structure of the instrument. We conducted an exploratory factor analysis of the 36 items using the maximum likelihood method with varimax rotation. A total of eight factors were identified with an eigenvalue greater than unity. From a detailed look at the factor loadings of these eight factors, it was found that the first four factors with the largest eigenvalues basically represented the four hypothesized EI dimensions. For example, seven out of the nine items measuring the first EI dimension of SEA loaded on the same factor with loadings larger than .50. Similarly, for the other three EI dimensions, at least six of the nine items loaded on their respective factor with loadings greater than .50. The remaining four factors captured only some random or error variances of individual items. All of the remaining four factors consisted of a maximum of only one item with a loading greater than .50.

To improve the psychometric properties of our EI scale, we selected only the four items with the largest factor loadings from each of the first four factors to represent the four EI dimensions. When a second factor analysis was conducted with only these 16 items, a clear four-factor structure emerged. The first part of Table 2.1 shows the results of this factor analysis. The average loadings of

Table 2.1 Factor Analysis and correlations for the item selection sample

(a) Factor Analysis

Items	Factor 1	Factor 2	Factor 3	Factor 4
SEA1	.05	**.89**	.13	.06
SEA2	.04	**.86**	.01	.16
SEA3	.10	**.74**	.11	.07
SEA4	−.01	**.87**	.05	.17
ROE1	.07	−.01	**.82**	.20
ROE2	.10	.15	**.76**	.04
ROE3	.11	.08	**.76**	.13
ROE4	.04	.08	**.80**	.26
UOE1	.17	.22	.09	**.76**
UOE2	.12	.37	.09	**.76**
UOE3	.06	.08	.19	**.83**
UOE4	.03	−.06	.33	**.66**
OEA1	**.85**	.09	.15	.10
OEA2	**.91**	.03	.07	.07
OEA3	**.88**	.01	.05	−.04
OEA4	**.83**	.07	.08	.26
Eigenvalue	5.01	2.70	2.27	1.46
% of variance explained	31.3	16.9	14.2	9.1

(b) Correlation Coefficients

	1	2	3	4	5	6	7	8
1. SEA	(.87)							
2. ROE	.20**	(.83)						
3. UOE	.34**	.42**	.84)					
4. OEA	.13⁺	.21**	.25**	(.90)				
5. LS	.38**	.46**	.33**	.16*	(.91)			
6. PWL	−.31**	−.29**	−.39**	−.13⁺	−.38**	(.67)		
7. IQ	.06	−.16*	−.05	−.19*	−.06	.03	−	

Notes

n = 189. Numbers in the diagonal are coefficient alphas. SEA = self emotional appraisal; OEA = other's emotional appraisal; ROE = regulation of emotion; UOE = use of emotion; LS = life satisfaction; PWL = powerlessness; IQ = intelligence as measured by Eysenck's test.

+p < .10; *p < .05; **p < .01 (two-tailed tests).

the 16 items on their respective EI dimensions was .80. Cross-loadings were negligible. Internal consistency reliability for the four factors (each with four items) ranged from .83 to .90. The distribution of each item appeared to be similar. The means ranged from 4.25 to 4.94, with standard deviations ranging from 1.20 to 1.43.

Results of scale correlation

The correlations among the four EI factors and the criterion variables were all within reasonable limits. The second part of Table 2.1 shows the correlation coefficients. The EI dimensions were all mildly correlated (ranging from $r = .13$ to $r = .42$), which indicated that they were related but not identical dimensions. All EI dimensions correlated significantly with life satisfaction. The correlation ranged from .16 to .46. All EI dimensions correlated moderately and negatively with the powerlessness measures. The correlation ranged from $-.13$ to $-.39$. Individuals with a high level of EI should have a low chance of experiencing powerlessness. Finally, as expected, the EI dimensions had minimal correlations with the IQ estimate. It is notable that OEA and ROE actually correlated negatively and significantly with Eysenck's IQ measure. In other words, individuals with a higher level of cognitive intelligence will be less able to recognize others' emotions.

Cross-validation samples on factor structure and relationship with criteria

Samples, sampling procedures, and measures

To assure that the factorial structure of the 16 EI items and the correlations of the EI dimensions with the criterion variables could be generalized to other samples, we collected data from two independent samples in Hong Kong. These students enrolled in different management courses and were invited to participate in this study. The first sample consisted of 72 undergraduate students. They were asked to respond to a questionnaire containing the 16 EI items as well as the powerlessness and life satisfaction items. The second sample consisted of another 146 undergraduate students who were asked to respond to the same measurement items.

Results of the first cross-validation sample

We conducted a confirmatory factor analysis of the EI items using the computer program LISREL (Jöreskog & Sörbom, 1993). With the specified four items loading on their respective EI dimensions, the model χ^2 of the confirmatory factor analysis was 132.41 (d.f. = 98). The standardized root mean residual (RMR) of the model was .08, the comparative fit index (CFI; Bentler, 1990) was .95, and the Tucker-Lewis Index (TLI; Tucker & Lewis, 1973) was .93. All model fit indices showed that the four-factor model fitted the data reasonably well. Correlations among the four EI dimensions, as well as their correlations with powerlessness and life satisfaction, are shown below the diagonal in Table 2.2.

All of the observed correlations matched well with our hypotheses. All EI dimensions were negatively correlated with powerlessness and positively correlated with life satisfaction. In addition, the size of the correlations were similar to those found in the item-selection sample.

Results of the second cross-validation sample

The confirmatory factor analysis results for this cross-validation sample were similar to those of the first cross-validation sample. Model χ^2 for the four-factor model for the 16 EI items was 179.33 (d.f. = 98). The standardized RMR was .07, the CFI was .91, and the TLI was .89. Again, all model fit indices showed that the four-factor model fitted the data reasonably well. Correlations of the four EI dimensions with powerlessness and life satisfaction are shown in the upper half of Table 2.2. The magnitudes of these correlations were extremely similar to those found in the first cross-validation sample, and quite similar to

Table 2.2 Correlations among the emotional intelligence dimensions and criterion variables for the cross-validation samples

	SEA	ROE	UOE	OEA	PWL	LS
Self emotional appraisal (SEA)	(.89/.87)	.45**	.28**	.34**	−.14	.23*
Regulation of emotion (ROE)	.35**	(.74/.71)	.33**	.29**	−.26**	.29**
Use of emotion (UOE)	.34**	.24*	(.87/.87)	.31**	−.29**	.40**
Other's emotional appraisal (OEA)	.34**	.34**	.37**	(.89/.88)	−.08	.12
Powerlessness (PWL)	−.27	−.14	−.28*	.03	(.91/.90)	−.37**
Life satisfaction (LS)	.29*	.18	.31**	.26*	−.36**	(.71/.73)

Notes
n = 72 for the first validation sample (lower triangle); n = 146 for the second validation sample (upper triangle). Numbers in the diagonal are coefficient alphas, and the first and second numbers are from the first and second validation samples, respectively. SEA = self emotional appraisal; OEA = other's emotional appraisal; ROE = regulation of emotion; UOE = use of emotion; LS = life satisfaction; PWL = powerlessness.

†p < .10; *p < .05; **p < .01 (two-tailed tests).

those in the first developmental sample. We concluded that the 16-item EI scale effectively captured the EI dimensions. The resulting 16 EI items are shown in Appendix 2.1.

Samples testing convergent, discriminant, and incremental validity

Samples, sampling procedures, and measure

Davies, Stankov, and Roberts (1998) argued that the construct of EI was elusive because self-reported EI measures had salient loadings on well-established Big Five personality factors. To test the convergent and discriminant validities of the 16-item EI scale we developed, we collected additional data from two independent samples. The first sample consisted of 110 undergraduate business students. These students completed a questionnaire containing the 16 EI items, another existing measure of EI (the 30-item Trait-Meta-Mood Scale by Salovey et al., 1995), the 80-item Big Five personality measure (McCrae & Costa, 1987), and the same life satisfaction scale as in our earlier samples. As with the previous samples, the response format for all measures was a 7-point scale.

The second sample consists of 116 non-teaching employees from a Hong Kong university. To include a variety of employees from various jobs, questionnaires were distributed to different units to include administrative, clerical, and technical staff. These employees were selected from the telephone directory randomly. One hundred and fifty employees were contacted by telephone, and those who agreed to participate (i.e., 116) received, in person, a copy of the questionnaire from a research assistant. Respondents were instructed to complete the questionnaire within one week, and the research assistant collected the questionnaire in person. Two personality and two EI measures were included in the questionnaire. The first personality scale consisted of the 60-item short form of the Neuroticism-Extraversion-Openness (NEO) Personality Inventory (Costa & McCrae, 1985), and the second was the adjective scale used in the previous sample. To avoid a long questionnaire, we randomly selected six items for each Big Five personality dimension from the 80-item adjective scale used in the previous sample. The first EI scale was the 16-item scale developed in previous samples. The second scale consisted of 20 items from Bar-On's EQ-i. Specifically, we randomly selected five items for each of the four dimensions of Bar-On's EQ-i (i.e., emotional self-awareness, empathy, impulse control, and optimism), which appeared to be most relevant to our EI definition. Reliability estimates (coefficient alphas) for the four dimensions of SEA, UOE, ROE, and OEA were .92, .91, .84, and .93, respectively.

Results of the first convergent, discriminant, and incremental validity sample

To test the convergent and discriminant validities of our measure, we conducted exploratory factor analysis on the EI and personality measures. Because of the

Table 2.3 Exploratory factor analysis of Big Five and emotional intelligence indicators of the convergent, discriminant, and incremental validity sample

	Factor 1	Factor 2	Factor 3	Factor 4	Factor 5	Factor 6	Factor 7
NEURO1	−.18	**−.57**	−.18	−.26	−.21	−.05	.31
NEURO2	−.19	**−.50**	−.14	−.38	.01	−.03	.53
EXTRA1	.07	−.25	−.21	.29	**.53**	−.16	.31
EXTRA2	.11	.07	.09	.43	**.46**	.06	.03
OPEN1	.13	.02	−.06	−.07	**.89**	.13	.00
OPEN2	.09	.15	.16	.02	**.85**	.01	−.14
AGREE1	.14	.06	.04	**.76**	−.03	.15	−.17
AGREE2	.00	.07	.09	**.87**	.03	.04	.00
CONSC1	.21	.13	**.64**	.16	−.12	.07	−.59
CONSC2	.23	.25	**.65**	.26	.21	.07	−.44
ATTEND	.36	**.40**	.30	.36	.12	.04	.15
ATTEND	.28	.25	.24	**.49**	.17	.16	.17
CLARITY	.26	.00	.05	.02	−.02	.18	**.42**
CLARITY	.33	−.03	.02	.09	−.06	.30	**.34**
REPAIR	**.71**	.02	.09	−.04	.25	.15	−.07
REPAIR	**.69**	.14	.16	.06	.06	.17	−.01
SEA1	**.71**	.15	.15	.19	.01	.08	.14
SEA2	**.77**	.12	.05	.13	.08	.16	.01
UOE1	.09	**.89**	.23	.10	.02	−.03	−.07
UOE2	.11	**.93**	.05	−.01	−.01	.06	.02
ROE1	.12	.19	**.82**	.12	−.11	.02	.10
ROE2	.12	.10	**.86**	.03	.14	.04	−.02
OEA1	.32	.03	.07	.13	.02	**.76**	.05
OEA2	.22	.04	.03	.12	.12	**.96**	.08
Eigenvalue	2.79	5.33	1.96	1.79	1.68	1.72	.95
% of variance explained	11.6	22.2	8.2	7.5	7.0	7.2	4.0

Notes

n = 110. NEURO, EXTRA, OPEN, AGREE, and CONSC = neuroticism, extraversion, openness, agreeableness, and conscientiousness, the Big Five personality dimensions; ATTEND, CLARITY, and REPAIR = the three EI dimensions of the Trait-Meta-Mood Scale; SEA, UOE, ROE, and OEA = self emotional appraisal, use of emotion, regulation of emotion, and other's emotional appraisal. The number after each dimension represents the indicator used for the latent construct. For example, NEURO1 represents the first indicator of the neuroticism dimension of the Big Five personality traits.

large number of Big Five personality items compared to the sample size, we randomly averaged the items and formed two indicators for each personality dimension. Table 2.3 shows the results of the exploratory factor analysis. The Big Five personality indicators loaded heavily on their respective dimensions except for neuroticism and conscientiousness. The UOE dimension of EI and neuroticism both loaded on Factor 2. The ROE dimension of EI and conscientiousness loaded on the same factor, Factor 3. The other two EI dimensions, SEA and OEA, did not cross-load with the Big Five factors.

To show the incremental validity of our EI measure as compared with the Trait-Meta-Mood Scale, we conducted hierarchical regression using life satisfaction and powerlessness as criterion variables. We first entered the Big Five personality dimensions as control variables. These were followed by the three Trait-Meta-Mood dimensions. Finally, our four EI dimensions were entered into the regression equation as predictors. For life satisfaction as the dependent measure, the changes in model R^2 when the three sets of predictors were entered hierarchically were .466 (p < .01), .029 (p > .10), and .077 (p < .01), respectively. The Big Five dimensions shared a significant portion of the variances of life satisfaction. The Trait-Meta-Mood dimensions did not explain incremental variances of life satisfaction on top of the Big Five dimensions. In contrast, our EI dimensions provided significant incremental contributions in predicting life satisfaction on top of the Big Five dimensions.

When powerlessness was used as the dependent measure, the changes in the model R^2 when the three sets of predictors were entered hierarchically were .247 (p < .01), .077 (p < .05), and .059 (p < .10), respectively. Our EI measure still provided incremental variance explanation marginally on top of the Big Five dimensions and the Trait-Meta-Mood Scale. The first two columns in Table 2.4 show the beta coefficients for the final step of the regression when life satisfaction and powerlessness were analyzed as dependent variables.

Results of the second convergent, discriminant,
and incremental validity sample

We conducted a confirmatory factor analysis with our 16 EI items and the Big Five personality dimensions. To avoid too many indicators for the Big Five measures, we formed three indicators for each dimension by randomly averaging two items from the respective dimension. Results show reasonably good fit for the nine-factor model (i.e., four EI and five personality factors). The model χ^2 was 591.59 (d.f. = 398), the standardized RMR was .08, the CFI was .90, and the TLI was .89. These results indicate good convergent and discriminant validity between our EI and the Big Five personality dimensions. To cross-validate the incremental predictive validity of our EI measure on the Big Five personality dimensions and the EQ-i, hierarchical regression was conducted on life satisfaction by entering the Big Five personality dimensions and EQ-i in the first step and our EI measure in the second step. The changes in model R^2 when the two sets of predictors were entered hierarchically were .099 (p < .01), and .023

Table 2.4 Regression results for the discriminant, convergent, and incremental validity samples of Study 2.1

	Sample 1 (n = 110)		Sample 2 (n = 116)
	Life Satisfaction	Powerlessness	Life Satisfaction
NEURO	−.13	.12	−.01
EXTRA	.19*	.00	−.03
OPEN	.06	−.10	−.00
AGREE	.20*	.09	−.01
CONSC	.20*	−.15	−.08
ATTEND	.05	−.28*	—
CLARITY	.03	.06	—
REPAIR	−.17*	.08	—
EQ-i	—	—	.22⁺
EI	.35**	−.22⁺	.23⁺
R²	.57**	.38**	.20**

Notes
NEURO, EXTRA, OPEN, AGREE, and CONSC = neuroticism, extraversion, openness, agreeableness, and conscientiousness, the Big Five personality dimensions; ATTEND, CLARITY, and REPAIR = the three emotional intelligence dimensions of the Trait-Meta-Mood Scale; EQ-i = the estimate of emotional intelligence by the Bar-On Emotional Quotient Inventory items; EI = the estimate of emotional intelligence using the 16 items developed in this study.

$^+p < .10$; $*p < .05$; $**p < .01$ (two-tailed tests).

(p < .10), respectively. Thus, the incremental validity was cross-validated in this non-student sample. The third column in Table 2.4 shows the beta coefficients for the final step of this regression analysis. Finally, descriptive statistics and correlation among the measures for this sample are shown in Table 2.5. Table 2.5 may be regarded as a multi-trait multi-method correlation matrix, as we have two measures of both the Big Five personality dimensions and EI. The results clearly indicate the convergence between our EI measure and the EQ-i (r = .63) and its discriminant validity with regard to the Big Five personality dimensions. The patterns of correlations of our EI measure and the EQ-i with the Big Five personality dimensions were very similar, and they were all smaller than the correlation between the EI and EQ-i measures.

Estimation of the EI construct from its dimensions

Based on the above analyses of the three groups of samples showing evidence of factor structure, internal consistency, convergence, and discriminant and incremental validity, we concluded that our EI measure should be of reasonable reliability and validity to be adopted for further studies. However, as EI is a multidimensional construct, one final issue is the estimation of the overall EI

Table 2.5 Correlation matrix for the second convergent, discriminant, and incremental validity sample

	Mean (S.D.)	1	2	3	4	5	6	7	8	9	10	11	12
1. NEURO1	3.06 (.57)	(.83)											
2. NEURO2	3.52 (.76)	.64	(.79)										
3. EXTRA1	3.17 (.42)	-.40	-.21	(.68)									
4. EXTRA2	3.91 (.68)	-.21	-.03	.69	(.77)								
5. OPEN1	3.17 (.40)	.14	.21	.08	.25	(.62)							
6. OPEN2	3.79 (.64)	-.01	.04	.18	.44	.36	(.72)						
7. AGREE1	3.26 (.42)	-.06	-.02	.14	.08	.16	-.02	(.67)					
8. AGREE2	4.31 (.63)	.09	.20	.18	.30	.06	.15	.58	(.78)				
9. CONSC1	3.33 (.46)	-.28	-.20	.15	.13	-.17	-.02	.32	.23	(.74)			
10. CONSC2	3.93 (.60)	-.27	-.17	.23	.34	-.01	.17	.27	.30	.59	(.70)		
11. EQ-i	4.86 (.54)	-.27	-.15	.22	.25	.04	.13	-.04	.04	.25	.30	(.78)	
12. LS	3.74 (.95)	-.17	-.08	.09	.10	.00	.05	.04	-.01	.25	.24	.39	(.92)
13. EI	4.95 (.79)	-.40	-.24	.24	.27	.07	.13	.17	.19	.50	.51	.63	.41

Notes

n = 116. Numbers in the diagonal are coefficient alphas. NEURO, EXTRA, OPEN, AGREE, and CONSC = neuroticism, extraversion, openness, agreeableness, and conscientiousness, the Big Five personality dimensions; EQ-i = the estimate of emotional intelligence based on the Bar-On Emotional Quotient Inventory items; LS = life satisfaction; EI = the estimate of emotional intelligence using the 16 items developed in this study. The number after each dimension represents the measure used for the latent construct. For example, NEURO1 represents the first measure of the neuroticism dimension of the Big Five personality elements. The first and second personality measures are the Neuroticism-Extraversion-Openness (NEO) Personality Inventory and the adjective scales, respectively. The NEO Personality Inventory is measured by a 5-point scale, and the EQ-i and EI are measured by 7-point scales, while all others are measured by 6-point scales.

construct from its dimensions. Law, Wong, and Mobley (1998) pointed out that there are three types of multidimensional constructs, namely, profile, aggregate, and latent. For the profile and aggregate types, individual dimensions of the multidimensional construct may be unrelated to each other. As the EI construct represents interrelated sets (dimensions) of abilities, it mostly fits the latent type. That is, the EI construct exists at a deeper level than its dimensions, and the dimensions should be interrelated because they are manifestations of the EI construct. This definition is also comparable to the traditional intelligence construct, which is defined as the common factor behind various sets (dimensions) of abilities in verbal comprehension, word fluency, spatial reasoning, numerical manipulation, memory, and reasoning (Eysenck, 1964).

To test whether the EI items that were developed fit this description, we followed the recommendation of Law et al. (1998) to perform a second-order confirmatory factor analysis on the EI items. Specifically, we compared the results of two confirmatory factor analyses. The first specified a single factor behind all the 16 items, while the second specified the four dimensions from their respective items and then a second-order factor behind the four EI dimensions. For all of the samples in Study 2.1, the results of the single-factor model were unacceptable, while the second-order model fitted the data reasonably well. For example, the non-student sample (i.e., the second convergent, discriminant, and incremental validity sample with n = 116) had an extremely poor fit for the single-factor model (χ^2 = 942.95 with d.f. = 104; CFI = .44; TLI = .35; standardized RMR = .20), while it fitted well the second-order model (χ^2 = 211.85 with d.f. = 100; CFI = .93; TLI = .91; standardized RMR = .08). From these results, we conclude that the EI items developed in Study 2.1 can serve as a reasonable estimate of their dimensions, and that the dimensions in turn can represent an underlying multidimensional EI construct.

Study 2.2: testing the interaction between the EI of followers and their emotional labor

There are two limitations of the design in the series of analyses conducted in Study 2.1. First, all of the dependent and independent variables are self-reported by the same respondents. It is difficult to tell how much of the covariance between EI and the criterion variables (life satisfaction and powerlessness) is caused by the problem of common method variance. Second, all the samples except the last one used to test the EI scale developed are from undergraduate students. The results may not be generalizable to experienced workers in an organization. To deal with these two concerns, we conducted our second study with practicing managers to test the hypothesis that the EI of followers is related to their job performance and that the relationship is moderated by emotional labor.

Sample and procedures

The sample for this study consisted of 149 supervisor–subordinate dyads. The supervisors were 60 middle- and upper-level managers enrolled in a part-time management diploma course at a large Hong Kong university. These managers were asked to evaluate the emotional labor and job performance of four of their subordinates. Respondents with fewer than four subordinates were asked to evaluate as many subordinates as they had. After completing the evaluations, the managers were asked to give a sealed envelope to each of their subordinates. The envelope contained (1) a cover letter explaining the objectives of the study and a statement ensuring that responses would be confidential, (2) a stamped reply envelope addressed to the authors of this study, and (3) a short questionnaire containing our 16-item EI scale and scales designed to measure emotional labor, job satisfaction, organizational commitment, and turnover intention. Each subordinate questionnaire was marked with an identification code so that the evaluation of the supervisors could be matched with the responses of their subordinates. According to the supervisors, 160 subordinate questionnaires were given and 149 completed questionnaires were received. The mean age of these subordinates was 29.02 (with a standard deviation of 6.97), and 52.8% were female.

Measures

EI

The 16 items developed from Study 2.1 were used to measure the EI of the subordinates. The response format was a 7-point Likert-type scale. Reliability estimates (coefficient alphas) for the four dimensions of SEA, UOE, ROE, and OEA were .89, .88, .76, and .85.

Emotional labor: supervisor judgments

Because emotional labor is a requirement of the organization, and supervisors are responsible to ensure that their subordinates fulfill this requirement, we believe that supervisors should be the most reasonable people to judge the emotional labor of subordinates. Therefore, we trained the supervisors for about an hour in the concept of emotional labor. After introducing the concept, we showed the supervisors the Adelmann (1989, pp. 22–24) tables, which contrast high and low emotional labor jobs in different occupations. The classification system was explained. Then samples of job descriptions were presented, and the supervisors were asked to judge whether these jobs should be classified as high or low in emotional labor. The training session ended when the supervisors reached a consensus on the classification of these jobs. The supervisors were asked to judge whether the jobs of their subordinates should be classified as requiring a high (coded as 1) or low degree of emotional labor (coded as 0) before they evaluated the performance and organizational citizenship behavior of their subordinates. They were instructed to select subordinates with both high and low emotional labor jobs whenever possible.

Emotional labor: subordinate ratings

Past studies either were case studies (e.g., Rafaeli & Sutton, 1987; Sutton, 1991; Van Maanen & Kunda, 1989) or used an ad hoc measure that was suitable only for a particular occupation or sample (e.g., Morris & Feldman, 1997; Wharton, 1993; Wharton & Erickson, 1995). To provide cross-validation evidence for the supervisor judgments, we also included five emotional labor items in the incumbent questionnaire. We designed these items according to the Hochschild (1983) characteristics of jobs with a high degree of emotional labor, and the items used by Adelmann (1989). These five items are shown in the Appendix 2.1. The response format was a 7-point Likert-type scale, and the coefficient alpha of these five items was .69.

Job satisfaction

The four items from the Job Diagnostic Survey (Hackman & Oldham, 1975), which measure satisfaction with the work itself, were adopted. These items asked respondents to evaluate their extent of satisfaction in four dimensions of performing their jobs (including, for example, the amount of personal growth and development and the feeling of worthwhile accomplishment). The response format was a 5-point Likert-type scale. The coefficient alpha of these four items was .77.

Organizational commitment

The six items measuring the affective commitment to the organization as developed by Meyer, Allen, and Smith (1993) were adopted. An example of such items is "I really feel as if this organization's problems are my own." The response format was a 5-point Likert-type scale. The coefficient alpha of the six items was .74.

Turnover intention

The three items from Cammann, Fichman, Jenkins, and Klesh (1979) were modified so that a Likert-type response scale could be used. An example of such items is "I will probably look for a new job in the next year." The response format was a 5-point Likert-type scale, and the coefficient alpha of the three items was .81.

Job performance

The five items developed by Williams (1988) and used by Hui, Law, and Chen (1999) were adopted. An example of such items is "This subordinate always completes the duties specified in his/her job description." The response format was a 7-point Likert-type scale, and the coefficient alpha of the three items was .81.

Results

Two preliminary analyses were conducted to check the appropriateness of the EI and emotional labor measures. Using the LISREL program, confirmatory factor analysis was conducted on the 16 EI items to determine whether they conformed to the four-factor model as designed. To maximize our sample size, we invited the 60 supervisors to evaluate their own EI level, and we included these 60 data points in the confirmatory factor analysis. In other words, the total sample size of the confirmatory factor analysis was 209. The results of the analysis showed that the four-factor model fitted the data very well. The model χ^2 was 233.53 (d.f. = 98), the CFI was .94, the TLI was .92, and the standardized RMR was .05. The reliability estimates for each dimension (ranging from .76 to .89) were also acceptable. As with the samples in Study 2.1, the second-order model also resulted in a reasonably good fit (χ^2 = 243.59, with d.f. = 100; CFI = .93; TLI = .92; standardized RMR = .07), while the single-factor model was unacceptable (χ^2 = 488.20, with d.f. = 104; CFI = .82; TLI = .80; standardized RMR = .20). Thus, these dimensions may be combined to form an estimate of the underlying EI construct.

Moreover, the convergence of the supervisor judgments and incumbent ratings of emotional labor were examined. As a supervisor's judgment is a dichotomous variable, the point-biserial correlation coefficient was calculated. It was 0.77 ($p < .01$) between the two ratings, which indicated strong agreement between the supervisors and incumbents concerning the emotional labor of incumbent jobs.

We conducted another preliminary analysis for the performance data because, in our data, 41 supervisors rated the performance of more than one subordinate. The independence of the performance data may have created a problem in data analysis. Thus, we calculated the within-group inter-rater reliability for these 41 supervisors according to the formula provided by L. R. James, Demaree, and Wolf (1984). To be conservative, we did not consider any response bias and assumed a triangular null distribution. The mean inter-rater reliability for the 41 groups of performance ratings was 0.65, and its standard deviation was 0.31. Over half of these reliability coefficients (53.7%) were less than 0.70. George and Bettenhausen (1990) argued that an inter-rater reliability greater than 0.70 could be considered as an indicator of good within-group agreement. From this result, we believe that the performance ratings may be regarded as independent and the results will not be affected significantly.

To test the proposed moderating effect of emotional labor on the follower EI–job outcome relationship, moderated regression analyses were conducted for each job outcome using both the measures of emotional labor (supervisor and subordinate assessment). Specifically, the main and interaction terms were entered into the regression equation step by step, and the change in R^2 was examined when the interaction term was entered into the equation.

Descriptive statistics and correlations among variables are shown in Table 2.6. It should be noted that the judgments by supervisors of a low degree of emotional labor were coded as 0, and those of a high degree of emotional labor were coded

Table 2.6 Descriptive statistics and correlations among variables for Study 2.2

	$\bar{X}$	S.D.	1	2	3	4	5	6	7	8	9	10	11
1. SEA	4.70	.97	(.89)										
2. ROE	4.71	.91	.68**	(.76)									
3. UOE	4.50	.96	.73**	.60**	(.88)								
4. OEA	4.59	.96	.74**	.76**	.65**	(.85)							
5. EI	4.63	.83	.90**	.86**	.85**	.90**	(.94)						
6. EL (Sup.)	.51	.50	.32**	.37**	.16	.39**	.35**	—					
7. EL (Sub.)	4.42	.79	.44**	.47**	.33**	.49**	.49**	.77*	(.88)				
8. JP	5.00	.91	.15	.26**	.08	.27**	.21**	.31**	.25**	(.81)			
9. JS	3.27	.67	.34**	.45**	.27**	.36**	.40**	.29**	.44**	.27**	(.77)		
10. OC	3.95	.78	.15	.17*	.14	.02	.14	.29**	.40**	.13	.45**	(.74)	
11. TI	3.78	1.31	−.00	−.01	.01	.11	.03	−.10	−.08	−.10	−.34**	−.53**	(.81)

Notes

n = 149. SEA, ROE, UOE, and OEA = self emotional appraisal, regulation of emotion, use of emotion, and other's emotional appraisal; EI = the mean score of the four EI dimensions; EL (Sup.) = emotional labor estimated by supervisor; EL (Sub.) = emotional labor estimated by incumbents; JP = job performance; JS = job satisfaction; OC = organizational commitment; TI = turnover intention.

$^+$p < .10; *p < .05; **p < .01 (two-tailed tests).

as 1. EI (as represented by the mean score across the four EI dimensions) had a significant correlation with job performance ($r = .21$, $p < .01$) and job satisfaction ($r = .40$, $p < .01$) but a non-significant correlation with organizational commitment ($r = .14$, n.s.) and turnover intention ($r = .03$, n.s.). As a result, we conclude that hypotheses 2.1 and 2.2 are supported, while hypotheses 2.3 and 2.4 are not. EI is related to job performance and job satisfaction but not to organizational commitment and turnover intention.

The results of the moderated regression analyses are shown in Table 2.7. As an exploratory effort, we conducted these analyses for both the overall measure of EI and its individual dimensions. As the results are quite similar, we focus on the mean EI score as a representation of the EI construct to simplify our discussion. As shown in the two parts of Table 2.7, the interaction terms are significant when organizational commitment and turnover intention are used as the dependent variables. It does not matter whether supervisor or job incumbent assessments of emotional labor are used. Therefore, hypotheses 2.7 and 2.8 are strongly supported. Emotional labor is a significant moderator of the EI–job performance relationship when incumbent assessments of emotional labor are used. When supervisor assessments of emotional labor are used, the

Table 2.7 Change in the model R^2 of the moderated regression analysis

	Dependent Variables			
	Job Performance	Job Satisfaction	Organizational Commitment	Turnover Intention
(a) Using Supervisor Assessments of Emotional Labor				
SEA* EL	.02[+]	.02[+]	.06**	.06**
OEA * EL	.01	.01	.06**	.08**
ROE * EL	.02[+]	.01	.05**	.04*
UOE * EL	.01	.01	.07**	.06**
EI * EL	.02[+]	.02[+]	.09**	.08**
(b) Using Job Incumbent Assessments of Emotional Labor				
SEA* EL	.03*	.00	.03*	.04*
OEA * EL	.03*	.00	.02[+]	.06**
ROE * EL	.02	.00	.04*	.06**
UOE * EL	.00	.01	.04**	.04*
EI * EL	.03*	.01	.04[+]	.06**

Notes
n = 149. SEA, OEA, ROE, and UOE = self emotional appraisal, other's emotional appraisal, regulation of emotion, and use of emotion; EL = emotional labor; EI = the mean score of the four EI dimensions.

[+]p < .10; *p < .05; **p < .01 (two-tailed tests).

Table 2.8 Beta coefficients for the regression of job outcomes on emotional intelligence for the groups with high and low levels of emotional labor as judged by supervisors

	Low EL Group (n = 73)			High EL Group (n = 76)		
	b_0	b_1	R_{xy}	b_0	b_1	R_{xy}
Job performance	4.71	.00	.00	3.70	.32	.26
Organizational commitment	4.61	–.21	–.26	2.17	.41	.34
Turnover intention	1.76	.50	.36	5.85	–.45	–.22

Notes
The low and high emotional labor (EL) groups represent the jobs which were judged to involve low and high emotional labor, respectively, by their supervisors; b_0 is the intercept of the regression line, and b_1 is the slope of the regression line; R_{xy} is the Pearson correlation between EI and the outcome variable.

moderating term is marginally significant. As a whole, we conclude that hypothesis 2.5 is generally supported. In contrast, the product term is marginally significant when job satisfaction is used as the dependent variable and emotional labor is assessed by the supervisor. When emotional labor is assessed by incumbents, the product term is not significant. Therefore, hypothesis 2.6 is not supported.

To examine the direction of the interaction term, we calculated the intercepts (b_0), slope (b_1), and correlation coefficients for the high and low emotional labor sub-groups according to supervisor judgments of emotional labor. The results are shown in Table 2.8. These results provide strong support for our hypotheses.

The correlation between EI and job performance was virtually zero in the low emotional labor group, while it was highly significant (r = .26) in the high emotional labor group. The results for organizational commitment and turnover intention are even more dramatic. EI showed the expected positive correlation with organizational commitment (r = .34) and a negative correlation with turnover intention (r = –.22) only in the high emotional labor group. In the low emotional labor group, the observed correlations are opposite to the expected relationships. These differences in correlation coefficients are all statistically significant (p < .05).

Study 2.3: testing the influence of leader EI on followers' job outcomes

Study 2.2 demonstrated the relationship between follower EI and job outcomes. In Study 2.3, we test the relationship between the EI of leaders and their effectiveness by examining the relationship between leader EI and follower job outcomes.

Sample and procedures

To control for organizational differences, the sample for this study consisted of 146 middle-level administrators in the Hong Kong government. These administrators were asked to evaluate their own EI with the 16-item EI measure developed in Study 2.1, and the in-role and extra-role behaviors of one of their subordinates who reported to them directly. After completing the evaluations, these administrators were asked to give a short questionnaire containing the 16-item EI scale and items assessing job satisfaction, job characteristics, education level, and tenure with the organization to the subordinate they had evaluated. These subordinates were given the short questionnaire in a sealed envelope that contained a cover letter explaining the objectives of the study, a statement ensuring that responses would be confidential, and a stamped reply envelope addressed to the authors of this study. Respondents mailed the completed questionnaire directly to the authors. Each questionnaire was marked with an identification code so that supervisor evaluations could be matched with subordinate responses. The mean age of these subordinates was 28.90 (with a standard deviation of 6.30), and 61.9% were female.

Measures

EI

Reliability estimates (coefficient alphas) for the four dimensions of SEA, UOE, ROE, and OEA were .83, .89, .83, and .90 for the supervisor responses. These reliability estimates were .86, .85, .79, and .82 for the subordinate responses.

Job satisfaction

The 14 items from the Job Diagnostic Survey (Hackman & Oldham, 1975) that measures job satisfaction were adopted. The response format was a 5-point Likert-type scale, and the coefficient alpha of these 14 items was .87.

Job perception

Although we chose a relative homogeneous sample in terms of organizational culture and reward systems, job characteristics were statistically controlled because respondents came from different units of the government service. Thus, we measured their job characteristics by the 15 items of the Job Diagnostic Survey (Hackman & Oldham, 1975). The response format was a 7-point Likert-type scale, and the reliability for each dimension was skills variety, .73; job identity, .85; job significance, .80; autonomy, .80; and feedback, .61.

In-role and extra-role behavior

The five items used in Study 2.2 measuring in-role behavior (i.e., job performance) were adopted. The response format was a 7-point Likert-type scale, and the coefficient alpha in this sample was .81. Extra-role behavior (i.e., organizational citizenship behavior) was measured by items from Podsakoff, MacKenzie, Moorman, and Fetter (1990). These 36 items measured seven dimensions of organizational citizenship behaviors. The response format was a 7-point Likert-type scale, and the coefficient alphas were altruism, .88; peace-making, .78; cheerleader, .92; conscientiousness, .84; civic virtue, .83; courtesy, .83; and sportsmanship, .80.

Education and tenure with organization

Education level and job tenure were also assessed in this study. Education level was measured by a multiple-choice item. Primary, secondary, and tertiary education levels were coded as 1, 2, and 3. Tenure with the organization was measured by an open question asking respondents to indicate their tenure with their organizations in terms of the number of months.

Results

Descriptive statistics and the correlations among measures are shown in Table 2.9. To test for the relationship between leader EI and follower job outcomes, hierarchical regression was conducted. The results are shown in Table 2.10. After controlling for the subordinate job perceptions, EI, education level, and tenure with the organization, the EI of supervisors still had a marginally significant relationship with the job satisfaction of subordinates and a significant relationship with their extra-role behaviors. However, no relationship was found

Table 2.9 Descriptive statistics and correlations among variables for Study 2.3

	Mean	S.D.	1	2	3	4	5	6	7
1. Subordinate's EI	4.84	.76	—						
2. Supervisor's EI	5.32	.72	.05	—					
3. Job perception	4.42	.93	.23**	.25**	—				
4. Job performance	5.07	.89	.05	.13	.14+	—			
5. Job satisfaction	3.25	.52	.22**	.26**	.55**	.16+	—		
6. Organizational citizenship behavior	4.39	.72	.15+	.21*	.29**	.63**	.21*	—	
7. Education level	2.35	.55	.19*	−.13	−.09	−.01	−.14	.03	—
8. Tenure	45.54	46.34	−.11	.10	.05	.10	.12	−.07	−.28**

Notes
n = 146. EI = emotional intelligence as measured by the 16 items developed in this study.
+p < .10; *p < .05; **p < .01 (two-tailed tests).

Table 2.10 Results of regression analyses of leader EI on follower job outcomes

Independent Variables	Dependent Variables					
	Job Performance		Job Satisfaction		Organizational Citizenship Behavior	
	Model 1	Model 2	Model 1	Model 2	Model 1	Model 2
Job perception	.13	.10	.51**	.48**	.23**	.21*
Subordinate's EI	.02	.01	.14+	.14+	.08	.08
Education level	.04	.05	−.09	−.07	.03	.04
Tenure	.10	.09	.09	.08	−.08	−.09
Job satisfaction	–	–	–	–	.07	.04
Supervisor's EI	–	.122	–	.13+	–	.18*
R^2	.026	.040	.333**	.348**	.100*	.128*
ΔR^2	–	.014	–	.015+	–	.028*

Notes
n = 146. EI = emotional intelligence as measured by the 16 items developed in this study.

+$p < .10$; *$p < .05$; **$p < .01$ (two-tailed tests).

for job performance. Thus, hypothesis 2.9 was not supported, while hypotheses 2.10 and 2.11 were supported.

Discussion and conclusion

Recently, increasing numbers of scholars have argued that EI is a core variable that affects the performance of leaders (see, e.g., Day, 2000; Sternberg, 1997). Unfortunately, there has been a lack of a psychometrically sound yet practically short EI measure for leadership and management research. There is also little evidence concerning the relationship between the EI of leaders and followers and job outcomes. The purpose of this study was to develop such a measure and provide evidence concerning the relationship between EI and job outcomes to aid future leadership and management research.

Our study yielded some interesting results. First, apart from acceptable reliability and validity, the EI measure developed shows good convergence with some of the past EI measures such as the Trait-Meta-Mood Scale and the EQ-i. However, our measure appears to perform better in predicting external criterion variables such as life satisfaction. As the EI measure developed is relatively simple, it may be beneficial for future leadership and management research.

For the EI of followers, our study has provided preliminary evidence that the EI–job outcome relationship is more complicated than recent proposals have suggested (e.g., Abraham, 1999; Ashkanasy & Hooper, 1999; Goleman, 1998).

Specifically, job performance is significantly correlated with EI, and this relationship appears to be moderated by emotional labor, as proposed in Figure 2.1. Job satisfaction is significantly correlated with EI, but emotional labor does not moderate the EI–job satisfaction relationship. In contrast, organizational commitment and turnover intention have a low and non-significant correlation with EI, but emotional labor strongly moderates the EI–commitment and EI–turnover intention relationship. In other words, EI has a strong positive relationship with job satisfaction regardless of the nature of the job. In contrast, EI might have a desirable relationship with organizational commitment and turnover intention only in jobs that require high emotional labor, while the relationship is undesirable in jobs that require low emotional labor. Perhaps this is because employees with high EI find it difficult to commit to a workplace that is not conducive to the emotional impact they consider good. Alternatively, they may feel that their abilities are not appreciated or utilized in low emotional labor jobs. These results are sensible on a post-hoc basis, although they were unexpected when the study was designed.

Our study provides some preliminary support for researchers who have proposed the importance of leader EI (e.g., Boal & Hooijberg, 2000; Hooijberg, Hunt, & Dodge, 1997; Sternberg, 1997). Our results show that the EI of leaders is positively related to the job satisfaction and extra-role behavior of followers, as expected. However, no relationship between the EI of leaders and the job performance of their followers has been found. This may be due to our sample, which consists of government administrators, who have a culture of distorting the performance ratings of their subordinates. Future research should use different samples to cross-validate this finding.

Despite these unexpected findings and limitations, we believe there are both theoretical and practical implications of this study. Theoretically, we have applied the emotion regulation model to explain the importance of EI in social interactions in the workplace. As some or most of the social interactions in the workplace may be related to job duties, we hypothesize a positive relationship between EI and job outcomes. As an exploratory effort, we focus on demonstrating these relationships. As the results of this study provide support for these relationships, it is worthwhile to investigate further the role of emotion regulation in the workplace. For example, the emotion regulation model has specified two types of actions to regulate emotions, namely, antecedent- and response-focused emotion regulation. It is worthwhile to investigate the specific actions taken by both the leaders and the incumbents in the workplace. What are the factors affecting the choices of actions made by leaders and incumbents? Will some actions be more effective under certain circumstances? Will some actions be more effective for some jobs? These are interesting questions that future leadership and management research should address.

Furthermore, new studies should be conducted to investigate the role of EI in the workplace. Proponents have argued for the benefit of hiring employees with high levels of EI. However, few empirical studies have been conducted to test this argument. The results of this exploratory study provide clear evidence that EI may play a role in the workplace in bringing about important job outcomes that management desires.

The results of this study also have certain practical implications. First, it is generally believed that individuals with a high level of EI are better employees. For example, Goleman (1995) contends that "emotional intelligence, the skills that help people harmonize should become increasingly valued as a workplace asset in the years to come" (p. 160). The results of this study indicate that although it may be nice to have leaders and employees with a high level of EI because these employees tend to have higher job satisfaction, it is still important to ensure the match between employee levels of EI and job requirements. It may be a waste of resources and time to stress the importance of the level of employee EI when it is not required in the job.

Second, in contrast to our expectations, strong interaction effects were observed for organizational commitment and turnover intention. That is, the relationship between follower EI and organizational commitment and turnover intention is undesirable for low emotional labor jobs. If this finding is further verified by future research, then it will mean that employees with high levels of EI who do not have the opportunity to use these skills in their jobs may be less committed to their organizations and have a higher chance of quitting. This finding is worthy of further research. It is also interesting that this strong moderation does not hold for other job outcomes such as job performance. Perhaps employees with a high level of EI are still able to concentrate on performing their jobs although they know that their skills are under-utilized. Thus, having employees with a high level of EI may be advantageous to the organization.

To conclude, this study has provided some preliminary evidence for the role of leader and follower EI and for the moderating effect of emotional labor on the EI–job outcome relationship. As an exploratory effort, we believe that we have provided sufficient evidence for future leadership and management research to investigate the role of emotions in the workplace. Thus, more research on the role of both leader and follower EI in the workplace is necessary.

Appendix 2.1
EI and emotional labor items

EI items

Self emotional appraisal (SEA)

1. I have a good sense of why I have certain feelings most of the time.
2. I have good understanding of my own emotions.
3. I really understand what I feel.
4. I always know whether or not I am happy.

Other's emotional appraisal (OEA)

5. I always know my friends' emotions from their behavior.
6. I am a good observer of others' emotions.
7. I am sensitive to the feelings and emotions of others.
8. I have good understanding of the emotions of people around me.

Regulation of emotion (ROE)

9. I always set goals for myself and then try my best to achieve them.
10. I always tell myself I am a competent person.
11. I am a self-motivated person.
12. I would always encourage myself to try my best.

Use of emotion (UOE)

13. I am able to control my temper and handle difficulties rationally.
14. I am quite capable of controlling my own emotions.
15. I can always calm down quickly when I am very angry.
16. I have good control of my own emotions.

Emotional labor items

To perform my job well, it is necessary for me to:

1. spend most of my work time interacting with people (e.g., customers, colleagues, and other workers in this organization).
2. spend a lot of time with every person whom I work with.
3. hide my actual feelings when acting and speaking with people.
4. be considerate and think from the point of view of others.
5. hide my negative feelings (e.g., anger and depression).

3 Sufficient evidence to make yourself comfortable?

As reported in Chapter 2, we were invited to submit our Academy of Management conference paper to the *Leadership Quarterly* in spring of 2000. We felt happy and believed that the paper would soon be published in this mainstream management journal. However, it still took us three revisions, and we needed to add in the results of two more independent samples before the paper was accepted. As far as we know, this paper might be an important breakthrough because the emotional intelligence (EI) construct was not accepted in mainstream psychology and management literature up to the year 2002. One of the major reasons was that in 1998 a paper published in a very influential psychology journal severely criticized the EI construct (Davies, Stankov, & Roberts, 1998). In that paper, the authors used the EI measurement scales reported from 1990 to 1998 and the traditional Big Five personality scales to collect data from multiple samples. Using the technique of factor analysis, they found that the items of the so-called EI measurement scales could not form an independent factor. Instead, they all loaded heavily on the traditional Big Five personality factors. Thus, they concluded that EI was only an "elusive" construct and implied that scholars should stop investigating this construct and that it would not be appropriate to use the EI construct to help explain psychological phenomena.

We were aware of Davies et al.'s paper as soon as it was published. At that time, we were collecting data to develop our practical EI measure. In fact, we agreed that the EI measurement scales reported from 1990 to 1998 were not adequate EI measures. This was why we decided to develop a practical EI measurement scale as the first step of our investigation in this line of research. However, we did not agree that EI itself was an elusive construct. We believed that if defined and measured adequately, EI could be a scientifically rigorous and valuable construct. The reason for Davies et al.'s findings was that most of the measurement items were not valid for two reasons. First, the investigation was at a very initial stage, and so it was difficult to have excellent measures. Second, the domain of EI was not clear, and so some people had added a lot of dimensions to the measurement scales. This created a lot of confusion about the definition of the EI construct and the resulting measurement scale. To show the validity of EI construct, these two points must be addressed.

Lesson 4: is the construct and related conceptualization scientifically sound?

The original proponents of the EI construct were aware of the problem of the unclear definition and domain of the EI construct at that time. On one hand, they tried to clarify the definition and domain of the EI construct. The major direction was to define the construct as a particular type of intelligence or ability. I totally agreed with this direction. For Chinese characters, we have a saying which means "recognizing the meaning from the words themselves." I think this is applicable to the case of EI. By putting the words "emotional" and "intelligence" together to form a concept, the only sensible definition to me is "the intelligence to deal with problems or issues that are related to emotions." Anything other than this will be excessive. As intelligence means problem-solving ability, anything that is not related to abilities, such as personality, should not be part of the concept. As the problem that needs to be solved should be related to emotions, other types of abilities such as abstract thinking and interpersonal relationships should not be part of the concept. Logically, we may argue that abstract thinking may be one of the antecedents or correlates of EI and inter-personal relationships may be a consequence of EI, but they should not be part of the EI concept.

Several years ago I had a chance to discuss the concept of EI with a very famous psychologist in mainland China just before his retirement. I said that intelligence is intelligence, and personality or anything else should never be confused with intelligence. I therefore disagree with some scholars who have used "trait EI" versus "ability EI" to distinguish personality and ability components of EI. If the concept is about a trait, then it is not EI. He agreed and said that it was a pity that graduate students or young researchers nowadays lacked the confidence to make this type of statements in conceptualizing constructs. They were easily confused when they read the literature and forgot the fundamental nature of different types of constructs such as perception, attitudes, personality, and abilities. However, this type of confidence and clarity about scientific constructs is extremely important in building up rigorous arguments concerning the constructs as well as relationships among them.

I think I am quite fortunate that at the early stage of my investigation of the EI construct, I was already very firm on the basic definition of "the intelligence to deal with problems or issues that are related to emotions." When I attempted to develop reasonable domains and measurement items, I did not include any other types of variables in the EI construct, and I was not surprised by Davies et al.'s findings. I was able to continue my investigation instead of accepting their conclusion that EI was an elusive construct.

The other related and important conceptualization that I firmly believed at the very beginning was the utility of EI in organizational behavior and human resource management. In my area, the fit between a person and a job is an important framework. If a person's abilities match the job requirements, then he/she can perform the job well. Thus, EI would affect job outcomes such as job performance only if the job requires incumbents with this type of ability to perform. In providing validation evidence for our practical EI measure, we incorporated the concept of emotional labor, which represents job requirements that match this person–job fit framework.

There are two possible definitions of emotional labor. The first is to define how the employees handle their emotions in order to perform their jobs. The well-established classification of ways to handle emotional requirements is deep acting versus surface acting. Deep acting means the employees internalize the needed emotions in performing their job, while surface acting means the employees only pretend they have those required emotions.

The second possible definition of emotional labor is to regard it as the extent to which the job requires employees to handle issues or problems related to emotions. We adopt this definition because it matches the fundamental conceptualization in my area. There should be little debate that EI, as the ability to handle problems related to emotions, may be more important for jobs that require employees to handle a lot of duties that involve emotions. Up to the present moment, I am still very confident that my basic definition of EI as a particular type of intelligence or ability and my argument that it will be more important for jobs with a high emotional labor requirement are reasonable. The EI construct and its relationships with various job outcomes and emotional labor can be subject to rigorous scientific investigation. Without the belief and understanding of the basic nature of the constructs and the area of investigation, I think it would be difficult for me to build up a line of research with various questions that are of interest to me over a relatively long period of time.

Lesson 4: Before collecting empirical evidence, can we be confident that we are able to define our constructs and their relationships in a reasonable manner? Can we use relatively simple language that we believe that a reasonable person without training in our field can understand and agree? If yes, then we can proceed with empirical investigation. If not, we better rethink them?

Lesson 5: patience and persistence in gathering evidence

If I did not have the confidence and a reasonable conceptualization, I think we probably would have stopped our investigation once Davies et al.'s (1998) paper was published. However, it did not mean that their findings had no impact on our investigation. We became even more careful to show that EI should be a correlated but distinct construct when compared to the Big Five personality dimensions. For example, we included Big Five personality measures in some of our samples in order to have evidence showing the distinctiveness of personality and EI. In the employee samples, we also attempted to show that EI had incremental predictive power for important job outcomes such as performance and satisfaction.

When we formally submitted our Academy of Management conference paper to the *Leadership Quarterly*, the major comment of the editor and reviewers was that they wanted us to provide stronger evidence about the impact of EI on job outcomes. In fact, we were a little bit surprised because, as we had been invited to submit our paper, we did not expect we still needed to report additional data. We were probably wrong in this expectation because our submission was being treated as an ordinary submission. We did not receive any preferential treatment from the editor.

We believed the comment was reasonable at that time. Thus, we reported the results of our seventh sample with data collected from supervisor–subordinate dyads. In this sample, we showed the impact of EI on traditional job outcomes including performance, satisfaction, turnover intention, and organizational commitment. We framed our original six samples as the first study of developing the measurement scale, while this seventh sample was the second study. The purpose of the second study was to provide a test of the interaction effect between EI and emotional labor on job outcomes.

After another round of revision, all three reviewers and the editor were satisfied with the evidence we provided. However, one reviewer had one last "minor" concern about the theme of our paper. He/she said that our study had nothing to do with leadership, and so it might not fit the journal. The editor agreed with this concern and said that if we could not show any relevance to the area of leadership, the paper could not be accepted. My co-author was quite angry at that time because the editor was well aware of the theme of our study when he invited us to submit the paper. If this issue was a critical concern, it should have been raised during the invitation. I remember that I gave my co-author a big smile and told him that I already had data from another sample that could show the relevance of EI in leadership. As I was interested in the topic, I tried to collect more evidence whenever I got the chance to do so. Just a few months before I had been invited to conduct a training session for some government officials. In exchange, I collected some data from the trainees and their subordinates. In that dataset, I investigated the impact of the supervisors' EI on their subordinates' job outcomes. Thus, we were able to report this sample as the third study of the paper. We wrote up the revision, and this time the paper was formally accepted.

The important lesson I learned is that we have to be patient and persistent in pursing some new and risky constructs or research questions. We need empirical evidence to demonstrate the validity of the constructs and their relationships. Even though we may be keen on showing that our expectations are correct, we have to be patient in collecting empirical evidence to test our expectations. During the first few years when I began to work on the EI construct, I tried to get evidence to show its validity whenever I got a chance to do so. We never know whether the end results will be as expected or whether we will actually be able to publish the data. The reason for the continuous efforts should not be too focused on publications. We have to keep the purpose of simply wanting to know and testing our expectations. Although publication is the name of the game, being curious and having the desire to test our expectations and theories should never be forgotten. Otherwise, we may miss the opportunity when it arises.

Lesson 5: Once we are confident about the constructs and the expected relation-ships among them, we should be patient and persistent in gathering empirical evidence to test them. Never replace pure curiosity with the instrumental purpose.

Lesson 6: editors and reviewers have their concerns

On top of the leadership sample, I had been collecting other data to test the validity of the EI construct during the first few years. I felt this was especially important after the publication of Davies et al.'s (1998) paper. I realized that it would become even more difficult for us to convince the editors and reviewers of mainstream journals that we were investigating something that would be worthwhile. I decided to go in two directions. First, I would try to work on related ideas as much as possible and present the evidence in whatever outlets I could. It would be very difficult to convince editors and reviewers in main-stream journals because they would definitely become more skeptical about the EI constructs after Davies et al.'s paper.

When I discussed this with my co-authors, I said we should use Chairman Mao Zedong's strategy in guerrilla warfare. That is, in order to get the cities, we first encircled them with rural areas. Instead of putting our hope solely in getting publications in the mainstream journals, we should present and publish as much as we could by whatever means. When there was sufficient information and attention from more scholars, the editors and reviewers of mainstream journals would change.

In my experience, many editors and reviewers of mainstream management journals are often quite conservative. They are not very receptive to really new and innovative constructs and theories, but they are very keen on rigorous scientific methods in empirical studies. On one hand, this may make it difficult to have a so-called paradigm shift in scientific investigation. This has been well discussed by some scholars such as Thomas Kuhn (1970). On the other hand, this may be necessary because once papers are published in mainstream journals, their findings and conclusions become influential and scholars will follow them as if they are the truth. Seldom will scholars severely criticize or be very skepti-cal regarding papers published in mainstream journals. It is a norm for scholars to frame their studies as following what has already been published and to argue that they are filling gaps in the existing literature instead of trying to create a new paradigm. A well-known saying is that we are standing on the shoulders of the giants, and *giants* refers to the extant literature. Thus, it is the respon-sibility of the editors and reviewers of mainstream journals to be very keen on the validity of the data that empirical studies report.

Unfortunately, it is relatively difficult for a single study on a really new and innovative idea to present comprehensive and convincing evidence compared to studies that are simply filling a particular research gap. As we had chosen to work on something that editors and reviewers of mainstream journals would be skeptical of, we were prepared to get rejections more often than those publish-ing on more established constructs and theories. Fortunately, we were not alone.

We later found out that a lot of management scholars were interested in studying emotions and EI during those years before publications could be found in mainstream management journals. I remember my co-author telling me that more than 300 people had shown up at a conference session with the theme of EI in the year 2002.

The second direction we adopted was to take Davies et al.'s study very seriously and try to show that the problem was with the early EI measurement scales, not the EI construct itself. Therefore, on top of the data for the first paper, we also collected data from two relatively large student samples to replicate Davies et al.'s study with two extensions. The first extension was to show that the items of our new measure would form a distinct factor instead of being part of the Big Five personality traits. Second, we added in criterion variables such as life satisfaction to show the incremental validity of EI over the Big Five personality dimensions.

We wrote a paper based on the two samples and submitted it to the journal where Davies et al.'s paper had been published. We tried our best not to frame our paper as a criticism of their paper. We simply argued that Davies et al.'s findings had no problem but that the conclusion was too strong. Instead of regarding EI as an elusive construct, we needed to be very careful in defining the domain of EI when we developed measurement instruments for the EI concept. When measurement items are purely ability based, they would not load on the Big Five personality factors.

Unfortunately, the paper was desk rejected. It was not a total surprise to me, and it took only a very short period of time for me to refocus on how I could further improve the paper. I discussed it with my co-authors and decided to get employee samples so that we could try to sell the idea to management journals. We also decided to collect more rigorous and convincing data such as using multiple sources of data collection to avoid common method variance (i.e., both the independent and dependent variables are reported by the same respondent). At that time, the problem of common method variance was becoming a more and more critical concern in management studies. So we continued with the idea and tried to strengthen our paper with more convincing evidence instead of giving up.

Lesson 6: Editors and reviewers of mainstream journals have their concerns. We have to respect their concerns and not be easily disappointed. The acceptance rate of these journals is usually less than 5%. Rejection is the rule, while acceptance is the exception. We need to be "emotionally intelligent" enough to face rejections.

Second published paper in a mainstream management journal

After spending more than a year collecting data from two samples in mainland China, we framed the original two student samples as the first study. The two new samples were reported as the second study of the paper. By that time, the *Leadership Quarterly* paper had been formally accepted, and so we framed this second paper as providing further evidence for our newly developed EI scale. We submitted this paper to the *Journal of Applied Psychology*, and, fortunately, after several rounds of revisions, the paper was accepted (Law, Wong, & Song, 2004). As far as we know, this is the second EI paper to be published in a mainstream management journal. In the next chapter, I will report some experiences from our "encircling the cities" strategy.

The following are the major contents of the paper.

Law, K. S., Wong, C. S., & Song, L. J. (2004). The construct validity of emotional intelligence and its potential utility for management studies. *Journal of Applied Psychology*, 89(3), 483–496; these contents are reprinted with permission.

Abstract. Despite the growing interest in emotional intelligence (EI), there has been considerable debate on whether EI is an elusive construct, what its dimensions are, and whether it can be considered as a dimension of intelligence. Some empirical evidence has been reported demonstrating that most EI-related scales fail to capture a construct that is distinct from traditional personality dimensions. In this study, we review the definition and domain of EI and argue that, when properly defined, EI is conceptually distinct from personality. To investigate the distinctiveness and potential utility of the EI construct, we used a two-study, four-sample design with participants from Hong Kong and the People's Republic of China. In Study 3.1, we used confirmatory factor analyses to show that, when properly defined and measured, EI is related to yet distinct from personality dimensions and has incremental predictive power on life satisfaction. In Study 3.2, multi-trait multi-method (MTMM) analyses were utilized to examine the construct validity of self-reports and others' ratings of EI. In a student sample, parents' ratings explained additional variance in the students' life satisfaction and feelings of powerlessness after controlling for the Big Five personality dimensions. The results of the MTMM analyses were cross-validated on an employee sample with peer ratings of EI. These peer ratings were found to be significant predictors of job performance ratings provided by supervisors, after controlling for the Big Five personality dimensions. We conclude that, when defined and measured properly, EI is a distinct and useful construct for psychological and management research. Other implications for future research on EI are discussed.

Emotional intelligence (EI) has been an emerging topic among social and organizational psychologists in recent years (see, e.g., Fineman, 1993; Mayer & Salovey, 1997; Schutte et al., 2001). There have been serious academic discussions on whether EI is an elusive construct (Davies, Stankov, & Roberts, 1998), what its dimensions are (Salovey & Mayer, 1990), and whether it should be considered as a dimension of intelligence (Mayer, Caruso, & Salovey, 2000a; Mayer & Salovey, 1997). Proponents of the EI construct have argued that it is distinct from traditional personality traits and general mental abilities and that it is a meaningful construct that can be used to explain various psychological and managerial phenomena. These proponents have developed various EI-related scales to measure the construct. However, some scholars have voiced strong reservations concerning the reliability and validity of these scales. For example, Davies et al. (1998) reviewed all of the existing EI-related scales and demonstrated, through exploratory factor analyses, that most of the scales had salient cross-loadings on personality dimensions. However, Wong and Law (2002) re-examined the definition and domain of the EI construct and developed a new EI scale. Using this new EI scale, they showed that on top of general mental abilities, EI was a good predictor of job performance. Given these opposing views of EI, some researchers continue to develop new and revised EI measures (see, e.g., Salovey, Mayer, Caruso, & Lopes, 2003; Schutte et al., 1998; Stough & Palmer, 2002), while others continue to take a conservative position and question the usefulness of EI for serious scientific research (see, e.g., Petrides & Furnham, 2000b).

The major purposes of this study are threefold. First, we review the definition and domain of the EI construct and argue that when EI is properly defined, it is conceptually distinct from personality dimensions. Second, we examine a newly developed EI scale under the generally agreed EI definition and demonstrate empirically that, as measured by this new scale, EI is distinct from personality dimensions. Third, in addition to conceptual and empirical distinctiveness, we also try to establish the predictive validity of EI in social and organizational settings. We use self and others' ratings of EI and investigate its construct validity using multi-trait multi-method (MTMM) analyses. Furthermore, we illustrate the incremental predictive power of others' ratings of EI on psychological and work outcomes, over and above personality dimensions, using a series of hierarchical regression analyses.

The definition and domain of EI

Psychology and management researchers were interested in studying human emotions long before the construct of EI was proposed. Salovey and Mayer (1990) were among the earliest to suggest the name "emotional intelligence" to refer to the ability of a person to deal with his/her emotions. They defined EI as "the subset of social intelligence that involves the ability to monitor one's own and others' feelings and emotions, to discriminate among them and to use this information to guide one's thinking and actions" (p. 189). Despite this early definition of EI, there has been confusion regarding the exact meaning and domain of this construct. During the early stage of the development of the EI construct, different researchers have used slightly different definitions of EI, which has led to some variations in the domain of the construct. As Mayer, Caruso, et al. (2000a) commented, some of "these alternative conceptions *of emotional intelligence* include not only emotion and intelligence per se, but also motivation, non-ability dispositions and traits, and global personal and social functioning" (p. 268, emphasis added). The Bar-On Emotional Quotient Inventory (EQ-i; Bar-On, 1997) is a well-known EI scale that belongs to this category.

Among various academics who have contributed to the development of the EI construct, two groups of scholars have been of prime importance. They are Davies et al. (1998) and Salovey and Mayer (1990). In 1998, Davies et al. qualitatively summarized the EI literature and developed from it a four-dimensional definition of EI. However, they did not develop any measure of EI. Instead, they utilized earlier work on EI and used a group of "EI-related measures" to show that these measures loaded on the same factors as the Big Five personality dimensions. Based on these cross-loadings in a series of exploratory factor analyses, Davies et al. (1998) concluded that EI was elusive as a construct. Ironically, while building up the foundation of EI by drawing a four-dimensional definition of EI from the literature, they used early EI scales that were not based on this four-dimensional definition and concluded that EI was an elusive construct.

Two years later, Mayer, Caruso, and Salovey (2000b) used a slightly different definition of EI and developed the Multi-factor Emotional Intelligence Scale (MEIS). Mayer, Caruso, et al. (2000b) followed the conceptualization developed by Salovey and Mayer (1990) and defined EI as a set of inter-related skills that can be classified within the following four dimensions: "the ability to perceive accurately, appraise, and express emotion; the ability to access and/or generate feelings when they facilitate thought; the ability to understand emotion and emotional knowledge; and the ability to regulate emotions to promote emotional and intellectual growth" (Mayer and Salovey, 1997, p. 10).

While the definitions of EI used by Davies et al. (1998) and Mayer, Caruso, et al. (2000b) were not identical, the differences in the definitions were minor. As Ciarrochi, Chan, and Caputi (2000) commented in a review of the EI literature, "while the definitions of EI are often varied for different researchers, they nevertheless tend to be complementary rather than contradictory" (p. 540). They further pointed out that "in general, the various measures *(of EI)* cover . . . four distinct areas: emotion perception, regulation, understanding, and utilization" (p. 540, emphasis added).

In this study, we use the four-dimensional definition of EI developed by Davies et al. (1998). These four EI dimensions are appraisal and expression of emotion in one's self, appraisal and recognition of emotion in others, regulation of emotion in one's self, and use of emotion to facilitate performance.

We use Davies et al.'s definition of EI because it is more representative of the entire EI literature. Davies et al.'s (1998) review considered Salovey and Mayer's (1990) definition of EI. In addition, Davies et al.'s definition of EI is, in fact, quite similar to that of Salovey and Mayer and also matches well with Ciarrochi et al.'s (2000) summary of the four basic areas of EI. Davies et al.'s definition of the dimensions of EI allows us to focus on the nature and characteristics of the EI construct.

The nature of EI

EI has its roots in the concept of "social intelligence" first identified by Thorndike in 1920. Thorndike (1920) defined social intelligence as "the ability to understand and manage men and women, boys and girls – to act wisely in human relations" (p. 228). Following Thorndike's ideas, Gardner (1983) included interpersonal and intrapersonal intelligences in his theory of multiple intelligences. According to Gardner, social intelligence, which is one among seven intelligence domains, is comprised of an individual's interpersonal and intrapersonal intelligences. Intrapersonal intelligence relates to one's ability to deal with oneself and to perceive and organize complicated and highly differentiated sets of feelings within the self. Interpersonal intelligence relates to one's ability to deal with others and to "notice and make distinctions among other individuals and, in particular, among their moods, temperaments, motivations and intentions" (p. 239). EI can be viewed as a combination of the intrapersonal and interpersonal intelligence of an individual.

Given its roots in social intelligence, Mayer, Caruso, et al. (2000a) argued that the conceptual background of EI meets traditional standards for intelligence measures. They highlighted three criteria that qualify EI as a facet of intelligence. These are conceptual, correlational, and developmental criteria. The conceptual criterion requires that EI must reflect mental abilities instead of preferred ways of behaving. Intelligence refers to the ability of a person. Gardner (1993) defined intelligence as "the *ability* to solve problems, or to fashion products, that are valued in one or more cultural or community settings" (p. 7). In order to fulfill the conceptual criterion and label EI as an intelligence facet, one must provide evidence that EI is not a personality trait or a preferred way of behaving but is itself a set of abilities. We argue conceptually that EI is defined as a set of abilities based on its theoretical definition. We also cite empirical evidence that EI has been shown to be distinct from personality dimensions as follows.

As defined earlier, EI consists of a set of abilities that a person uses to understand, regulate, and make use of his/her emotions. Emotional understanding, regulation, and utilization reflect the capability of a person to manage his/her emotions. Some people have higher competence to do so; some have less competence. As a particular type of competence, it is different from personality traits that reflect tendencies to think, feel, and behave in certain ways. In this competence sense, the four-dimensional definition qualifies EI as abilities and, therefore, as one possible facet of intelligence (see, e.g., Mayer, Caruso, et al., 2000a; Mayer & Salovey, 1997; Salovey & Mayer, 1990). There is also empirical evidence that EI abilities are distinct from personality traits. When developing the MEIS, Mayer and Salovey provided some preliminary data to show that EI was different from personality traits. Wong and Law (2002) also showed in multiple samples that EI, as measured under Davies et al.'s four-dimensional definition, was empirically distinct from the Big Five personality dimensions.

Mayer, Caruso, et al.'s (2000a) second criterion is the correlational criterion. If EI were an intelligence facet, it "should represent a set of correlated abilities that are similar to, but distinct from, mental abilities" (p. 270). In other words, if EI were an intelligence facet, it should correlate with other intelligence facets, such as general mental abilities. These correlations cannot be too high (discriminant validity), nor can they be too low (convergent validity). Both Mayer, Caruso, et al. (2000a) and Wong and Law (2002) showed empirically that the dimensions of EI were moderately correlated among themselves but only mildly correlated with general mental abilities. There is, therefore, some empirical evidence that EI meets the correlational criterion of an intelligence facet.

Mayer, Caruso, et al.'s (2000a) third argument that EI could be conceptualized as an intelligence facet is that intelligence should be developmental in nature. The verbal ability of a person, for example, should increase as one becomes more mature. Wong, Wong, and Law (2002) found that EI is positively correlated with age among incumbents of six different types of jobs. Mayer, Caruso, et al. also showed with a series of studies that EI increased with age and experience, which qualifies it as an ability rather than a personality trait.

Discriminant and predictive validity of EI

Based on the above discussion, it is clear that the definition and domain of EI have been gradually established. It also seems clear, however, that further and stronger evidence that EI possesses the three basic characteristics of an intelligence facet as suggested by Mayer, Caruso, et al. (2000a) is needed. In order to establish the construct validity of EI, we need to "demonstrate its partial (or complete) independence from other, seemingly analogous, concepts" (Davies et al., 1998, p. 989). As mentioned earlier, Davies et al. factor analyzed some existing EI-related scales and personality measures in multiple samples and concluded that EI was elusive.

One possible reason for Davies et al.'s finding was that the "EI-related scales" used in their investigations were early scales related to EI. During that time, a definition of EI had not been systematically developed. Davies et al. also admitted that the scales they identified were only "EI-related" scales. These scales were not developed according to the four-dimensional view then proposed by Davies et al. In fact, some earlier scales had not even been identified as EI scales by their developers. Their use in identifying EI may, therefore, be questionable and unfair. In response to the findings by Davies et al., Wong and Law (2002) developed a new EI scale (labeled as the Wong and Law EI Scale, WLEIS, for easy reference) following the four-dimensional definition of EI as introduced by Davies et al. They used both exploratory and confirmatory factor analyses in the scale development and validation process to show that EI as measured by the WLEIS was distinct from the Big Five personality dimensions. To examine the overall usefulness of the EI construct, we use confirmatory factor analyses in this study to compare the distinctiveness of the WLEIS and various EI-related scales included in the Davies et al. study compared to the Big Five personality dimensions. Based on the data collected, we found that the WLEIS is distinct from the Big Five personality dimensions, although they were moderately correlated owing to conceptual overlaps.

Because EI is conceptualized as an intelligence facet, it is an ability measure instead of a personality measure. This leads to our first hypothesis, which is the core focus of Study 3.1:

Hypothesis 3.1: EI is distinct from, but correlated with, the Big Five personality dimensions.

The construct validity of the WLEIS is further investigated by the MTMM method with self and others' ratings of EI. In Study 3.2, we deliberately choose two criterion variables from the EI literature, life satisfaction and powerlessness, which should have positive and negative correlations with EI, respectively. Life satisfaction is used as a criterion variable because proponents of EI have argued that, theoretically, life satisfaction should be positively related to EI. Intrapersonal emotion recognition and management will help an individual to deal with his/her emotions. A person with high EI should be able to recognize his/her emotions, to regulate these emotions, and to use these emotions to facilitate performance. As a result, this person should be happier as a whole in life. Several empirical studies have provided evidence of this positive relationship (e.g., Wong & Law, 2002; Wong et al., 2002). Powerlessness refers to the extent to which one regards one's experiences as being fatalistically determined, in contrast to being under one's own control (Pearlin & Schooler, 1978). Specifically, it is similar to a temporal variable showing one's state of mind toward one's control over life problems and experiences. A person with high EI would be less affected by his/her emotions, be able to direct emotions in a positive direction, and have lower chances of feeling depressed. EI also includes a dimension of "understanding others' emotions." A person with high EI would also be able to interpret others' moods correctly and therefore have a higher chance of forming close relationships and getting social support in general. As a result, this person should be less likely to feel powerless. There is some evidence in the literature that feelings of powerlessness are related to negative emotions such as sadness and fear (e.g., Roseman, Dhawan, Rettek, & Naidu, 1995). These ideas lead to our second and third hypotheses:

Hypothesis 3.2: EI is positively associated with life satisfaction.

Hypothesis 3.3: EI is negatively associated with one's feeling of powerlessness.

Finally, EI will be a useful construct for management studies if it has predictive power for job performance. It is intuitive that EI would affect job performance. Understanding and regulation of one's emotions as well as understanding of others' emotions are the core factors affecting intrapersonal well-being and interpersonal relations. In a negative sense, a person who is not sensitive to his/her own emotions and unable to regulate emotions would have problems interacting with others. Since interpersonal interactions are a basic component of many jobs, it is reasonable to hypothesize that EI would affect job performance in general.

On the positive side, the "use of emotion" dimension of EI describes one's ability to direct emotions to performance. A person with high EI would be able to direct positive emotions to high performance and redirect negative emotions to generate constructive performance goals. As Mayer and Salovey (1997) summarized, "using the emotions as one basis for thinking, and thinking with emotions themselves, may be related to important social competencies and adaptive behavior" (p. 22).

Theoretically, if we follow the social exchange framework (Blau, 1964), in which organizations use different types of exchanges to facilitate performance and social exchange is one important type of exchange in organizations, then we know that factors that facilitate social exchanges improve employee performance. Social exchange involves interactions. As we argued above, emotional understanding, regulation, and utilization would help to cultivate positive social interactions and exchanges in an organization and, as a result, facilitate employee performance.

There have also been similar arguments used in the previous literature to justify an EI–performance link. Based on Atwater and Yammarino's (1992) work on self–other rating agreements, Sosik and Megerian (1999) argued that one's understanding of one's and others' affective ratings (as a result of one's EI) would influence self–other rating agreements, which, in turn, would influence performance outcomes. Lam and Kirby (2002) showed that overall EI explains individual cognitive-based performance over and beyond the level attributable to general intelligence. Dulewicz and Higgs (2000) showed that EI is predictive of the career success of 100 managers.

On top of showing a main effect of EI on job performance, Wong and Law (2002) argued that emotional labor moderates the EI–performance link and provided preliminary evidence for EI's predictive validity in job performance. Emotional labor refers to the extent to which an employee is required to present an appropriate emotion in order to perform a job in an efficient and effective manner (Hochschild, 1983). Both Lam and Kirby (2002) and Wong and Law (2002) use self-ratings of EI. In this study, we used colleagues' ratings of EI to predict supervisory ratings of job performance. This design provides much stronger support for the utility of the EI construct in management studies. The above discussion leads to the final hypothesis of this study:

> Hypothesis 3.4: EI is positively associated with employees' job performance.

The first hypothesis was tested in samples 1 and 2 of Study 3.1. Hypotheses 3.2 and 3.3 were tested with sampl`e 1 of Study 3.2. Hypothesis 3.4 was tested with sample 2 of Study 3.2.

Study 3.1

In this study, we collected data that are comparable to the Davies et al. data, which enabled a more rigorous test of the distinctiveness of the EI construct using confirmatory factor analyses (CFA). The aims of Study 3.1 are threefold. First, a series of CFAs on sample 1 illustrates that the EI-related scales used by Davies et al. are not psychometrically sound. Second, CFAs of the new WLEIS developed based on Davies et al.'s four-dimensional view show that EI is distinct from the Big Five personality dimensions. This result is cross-validated with sample 2. Third, the WLEIS explains incremental variance in life satisfaction over and above that accounted for by the Big Five personality dimensions in both samples 1 and 2.

Data for the first sample in Study 3.1 were collected from university students in two stages. In the first stage, we included only three of the five self-report EI-related scales that were used in the Davies et al. study, because two of the EI-related scales were not made available to us. After all five EI-related scales were made available, we collected data using all of the scales from an additional sample of students. The data collected during these two stages were combined to form sample 1 of Study 3.1. In both stages of data collection, we also used the WLEIS. Given the positive results from sample 1, which confirmed our arguments, we cross-validated the results with another sample of university students. This cross-validation sample formed sample 2 of Study 3.1.

Sample and procedures

Sample 1 of Study 3.1 consisted of 202 undergraduate students at a large university in Hong Kong. The students were asked to make self-assessments on EI-related scales, Big Five personality scales, and life satisfaction measures in an introductory management course. We included most of the self-report measures that were examined by Davies et al. for easy comparison. The EI-related scales that were included at this stage were the Trait-Meta-Mood (TMM) Scale, the Emotional Empathy Scale (EES), and the Toronto Alexithymia Scale (TAS). After obtaining items for the Emotional Control Questionnaire (ECQ) and the Affective Communication Test (ACT), in our second stage of data collection, we added these two scales to all of the measures that were used in the first stage. The respondents in the second stage consisted of 216 undergraduate business students from another large university in Hong Kong. They filled out this survey as a partial fulfillment of the course requirements for an introductory organizational behavior course. Data collected in these two stages were pooled together to form sample 1 of Study 3.1. The sample size for the Big Five personality scales, TMM, EES, and TAS was 418, while the sample size for the ECQ and ACT scales was 216.

Having obtained evidence to confirm our arguments, a further sample was collected to provide cross-validation data on personality measures, WLEIS, and life satisfaction. This sample consisted of 314 undergraduate students, from the same university as the participants in the first stage of sample 1. All questionnaires were administered in English to the Hong Kong subjects.

Measures

EI-RELATED MEASURES

We used the same self-report EI-related measures as Davies et al. These include (1) the 30-item TMM (Salovey, Mayer, Goldman, Turvey, & Palfai, 1995), which measures three EI subscales: attention, repair, and clarity;

(2) the 33-item EES (Mehrabian & Epstein, 1970); (3) the 20-item TAS (Bagby, Taylor, & Parker, 1994), which measures EI with three subscales: difficulty identifying feelings, difficulty describing feelings, and externally oriented thinking; (4) the 32-item ECQ (Roger & Najarian, 1989), which measures four EI-related subscales: rehearsal, emotional inhibition, benign control, and aggression control; and (5) the 13-item ACT (Friedman, Prince, Riggio, & Dimatteo, 1980).

Since all of the above EI-related scales did not measure EI based on Davies et al.'s proposed four-dimensional definition, we also included the newly developed 16-item WLEIS as a final measure of EI. The response format of WLEIS was a 7-point Likert-type scale ("1" means totally disagree). A sample item from the "self emotional appraisal" is "I really understand what I feel." A sample item from the "use of emotions to facilitate performance" dimension is "I would always encourage myself to try my best." A sample question from the "regulation of emotions" dimension is "I can always calm down quickly when I am very angry." A sample item from the "other's emotional appraisal" is "I have good understanding of the emotions of people around me."

PERSONALITY

In sample 1, we used the short form of the Neuroticism-Extraversion-Openness Personality Inventory (NEO-PI) to capture the Big Five personality dimensions (Costa & McCrae, 1985). Each dimension contained 12 items. In sample 2 (the cross-validation sample), we used the Big Five adjective scale that was developed by McCrae and Costa (1987). Since all the data were collected in class as an exercise on dispositional variables, we had limitations on the length of the questionnaires. In order to be fully comparable to the Davies et al. study, we included all five EI-related scales. To limit the length of the questionnaire, we randomly selected six items for each of the Big Five personality dimensions from the original 80-item scale, resulting in a 30-item measure. Since all the items within each Big Five dimension of the McCrae and Costa scale measure the same construct, random selection of six items from each dimension would not affect their validity. Classical measurement theory argues that fewer items from each dimension might lower the reliability of the measures. However, our results showed that reliabilities of the Big Five dimensions were comparable to the original 80-item scale in the literature (Costa & McCrae, 1985). In fact, the coefficient alphas of the five personality dimensions were higher than those of the short form of the NEO-PI in sample 1, indicating that the reliabilities of these 30 items were acceptable.

LIFE SATISFACTION

The nine-item life satisfaction measure constructed by A. Campbell, Converse, and Rodgers (1976) was adopted. This is a well-established measure of the general satisfaction of an individual with his or her life.

Analyses

We conducted two sets of analyses of sample 1. In the first set of analyses, we randomly grouped the items to form three indicators for each EI-related and personality dimension and used these indicators as inputs in the CFA. This method of averaging indicators to form new indicators, in order to reduce the number of observed variables in CFAs, is quite common in the literature (see, e.g., Mathieu & Farr, 1991; Mathieu, Hofmann, & Farr, 1993). We used confirmatory instead of exploratory factor analysis because the factor structure of all the constructs was known. Our purpose in Study 3.1 was to confirm the factor structure of the EI and personality scales and to study their inter-factor correlations to test whether they are distinct constructs.

In the second set of analyses, we conducted a series of hierarchical regressions to show the incremental validity of the WLEIS in predicting life satisfaction over and beyond the Big Five personality dimensions. We first entered the personality dimensions as control variables for predicting life satisfaction. The four dimensions of the EI scale were then added as the next set of predictors. If the change in model R^2 after adding the WLEIS were significant, EI would have incremental explanatory power in predicting life satisfaction over and beyond the personality dimensions. This would be considered an additional piece of evidence to demonstrate that EI and the personality dimensions are distinct constructs.

On the cross-validation sample (sample 2 of Study 3.1), we conducted a CFA and hierarchical regression to cross-validate the results of the WLEIS used in sample 1.

Results

Summary statistics

Descriptive statistics, coefficient alphas, and correlations among all the measures for the two samples are presented in Tables 3.1 and 3.2. The results in Table 3.1 indicate that most of the measures have acceptable reliability estimates. Table 3.2 shows that some personality and EI-related dimensions were moderately correlated, although none of the correlations exceeded .50 except that between the ACT and extraversion (r = .59).

CFAs of the factorial structure of EI

Table 3.3 shows the results when each EI-related measure was factor analyzed with the Big Five personality dimensions using CFA. We included only one EI-related measure in each CFA for two reasons. First, the sample size of n = 216 did not allow us to include more measures without a severe loss of statistical power. Second, and more important, we can examine the structure and goodness-of-fit of *each* EI-related measure if we study each one independently.

Table 3.1 Descriptive statistics and coefficient alphas among all measures in Study 3.1

	No. of Items	Sample 1			Sample 2		
		Mean	S.D.	α[a]	Mean	S.D.	α[a]
NEURO	12/6	3.10	.60	.81	3.50	.77	.75
EXTRA	12/6	3.28	.46	.70	3.84	.76	.79
OPEN	12/6	3.19	.41	.57	3.72	.64	.61
AGREE	12/6	3.29	.41	.62	4.28	.60	.67
CONSC	12/6	3.30	.45	.67	4.00	.71	.70
TMM1 (repair)	6	3.36	.65	.70	—	—	—
TMM2 (attention)	13	3.52	.46	.73	—	—	—
TMM3 (clarity)	11	3.13	.45	.66	—	—	—
EES (emotional empathy)	33	3.30	.31	.74	—	—	—
TAS1 (difficulty identifying feelings)	7	2.72	.68	.79	—	—	—
TAS2 (difficulty describing feelings)	5	2.90	.68	.69	—	—	—
TAS3 (externally oriented thinking)	8	2.74	.44	.46	—	—	—
ECQ1 (rehearsal)	8	2.86	.68	.76	—	—	—
ECQ2 (emotional inhibition)	8	2.67	.60	.69	—	—	—
ECQ3 (benign control)	8	2.94	.55	.64	—	—	—
ECQ4 (aggression control)	8	3.05	.44	.49	—	—	—
ACT (affective communication)	13	3.06	.46	.68	—	—	—
EI1 (self emotional appraisal)	4	4.01	1.05	.89	4.84	1.09	.90
EI2 (regulation of emotion)	4	3.78	1.12	.89	4.27	1.20	.89
EI3 (use of emotion)	4	4.09	.92	.80	4.57	.99	.79
EI4 (others' emotional appraisal)	4	4.15	.96	.89	4.60	1.15	.93
LS	9	4.92	.89	.90	4.80	.89	.90

Notes
n = 418 for all variables in sample 1, except for ACT and ECQ, where n = 216; n = 314 for sample 2. NEURO, EXTRA, OPEN, AGREE, and CONSC = neuroticism, extraversion, openness, agreeableness, and conscientiousness; TMM1, TMM2, and TMM3 = the three dimensions of the Trait-Meta-Mood Scale; EES = the Emotional Empathy Scale; TAS1, TAS2, and TAS3 = the three dimensions of the Toronto Alexithymia Scale; ECQ1, ECQ2, ECQ3, and ECQ4 = the four dimensions of the Emotional Control Questionnaire; ACT = the Affective Communication Test; EI1, EI2, EI3, and EI4 = the four dimensions of the recently developed emotional intelligence scale introduced in this study; LS = life satisfaction.

[a] α is the coefficient alpha of the scale or dimension.

Table 3.2 Correlations among measures in sample 1 and sample 2 of Study 3.1

	1	2	3	4	5	6	7	8	9	10	11	12	13	14	15	16	17	18	19	20	21	22
1. NEURO	1.0	.01	.13	-.05	-.24	—	—	—	—	—	—	—	—	—	—	—	—	-.26	-.45	-.24	-.07	-.35
2. EXTRA	-.38	1.0	.13	.39	.24	—	—	—	—	—	—	—	—	—	—	—	—	.23	-.01	.22	.19	.27
3. OPEN	-.01	.13	1.0	.00	.10	—	—	—	—	—	—	—	—	—	—	—	—	.13	-.13	.16	.20	.03
4. AGREE	-.20	.23	.10	1.0	.21	—	—	—	—	—	—	—	—	—	—	—	—	.19	.12	.05	.08	.20
5. CONSC	-.29	.25	.03	.30	1.0	—	—	—	—	—	—	—	—	—	—	—	—	.28	.26	.36	.21	.13
6. TMM1	-.48	.15	.47	.31	.26	1.0	—	—	—	—	—	—	—	—	—	—	—	—	—	—	—	—
7. TMM2	-.09	.18	.25	.22	.05	.09	1.0	—	—	—	—	—	—	—	—	—	—	—	—	—	—	—
8. TMM3	-.36	.17	.14	.16	.37	.29	.16	1.0	—	—	—	—	—	—	—	—	—	—	—	—	—	—
9. EES	.25	.11	.28	.35	.05	.08	.40	.03	1.0	—	—	—	—	—	—	—	—	—	—	—	—	—
10. TAS1	.45	-.19	-.04	-.37	-.35	-.33	-.17	-.53	-.09	1.0	—	—	—	—	—	—	—	—	—	—	—	—
11. TAS2	.36	-.24	-.08	-.20	-.24	-.21	-.12	-.48	-.04	.48	1.0	—	—	—	—	—	—	—	—	—	—	—
12. TAS3	.06	-.21	-.40	-.21	-.13	-.24	-.36	-.25	-.40	.25	.20	1.0	—	—	—	—	—	—	—	—	—	—
13. ECQ1	.39	-.27	-.15	-.30	-.24	-.38	.05	-.34	-.07	.42	.23	.15	1.0	—	—	—	—	—	—	—	—	—
14. ECQ2	.01	-.37	-.12	-.18	-.15	-.22	-.23	-.33	-.37	.23	.53	.30	.14	1.0	—	—	—	—	—	—	—	—
15. ECQ3	.43	-.09	-.06	-.35	-.38	-.26	.05	-.40	-.06	.45	.32	.26	.25	.05	1.0	—	—	—	—	—	—	—
16. ECQ4	-.01	.12	.12	-.34	.11	.10	.00	-.02	-.09	.10	-.08	-.14	.12	-.05	.05	1.0	—	—	—	—	—	—
17. ACT	-.23	.59	.29	.13	.18	.31	.20	.20	.22	-.07	-.36	-.34	-.12	-.43	-.05	.21	1.0	—	—	—	—	—
18. EI1	-.30	.06	.15	.09	.30	.19	.19	.02	.48	-.04	-.04	-.31	-.04	-.12	-.33	-.25	.04	1.0	.34	.30	.45	.25
19. EI2	-.43	.06	.03	.06	.27	.21	-.14	.28	-.25	-.19	-.08	.05	-.25	.08	-.43	-.10	.03	.54	1.0	.52	.14	.13
20. EI3	-.22	.11	.22	.02	.44	.23	-.01	.32	-.09	-.11	-.12	-.07	-.16	-.27	-.12	.18	.24	.54	.52	1.0	.44	.32
21. EI4	-.01	.03	.16	.04	.22	.05	.00	.16	.07	-.06	-.13	-.03	.00	-.27	-.14	.14	.21	.41	.33	.27	1.0	.12
22. LS	-.48	.44	.18	.26	.33	.48	.19	.33	.11	-.29	-.23	-.24	-.35	-.31	-.21	.16	.41	.34	.33	.37	.17	1.0

Notes
See Table 3.1 for key to variables. Figures in the lower triangle are correlations for sample 1; numbers in the upper triangle are correlations for sample 2.

Table 3.3 Results of confirmatory factor analyses for Study 3.1

Measure	Model Fit Indices					Factor Correlations					
	χ^2 (d.f.)	RMSEA	TLI	CFI	IFI	Dimension	NEURO	EXTRA	OPEN	AGREE	CONSC
TMM	M_1 = 568.60 (224)	.062	.85	.88	.88	TMM1	-.59	.66	.25	.42	.36
						TMM2	.11	.23	.49	.35	.08
						TMM3	-.46	.28	.15	.30	.54
	M_2 = 714.72 (234)	.072	.81	.83	.84	Second-order	-.72	.78	.39	.59	.60
EES	336.50 (120)	.066	.86	.89	.89	—	.33	.16	.54	.49	.08
TAS	M_1 = 485.79 (224)	.055	.88	.90	.90	TAS1	.57	-.26	-.06	-.50	-.52
						TAS2	.46	-.32	-.09	-.27	-.36
						TAS3	.10	-.04	-.81	-.39	-.26
	M_2 = 609.72 (234)	.064	.84	.86	.86	Second-order	.61	-.34	-.15	-.52	-.55
ECQ	M_1 = 520.94 (288)	.062	.81	.85	.85	ECQ1	.51	-.40	-.05	-.46	-.37
						ECQ2	.07	-.53	-.22	-.25	-.27
						ECQ3	.56	-.14	-.09	-.56	-.65
						ECQ4	.02	.18	.21	-.64	.21
	M_2 = 618.71 (305)	.071	.76	.79	.80	Second-order	.92	-.50	-.18	-.87	-.95
ACT	287.60 (120)	.077	.80	.85	.85	—	-.29	.78	.35	.18	.28

	χ²(df)	RMSEA				Dimension					
EI (Sample 1)											
	M₁ = 846.41 (398)	.053	.91	.92	.92	EI1	-.37	.11	-.12	.11	.42
						EI2	-.50	.09	-.22	.10	.38
						EI3	-.25	.13	.02	.00	.59
						EI4	.00	.04	-.01	.06	.29
						Second-order	-.44	.14	-.12	.09	.59
	M₂ = 946.96 (415)	.057	.90	.91	.91						
EI (Sample 2)											
	M₁ = 794.07 (398)	.056	.90	.92	.92	EI1	-.31	.28	.19	.23	.36
						EI2	-.53	.00	-.17	.16	.28
						EI3	-.32	.30	.25	.10	.47
						EI4	-.08	.21	.27	.09	.25
						Second-order	-.52	.37	.26	.27	.59
	M₂ = 881.43 (415)	.060	.89	.90	.90						

Notes

M_1 means the model specifies only first-order dimensions for the EI measure under investigation. M_2 means the model specifies a second-order latent construct behind the dimensions for the EI measure. RMSEA = root mean square error approximation; TLI = Tucker and Lewis Index; CFI = comparative fit index; IFI = incremental fit index; NEURO, EXTRA, OPEN, AGREE, and CONSC = neuroticism, extraversion, openness, agreeableness, and conscientiousness; TMM1, TMM2, and TMM3 = the three dimensions of the Trait-Meta-Mood Scale; EES = the Emotional Empathy Scale; TAS1, TAS2, and TAS3 = the three dimensions of the Toronto Alexithymia Scale; ECQ1, ECQ2, ECQ3, and ECQ4 = the four dimensions of the Emotional Control Questionnaire; ACT = the Affective Communication Test; EI1, EI2, EI3, and EI4 = the four dimensions of the recently developed emotional intelligence scale introduced in this study.

The first row of Table 3.3 shows that when the nine TMM indicators (three indicators for each TMM dimension) were factor analyzed with the 15 Big Five personality indicators (three indicators for each Big Five personality dimension) and eight latent factors were specified, the model fit indices were very marginal (comparative fit index [CFI] = .88; Tucker-Lewis Index [TLI] = .85; root mean square error approximation [RMSEA] = .062). The last row under TMM in Table 3.3 (that is, the fourth row in the table) shows that when a second-order factor was added underlying the three TMM factors, the model fit indices dropped significantly (CFI = .83; TLI = .81; RMSEA = .072). These results led to two conclusions concerning the TMM scale. First, the scale might not have a clear factorial structure distinct from the Big Five dimensions. Second, there might not be a higher-order factor underlying the three TMM dimensions.

Table 3.3 shows that the results of the CFA for many of the EI-related scales also have quite unsatisfactory fit indices. For example, the fit indices for the ECQ were quite low (less than .85) for both the first-order and the second-order model. The same was true for the ACT (CFI = .85; TLI = .80; RMSEA = .077). The first-order model for TAS was marginal (CFI = .90; TLI = .88; RMSEA = .055), while the second-order model (three TAS factors, one second-order TAS factor, and five Big Five personality factors) was quite low (CFI = .86; TLI = .84; RMSEA = .064). The above analyses lead to another possible explanation of Davies et al.'s results. While it may still be true that these EI-related measures are cross-loaded with the Big Five personality dimensions, the cross-loadings may be a result of their poor representation of the EI construct. In other words, Davies et al.'s findings might be due to the construct validity of the EI-related scales that were included in their investigation.

The last two rows of Table 3.3 show the CFA results when the WLEIS was analyzed with the Big Five dimensions. In sample 1, both the first-order model (CFI = .92; TLI = .91; RMSEA = .053) and the second-order model (CFI = .91; TLI = .90; RMSEA = .057) showed good model fit. Again, in the cross-validation sample (sample 2), the first-order model (CFI = .92; TLI = .90; RMSEA = .056) showed good model fit, and the second-order model (CFI = .90; TLI = .89; RMSEA = .060) showed marginal fit.

These results support two important conclusions regarding the four-dimensional EI construct. First, the four EI dimensions, as measured by the WLEIS, were distinct from the Big Five dimensions. While some EI dimensions were moderately correlated with neuroticism (r = .44 and .52 in samples 1 and 2) and conscientiousness (r = .59 in both samples), EI is different from these personality dimensions. The correlations are expected because EI is conceptually related to these dimensions. For example, neuroticism is a general tendency to over-react to negative stimuli from the environment. While neuroticism is conceptually distinct from EI, which reflects one's ability to understand, regulate, and utilize one's emotions, a person with low EI would quite likely be a neurotic person as well. We therefore see the moderate correlations between EI and some personality dimensions as expected. On the other hand, the results of the CFA clearly showed that EI is distinct from the Big Five personality dimensions.

The second conclusion regarding the EI scale, as illustrated in Table 3.3, is that a meaningful overall construct underlies the four EI dimensions. The second-order model for the EI scale generated acceptable fit indices in both the first sample and the cross-validation sample. Based on the above analyses, we conclude that EI is an overall latent construct underlying its four dimensions. In addition, when properly defined, EI is related to, yet different from, the Big Five personality dimensions. Hypothesis 3.1 was supported by the data.

Hierarchical regression analyses

Table 3.4 shows the results of the hierarchical regression for both sample 1 and the cross-validation sample (sample 2). The results were quite similar in both of these samples. Neuroticism, extraversion, and agreeableness were the three major personality traits affecting life satisfaction. When the four EI dimensions were added to the regression model, the increases in model R^2 were significant ($p < .01$), although the absolute magnitude was not large ($\Delta R^2 = .05$

Table 3.4 Results of regression analyses on life satisfaction after controlling for personality in Study 3.1

| | Life Satisfaction | | | | | |
| | Sample 1 | | | Sample 2 | | |
	β	R^2	ΔR^2	β	R^2	ΔR^2
Step 1:						
NEURO	−.32**			−.36**		
EXTRA	.24*			.13*		
OPEN	.13**			−.03		
AGREE	.08*			.25**		
CONSC	.15*	.354**		−.01	.203**	
Step 2:						
EI1	.09+			.10		
EI2	.04			−.09		
EI3	.19**			.23**		
EI4	.00	.406**	.052**	−.01	.265**	.062**

Notes
n = 418 for sample 1; n = 314 for sample 2. The regression weights of the control variables are the weights at step 1 only; the beta-weights for the other variables are the final regression weights after these variables were added to the model. NEURO, EXTRA, OPEN, AGREE, and CONSC = neuroticism, extraversion, openness, agreeableness, and conscientiousness; EI1, EI2, EI3, and EI4 = the four dimensions of the recently developed emotional intelligence scale introduced in this study.

+p < .10; *p < .05; **p < .01.

and .06). The 5% to 6% additional variance accounted for in life satisfaction is understandable, because, as we saw in Table 3.2, EI is moderately correlated with the Big Five personality dimensions. In addition, life satisfaction was moderately correlated with the personality dimensions; the Pearson correlations between life satisfaction and neuroticism, extraversion, openness, agreeableness, and conscientiousness were .48, .43, .18, .26, and .33, respectively. There was limited room for additional variance to be accounted for by EI when the Big Five personality dimensions were in the model. As a result, we interpreted the additional 5% to be of reasonable practical significance.

Study 3.2

Our major purpose in Study 3.1 was to show that, with appropriate measures, EI is distinct from the Big Five personality dimensions. EI also accounts for a significant proportion of the variance in life satisfaction, over and above that of the Big Five personality dimensions. However, the self-report nature of the WLEIS limited the validity of the evidence in Study 3.1. For example, its explanatory power for life satisfaction may be due to common method variance (see, e.g., Bagozzi & Yi, 1990; Williams & Brown, 1994). Therefore, we need additional evidence to demonstrate the predictive power of EI using non-self-report measures of EI.

Study 3.2 addresses this issue by providing evidence of discriminant and convergent validity, using multiple raters to assess EI. Study 3.2 consists of two samples: one of high school students and their parents, the other a work sample with self, peer, and supervisor ratings of EI and job performance.

Study 3.2 contributes to the criterion validity of EI, as well as to its construct validity. To demonstrate the construct validity of EI, we used multiple assessors (parent and self-rating of students in sample 1; self, peer, and supervisor ratings in sample 2) to measure EI and related constructs and analyzed the data using the MTMM technique. To demonstrate the criterion validity of EI, we used parents' ratings of EI to predict students' self-rating of life satisfaction and feelings of powerlessness, after controlling for the Big Five personality dimensions. By making use of the work sample in sample 2, we showed that peers' ratings of an employee's EI were a useful predictor of a supervisor's rating of the job performance of the same employee, after controlling for relevant variables and personality dimensions. In both cases, common method variance could be avoided because the dependent variable and the predictor (i.e., EI) were collected from different sources.

Method

Participants

SAMPLE 1

In this first sample, we collected data by distributing 560 sets of questionnaires in two high schools in Anhui Province of the People's Republic of China. All respondents were students in grade 12 of high school. Each questionnaire set included one self-rating questionnaire to be completed by the students, and one parent rating questionnaire for their parents to complete. Each student was asked to fill in their self-rating questionnaire, which assessed their own EI, the Big Five personality dimensions, their life satisfaction, and their perception of powerlessness. One parent of each student received the parent questionnaire, which asked them to evaluate the EI and personality of their son/daughter. Out of the 560 sets of questionnaires (i.e., 1,120 questionnaires), we received 889 valid responses, a return rate of 79.4%.

SAMPLE 2

We collected data from a cigarette factory in Anhui province. One hundred and eighty-one sets of questionnaires were distributed to first-line supervisors in the factory. In each set, there were three questionnaires, sealed in separate envelopes. Each supervisor received one set of questionnaires in which he/she was asked to rate two of his/her immediate subordinates (subordinates A and B). The supervisor was then instructed to give the two "subordinate questionnaires" to subordinates A and B separately. Subordinate A was required to rate his/her own EI and job performance as well as the EI and job performance of his/her peer (i.e., subordinate B), whose name was written on the questionnaire by the supervisor. Similarly, subordinate B was asked to rate his/her own EI and job performance as well as that of subordinate A. All the questionnaires were sealed in envelopes and returned to the human resource management office of the factory within two weeks of dissemination. With the enthusiastic support and encouragement of the factory managers, we received 165 valid response sets (response rate = 90.7%). Since the English standard of students and workers in mainland China is not high, we followed the standard translation–back-translation procedure (Brislin, 1980) to translate all the items into Chinese.

Measures of Sample 1

EI AND PERSONALITY

We used the same EI scale, the WLEIS developed by Wong and Law (2002), as used in Study 3.1. Coefficient alphas for the EI dimensions of self emotional appraisal, other's emotional appraisal, regulation of emotion, and use of emotion, as assessed by parents, were .69, .84, .78, and .72, respectively. For the students' self-ratings, the coefficient alphas for the four EI dimensions were .69, .84, .81, and .72, respectively. For the personality dimensions, we used the 80-item Big Five personality measure of McCrae and Costa (1987). Coefficient alphas for parents' ratings of neuroticism, extraversion, openness, agreeableness, and conscientiousness were .79, .83, .85, .85, and .90, respectively. The coefficient alphas for the students' self-ratings were .77, .80, .82, .83, and .86, respectively.

LIFE SATISFACTION

Life satisfaction was measured by four items that were adopted from the life satisfaction scale developed by A. Campbell et al. (1976). A sample item is "In general, I feel very happy." The coefficient alpha for these four items was .75.

POWERLESSNESS IN LIFE MASTERY

This was measured by the seven-item scale constructed by Pearlin and Schooler (1978). An example is "I have little control over the things that happen to me." The coefficient alpha for the seven items was .64.

CONTROL VARIABLES

We collected data on students' gender (0 for male, 1 for female), whether the student's mother worked outside the home (0 for full-time, 1 for not employed), and the educational level of the student's father and mother (with 1 to 6 indicating primary school, junior-high school, high school, two-year college program, four-year university program, and graduate school) as control variables.

Measures of Sample 2

EI AND PERSONALITY

We used the same EI scale, the WLEIS developed by Wong and Law (2002), as in sample 1. Coefficient alphas for the four EI dimensions ranged from .76 to .90 for supervisory ratings, .72 to .89 for self-ratings, and .77 to .91 for peer ratings. For personality dimensions, we used the 80-item Big Five personality measure introduced by McCrae and Costa (1987). Only self-ratings of the Big Five personality traits were available. Coefficient alphas for neuroticism, extraversion, openness, agreeableness, and conscientiousness were .79, .80, .87, .85, and .90, respectively.

TASK PERFORMANCE

Task performance was assessed by supervisors, subordinates (self), and peers with three items derived from a general performance measure (Farh & Cheng, 1997). A sample item is "My performance is very good as compared with other employees on the same job." The coefficient alphas for the three items, as reported by supervisor, peer, and self, were .80, .82, and .82, respectively. This variable is labeled "task performance" below.

CONTEXTUAL PERFORMANCE

Contextual performance was measured with the scale developed by Van Scotter and Motowidlo (1996). The scale includes 15 items, which capture two dimensions, interpersonal facilitation and job dedication. Seven items are used to capture interpersonal facilitation and eight items to assess job dedication. The coefficient alphas for supervisory, peer, and self-ratings of interpersonal facilitation were .82, .86, and .85, respectively. For job dedication, coefficient alphas for the three rating sources were .85, .89, and .83, respectively. Since the rater and ratee varied when different respondents (supervisor, self, and peer) were responding to the task and contextual performance items, the leading words in the questionnaire were adjusted accordingly.

CONTROL VARIABLES

Loyalty to supervisor, trust in supervisor, and the demographic characteristics of the subordinates were used in the regression analyses to control for variables that might affect job performance. To measure loyalty to supervisor, we used a nine-item scale developed by Becker, Billings, Eveleth, and Gilbert (1996). The coefficient alpha was .89. A three-item scale to measure trust in supervisor (Chen, 1997) was used. The coefficient alpha was .84. Age, gender (coded as 2 for female and 1 for male), education (months of education after graduation from high school), and tenure (months of experience with the immediate supervisor) were the other demographic control variables.

Analysis and results

MTMM approach

SAMPLE 1

Table 3.5 shows the descriptive statistics and results of our MTMM analyses of sample 1. First, the reliabilities are shown in parentheses on the main diagonal. EI was reliably measured by the two methods of self-rating and parent rating. The coefficient alphas were .78 and .81, respectively. Acceptable reliability was found with the Big Five personality measures rated by the students (self) as well as by their parents. The coefficient alphas ranged from .77 to .90. Second, the values of the hetero-trait mono-method triangles are shown in italics. Third, the values of the hetero-trait hetero-method triangle are underlined. Finally, the values presented in bold type are the mono-trait hetero-method values.

Our results from sample 1 concur with the requirements set by D. T. Campbell and Fiske (1959). First, the coefficients on the reliability diagonal (numbers in brackets) are the highest in the matrix. Second, the coefficients on the validity diagonals (numbers in bold) are significantly different from zero and high enough to warrant further investigation. The correlation between self-rating EI and parent rating EI was .28. Similar correlations for the Big Five personality dimensions ranged from .20 to .37. The data showed discriminant validity, which requires that the validity coefficient be higher than all of the values in the column and row in which it is located. The correlation between parents' EI ratings and students' EI ratings of .28 seems a bit low. One possible reason is that these are high school students who may not yet have clear and stable

Table 3.5 Results of the 6-traits-by-2-methods multi-trait multi-method analyses in sample 1 of Study 3.2

Traits		Mean	S.D.	Self-Rating						Parent Rating					
				EI	NEURO	EXTRA	OPEN	AGREE	CONSC	EI	NEURO	EXTRA	OPEN	AGREE	CONSC
Self-rating	EI	3.60	.46	(.78)											
	NEURO	3.67	.93	−.39	(.77)										
	EXTRA	4.74	.94	.15	−.08	(.80)									
	OPEN	4.93	.95	.30	−.12	.45	(.82)								
	AGREE	5.21	.74	.26	−.36	.29	.14	(.83)							
	CONSC	5.04	.77	.55	−.46	.10	.27	.47	(.86)						
Parent rating	EI	3.57	.45	**.28**	−.12	.00	.01	.02	.22	(.81)					
	NEURO	3.56	.98	−.18	**.34**	.04	−.02	−.18	−.20	−.30	(.79)				
	EXTRA	4.65	1.04	.06	−.02	**.37**	.21	.02	−.02	.00	.08	(.83)			
	OPEN	4.28	1.10	.15	−.04	.14	**.32**	−.10	.08	.15	.08	.55	(.85)		
	AGREE	5.34	.88	.07	−.14	.01	−.02	**.20**	.14	.16	−.16	.28	.09	(.85)	
	CONSC	5.13	.95	.17	−.11	−.13	−.02	.05	**.34**	.42	−.21	.11	.24	.58	(.90)

Notes
The six traits are emotional intelligence (EI), neuroticism (NEURO), extraversion (EXTRA), openness (OPEN), agreeableness (AGREE), and conscientiousness (CONSC). The two methods are self-rating and parent rating. The numbers on the diagonal are the coefficient alphas. The numbers in italics are in the hetero-trait mono-method triangles; the numbers underlined are in the hetero-trait hetero-method triangle; the numbers in bold are the results of the mono-trait hetero-method.

understandings of their own EI. Meanwhile, some Chinese parents are quite protective of their children. In the minds of these Chinese parents, their kids are always kids, and the EI of their kids is always quite low. The first reason implies that parents' EI ratings may be more accurate than students' self-ratings. The second reason implies that parents' EI ratings of their kids are biased because some parents would underestimate the EI of their kids but some would not. Without additional information, both arguments seem to be plausible.

Fourth, some validity coefficients (numbers in bold) are smaller than some coefficients in the hetero-trait mono-method (numbers in italic) triangles, which may imply that we have a common method variance problem in the dataset. However, these results should not be a worry. D. T. Campbell and Fiske (1959) commented that this was a frequent phenomenon in research on individual differences. Finally, we see the same pattern of interrelationships among different traits in the two hetero-trait mono-method triangles and the hetero-trait hetero-method triangle.

While Campbell and Fiske's recommended analyses are standard, they were not sufficiently precise or normative to evaluate the goodness-of-fit of the data with respect to the prescribed model. Therefore, we used the factor analysis approach of MTMM and ran a CFA with six traits (EI and the Big Five) and two methods (self-rating and parent rating) on the data. As in Study 3.1, we randomly grouped the items to form three indicators for each of the 12 constructs (six traits, each with two rating sources). In the CFA, we specified a latent trait factor for each of the six traits from the two sources (self-rating and parent rating). We also prescribed two method factors for all the traits that were assessed by self-rating and parent rating. However, since we had only two methods (sources), the model was not identified. To solve this problem, we followed Marsh and Hocevar's (1983) approach to obtain a priori estimates of the error variances of all the indicators. We conducted an exploratory factor analysis on all 36 indicators and used one minus the estimated communality for each indicator as the estimate of the error variance of each indicator.

Results of the CFA with EI, the Big Five personality dimensions, and the two method factors of self and parent were encouraging. The degree of freedom and model χ^2 for this two-method, six-trait model were 649 and 3906.87, respectively. The CFI was .87, and the TLI was .85. We also tested two alternative models. Model A, which included only two methods, had a model χ^2 of 15048.18, CFI of .41, and TLI of .38. Model B, which included only six traits, had a model χ^2 of 8449.92, CFI of .68, and TLI of .66. The changes in the model χ^2 of the two-method, six-trait model over these two trait-only and the method-only models were both significant. Using a variance partitioning approach, we found that the six traits explained 41.49% of the total observed variance; the two methods explained 22.26% of the observed variance; and the remaining 36.26% was attributed to random error.

SAMPLE 2

Table 3.6 shows the descriptive statistics and results of our MTMM analyses of sample 2. The results are very similar to the results from sample 1. First, the

Table 3.6 Results of the 3-traits-by-3-methods multi-trait multi-method analyses in sample 2 of Study 3.2

	Mean	S.D	Self-Rating				Peer Rating				Supervisor Rating			
			EI_S	$Task_S$	IF_S	JD_S	EI_P	$Task_P$	IF_P	JD_P	EI_M	$Task_M$	IF_M	JD_M
EI_S	3.90	.46	(.89)											
$Task_S$	3.90	.58	.54	(.79)										
IF_S	4.06	.45	.65	.47	(.82)									
JD_S	3.99	.48	.67	.58	.78	(.85)								
EI_P	3.75	.47	**.41**	.25	.34	.38	(.89)							
$Task_P$	3.87	.63	.15	**.39**	.18	.29	.49	(.82)						
IF_P	3.92	.52	.27	.17	**.38**	.34	.68	.46	(.86)					
JD_P	3.87	.57	.17	.18	.29	**.33**	.67	.62	.78	(.89)				
EI_M	3.65	.48	**.38**	.32	.19	.32	**.34**	.24	.15	.16	(.88)			
$Task_M$	3.75	.66	.18	**.31**	.17	.30	.32	**.38**	.20	.27	.51	(.82)		
IF_M	3.70	.53	.20	.19	**.26**	.27	.38	.26	**.39**	.31	.57	.44	(.85)	
JD_M	3.71	.51	.23	.27	.26	**.39**	.45	.35	.32	**.37**	.58	.63	.69	(.83)

Notes
Correlations among different raters of the same constructs (inter-rater reliability) are marked in bold. For the subscripts, $_S$ = self, $_P$ = peer, and $_M$ = manager or supervisor. EI = emotional intelligence; Task = task performance; IF = interpersonal facilitation; JD = job dedication.

coefficients on the reliability diagonal (numbers in brackets) are consistently the highest in the matrix. Second, all of the coefficients in the validity diagonals (numbers in bold) are significantly different from zero and high enough to warrant further investigation. This indicates high convergent validity. Third, the correlations between self-rating, peer rating, and supervisor rating of EI were .41, .38, and .34.

The CFA results of the MTMM in sample 2 were very similar to those of sample 1. In sample 1, we needed to create three random indicators for each construct because there were only two sources for each trait. Since we had three methods (i.e., self, peer, and supervisor) and four traits (EI, task performance, interpersonal facilitation, and job dedication) in sample 2, we used one single aggregate of each construct to simplify the model. In other words, the CFA consisted of 12 indicators from a combination of four latent traits and three latent methods. This three-method, four-trait model had a model χ^2 of 79.85 and 33 degrees of freedom. The CFI and TLI of this model were .98 and .95, respectively. Seventy percent of the total observed variance was due to the three methods; 25% was attributed to the four traits; and 5% was attributed to random error. The alternative model, with three methods only, had 51 degrees of freedom, a model χ^2 of 283.91, CFI of .88, and TLI of .84. The alternative model, with four traits only, had 48 degrees of freedom, a model χ^2 of 932.06, CFI of .53, and TLI of .36. Therefore, the results from sample 1 confirmed that the variance attributed to the traits is a major component of the total observed variance, while method (source) is the major component of total observed variance in sample 2.

Hierarchical linear regression

SAMPLE 1

To show the predictive validity of the EI construct, we ran a hierarchical linear regression of the parents' EI rating on the students' ratings of powerlessness and life satisfaction. After entering the control variables as the first step, we entered the Big Five personality dimensions as the second set of control variables. We then entered the parents' rating of EI as the final step. Table 3.7 shows the results of the hierarchical regression analyses. The parents' rating of EI was a significant predictor of the students' life satisfaction, after controlling for demographic variables and the Big Five personality dimensions (β = .16, p < .05; ΔR^2 = .02, p < .01). Hypothesis 3.2 was supported by the data. It was also a significant predictor of students' perceptions of powerlessness, over and above that of the Big Five personality dimensions (β = −.17, p < .05; ΔR^2 = .02, p < .05). Hypothesis 3.3 was supported by the data.

SAMPLE 2

In sample 2, we had three dependent variables in the hierarchical regression analyses: task performance, interpersonal facilitation, and job dedication. We

Table 3.7 Results of the regression analyses of parent rating of EI on academic results, life satisfaction, and powerlessness

	Life Satisfaction (n = 388)			Powerlessness (n = 387)		
	Model 1	Model 2	Model 3	Model 1	Model 2	Model 3
Gender	.05	.04	.04	-.08	-.09	-.09
Working mother	-.07	-.09	-.09	-.02	-.01	-.01
Father's education	.11	.08	.08	-.08	-.05	-.05
Mother's education	.06	.01	.01	.07	.11	.11
NEURO (parent)	—	-.17**	-.14*	—	.14*	.10
EXTRA (parent)	—	.14+	.14*	—	.09	.08
OPEN (parent)	—	.10	.08	—	-.25**	-.23**
AGREE (parent)	—	.21**	.22**	—	-.06	-.07
CONSC (parent)	—	-.03	-.10	—	-.07	.01
Parent rating EI	—	—	.16*	—	—	-.17*
R^2	.04*	.16**	.18**	.01	.10**	.12**
ΔR^2	—	.13**	.02**	—	.09**	.02*
d.f.$_1$, d.f.$_2$	4, 284	5, 279	1, 278	4, 284	5, 279	1, 278

Notes
The Big Five variable scores are parents' ratings. NEURO, EXTRA, OPEN, AGREE, and CONSC = neuroticism, extraversion, openness, agreeableness, and conscientiousness; EI = emotional intelligence.

$^+p < .10$; $^*p < .05$; $^{**}p < .01$.

first entered the demographic variables as controls (age, gender, education, and tenure with supervisor) in the first step of the regression. Loyalty to supervisor and trust in the supervisor were entered in the second step, and peer rating or employees' self-rating of EI was added in the final step. Table 3.8 presents the results of these regression analyses.

Table 3.8 (column M_{4a}) shows that the peer rating of EI has significant predictive power on task performance after controlling for demographics, loyalty to supervisor and trust in the supervisor, and the Big Five personality dimensions ($\beta = .42$; $\Delta R^2 = .17$, $p < .01$). Similar significant results were found for the two contextual performance dimensions. When contextual performance was used as the dependent variable, the peer rating of EI was a significant predictor of interpersonal facilitation ($\beta = .44$; $\Delta R^2 = .18$, $p < .01$) and job dedication ($\beta = .50$; $\Delta R^2 = .24$, $p < .01$). Table 3.8 (column M_{4b}) shows the results when employees' self-rating of EI was used as a predictor of the supervisor's rating of performance. Employees' self-rating of EI was a significant predictor of task performance ($\beta = .17$; $\Delta R^2 = .03$, $p < .05$), interpersonal facilitation ($\beta = .26$;

Table 3.8 Results of regression analyses of peer rating and self-rating of EI on job performance

	Task Performance					Interpersonal Facilitation					Job Dedication				
	M_1	M_2	M_3	M_{4a}	M_{4b}	M_1	M_2	M_3	M_{4a}	M_{4b}	M_1	M_2	M_3	M_{4a}	M_{4b}
Age	.00	.05	.05	.04	.05	.11	.13	.13	.11	.13	.02	.05	.05	.02	.04
Education	-.09	-.07	-.07	-.06	-.06	-.08	-.07	-.08	-.08	-.07	-.06	-.05	-.07	-.07	-.06
Tenure with supervisor	.16+	.12	.13	.15*	.12	-.06	-.07	-.07	-.03	-.07	.02	-.00	.00	.03	-.01
Gender	.13+	.14+	.14+	.15*	.13+	-.05	-.03	-.02	-.01	-.03	.10	.12	.14+	.14*	.12
NEURO (self)	—	-.03	.01	-.02	.03	—	.04	.09	.07	.12	—	.08	.12	.11	.16+
EXTRA (self)	—	-.04	-.04	.00	-.05	—	-.01	-.01	.04	-.01	—	-.05	-.04	.01	-.05
OPEN (self)	—	.06	.06	.04	.03	—	.01	.00	.00	-.03	—	-.01	-.01	-.02	-.06
AGREE (self)	—	.26*	.26**	.27**	.26*	—	.12	.13	.13	.12	—	.17+	.18+	.18*	.17+
CONSC (self)	—	-.07	-.06	-.10	-.06	—	-.01	.01	-.03	.01	—	.05	.07	.02	.06
Loyalty	—	—	.12	.06	.10	—	—	.17+	.13	.15	—	—	.22*	.16+	.19*
Trust	—	—	-.03	-.07	-.06	—	—	-.10	-.15+	-.15	—	—	-.19*	-.25**	-.25**
EI (peer)	—	—	—	.42**	—	—	—	—	.44**	—	—	—	—	.50**	—
EI (self)	—	—	—	—	.17*	—	—	—	—	.26**	—	—	—	—	.31**
ΔR^2	.05+	.05	.01	.17**	.03*	.02	.01	.02	.18**	.06**	.01	.04	.04+	.24**	.08**
ΔF	2.06+	1.81	.88	35.97**	4.50*	.91	.39	1.56	36.11**	9.71**	.58	1.19	3.05+	54.55**	15.29**
d.f.$_1$, d.f.$_2$	4, 163	5, 158	2, 156	1, 155	1, 155	4, 161	5, 156	2, 154	1, 153	1, 153	4, 163	5, 158	2, 156	1, 155	1, 155

Notes

$n = 168$. M_1 has only the demographic variables as predictors; M_2 has the demographic variables plus the Big Five personality dimensions; M_3 adds in loyalty to supervisor (Loyalty) and trust in supervisor (Trust) as predictors; M_{4a} has all predictors in M_3 plus peer rating of emotional intelligence (EI); M_{4b} has all predictors in M_3 plus self-rating of EI. NEURO, EXTRA, OPEN, AGREE, and CONSC = neuroticism, extraversion, openness, agreeableness, and conscientiousness.

$^+$p < .10; *p < .05; **p < .01.

$\Delta R^2 = .06$, $p < .01$), and job dedication ($\beta = .31$; $\Delta R^2 = .08$, $p < .01$). Hypothesis 3.4 was therefore supported by the data.

Discussion

In this paper, we reviewed the definition and domain of the EI construct and argued that it should be conceptually distinct from traditional personality dimensions. We then used a two-study, four-sample design to investigate the validity and utility of the EI construct. We followed Davies et al. and other recent work on EI (e.g., George, 2000; Mayer, Caruso, et al., 2000a; Mayer & Salovey, 1997) in defining EI as a four-dimensional construct, comprising the ability to understand one's own and other's emotions, to regulate one's emotions, and to utilize one's emotions. This definition of EI as a set of abilities conceptually distinguishes it from personality traits, which are behavioral preferences.

On top of this conceptual argument, we dealt with the empirical conclusions of Davies et al. by using CFAs to investigate various EI-related scales and a newly developed EI scale (the WLEIS) based on the four-dimensional view in Study 3.1. We replicated Davies et al.'s results for earlier EI-related scales, but we further found that the WLEIS captured a construct that may be distinct from the Big Five personality dimensions. A CFA using the data from a second sample in Study 3.1 replicated the structural distinctiveness of the EI construct from the Big Five personality dimensions. In Study 3.2, we obtained data on others' ratings of EI to show the convergent and discriminant validity of EI using MTMM analyses. Parents' ratings of EI were also shown to account for incremental variance in life satisfaction and powerlessness beyond the Big Five personality dimensions, in a student sample. Peers' ratings of EI were found to be predictive of supervisor ratings of in-role and extra-role performance in an employee sample.

There are at least three important implications arising from the results of this paper. First, if EI does indeed measure emotion-related abilities that are distinct from personality traits, we certainly advocate continued research on EI and the development of scales that do not rely on self-reports. Furthermore, given the confusion over the definition and domain of the EI construct in the past, we believe that it will be beneficial to EI researchers to adopt a mutually acceptable definition of the construct and to develop more standardized measures according to this definition. As reviewed in this paper, the four-dimensional definition adopted here appears to be a reasonable direction for future EI research. More research should be conducted according to this framework to avoid further confusion.

Second, our two studies provided evidence to support that EI is related to but distinct from the Big Five personality dimensions. Furthermore, sample 2 of Study 3.2 showed that EI might be a good predictor of job performance. After controlling for relevant variables and the Big Five personality dimensions, EI still accounts for more than 10% of the variance in in-role and extra-role performance when peer ratings of EI were used. It should be noted that neither

EI nor job performance was assessed by the employees themselves. The results are therefore not confounded by self-reporting. Given these initial positive results, researchers are encouraged to develop more rigorous non–self-report measures of EI. One possible direction would be the development of forced-choice EI questions, whereby participants are asked to select the response that most closely represents their EI level, rather than evaluating their own abilities directly.

Third, the criterion variables examined in this study included life satisfaction, the feeling of powerlessness, and job performance. Conceptually, EI may be more important for criterion variables such as psychological well-being and occupational stress experienced by workers. Future research should investigate the relationship between EI and criterion variables other than job performance. Furthermore, if EI is related to job performance and other important variables in the workplace, training in EI may be as important as selecting applicants with high EI. Future research may attempt to develop effective EI training programs. The predictive power of EI for job performance, as compared with general mental abilities, could also be an interesting research direction. While we have some evidence that EI can predict performance over and beyond general mental abilities, past studies used self-report measures of EI. It would be interesting to compare the predictive validity of EI and general mental abilities when EI is assessed by aptitude tests.

There are, however, two limitations of this EI project. First, while we have provided evidence for the validity of non–self-report assessment of EI in Study 3.2, "tests" of EI might be important because EI is defined as an ability facet. Traditionally, abilities are measured by tests instead of self-report measures. The recent development of the Mayer-Salovey-Caruso Emotional Intelligence Test (MSCEIT; Mayer, Caruso, & Salovey, 2000b) may be one possible move in this direction. The major contribution of our study is to provide some preliminary evidence of the validity of EI. By helping to open up this line of research, we hope that there might be development of rigorous tests of EI in the future, as well as evidence of its relationship with other organizational constructs.

Our second limitation is that all the data in this project were collected in Hong Kong and the People's Republic of China. Cross-cultural generalizability of the results may be a concern. We do not know whether EI would vary across different cultures. However, when we go back to the EI literature, we do not find any discussion of EI across cultural boundaries. Our position is that one's abilities to understand, regulate, and utilize one's emotions in constructive ways are general human abilities. There is no immediate evidence that the validity of EI, as defined under our four-dimensional view, should vary across cultures. While further studies may be needed to verify this position, we take the general scientific attitude that psychological and management phenomena are considered as universal unless there are theories or evidence showing their cross-cultural variations.

While the EI construct may be universal, we agree that behaviors resulting from the EI of an individual may vary across cultures. For example, a non-reactive quiet response by the subordinate when one's boss is making unreasonable demands may reflect high EI among Chinese but probably not among non-Chinese. In this respect, our use of a self-report measure of EI may, in fact, be a plus because we asked respondents about their final judgment of the EI of the target person irrespective of the assessment clues or methods they would use. By doing so, we may be able to avoid some cross-cultural differences regarding expressing emotions or diagnosing emotions because the assessors would be able to use the clues or methods that are appropriate for their specific culture. This issue may have to be considered when behavior- or outcome-oriented tests of EI, such as the MSCEIT, are used across cultural boundaries.

4 Provide convincing evidence after the initial stage

As reported in Chapters 2 and 3, we realized that we needed to provide as much evidence as possible to show that the emotional intelligence (EI) construct was a worthwhile topic for scientific investigation during the first few years of our investigation. Shortly after the *Leadership Quarterly* invited us to submit our first paper, I was thinking about how to show the validity of the EI construct from another angle. We were still following the basic idea that EI should have a stronger relationship with job outcomes for jobs requiring a high level of emotional labor. The idea was not new because it was basically a replication. The challenge was how we could have constructive extensions in a replication study. In other words, we needed to convince readers that the additional evidence was reasonable and of sufficient meaning.

This is probably a common situation for research ideas that have just gone through their initial stage. I think quite a few doctoral theses face a similar situation. If adequately conducted, research for a doctoral thesis might involve some innovative ideas and make some important contributions. After the thesis is published, follow-up studies may be worthwhile. In most situations, the first publication from the thesis may not include everything that was discussed in the thesis itself. So we do not start from zero, but the biggest challenge is how to convince readers that incremental contributions can be made after the major contributions of the first paper prepared from the thesis. We have to decide what additional arguments and data might be necessary in order to make the follow-up paper convincing.

Lesson 7: observe the code of ethics

An additional constraint is the ethical standard in scientific research that we should not commit self-plagiarism. At least two points have to be noted. First, for the conceptual part, we need to cite the previous study to let readers know that some of the theoretical arguments have already been published. The editor and reviewers can judge whether sufficiently new contributions have been made.

Second, we should be careful not to have the same data reported in multiple studies. Although it is fine to report data from the same sample in more than one study, the general guideline is that at least the key variables involved should be different. To play it safe, it is always a good practice to inform the editor that other data from the same sample have been published when the paper is submitted. In the past ten years, I have attended some workshops in Asia and heard some speakers telling junior faculty members to use the same idea or dataset to write up multiple papers so that they can have a larger number of publications within a shorter period of time. Whenever I heard this said, I would try to politely explain that this is not correct. Also, if the papers got published, we could not deny that we had reported the same dataset in multiple papers. This may have serious consequences for our academic record. Although the number of publications is very important in the short run, I still want to make a strong appeal here to junior faculty colleagues that it will be very important to follow the ethical standards for conducting scientific research.

Different professional associations have their own code of ethics or conduct, and it is best to study and follow them. The Academy of Management has a clear code of conduct. Unfortunately, as far as I know, only a small percentage of the academy members have read the code in detail. I would strongly recommend doctoral students and junior faculty to study them carefully. I remember that during the first few years of my study of the EI construct, I was very careful to file the records of each sample and kept the evidence showing that they were independent samples. As for the research ideas that each sample could demonstrate, I kept very good records of the initial intention and the amendments whenever necessary. Hard copies of those records were kept in my office for about ten years.

Lesson 7: It is important to study the code of ethics or conduct of the professional academic body you are affiliated with. Try to make it a habit to follow the code. This can make you really a professional researcher and avoid unnecessary troubles.

Lesson 8: something new in theory and/or data

My decision at that time for the extensions of our third paper was to go in two directions. First, I wanted to add in some completely new conceptual extensions. Second, I collected data from a source which was quite different from the other samples I had been studying. I believed that if I could achieve these two points, they should be sufficiently good selling points to readers that the paper deserved publication.

The idea could work because I had been involved in another line of projects about career interests since 1997. A prominent scholar in the area of career counseling visited Hong Kong and wanted to discuss with local scholars about the applicability of the career interest model in the local environment. I read through the literature and provided some ideas about the local situation. I was involved as a junior author for that project, and we got one paper published.

Through this experience, I learned about the most popular career interest model and its related constructs and findings in the career counseling area (Holland, 1985). This model classified job duties into six major types. I discovered that the six types could be a proxy for different levels of emotional labor. For example, one type of job duty is "social," which means interacting with people. This certainly should require a high level of emotional labor. Another type of job duty is "realistic," which means working with instruments or machines. This certainly should have a very low level of emotional labor requirement.

Although each job would usually involve more than one type of duties, Holland's theory argues that for most occupations, we could identify one dominant type of duties. Thus, conceptually, I tried to link up the career interest model with the concept of emotional labor requirement. The advantage of doing this was that it could provide an objective indicator of the level of emotional labor and link the EI construct with the well-established career counseling literature. The objective indicator of emotional labor could be compared to the traditional ratings of emotional labor judged by job incumbents. However, in so doing, I needed data from six typical types of occupations. As I had been helping some labor unions in Hong Kong as a volunteer, I was able to survey union members in different types of occupations. The only occupation type that I did not need the unions for was "social," because it would be relatively easy for me to get secondary school teachers to complete questionnaires.

The unique strength of this sample was that it was very different from my other samples. However, I could not get data from multiple informants, such as both employees and their supervisors. I had to limit the job outcome variables to satisfaction or other types of subjective ratings by the job incumbents. This might make the results not as convincing, as common method variance would be a threat. To overcome this weakness, I added another variable, which was life satisfaction. My expectation was that the effect of EI on job satisfaction would be moderated by emotional labor. However, as life satisfaction would have a relatively small or even no relationship with the job, the effect of EI on life satisfaction would not be moderated by emotional labor. If both expectations were supported in the same sample, the evidence would be much more convincing because we could largely rule out the possibility that the results were merely due to chance. It would be very much like having an independent sample to cross-validate the findings.

Although showing the effect of EI on job satisfaction was not a big idea, I believed adding the proxy measure of emotional labor from Holland's career interest model and the differential moderating effect of emotional labor on life satisfaction were good extensions. These extensions made the study not just a replication.

I remember that one doctoral student asked me how I came up with Holland's model and life satisfaction as two extensions. Frankly speaking, I myself was not very sure. All I could say was that it did not come from a formal procedure or systematic analysis. At that time, I was working on Holland's model for other projects, and the idea of using life satisfaction to validate the EI measure had already been employed in other student samples. I believe this may reflect a fundamental nature of scientific research. We are limited by our own exposure to different topics and areas. It is always advisable to keep a broad horizon and not limit ourselves to one single project. Practically, as the risk of not finally getting our research project published is high, it is better for us to work on multiple projects from time to time. Otherwise, we may not be able to come up with various ways to enrich our research project and study design so that our evidence can be more convincing.

Lesson 8: It is both interesting and practical to work on multiple projects from time to time. It can broaden our horizon and stimulate us to come up with more innovative or convincing ideas. We never know when this might happen, but without a broader background, our innovativeness may be limited.

Lesson 9: publication outlets

It took me about nine months to collect the data as planned and to write up a draft report of this project. As my co-author was an Australian citizen and had a planned trip back to Australia, we submitted the paper to a specialized conference with the topic of emotions in organizations held in Australia. The paper was accepted for presentation (Wong & Law, 2002), and the organizer invited us to publish the paper as one of the chapters in an edited book which consisted of the best papers presented at the conference. At that time, we were sure that our submission to the *Leadership Quarterly* would be accepted for publication. We believed it would be nice to have more evidence for the validity of the EI construct published as soon as possible. Therefore, we did not submit this paper to journals but accepted the offer of the organizers of the conference. We further revised the conference paper by incorporating the comments of the editors, and the paper was formally published in 2005 (Wong, Wong, & Law, 2005).

When I told the above story to some of my colleagues and graduate students, they usually would ask why we did not submit our paper to journals. This was a difficult question to answer. Choosing a publication outlet for a particular paper may not be a systematic process. Practically, it is advisable to plan our research projects to target mainstream journals in the first place. This is probably very good advice to junior faculty members because they need this type of publications to get tenure. However, if this is the only type of target throughout one's academic career, I think it will be too narrow. Also, there are some projects that inherently would not be publishable in mainstream journals but that are worthwhile for other reasons. One example was the career interest project that I was involved in. Career counseling is definitely not a mainstream topic in the area of business management. However, after finishing that paper, I got the chance to design a career interest and related assessment instruments for Hong Kong young people. The project was funded by the Hong Kong government, and we set up two career counseling centers to serve young people in Hong Kong. From the year 2008 on, it has been providing career education and related services free of charge to thousands of young people each year in Hong Kong. This project carried relatively little weight in my academic publications, but it was certainly a meaningful project.

Once we are able to get tenure, I still believe we should not worry too much about whether our research projects are published in mainstream journals or not. Instead, we should pay more attention to their rigor and contribution to knowledge, and probably impact on practitioners as well. So far as the outlet is adequate to inform our colleagues who are interested and working in the same area, we should consider publishing there. To me, the book chapter at that time was a very good outlet to inform other scholars interested in studying emotions in organizations. We believed this was why the organizers of the conference invited us to publish the paper in the specialized book at that time.

Lesson 9: While it is nice to target our research projects at mainstream journals, this should not limit our research efforts in projects that may not be suitable for those journals. This is especially true for scholars who already have tenure. Otherwise, various meaningful projects and academic works would be ignored, and this would not be healthy for the academic world.

The following are the major contents of the paper.

Wong, C. S., Wong, P. M., & Law, K. S. (2005). The interaction effect of emotional intelligence and emotional labor on job satisfaction: A test of Holland's classification of occupations. In Härtel, C.E.J., Zerbe, W. J., & Ashkanasy, N. M. (Eds.), *Emotions in organizational behavior*, pp. 235–250. Mahwah, NJ: Lawrence Erlbaum; these contents are reprinted with permission.

Abstract. Although emotional intelligence has been a popular concept in the media, there have been few scientifically rigorous studies designed to examine its roles in the workplace. Following the exploratory evidence provided by a recent study, the study reported in this study replicated the finding that emotional intelligence and the nature of the job requirement (i.e., emotional labor) would have an interacting effect on job satisfaction. Using a sample of 307 respondents from six different jobs, this interaction effect was confirmed. Furthermore, this study argued that the nature of the job requirement could be estimated from Holland's occupational model. The results supported this argument. Implications for future career and human resource management research concerning emotional intelligence are discussed.

Emotional intelligence (EI) has been an emerging topic for psychological, educational, and management researchers and consultants in recent years. In general, EI has been defined as the ability to perceive, understand, and manage one's emotions (Salovey, Hsee, & Mayer, 1993; Salovey & Mayer, 1990). Although lacking solid research supports, proponents of the EI concept argue that EI affects people's physical and mental health as well as career achievements (e.g., Goleman, 1995). Some emerging leadership theories also imply that emotional and social intelligence are even more important for leaders and managers because cognitive and behavioral complexity and flexibility are important characteristics of competent leaders (Boal & Whitehead, 1992). However, up to now, there is little empirical evidence in the literature about the relationship between EI and job outcomes such as performance and job satisfaction. There are at least three major reasons for such a lack of empirical evidence. First, as a new construct, scholars have not adopted a uniform domain of the EI construct. Political sensitivity, social awareness, service orientation, achievement drive, and some other personality dimensions have been argued to be part of EI by some authors (e.g., Bar-On, 1997), while other scholars would confine EI to the domain of one branch of social intelligence (see, e.g., Mayer, Caruso, et al., 2000a). Second, since different domains of the construct are being used, a simple and psychometrically sound EI measure that can be used practically in management studies has not been developed. Third, there is no conceptual framework that defines the role of EI in the area of management and its relationships with job outcomes.

In response to these deficiencies in the literature, Wong and Law (2002) derived specific hypotheses concerning the relationship between EI and job outcomes. These were based on Mayer, Caruso, et al.'s (2000a) theoretical view that EI could be viewed as one facet of intelligence and on the conceptual framework of Gross' model of emotional regulation (Gross, 1998a, 1998b). Specifically, Wong and Law hypothesized that the relationship between EI and job outcomes would depend on the nature of the job requirements. Borrowing the concept of emotional labor from Hochschild (1983), they argued that if the job required incumbents to present a particular form of emotion regardless of their true emotions (i.e., high emotional labor requirement), the relationship between EI and job outcomes would be stronger. After clarifying the domain of EI and developing a 16-item EI measure, Wong and Law (2002) provided exploratory evidence supporting their hypotheses.

There are two main purposes of this study. First, we extend and build on Wong and Law's results concerning the interaction effect between EI and emotional labor on job satisfaction. To provide a stronger test of the interaction between EI and emotional labor, it is necessary to control for the most common predictors of job satisfaction, which was not done in the Wong and Law study. Also, to further illustrate the authenticity of the interaction effect, we compared the interaction between EI and emotional labor on job-related outcomes (job satisfaction) and a non-job outcome (life satisfaction). Life satisfaction is chosen as the non-job outcome because it has been shown repeatedly that EI has a main effect on life satisfaction (see, e.g., Ciarrochi, Chan, & Caputi, 2000; Martinez-Pons, 1997; Wong & Law, 2002). While the interaction between emotional labor and EI should have significant effects on job satisfaction, the interaction effect on life satisfaction should be insignificant.

Second, the concept of EI will have greater relevance in management and vocational psychology research if it can be extended to a well-established occupational model. Some researchers in vocational psychology have called for more studies concerning the role of emotions in career theories (e.g., Kidd, 1998). Since Wong and Law argued that the nature of the job would moderate the relationship between EI and job outcomes, it is very likely that this relationship would also differ among occupations. If this relationship can be systematically examined in a well-established occupational model, it would help to advance our understanding of career counseling, selection, and training for various occupations. In this study, we applied Holland's (1959, 1985) model of occupational interest and used it as a proxy of the emotional labor of the job.

In the following discussion, we will first briefly summarize the domain of EI and the occupational model that may be relevant to the differential relationships between EI and job outcomes. Then an empirical study will be reported which tested the applicability of the occupational model to explain the differential relationships between EI and job satisfaction.

Domain and measures of EI

EI has its roots in the concept of "social intelligence" first identified by Thorndike in 1920. Salovey and Mayer (1990) were some of the earliest to propose the name "emotional intelligence" to represent the ability of a person to deal with his/her emotions. They defined EI as "the subset of social intelligence that involves the ability to monitor one's own and others' feelings and emotions, to discriminate among them and to use this information to guide one's thinking and actions" (p. 189). In response to writers who expanded the domain of EI to personality traits and other psychological concepts, Mayer and Salovey (1997) attempted to confine its domain to a human's ability in dealing with emotions. These emotion-handling abilities comprised four distinct dimensions, namely, appraising and expressing emotions in the self (self emotional appraisal), appraising and recognizing the emotions of others (other's emotional appraisal), regulating one's emotions in the self (regulation of emotion), and using one's emotions to facilitate performance (use of emotion).

The above definition of the construct of EI has several advantages. First, as we continue to argue that EI is one branch of social intelligence, this definition of EI makes it clear that it is one form of human intelligence (Gardner, 1993). Second, this definition of EI addressed an erroneous view of the EI construct in the past – that EI is only a mix of well-established constructs. This erroneous view of EI leads Davies, Stankov, and Roberts (1998) to draw the conclusion that EI is elusive and is a combination of personality traits. Under the above four-dimensional view, EI is an ability facet which is conceptually distinct from other well-established and -researched human characteristics such as personality, needs, and achievement drive. The final advantage of this four-dimensional view of EI is that it allows formal testing of the psychometric properties of measures designed to capture the underlying multidimensional EI construct (Law, Wong, & Mobley, 1998).

There is very limited empirical evidence of the impact of EI on job outcomes. Theoretically, employees with a high level of EI are those who can understand, master, and utilize their emotions and can therefore master their interactions with others in a more effective manner. Based on a work–family relations framework, Wharton and Erickson (1995) argued that emotional management affects individual consequences such as work–family role overload and work–family role conflicts. Mayer, Caruso, et al. (2000b) showed that EI is positively related to empathy, life satisfaction, and parental warmth. Using Gross' model of emotion regulation (Gross, 1998a, 1998b), Wong and Law (2002) showed preliminary evidence that EI was positively related to job satisfaction. Therefore, employees with a high level of EI are those who understand their emotions, are able to regulate them, and are able to use them in a constructive way to enhance job performance. The continual presence of positive emotional states in the employees should also lead to positive affection toward their job. As a result, they should have a higher level of both general satisfaction and satisfaction toward their job. Based on these findings, we proposed:

Hypothesis 4.1: EI is positively related to life satisfaction.

Hypothesis 4.2: EI is positively related to job satisfaction.

Emotional labor and Holland's model of vocational choice

Kidd (1998) argued that traditional theories of occupational choice and career development were largely driven by the assumption of rationality in behavior at work. As such, the roles of feelings and emotions such as anger, worry, enthusiasm, hurt, and so forth are rarely elaborated in any detail in career theories (p. 277). This may due to the fact that these theories are largely applied to fresh graduates entering employment for the first time. However, as more and more employees and job seekers experience redundancy or become unemployed and need to find a job of a different nature owing to economic restructuring, the role of emotions may become more important to career theories.

By applying the concept of emotional labor, Brotheridge and Grandey (2002) attempted to investigate differences among occupations. Their results suggested the existence of a hierarchy of emotional labor expectations, with human service professionals reporting the highest levels of frequency, variety, intensity, and duration of emotional display and expectations for control over emotional expressions. Thus, it appears worthwhile to further investigate the role of emotions among occupations. Unfortunately, Brotheridge and Grandey did not incorporate their findings into existing career theories. In this section, we will review the concept of emotional labor and examine how this can be incorporated in a well-established model of vocational choice.

In the economics literature, many scholars view employee emotions as a commodity provided by the employees in exchange for individual rewards (see, e.g., Hochschild, 1983; Morris & Feldman, 1996, 1997; Sutton, 1991). On top of the traditional mental and physical labor, they argue that there is a third type of labor, emotional labor, which can be offered by employees in exchange for a wage or salary. According to this view, "mental labor" refers to the cognitive skills and knowledge as well as the expertise that can be offered by the employees. "Physical labor" refers to the physical efforts of employees to achieve organizational goals. "Emotional labor" refers to the extent to which an employee is required to present an appropriate emotion in order to perform the job in an efficient and effective manner. Examples of jobs requiring a high level of emotional labor are restaurant servers, bank tellers, and flight attendants. These jobs require employees to be amiable. Even if they are in bad mood, they have to regulate their emotions in order to achieve high performance. In contrast, the emotional labor of auto mechanics would be quite low. They have very infrequent interaction with customers and spend most of their work time dealing with machines. As a result, there is not a strong requirement from the job that they need to regulate their emotion. Subsequently, scholars studying emotional labor have argued that the extent of emotional labor required may vary across occupations.

Wong and Law (2002) argued that the emotional labor of the job would moderate the EI–job satisfaction link. In particular, for jobs with high emotional labor, EI would have a strong impact on job satisfaction, whereas if the job required low emotional labor, the relationship between EI and job satisfaction would be less significant. This study further extends Wong and Law's argument. First, we argue that it would be a better test of the interaction effect if we can control for major variables affecting the outcome variable, namely, job satisfaction. Second, we compare the interaction effect of EI and emotional labor on job satisfaction as well as life satisfaction. Life satisfaction refers to "'global' well-being, that is, happiness or satisfaction with life-as-a-whole or life in general" (Andrews & Robinson, 1991, p. 61). Theoretically, emotional labor is a job characteristic and so should not interact with EI in affecting overall life satisfaction. As a result, the interaction effects of EI and emotional labor on life satisfaction should be insignificant, while their interaction effects on job satisfaction should be significant. Finally, we also use Holland's model of vocational choice as an operationalization of emotional labor in this study.

Holland's model of vocational choice (Holland, 1959, 1985) has been one of the most widely chosen models used to describe an individual's career interests and to classify occupations (Borgen, 1986; Brown & Brooks, 1990). This model describes individuals' career interests toward six types of occupations, which lie at the vertices of a hexagon: realistic (e.g., plumbers and machine operators), investigative (e.g., mathematicians and computer programmers), artistic (e.g., artists and designers), social (e.g., teachers and social workers), enterprising (e.g., managers and salespeople), and conventional (e.g., clerks and accountants). For this reason, it is sometimes referred to as the RIASEC model (using the first letter of each career type in their specified order). The basic argument in Holland's theory is that "people search for environments that will let them exercise their skills and abilities, express their attitudes and values, and take on agreeable problems and roles" (1985, p. 4). Consequently, realistic people seek realistic environments (or jobs), social people seek social environments, and so forth. Another important feature of Holland's model is the concept of calculus, which specifies the relationship within and between types or environments. Holland argued in the calculus assumption that the six types can be ordered as the vertices of a hexagon, in which the distances between the types are inversely proportional to the theoretical relationships between them. In other words, the distance between a realistic job and a social job is three times the distance between a realistic job and an investigative job. Similarly, the distance between a realistic job and an artistic job is double the distance between a realistic job and an investigative job.

According to Holland's (RIASEC) model, social jobs would have the highest level of emotional labor because they (1) involve a lot of interpersonal interactions and (2) require incumbents to serve their clients or customers in some form of appropriate manner. For example, those in educational occupations, such as teachers and social workers, must be able to present the appropriate type of empathic emotion when they are interacting with their students and clients. In contrast, realistic and investigative types of occupations involve less interpersonal interaction, and there is a much smaller demand on the incumbents to present an appropriate emotion when performing their jobs. In agreement, occupations with high emotional labor as identified by Hochschild (1983) are mostly jobs in service industries that require substantial amount of interpersonal interaction. Thus, it is reasonable to argue that the relationship between EI and job outcomes is strongest for social jobs. In addition, according to the calculus assumption of Holland's (RIASEC) model, the strength of this relationship will decrease according to the distance of the particular occupation type from the social type. That is, this relationship will be similar for the adjacent types (i.e., artistic and enterprising) but weaker than for the social type. The relationship will also be similar for the alternate types (i.e., investigative and conventional) but weaker than for the adjacent types. Finally, the relationship will be weakest for the opposite type (i.e., realistic). As a result, we proposed:

> Hypothesis 4.3: The effects of EI on job satisfaction are dependent on the emotional labor of the job. Specifically, the higher the emotional labor of the job, the stronger the effects of EI on job satisfaction.

> Hypothesis 4.4: Following Holland's model of vocational choice, the effects of EI on job satisfaction would be highest for the social type of jobs. The effect sizes of the EI–job satisfaction relationship for different types of jobs will follow Holland's calculus assumption.

> Hypothesis 4.5: The effects of EI on life satisfaction are independent of the emotional labor of the job.

Methods

Sample and sampling procedure

The sample for this study came from two sources. The first source is union members in five types of jobs. The five jobs included bus driver (realistic), computer programmer (investigative), art designer for advertising companies (artistic), shop manager in a retail shop (enterprising), and clerk (conventional). A total of 300 questionnaires were given to the union, and 218 valid responses were returned, representing a response rate of 72.7%. However, since there are no social jobs in the union, our second sample source was teachers at two secondary schools. One hundred and ten questionnaires were sent to all the teachers of the two schools, and 89 valid responses were returned, representing a response rate of 80.9%. Thus, the final sample consisted of 307 respondents (46 bus drivers, 103 clerks, 17 computer programmers, 9 art designers, 43 shop managers, and 89 secondary school teachers). The average age was 37.5 years with a standard deviation of 8.2. Fifty-one percent of this sample were male, and 62.6% were married.

Measures

EI

The 16-item measure developed by Wong and Law (2002) was adopted in this study. The internal consistency reliability was .90 for this sample.

Emotional labor

In this study, the five-item measure from Wong and Law (2002) was used to measure the emotional labor of a job. The internal consistency reliability was .84 for this sample.

Proxy of emotional labor by Holland's occupational model

To test the importance of EI in various occupational types, we created a second proxy measure of emotional labor according to Holland's (RIASEC) model. As argued before, the social type of jobs would probably have the highest level of emotional labor because these jobs have the greatest requirement for social interaction. Following the calculus assumption of Holland's (RIASEC) model, the order of emotional labor will thus be social, its adjacent types (i.e., artistic and enterprising), its alternate types (i.e., investigative and conventional), and its opposite type (i.e., realistic). Thus, this proxy measure of emotional labor was coded as follows: the social type (i.e., secondary school teachers) was coded as 4, its adjacent types (i.e., art designers and shop managers) were coded as 3, the alternate types (i.e., computer programmers and clerks) were coded as 2, and the opposite type (i.e., bus drivers) was coded as 1.

Job satisfaction

The four items from the Job Diagnostic Survey (Hackman & Oldham, 1975) that measured satisfaction with the work itself were adopted in this study. These items asked respondents to evaluate the extent of their satisfaction in four dimensions of performing their jobs (including, for example, the amount of personal growth and development, and the feeling of worthwhile accomplishment). To be more comprehensive, we added one item asking for respondents' satisfaction with the overall job content. The internal consistency reliability of these five items was .89.

Life satisfaction

The nine items constructed by A. Campbell, Converse, and Rodgers (1976) were adopted to measure an individual's life satisfaction in this study. Items on this scale are pairs of opposite adjectives (e.g., "interesting" versus "boring," "enjoyable" versus "miserable") with a 7-point Likert-type scale of numbers between them. Respondents were requested to circle the number which best described their feeling toward their lives. The internal consistency reliability was .94 for this sample.

Organizational commitment

Since respondents worked for various organizations, it was necessary to control their attitudes toward their organizations in examining their level of job satisfaction. Six items measuring the affective commitment to the organization, developed by Meyer, Allen, and Smith (1993), were adopted in this study. An example of an item is "I really feel as if this organization's problems are my own." The response format was a 7-point Likert-type scale. The coefficient alpha of the six items was .92.

Job characteristics

Job characteristics are one of the most important factors affecting job satisfaction (Fried & Ferris, 1987; Loher, Noe, Moeller, & Fitzgerald, 1985). Thus, it is necessary to control this predictor of job satisfaction. The three items used by Wong (1997) were adopted in this study. These items were "The content of my job is complicated and complex," "My job is very challenging," and "The scope of my job is quite large." The internal consistency reliability was .79 for this sample.

Demographics

The demographics of respondents were also statistically controlled to avoid confounding results. Respondents were required to give their age and tenure in response to open-ended questions. Education level, gender, and marital status were measured by multiple-choice items.

Analysis

Hierarchical regression was conducted to test the main effect of EI and the interaction effect between EI and emotional labor on job satisfaction and life satisfaction. Specifically, the control variables, EI and emotional labor, were entered into the regression equation first. The product term of EI and emotional labor was entered in the last step to examine the significance of the change in R^2. To test for the utility of Holland's occupational model in predicting the differential importance of EI in various occupations, the proxy measure of EI calculated from Holland's model was used to replace the emotional labor measure in the hierarchical regression. Finally, to ensure that this result is applicable to job-related criterion, life satisfaction was used as the dependent variable to test for the interaction effect of EI and emotional labor.

Results

Descriptive statistics and correlations among variables are shown in Table 4.1. The univariate correlation coefficients between EI and job satisfaction ($r = .36$, $p < .01$) and EI and life satisfaction ($r = .30$, $p < .01$) are moderately high. Therefore, both hypotheses 4.1 and 4.2 are supported. EI has significant effects on both job satisfaction and life satisfaction, and the effects of EI on both job satisfaction and life satisfaction are of similar magnitude.

Before conducting the hierarchical regression analyses, we conducted a confirmatory factor analysis on the 16-item EI measure to cross-validate its factor structure and the assumption of an underlying second-order EI construct behind the four dimensions. The measurement model included the four respective items of each dimension specified as the indicators for each dimension as well as the four dimensions specified as the indicators of an underlying second-order EI construct. Using the LISREL 8 package (Jöreskog & Sörbom, 1993), the fit of this model is very reasonable ($\chi^2 = 356.65$, d.f. $= 100$; standardized root mean square [SRMR] $= .074$; the Tucker-Lewis Index [TLI] $= .92$; the comparative fit index [CFI] $= .93$; incremental fit index [IFI] $= .93$). These goodness-of-fit indices, together with the internal consistency reliabilities for the four dimensions, provide further evidence of the psychometric soundness of this 16-item EI measure.

Results of the hierarchical regression are shown in Table 4.2. Columns 1 and 2 show the regression results when job satisfaction and life satisfaction are regressed on the predictor variables. The first column shows that the incremental R^2 of the interaction term between EI and emotional labor in predicting job satisfaction is significant ($\beta = .64$, $p < .05$) after controlling for all other variables. The second column shows the regression results when life satisfaction is used as the dependent variable. As expected, this interaction term is not significant when life satisfaction is used as the dependent variable. Finally, columns 3 and 4 of Table 4.2 show the regression results when emotional labor is proxied using Holland's model of vocational choice. The results of these two regression analyses are almost exactly the same as in columns 1 and 2. Therefore, it is clear that emotional labor moderates the EI–job satisfaction relationship but does not moderate the EI–life satisfaction relationship. Thus, hypotheses 4.3 and 4.5 are supported. Hypothesis 4.4, which expected there to be differential impacts of

Table 4.1 Descriptive statistics and correlations among variables

	Mean	S.D.	1	2	3	4	5	6	7	8	9	10	11
1. EI	4.98	.88	1.00										
2. EL	4.78	1.01	.46**	1.00									
3. JS	4.40	1.19	.36**	.37**	1.00								
4. LS	4.51	1.14	.30**	.19**	.39**	1.00							
5. OC	4.30	1.34	.34**	.26**	.62**	.25**	1.00						
6. JC	4.64	1.28	.37**	.41**	.61**	.35**	.38**	1.00					
7. Age	37.49	8.21	.30**	.17**	.11	-.01	.31**	.20**	1.00				
8. Tenure	10.54	7.84	.22**	.07	.07	.06	.15*	.19**	.52**	1.00			
9. Edu	4.43	1.57	.15*	.20**	.15*	.26**	-.09	.20**	-.13*	-.00	1.00		
10. Gender	.49	.50	-.07	.03	.01	.10	-.08	.02	-.13*	-.07	.05	1.00	
11. MS	.63	.48	.25**	.13*	.11	-.04	.24**	.19**	.54**	.35**	-.12*	-.13*	1.00

Notes

For gender, male = 0, female = 1. For marital status, single = 0, married = 1. EI = emotional intelligence; EL = emotional labor; JS = job satisfaction; LS = life satisfaction; OC = organizational commitment; JC = job characteristics; Edu = education level; MS = marital status.

*p < .05; **p < .01.

Table 4.2 Results of the regression analyses testing the interaction effect

Independent Variables	EL Measured by Employees' Responses						Holland's Proxy as EL Measure					
	(1) Job Satisfaction			(2) Life Satisfaction			(3) Job Satisfaction			(4) Life Satisfaction		
	β	ΔF	ΔR^2	β	ΔF	ΔR^2	β	ΔF	ΔR^2	β	ΔF	ΔR^2
Tenure	-.05			.03			-.06			.01		
Gender	.04			.10			.02			.07		
Age	-.07			-.09			-.07			-.09		
MS	-.03			-.10			-.04			.16		
Edu	.11	3.20**	.06**	.16*	3.53**	.07**	.10	3.21**	.06**	.07	3.54**	.07**
JC	.40**			.21**			.40**			.06**		
OC	.48**	138.65**	.49**	.17*	15.30**	.10**	.49**	138.72**	.49**	.05*	15.38**	.10**
EI	-.30			-.15			-.18			.18		
EL	-.34	1.62	.01	-.50	4.48*	.03*	-.60*	1.09	.00	-.26	7.26**	.05**
EI * EL	.64*	4.84*	.01*	.69	3.06	.01	.62*	5.04*	.01*	.04	.01	.00
Model R²	.57**			.21**			.57**			.21**		

Notes
For gender, male = 0, female = 1. For marital status, single = 0, married = 1. EL = emotional labor; MS = marital status; Edu = education level; JC = job characteristics; OC = organizational commitment; EI = emotional intelligence.

*p < .05; **p < .01.

the moderating effect of emotional labor on the EI–satisfaction relationship, is also supported.

To further examine differences across occupations, Table 4.3 presents the means and standard deviations of EI, emotional labor, and job-related variables for the respondents from the six jobs. In general, the mean scores appear to support our expectation about differences among occupations, with the exception of bus drivers. For example, teachers and shop managers have the highest levels of EI and emotional labor, while other occupational groups have relatively low levels of these two variables. The unexpected results of bus drivers may result from two factors. First, bus drivers in this sample are relatively older than respondents in other occupational groups. As a set, older people should have better mastery of emotion-handling abilities (Mayer, Caruso, et al., 2000b). As shown in Table 4.3, the mean age of bus drivers in this sample is about five years older than for other groups. This difference is statistically significant in a t-test (t = 3.44, p < .01). Second, the bus companies in recent years have emphasized their services to the customers. Thus, although the main duty of bus drivers is still driving the bus (i.e., operating a machine), bus drivers may have perceived a higher level of emotional labor required when this study was conducted.

Discussion

The study reported in this paper serves two main purposes. First, it empirically investigates the interaction effect of EI and emotional labor on job satisfaction. Although EI has become a popular concept, there is relatively little scientific evidence concerning its impact on job outcomes. This study provides evidence that EI interacts with emotional labor in affecting job satisfaction. Furthermore, to ensure that the interaction found in this study did not happen by chance, we controlled for other antecedents of job satisfaction and contrasted this interaction effect between job satisfaction and life satisfaction. Clear support was found that EI, as an interrelated set of abilities, will interact with the nature of the job (i.e., the requirement of emotional labor) in affecting job outcomes.

The second purpose of the reported study was to follow recent studies in vocational psychology concerning the role of emotions in career theories. Specifically, we attempted to apply Holland's occupational model to further understand the role of EI and emotional labor in various occupations. We argue that the concept of emotional labor can be incorporated into Holland's classification of occupations. Specifically, social types of occupations should have the highest level of emotional labor, and thus Holland's classification can be used as a proxy measure of emotional labor. The results of our hierarchical regression show that the same conclusion concerning the interaction effect of EI and emotional labor can be drawn using this proxy measure. With few exceptions, the mean levels of emotional labor and EI for the six jobs included in this study are also consistent with our expectations based on the calculus assumption of the model.

Table 4.3 Mean scores (standard deviations) for emotional intelligence (EI), emotional labor (EL), job satisfaction (JS) and life satisfaction (LS), organizational commitment (OC), and job characteristics (JC) across the six occupations

Job	EI	EL	JS	LS	OC	JC	Age
Teachers (n = 89)	5.17 (.81)	4.94 (.80)	4.57 (.97)	4.91 (1.00)	4.30 (1.42)	5.07 (.93)	39.26 (6.77)
Shop managers (n = 43)	5.14 (.76)	5.32 (.81)	4.85 (1.40)	4.80 (1.26)	4.53 (1.34)	5.00 (1.38)	36.71 (7.29)
Art designers (n = 9)	4.90 (.97)	4.76 (1.17)	5.09 (.83)	4.79 (.78)	4.51 (1.06)	4.81 (.80)	28.67 (4.42)
Programmers (n = 17)	4.99 (.65)	4.73 (.81)	3.94 (1.26)	4.22 (.71)	3.43 (1.19)	4.06 (1.43)	33.24 (6.62)
Clerks (n = 103)	4.72 (1.00)	4.40 (1.16)	3.99 (1.06)	4.32 (1.07)	4.01 (1.19)	4.15 (1.27)	36.26 (8.57)
Bus drivers (n = 46)	5.07 (.79)	4.81 (.97)	4.57 (1.35)	3.92 (1.25)	4.99 (1.29)	4.75 (1.42)	41.29 (8.95)

These findings support our argument and the applicability of Holland's model in understanding the role of EI in different occupations.

There are at least five implications for future research and human resource practitioners. First, although there has been a lot of discussion about the importance of EI in the popular press, both a conceptual framework and scientifically rigorous empirical evidence concerning its relationship with job outcomes are hard to find. By defining EI as a set of interrelated abilities in dealing with emotions, it is possible to use the common conceptual framework concerning the interaction effect between individual abilities and a job's nature, affecting job outcomes. The results of the study reported in this paper provide further evidence supporting this argument. Thus, more scientific and rigorous research on this construct would be worthwhile.

Second, the study reported here is the first attempt to hypothesize and test the role of EI in various occupations based on a well-established occupational model. Results indicate that the role of emotions can be incorporated into Holland's career model. Not only does the level of emotional labor differ among the occupations specified by Holland's model, but the calculus assumption is also applicable to conceptualize the extent of differences among various occupational environments. This conclusion should be regarded as preliminary because this study did not control for the characteristics of incumbents in the six jobs. For example, the bus drivers in this sample are older than other respondents, and this makes their EI level unexpectedly high; also, the sample size for some jobs (e.g., art designer and programmer) may be too small. Future research may use more rigorous controls to further validate this conclusion.

While the results may be preliminary, they are encouraging and may lead to important implications for both the conceptual development of career theories and the practical application of human resource selection. For the development of career theories, it appears possible that the role of emotions can be incorporated in existing models. It may not be necessary to develop completely new theories in responding to the changes in demand for career counseling. A more efficient way for vocational psychology researchers to examine the role of emotions may be to review the present career theories and try to incorporate the element of emotions into these theories. For human resource selection, the element of emotional labor may need to be examined in job analysis, and EI may be used as a selection variable for jobs with high emotional labor. For employees, EI may be an important consideration in one's career choice and development. For human resource practitioners, EI may be used in selection and placement decisions for jobs with high emotional labor. Thus, more studies in this line of research concerning the roles of EI and emotional labor in career theories and human resource selection should be worthwhile.

The third implication of this study for future research and human resource practitioners concerns the role of EI in different job types. Although we argue that the six jobs used in this study are representative of their respective occupation type according to Holland's model, variations should exist mong jobs within the same occupation group. It is necessary to examine jobs in more occupations prescribed by Holland's model in order to ensure that the calculus assumption is really generalizable to most of the occupations. For applications in career counseling and human resource selection, it is also necessary to examine as many occupations as possible. Thus, future research should further investigate the roles of EI and emotional labor for more jobs both across and within occupational groups.

The fourth implication is that common method variance may be a problem for this study. This should be better addressed in future research. However, as the main purpose of this study is to investigate the interaction rather than the direct effect, and the interaction term was entered into the regression equation after controlling for all other variables, this issue may not be critical for the study reported here. However, it would be worthwhile for future research to use a non–self-report EI measure to examine its effect on job outcomes.

Finally, the simple correlation between emotional labor and job satisfaction is positive. This is somewhat counter-intuitive because emotional labor is basically a form of restriction on job incumbents' expression of their true feelings. Such restrictions may increase the chances that a job incumbent will have negative feelings toward his/her job. However, after controlling for job characteristics, the relationship is negative. This is probably due to the positive correlation between emotional labor and job characteristics. It is well known in the job design literature that trade-offs exist. That is, when we enrich the job characteristics of a job to increase its motivational value, some unavoidable negative consequences may result (see, e.g., Campion, 1988; Wong & Campion, 1991). The results of this study indicate that when jobs are enriched, their emotional labor may be increased as well. Future research may further examine the exact relationship among job characteristics, emotional labor, and job satisfaction.

5 Alternative measures of emotional intelligence

After finishing the three emotional intelligence (EI) projects reported in the previous three chapters, I was convinced that EI was a worthwhile construct that could be studied scientifically. However, one major issue may hinder this line of research. That is, using surveys and questionnaires to measure EI is quite different from our traditional way of assessing intelligence. To measure intelligence or ability, many scholars think that it is more appropriate to use a performance test instead of self-report questionnaire items.

The original proponents of the EI construct had been working very hard to develop a performance test of EI. One of the important achievements is the Mayer-Salovey-Caruso Emotional Intelligence Test (MSCEIT; Mayer, Salovey, & Caruso, 2002). I have a lot of respect for their efforts, and I think they have made very important contributions to the advancement of our knowledge in this area. However, I was concerned about several issues. First, when I studied the test items of the MSCEIT, I was not sure about its cross-cultural validity. As a native Chinese who grew up in Hong Kong, I found some of the test items might not be appropriate. For example, some of the items involved the judgment of expression of emotions from pictures and drawings. In Chinese culture, there are some specific meanings attached to different colors which I think may not be universal across cultures. This issue stimulated me to work on cultural issues in the study of EI, an issue I will discuss further in Chapter 6.

Second, the publisher of the MSCEIT charges a relatively high price for using the instrument. Even for non-profit research projects, we would need to pay quite expensive royalties to use the MSCEIT. I was trained during the 1980s as a doctoral student. I clearly remember that psychology and management scholars at that time seldom commercialized their measurement instruments. My doctoral thesis topic was job design, and one of the important questionnaire instruments was the Job Diagnostic Survey (Hackman & Oldham, 1980). The developers of the instrument stated explicitly that any other scholars could use the instrument for research purposes and there was no need to ask for permission. I believe this was the norm for most scientists at that time. Unfortunately, this practice is no longer the norm nowadays, and I regret this change. When science and scientific discovery become commercialized and instrumentalized, scientists cannot be as pure as they were before. The cost of carrying out research projects is particularly relevant to me because some Asian scholars may not have sufficient financial resources to pay for the relatively expensive instrument for their research.

Third, I do not totally agree that intelligence or ability must be measured with performance tests and that self-report measures must be invalid. I believe that some types of abilities can use self-report measures. For examples, most people should have an adequate assessment of their own eyesight or other physical abilities. As human beings need to handle issues related to emotions frequently in their daily lives, it is not surprising that most of us may be able to assess how well we can handle emotional issues. To me, the problem of self-assessment using the Likert-type response format is whether the respondents would be affected by social desirability or other factors that lead them to fake their answers. This is a particularly relevant concern for human resource practitioners because the measurement instrument may be used for selection purposes. It would be helpful to have an EI instrument that can minimize or even avoid faking behavior on the part of job candidates.

Lesson 10: serving as a stepping stone for others

Mostly because of the second and third concerns above, I decided to develop an alternative EI measure that could minimize faking behaviors for Chinese respondents. Of course, more evidence about the validity of the EI construct could be gathered through this project too. I would also like to state explicitly that the scale (if successfully developed) can be used by other Chinese and Asian scholars if they are interested in using it for their research. This decision results from my commitment to the development of management research in Asia in general and China in particular.

Modern business research with scientific rigor mostly originates in Western countries. When mainland China adopted the open door policy in the late 1970s, universities in mainland China began to establish business schools. Until that time, very few Chinese management scholars had been trained with the modern scientific approach. The Chinese University of Hong Kong at that time offered short-term courses to train mainland Chinese scholars whose background was not in the business disciplines. Many participants of these courses contributed significantly to the establishment of various business schools in mainland China in the 1980s. In the early 1990s, the majority of faculty members in these business schools still lacked exposure to and training in modern scientific methods. However, the situation was gradually improving as more and more overseas Chinese management scholars who were trained in Western universities returned to mainland China.

In other Asian countries and regions, the trend is also moving toward more emphasis on modern scientific rigor in conducting business research. As EI was a relatively new topic in management research in the late 1990s, I believed it might be of interest to other Asian scholars and graduate students too. Thus, the motive of working on this project was partially about a sense of calling, and my intention was to serve as a small stepping stone for other researchers. This did not appear to be important when I first thought about the design of the specific studies. However, it became a very important motive to push me not to give up later. This was because I had underestimated the time and effort that would be needed. Also, as the target audience was Asian scholars or even practitioners, it would be difficult to publish reports in North American or European management journals. Fortunately, the Asia Academy of Management had been established by that time, and they had acquired the *Asia Pacific Journal of Management* as their official journal. I believed that if we conducted our studies with acceptable scientific rigor, this should be an appropriate outlet.

When the first paper was drafted in early 2003, I put the following sentences in the concluding paragraph of the paper: "As the main purpose of this study is to facilitate EI research in Asia, interested researchers can contact the authors to obtain the scoring key of the scale items reported in the Appendix. For non-profit making studies, we offer it at no charge." However, my co-author strongly opposed this idea because he had never seen something like this in journal papers. I compromised but insisted on putting this sentence in the appendix which reported the scale items because this reflected my true intention for the whole project.

Lesson 10: Although this is not always the case, a sense of calling may be an important motive for scientists in conducting some of our research projects. This is especially true when we face unexpected difficulties. An intrinsic motivation will be more powerful in keeping us from giving up.

Lesson 11: be patient with the data collection and analysis process

In conducting this project, we faced some unexpected difficulties. The first was that I had underestimated the difficulties in generating items that would minimize or even avoid faking responses. For self-report items with a Likert-type response format, generating items is quite easy and straightforward. After one explains the definition and domains of the EI construct to people, they can easily generate items such as "I have good understanding of my own emotions," "I can calm down quickly when I am very angry," and so on. These items have good face validity. However, respondents can fake their answers easily if they want to.

After examining the items of the MSCEIT, I realized that it would be quite difficult for me to develop as many types of items as were included in the MSCEIT. Also, the MSCEIT was too long. To develop similar items, the MSCEIT also required a group of experts to judge the appropriateness of responses. These experts needed to be familiar with the social environment and able to judge the appropriateness of people's attitudes and behaviors according to the social values and norms.

I was not confident that I could find such a group of experts in Hong Kong or mainland China. The history of China in the past 170 years appears to make the Chinese society not in its normal state. We have been invaded by Western countries and the Japanese and tried a lot of reforms and revolutions. The latest revolution was communism. Although this was not formally admitted, China had given up most of the ideology of communism since the open door policy in the late 1970s. Economic growth in the past 35 years had been exceptionally fast, but a lot of social problems such as corruption were also very serious. A lot of people felt that we were not sure about our core values as a society, and some even believed that we did not have any values anymore except for materialistic gains. Although I am not as pessimistic as that, I seriously doubted that I could find a group of experts who could actually judge the norms of adequate responses in different social interactions. Another way to rate MSCEIT items is by consensus. That is, we could find a large group of respondents and take the majority view as the most appropriate response. This may be difficult for the Chinese society as well because a lot of people do not believe we still have any consensus.

Facing the above difficulties, I tried to design something that might be simpler and workable. I searched the literature and tried to find some insights as to what I could do. Finally, I thought some simple forced-choice scales might be possible. That is, for each item, I gave two options for the respondents and forced them to choose one option that they liked more. I could then use some criterion variables (i.e., variables that should have some relationship with EI) to see whether those who chose a particular option had a higher (or lower) score on the criterion variables. If I got a sufficient number of items that were related to the criterion variables, the aggregate results might reflect the EI level of the respondents. In this case, I could avoid using expert judges or consensus ratings.

I believed this should be the way to go and began to try. To make sure this idea would work, I invited a small pilot group of students and my former schoolmates who had managerial experience. I intended to create two types of forced-choice items. The first type was to provide a simple scenario with two response options. I hoped one response option would represent a high EI level and have a stronger relationship with the criterion variables. When I asked my invited group members to try to generate some scenarios and corresponding response options, I found this was not an easy task. Most of the scenarios and response options they generated were either too complicated or too obvious. After detailed discussion with the members, I found that it would be better to go into the dimensions of EI for them to think about the scenarios and response options. I also learned how to explain the EI definition and domains in a more concise and precise way within a short period of time.

After getting experience with the pilot group, I invited a large group of people to generate scenarios and responses. Despite my preparation with the pilot group, this session took much longer than I expected. A lot of the participants had questions in thinking about the scenarios. I originally planned to finish the session in 15 minutes, but in the end it took two hours until everyone seemed to be satisfied with their work. Finally, I got 112 scenarios and their response options. The seriousness of the participants motivated me to read their write-ups very carefully, and it took me several days' work to select 65 items and modify the wording. I thought most of the items were good ones, but I was wrong! When I got another large sample to respond to the scenarios and some criterion variables, I found that the internal consistency reliability as well as the criterion validity was poor if I used all 65 items. Thus, I had to examine each item individually. It took me almost two weeks to finally figure out the best 20 items. If I had not been committed to the project, I believe I would not have had such patience during the process and probably would have given up.

Lesson 11: Be prepared for a lot of unexpected results to come up in empirical studies. We have to be patient with the respondents and the data collection and analysis process. When we read published papers, usually the authors do not report the difficulties in detail, and we could easily think that everything went smoothly. This is usually not the case.

Lesson 12: try to get as much evidence as possible

Generating the second type of forced-choice items was more straightforward. I used the multiple intelligence argument and asked the participants to generate abilities that were either related to EI (e.g., working even harder when negative emotions are induced by previous failure) or not related to EI (e.g., lifting heavy weights) and paired them up. As I thought this task would be simple and direct, I did not try it on a pilot group but invited a large group of participants to generate items. After looking at the ability items, I suddenly realized that I might have made a serious mistake. As one of my original purposes was to develop a scale that could be used in personnel selection based on EI, it would not be appropriate to compare EI abilities with other abilities that were also relevant to the workplace. Otherwise, the non–EI-related abilities would also have predictive power for job outcomes. Thus, the items generated by the first sample could not be used, and they have never been presented nor published. Although it was not a happy experience, we needed to live with this kind of situation. From my 20 years of experience in conducting research, about half of my efforts, including development of ideas and data collection, did not result in publishable papers. My recommendation for doctoral students and junior faculty colleagues is that we had better be prepared for this reality. Our efforts may not relate directly to outputs because we are in the risky business of scientific discovery.

I therefore looked for other opportunities to complete this part of item generation and testing. Fortunately, I was invited to help a hotel group conduct an employee opinion survey at that time. In exchange, I requested the general manager of the hotel to allow me to collect data for my research, and I did not charge any consulting fee. With this deal, I was able to ask their human resource managers to help me generate items and the hotel employees to provide data for me to make a preliminary selection of 20 items and to test the validity of the selected items. After completion of the item generation from the two different perspectives, I tested the social desirability of the choices using a sample of students from an executive master of business administration (EMBA) program, and I used a student sample and a life-insurance-agent sample to test the predictive validity of the full scale (i.e., 40 forced-choice items). As the results were reasonable, I wrote up the paper and submitted it to the *Asia Pacific Journal of Management*. Fortunately, with two rounds of revisions, the paper was accepted (Wong, Law, & Wong, 2004).

After completion of this paper, I wished I had more evidence to show the practical utility of this forced-choice scale. I therefore tried to collect data from Hong Kong and mainland Chinese samples. Fortunately, I was invited by the hotel group to conduct another employee opinion survey a year later, and this time I could get data from another hotel within this hotel group. By helping the hotel group, I discovered that hotel employees might be a very good sample for studying the impact of EI in the workplace. This is because some employees, such as front-desk staff, are requested to provide service to customers with personal interactions. Certainly the jobs of these employees will have a relatively high emotional labor requirement. However, another group of hotel employees, such as housekeeping and maintenance staff, are required not to contact the customers. Their emotional labor is therefore very low. By studying hotel employees, I could have enough variation in this moderating variable and be able to control other variables such as the company culture and policies.

I also got the chance to conduct training for a sample of nurses in a mainland Chinese hospital. In exchange, I collected data using the forced-choice scale and examined whether it had predictive power for their job outcomes. The results of both the hotel and nurse samples were affirmative. However, I still had doubts about the potential impact of faking if this scale was used in selecting candidates. In our previous paper, we examined only the social desirability of the options in the forced-choice items and did not find significant differences. From another study I was involved in (Law, Mobley, & Wong, 2002), I knew that social desirability was not the only reason for faking responses in a personnel selection context. Thus, it would be better to test the impact of faking responses directly. Based on the experience acquired from the previous study, I used a longitudinal design and asked a group of undergraduate students to respond to the scale two times. The first time, students were told that it was for research purposes. The second time, I asked the students to fake their responses to increase their chances of getting a good evaluation from human resource practitioners who were seeking good job candidates. Those who were evaluated favorably could win a prize. Although we saw room for faking responses, the forced-choice scale still showed predictive validity on criterion variables in this student sample. We wrote up a paper reporting the evidence from these three samples and submitted it to the *Asia Pacific Journal of*

Management. Fortunately, after two rounds of revisions, the paper was accepted (Wong, Wong, & Law, 2007).

Since we had developed the forced-choice scale for Chinese respondents, I tried to collect data whenever I had the chance in order to examine the mean scores, variances, and other characteristics of the scale. I was puzzled by one issue. The internal consistency reliability coefficient was not very stable across samples. It ranged from as low as .60 to as high as .80. One possibility was that because two options were provided for each item, the score was either 0 or 1 for each item. Thus, the scale in effect consists of dichotomized items. In order to have more confidence in the reliability of the scale, I collected data from a social service organization and tried to compare the internal consistency reliability with the test–retest reliability over a three-month period. It turned out that although the internal consistency reliability was only about .60 both times, the test–retest reliability was .71. Shortly after I got this evidence, one of the professors at Nanjing University contacted me about a special issue of their journal. She was looking for papers that would not only have valuable content but also share some of the research experiences involved in preparing them. I informed her about the background of this work, and she agreed to publish the evidence together with my brief introduction of the background in her journal. So this short paper was published in Chinese (Wong, Cheung, & Peng, 2012).

Lesson 12: Whenever possible, we should try to convince ourselves with more evidence. Only with more empirical evidence can we be more confident that perhaps our conclusions are close to the reality. As management is an applied field, we want our suggestions to be based on sufficient evidence.

The following are the major contents of the paper in which we first reported on the development of the forced-choice survey.

Wong, C. S., Law, K. S., & Wong, P. M. (2004). Development and validation of a forced choice emotional intelligence measure for Chinese respondents in Hong Kong. *Asia Pacific Journal of Management*, 21(4), 535–559; these contents are reprinted with permission.

Abstract. There have been relatively few empirical studies on emotional intelligence (EI) conducted with scientific rigor, especially in Asia. A recent study clarified the definition of EI as a set of mental abilities related to emotions and developed a self-report EI measure by demonstrating the relationships between EI and life satisfaction, job performance, and job satisfaction for Chinese respondents. To facilitate future EI research and EI-related human resource practices in Asia, we develop an alternative EI measure in this series of four studies using forced-choice items. Scenarios with alternative responses showing different levels of EI were generated in the first study, and 20 items were selected empirically. In the second study, pairs of abilities were generated, and 20 EI items were paired with various ability facets. In the third study, we examined the social desirability of the 40 items developed in the first two studies. In the fourth study, these 40 EI items were cross-validated. The results indicated that this forced-choice EI scale had acceptable convergent, discriminant, and predictive validity using life satisfaction, job performance, and job satisfaction as criterion variables. We discuss the implications of our findings in the conclusion.

Purpose of the project

The main purpose of this project is to facilitate future emotional intelligence (EI) research or EI-related human resource practices in Asia by developing an alternative EI measure using a forced-choice format. In a recent study, Wong and Law (2002) developed a self-report EI scale based on the above definition of EI (labeled as the Wong and Law EI Scale, WLEIS, in the following discussion for easy reference). The WLEIS contains 16 Likert-type self-report statements (e.g., "I have a good understanding of my own emotions"; "I am able to control my temper and handle difficulties rationally") to capture the four dimensions of EI. Using this scale, they provided evidence that the EI of Chinese job incumbents was related to their job performance and satisfaction, especially for jobs that require incumbents to present a particular type of appropriate emotion. Examples of these jobs include flight attendants, who need to present themselves as friendly, and bill collectors, who need to present themselves as hostile when they are performing their jobs.

Furthermore, Davies, Stankov, and Roberts (1998) criticized past EI-related scales and illustrated that in factor analyses those EI scales loaded heavily on the traditional Big Five personality dimensions. While replicating Davies et al.'s findings on past EI scales, Law, Wong, and Song (2004) found that the WLEIS was able to measure a distinct EI construct from the Big Five personality traits. Furthermore, the EI construct measured has incremental predictive power on Chinese job incumbents' performance and satisfaction. They confirmed the importance of defining the EI construct as a set of abilities and designing the measure accordingly, as well as confirming the construct validity of the EI construct measured by the WLEIS.

Although the WLEIS is useful for scientific research, it suffers from some weaknesses. First, respondents may provide biased responses because of social desirability. Social desirability refers to the inclination to present oneself positively to others. As EI is a set of abilities, it is possible that people will have the inclination to respond positively to Likert-type self-report items. Furthermore, respondents may fake their responses when they have the incentive to do so (Law, Mobley, & Wong, 2002). For example, a job applicant may provide false information in a self-report scale if faking will increase his/her chances of getting the job. Finally, some people may not be able to judge their own emotional abilities accurately. Some studies in general mental abilities have found that the correlation between self-reports of ability and actual ability are quite low (e.g., Paulhus, Lysy, & Yik, 1998). To facilitate further EI studies for both researchers and practitioners in Asia, our purpose in this project is to develop an alternative

EI scale with forced-choice items that may avoid the problem of social desirability.

One possible alternative is to use performance test items with options to be chosen (e.g., Mayer, Caruso, & Salovey, 2000b). That is, respondents are assessed by EI-related tasks, and the option they choose will reflect their EI level. One feasible task that reflects the EI of respondents includes scenarios that require them to show their understanding, assimilation, regulation, and use of their emotions. In setting these performance task items, Mayer, Caruso, et al. (2000b) pointed out that the critical issue was the discrimination of right from wrong answers. This can be judged by the consensus of a group, experts, or some target criteria.

Although Mayer, Salovey, and Caruso (1997) developed an EI measure using mostly performance test items, it may not be useful for researchers in Asia for three reasons. First, it is quite obvious that cultural norms may affect the choice of the right answers in performance tests. For example, most Asian countries have a greater power distance than the United States (Hofstede, 1991). That is, Asians will accept a greater difference in power between superior and subordinate roles. Furthermore, Asians, especially Chinese, are trained to suppress and regulate their emotions, while Westerners are trained to express their emotions. Thus, a non-reactive quiet response when one's boss is making unreasonable demands may be regarded as a high-EI response in Chinese culture but probably not in Western cultures. EI performance tests developed in Western cultures may therefore not be applicable to Asian subjects.

Second, as far as we know, the coding system of this measure is based on a norm-referenced method. That is, the scores of the items will depend on the choices of a reference group or experts on EI. It is very possible that the choices of the reference group or experts may be biased by the social desirability of their cultural norms. For example, in Mayer et al.'s (1997) scale (which is in interactive CD-ROM format), there is a forced-choice item: "A woman loved someone and then felt secure. What happened in between? (a) she learned the other person loved her in return; (b) she decided not to express her feelings; (c) her love went away; (d) she told the other person that she loved him; (e) her love itself brought about security." In responding to this item, social desirability may play a significant role. In Western societies, option (b) may not be a socially desirable choice because it is desirable for Westerners to express their true feelings. However, in Chinese societies, option (d) is definitely not a socially desirable behavior because for Chinese it is desirable for women to be passive in love affairs. Thus, even though the items are in a forced-choice format, it is unclear whether the final scores will be totally free from social desirability. The applicability of scores based on the norms of Western judges to Chinese respondents is highly questionable.

Finally, researchers usually need to pay high costs for tests that have been developed in Western countries even when using them for pure research purposes, and they have no access to the coding systems of these tests. Furthermore, there is no reported evidence showing the validity of this EI measure in Asian respondents up to the present moment. With no access to the coding system, it is very difficult, if not impossible, for Asian researchers to take the initiative to test the reliability and validity of this EI measure. It is even more difficult to try to make the necessary modifications because of limited access and copyright issues. Thus, the development of an EI measure that would be available free of charge for research purposes and at a minimal charge for practitioners would definitely facilitate EI research in Asia.

Apart from scenario items with options, we also assessed the EI of a subject by another type of forced-choice items which can avoid the potential problem of social desirability. We asked respondents to choose between two equally desirable ability pairs, only one of which reflects the EI of the subjects (e.g., Zavalia, 1965). Proponents of the multiple intelligence theory that goes beyond the traditional concept of the intelligence quotient (IQ) argue that humans will differ in various intelligence dimensions and that it is quite uncommon to find a person who will be high on all dimensions (e.g., Gardner, 1993; Sternberg, 1985). For example, one may be high in IQ but low in EI (Goleman, 1995). Thus, if respondents are forced to compare their EI level with a variety of other intelligence dimensions, it is possible to capture their true EI level.

The purpose of this project is to develop a forced-choice EI scale consisting of scenarios and ability-paired items. There are two sets of criteria in the development process. Each set contains three rules. The first set of criteria relates to initial item selection. First, to be qualified as an alternative EI measure, the items selected should converge with the existing EI measures. We use the WLEIS as the convergent criterion for item selection. The WLEIS is used because it was developed in Asia and tested with Asian subjects. Second, the items selected must be able to differentiate respondents by their EI levels. If an overwhelming percentage of respondents select the correct answer in a performance test item, that item will not be useful. Third, the final EI scale should be of reasonable simplicity and length. If many respondents cannot understand the items and/or they need a very long time to complete it, then the scale is not practical for future administration. Our goal is to select a reasonable number of items so that an average adult can finish the final EI scale within half an hour.

The second set of criteria relates to the evaluation of the appropriateness of the selected items. Although it is impossible to include all the variables in the nomological network of the EI construct to test the validity of the developed items, we tried to use criterion variables that have different degrees of relationship with EI. First, researchers have argued that one's EI level should have little relationship with one's mental intelligence. Empirically, Ciarrochi, Chan, and Caputi (2000) and Pellitteri (1999) found a low correlation between EI and mental intelligence in their Western college student samples. For Chinese students and job incumbents, Wong and Law (2002) and Wong, Wong, and Chau (2002) also found small correlations between EI and mental intelligence. Thus, the items selected should show relatively small correlations with mental intelligence.

Second, EI should be related to some personality dimensions. For example, it should have a positive correlation with agreeableness and a negative correlation with neuroticism (Wong & Law, 2002). Davies et al. (1998) argued that the construct of EI was elusive because most of the self-report EI measures developed in Western countries had salient loadings on well-established Big Five personality dimensions in factor analyses. Thus, although correlated, selected EI items should be able to form a distinct factor from the Big Five personality dimensions.

Third, to be a meaningful construct, EI should have incremental predictive power on some meaningful criterion variables over and beyond the traditional mental intelligence and personality constructs. For students, we chose life satisfaction as the criterion variable because EI should theoretically be related to it, and this is a meaningful construct to cultivate from the educational point of view. For employees in the work setting, job-related outcomes such as job performance and job satisfaction are meaningful criterion variables. EI will be a meaningful new construct for education and/or management researchers and practitioners if it has incremental predictive power on these criterion variables.

With these two sets of criteria, we used four related studies to develop the forced-choice EI scale in this project. In Study 5.1, experienced managers were invited to generate EI scenario items. Twenty items were empirically selected according to the first set of criteria with a sample of 326 undergraduate students. In Study 5.2, human resource practitioners were invited to generate ability pairs. Twenty pairs were selected empirically using the first set of criteria with a sample of 470 hotel employees. In Study 5.3, we examined the social desirability of the choices of each forced-choice item selected in Studies 5.1 and 5.2 with a sample of 44 participants in an executive master of business administration (EMBA) program. In Study 5.4, we cross-validated the appropriateness of the 40-item EI scale we developed in Studies 5.1, 5.2, and 5.3 using the second set of criteria with two samples: 158 business majors and 102 life insurance agents. The following sections report the details of these four studies.

Study 5.1: development of scenario items

Item generation

We started with 112 experienced managers who were participants of a part-time business diploma course in a large university of Hong Kong. These managers were first introduced to the four dimensions of EI defined in this study. For each EI dimension, they were asked to write a real-life scenario and possible behavioral responses for each scenario based on their experience. They were then asked to judge which behavioral response represents the highest level of EI. One hundred and twelve scenarios (each with at least two possible behavioral responses) were generated. These scenarios and behavioral responses were examined carefully by one of the authors. Scenarios were deleted if (1) they were very similar to other scenarios, and/or (2) it was very easy to judge whether some of the responses were desirable or not. After this deletion, a total of 65 scenarios were chosen. The authors then modified the wordings of the scenarios and limited the possible behavioral responses for each scenario to two. The first behavioral response is the one with the highest EI level that was proposed by the original writer. For the second behavioral response, we tried to select the one that appeared to have the most similar degree of social desirability to the first.

Examples of these scenarios and behavioral responses include the following.

1. When you are upset, you will:

   a. talk to someone who is close to you about your feeling;
   b. concentrate on something else (e.g., your work, studies, or hobby) so that you can get away from your bad feeling. (self emotional appraisal)

2. Your friend has a rough relationship with his/her boyfriend/girlfriend because your friend has a bad temper. When your friend talks to you about the rough relationship, you will:

   a. pretend to agree with him/her that his/her boyfriend/girlfriend is not good enough;
   b. point out that it is your friend's own fault and hope that he/she will improve. (other's emotional appraisal)

3. When you have to do something you don't like, you will:

   a. try to find something interesting about it;
   b. try to finish it as soon as possible and forget about it. (regulation of emotion)

4. You have an important examination tomorrow and you are studying hard in your room. Your family is watching a television program which you like very much as well. Since your house is small, the noise of the television annoys you. You will:

   a. ask your family to turn off the television but videotape the program so that you and your family can watch it together tomorrow after your examination;
   b. although a little bit uncomfortable, you put headphones on (to reduce the noise) so that you can concentrate on your study. (use of emotion)

Item selection

Three hundred and twenty-six undergraduate students from a large university in Hong Kong were asked to respond to the 65 items developed in the previous step. For each scenario, the respondents were asked to choose the behavioral response they would be more likely to make in reality. They also responded to the WLEIS, as well as to items that assessed their personality and mental intelligence.

As the respondents had to respond to 81 EI assessment items, we tried to make the personality and mental intelligence assessments as short as possible. Six items were randomly selected from each dimension of the McCrae and Costa (1987) adjective scale capturing the Big Five personality dimensions and used as the personality measure. For mental intelligence, we used results of the Hong Kong Certificate Education Examination (HKCEE; Chinese, English, mathematics, and the three best subjects) as a proxy. Although there is no published study reporting the relationship between HKCEE results and mental intelligence, studies of public examinations that are regarded as equivalent to the HKCEE showed significant correlations between examination results and mental intelligence (e.g., Hale, 1984; Wilding, Valentine, Marshall, & Cook, 1999). The HKCEE is taken by all Hong Kong secondary students, and its results are the core decision criterion for university admission. Our grading system was basically a 5-point scale (5 = maximum). Each student received HK$100 (about US$12.80) as a motivation to complete the questionnaire.

The reliability of the WLEIS was acceptable (coefficient alpha = .87). Given the evidence that it is a reasonable scale to capture EI (Wong & Law, 2002), we used it as the criterion to select the scenario items in developing the forced-choice EI measure. To ensure that the selected items would have discriminating power on the EI of the respondents, a scenario was dropped if more than two-thirds of the respondents chose the same response. For the remaining items, the point-biserial correlation of each item with the total score of the WLEIS was calculated. The 20 items (5 for each dimension) that showed the largest point-biserial correlation were selected. These items were prepared in Chinese, and the first part of Appendix 5.1 contains their English translation, prepared by the back-translation method. One point was given to those who chose the behavioral response that was judged to represent a high EI level for each item by the original developer. Hence, the highest possible score in this 20-item assessment was 20. The correlation between this 20-item forced-choice EI instrument and the WLEIS was .41 (p < .01).

Preliminary validation evidence

We conducted correlational and factor analyses to check the validity of the items selected. We calculated the correlation coefficients between the score on the selected 20 items and the Big Five personality dimensions and the proxy for mental intelligence. The results are shown in Table 5.1. The newly developed EI items appeared to be distinct from the traditional mental intelligence and personality dimensions because their correlation coefficients were relatively small. The correlation of the 20 forced-choice EI items with the mental intelligence

Table 5.1 Descriptive statistics and correlations among measures for Study 5.1

	Mean (S.D.)	CEI	WLEIS	NEURO	EXTRA	OPEN	AGREE	CONSC
1. CEI	10.34 (2.58)	—						
2. WLEIS	4.57 (.77)	.41**	(.87)					
3. NEURO	3.51 (.77)	-.25**	-.37**	(.75)				
4. EXTRA	3.84 (.75)	.09	.21**	.01	(.79)			
5. OPEN	3.72 (.64)	-.03	.13*	.15**	.38**	(.60)		
6. AGREE	4.28 (.60)	.20**	.17**	-.04	.23**	-.00	(.67)	
7. CONSC	3.99 (.71)	.25**	.40**	-.25**	.21**	.10+	.20**	(.71)
8. HKCEE	3.92 (.54)	.13*	.04	.01	.06	-.04	.21**	.14*

Notes

n = 326. Numbers in parentheses are coefficient alphas. CEI = the 20 scenario emotional intelligence items selected in Study 5.1; WLEIS = the Wong and Law (2002) self-report emotional intelligence measure; NEURO = neuroticism; EXTRA = extraversion; OPEN = openness to new experiences; AGREE = agreeableness; CONSC = conscientiousness; HKCEE = Hong Kong Certificate Education Examination.

+p < .10; *p < .05; **p < .01.

proxy was .13. The average correlation with the Big Five personality dimension ranged from –.25 to .25, with an average of .16.

Davies et al. (1998) criticized past EI-related measures for having salient loadings on the Big Five personality dimensions when factor analysis was conducted, concluding that EI was an elusive construct. In response to this serious criticism, we examined the newly developed forced-choice items using Davies et al.'s factor analysis method (Wong & Law, 2002). We conducted a factor analysis on the newly developed EI and the 30 Big Five personality items to further examine the distinctiveness among them. As the number of items is relatively large compared to the sample size and the EI items are dichotomous variables with a score of either 0 or 1, we summed up the five items for each EI dimension to create four variables with scores ranged from 0 to 5. These four scores were then considered as indicators of the EI construct in the exploratory factor analysis. In this way, we can reduce the number of indicators, ensure the statistical power of the factor analysis, and create continuous variables as EI indicators. As the correlations between EI and the Big Five personality dimensions should not be zero, we used the direct oblimin instead of the usual varimax rotation (Davies et al., 1998). The results are shown in Table 5.2. With few exceptions, the corresponding indicators had the highest loadings on their respective factors, and the four EI indicators formed a distinct factor. With these results, we concluded that the 20 scenario items represent an overall EI construct that is reasonably distinct from the personality dimensions.

Study 5.2: development of ability-paired forced-choice items

Item generation

Two practitioners, the human resource director and the human resource manager of a large hotel in Hong Kong, were invited to participate in this study. The human resource director was asked to generate ability items that would not be used in most human resource decisions (e.g., selection and promotion). The purpose of generating this type of ability items was to avoid any confusion between EI abilities and non-EI abilities that are useful in practical situations. For example, if we pair up leadership ability with an EI-related ability in a forced-choice item, practitioners will find it difficult to use this item because both choices may be related to desirable job outcomes such as job performance and job satisfaction.

The human resource manager was introduced to the four EI dimensions and the WLEIS. She was asked to generate ability items that were similar to those embedded in the WLEIS. We then paired the two sets of ability items that were generated. For each ability pair, the first ability item was EI related. For the second one, we tried to select the one that appeared to have the most similar degree of social desirability to the first one. A total of 28 pairs were formed.

Table 5.2 Results of factor analysis for Study 5.1

	Factor 1	Factor 2	Factor 3	Factor 4	Factor 5	Factor 6
NEURO1	−.09	.77	.11	−.09	.11	−.02
NEURO2	−.15	.77	−.01	.08	.22	−.18
NEURO3	.14	.50	.07	−.12	−.17	−.04
NEURO4	−.03	.57	−.05	.02	−.13	.01
NEURO5	−.03	.38	.11	.01	−.07	.29
NEURO6	.12	.44	−.11	−.09	−.14	.27
EXTRA1	.75	.01	−.05	−.05	−.01	−.02
EXTRA2	.54	−.09	.20	.05	−.05	−.06
EXTRA3	.81	−.01	.02	−.08	−.05	.03
EXTRA4	.76	−.08	−.13	−.07	−.09	.14
EXTRA5	.32	.15	.18	.17	−.13	−.04
EXTRA6	.27	−.04	−.18	.15	−.42	.12
OPEN1	−.06	.05	.01	.09	−.30	.19
OPEN2	.14	−.06	−.08	.05	−.51	−.04
OPEN3	.07	.23	−.34	.17	−.30	−.15
OPEN4	−.10	.05	−.01	−.01	−.46	−.01
OPEN5	.12	.07	.14	−.22	−.45	−.42
OPEN6	.16	−.07	.00	−.10	−.49	−.02
AGREE1	.09	.04	.55	.01	−.11	−.22
AGREE2	.15	.01	.43	.07	−.20	−.27
AGREE3	−.07	−.09	.44	.28	−.09	−.18
AGREE4	−.05	.04	.51	.02	.15	.15
AGREE5	−.01	.06	.58	.05	.06	−.03
AGREE6	.44	−.02	.41	−.11	.03	.18
CONSC1	−.04	−.04	−.00	.64	.00	.11
CONSC2	−.01	−.11	.03	.66	−.14	.05
CONSC3	−.04	−.11	.24	.58	−.04	.08
CONSC4	.05	.08	.01	.49	.15	−.09
CONSC5	.23	−.04	−.15	.44	−.07	−.12
CONSC6	.50	.01	−.07	.26	.09	−.13
CEI-SEA	.02	−.06	.06	.10	.12	−.17
CEI-OEA	−.01	−.01	.03	−.01	.05	−.47
CEI-ROE	−.03	−.17	.09	−.02	−.02	−.11
CEI-UOE	−.05	−.08	.02	.16	−.03	−.20

(*Continued*)

Table 5.2 (Continued)

	Factor 1	Factor 2	Factor 3	Factor 4	Factor 5	Factor 6
Eigenvalue	4.65	3.62	2.54	2.20	1.53	1.46
% of variance explained	13.68	10.66	7.47	6.48	4.51	4.29

Notes
NEURO = neuroticism; EXTRA = extraversion; OPEN = openness to new experiences; AGREE = agreeableness; CONSC = conscientiousness (the number denotes the specific personality measurement items); CEI-SEA = the 5 scenario emotional intelligence (EI) items on self emotional appraisal; CEI-OEA = the 5 scenario EI items on other's emotional appraisal; CEI-ROE = the 5 scenario EI items on regulation of emotion; CEI-UOE = the 5 scenario EI items on use of emotion.

Examples of pairs include (1) ability to comprehend changes in emotions versus ability to learn how to dance some new steps (self emotional appraisal), (2) ability to understand others' true feelings by observing their behaviors versus ability to tolerate physical pain (others' emotional appraisal), (3) ability to calm down faster than others when feeling angry versus ability to run faster than others (regulation of emotion), and (4) ability to motivate oneself to face failure positively versus ability to learn to create an artistic object (e.g., pottery, painting) (use of emotion).

Item selection

Four hundred and seventy employees of the hotel were invited to respond to the 28 ability pairs, as well as the WLEIS and the 30 Big Five personality items that were used in Study 5.1. For each of the 28 ability pairs, the respondents were asked to choose the ability that they believed they were stronger in. Education level was used as a proxy for mental intelligence in this sample. It was measured by a multiple-choice item listing the various education levels recognized by the Hong Kong Civil Servants scale. The reliability of the WLEIS was acceptable (coefficient alpha = .91). Again, given the evidence showing its predictive validity, we used this measure as the criterion to select the ability pair items. As explained in Study 5.1, an item was dropped if more than two-thirds of the respondents chose one of its abilities to ensure that the chosen item could discriminate among respondents. Then, the 20 items (5 each for the four EI dimensions) that showed the highest point-biserial correlations with the WLEIS were selected. These items were prepared in Chinese, and the second part of the Appendix 5.1 contains their English translation prepared by the back-translation method. As in Study 5.1, we gave 1 point to those who chose the EI-related ability instead of the other ability. The maximum total score for these 20 items was therefore 20. The correlation between this total EI score and the WLEIS was .37 (p < .01).

Preliminary validation evidence

Like in Study 5.1, we calculated the correlation coefficients between the total score on the 20 ability-paired items and the Big Five personality dimensions and education level of the respondents. The results are shown in Table 5.3. The 20 forced-choice EI items appeared to be distinct from the mental intelligence proxy and personality dimensions because their correlation coefficients were relatively small. The correlation of EI with education level was .01. The average correlation of the 20 items and the Big Five personality dimensions ranged from –.21 to .18, with an average of .14.

To further examine the distinctiveness of the 20 ability pairs and the Big Five personality dimensions in response to Davies et al.'s (1998) criticism, we used the same strategy as in Study 5.1 and created an indicator for each of the four EI dimensions based on their respective items. A factor analysis was conducted using these four EI indicators and the 30 Big Five personality items. The results are shown in Table 5.4. With few exceptions, the corresponding

Table 5.3 Descriptive statistics and correlations among measures for Study 5.2

	Mean (S.D.)	APEI	WLEIS	NEURO	EXTRA	OPEN	AGREE	CONSC
1. APEI	13.37 (3.89)	—						
2. WLEIS	4.95 (.84)	.37**	(.91)					
3. NEURO	3.60 (1.06)	–.21**	–.25**	(.83)				
4. EXTRA	4.60 (1.05)	.12*	.23**	.01	(.82)			
5. OPEN	4.31 (.95)	.01	.30*	.04	.45**	(.74)		
6. AGREE	5.00 (1.06)	.18**	.31**	–.20**	.53**	.30**	(.86)	
7. CONSC	5.12 (1.05)	.16**	.40**	–.26**	.38**	.37**	.64**	(.83)
8. Edu	3.08 (1.24)	.01	.12*	.08+	.24**	.27**	.21**	.20**

Notes
n = 470. Numbers in parentheses are coefficient alphas. APEI = the 20 ability-pair emotional intelligence items selected in Study 5.2; WLEIS = the Wong and Law (2002) self-report emotional intelligence measure; NEURO = neuroticism; EXTRA = extraversion; OPEN = openness to new experiences; AGREE = agreeableness; CONSC = conscientiousness; Edu = education level.
+p < .10; *p < .05; **p < .01.

Table 5.4 Results of factor analysis for Study 5.2

	Factor 1	Factor 2	Factor 3	Factor 4	Factor 5	Factor 6
NEURO1	.15	**.69**	–.08	–.06	.03	.11
NEURO2	.07	**.82**	.04	.08	–.01	–.01
NEURO3	.04	**.65**	–.02	.02	–.19	–.07
NEURO4	.03	**.70**	–.02	.05	.04	–.04

(*Continued*)

Table 5.4 (Continued)

	Factor 1	Factor 2	Factor 3	Factor 4	Factor 5	Factor 6
NEURO5	–.19	**.61**	–.06	–.06	–.06	.09
NEURO6	–.22	**.53**	.01	–.19	–.04	.13
EXTRA1	.03	.11	.07	**–.65**	.04	.08
EXTRA2	.25	–.01	.05	**–.72**	.06	–.00
EXTRA3	–.04	–.04	–.02	**–.84**	–.02	.01
EXTRA4	–.12	–06	–.12	**–.61**	.05	–.16
EXTRA5	.17	–.05	–.09	**–.62**	–.04	–.12
EXTRA6	–.33	.02	–.29	**–.27**	–.10	–.08
OPEN1	–.23	.05	**–.46**	–.21	–.01	–.01
OPEN2	.02	–.18	**–.75**	–.02	–.02	–.08
OPEN3	–.14	.26	**–.44**	.09	.15	–.13
OPEN4	.12	–.01	**–.57**	.13	–.04	–.04
OPEN5	.12	–.03	**–.44**	–.16	–.09	.02
OPEN6	.02	–.01	**–.70**	–.03	.07	.09
AGREE1	**.71**	.00	–.14	–.17	–.03	–.11
AGREE2	**.54**	–.03	–.05	–.25	–.07	–.29
AGREE3	**.51**	–.00	–.01	–.19	.02	–.36
AGREE4	**.56**	.01	–.04	–.05	.15	–.17
AGREE5	**.33**	–.01	–.03	–.21	.16	–.22
AGREE6	**.31**	–.14	–.12	–.42	–.01	–.06
CONSC1	.01	–.10	.01	.00	.21	**–.57**
CONSC2	–.09	–.06	–.09	.01	.14	**–.73**
CONSC3	.04	–.01	.01	–.04	–.08	**–.72**
CONSC4	.11	.03	.09	.08	–.05	**–.65**
CONSC5	.04	–.11	–.26	–.13	–.08	**–.46**
CONSC6	.14	–.08	–.24	–.24	–.10	**–.46**
APEI-SEA	.05	–.02	.00	.05	**.64**	–.01
APEI-OEA	–.03	.03	–.05	–.16	**.24**	–.00
APEI-ROE	.17	–.08	–.04	.04	**.69**	.11
APEI-UOE	–.12	–.09	.11	–.03	**.53**	–.14
Eigenvalue	8.11	3.85	2.42	2.01	1.86	1.23
% of variance explained	23.84	11.31	7.12	5.90	5.46	3.62

Notes
NEURO = neuroticism; EXTRA = extraversion; OPEN = openness to new experiences; AGREE = agreeableness; CONSC = conscientiousness (the number denotes the specific personality measurement items); APEI-SEA = the 5 ability-pair emotional intelligence (EI) items on self emotional appraisal; APEI-OEA = the 5 ability-pair EI items on other's emotional appraisal; APEI-ROE = the 5 ability-pair EI items on regulation of emotion; APEI-UOE = the 5 ability-pair EI items on use of emotion.

indicators had the highest loadings on their respective factors, and the four EI indicators formed a distinct factor. With these results, we concluded that the 20 ability pairs are reasonably distinct from the Big Five personality dimensions.

Study 5.3: examination of the social desirability of the choices in the newly developed EI forced-choice scale

As stated before, one of the important advantages of a forced-choice scale over a Likert-type scale is its ability to avoid the influences of social desirability or faking in responses. However, the options for an item must be of comparable desirability so that respondents cannot choose socially desirable answers deliberately. In Studies 5.1 and 5.2, we used our best judgment to pair up the choices that appeared to have the most comparable degree of social desirability. However, there was no objective evidence showing that the choices were of similar social desirability. The purpose of Study 5.3 was to empirically examine the extent of similarity in the social desirability of the two choices for each of the 40 items developed in Studies 5.1 and 5.2.

Sample

To check the social desirability of the 80 choices, we invited 44 Chinese participants from the EMBA program of a large university in Hong Kong to rate the social desirability of the 80 choices on a 5-point Likert-type scale (1 = very undesirable, 5 = very desirable). These participants are senior managers with at least 10 years of work experience. We used this experienced managerial sample to examine the potential utility of the items in a practical situation. If these experienced managers' judgment was similar to the authors', we would be more confident in recommending the application of these items in human resource management decisions.

Analysis and results

For each item, a paired sample t-test was conducted for the two choices. None of the 40 items showed a significant difference at the .05 level. The mean differences of the two choices ranged from zero to .16, with a mean of .07. From these results, it appears that the options for each item are of comparable social desirability.

Study 5.4: cross-validation of the forced-choice scale

In Studies 5.1 and 5.2, we created 40 EI items, i.e., 20 forced-choice items based on scenarios and 20 forced-choice items based on ability pairs. These 40 items were shown to be distinct from the Big Five personality dimensions and had reasonable correlations with those personality dimensions and the mental intelligence proxies. In Study 5.3, we examined the social desirability of the two options for each item. The results indicated that for each item the two choices were of comparable social desirability.

In Study 5.4, we combined the 40 EI items into an EI scale and labeled it Wong's Emotional Intelligence Scale (WEIS). Study 5.4 served two purposes. First, we cross-validated the discriminant and convergent validities of the WEIS with the Big Five personality dimensions, mental intelligence, and the WLEIS. Second, we examined the predictive validity of the WEIS on life satisfaction and job outcomes (performance and satisfaction) after controlling for the Big Five personality dimensions and other relevant variables.

Sample

This cross-validation sample consisted of two groups of participants. The first group included 158 undergraduate students majoring in business administration at a large university in Hong Kong. The second group included 102 life insurance agents under the same sales supervisor in a large insurance company in Hong Kong. With the permission of the sales supervisor, a life insurance agent was hired as a temporary assistant. This assistant contacted her colleagues in person one by one, explained the purpose of the study, and collected the completed questionnaires. Each participant (both students and life insurance agents) received HK$50 (about US$6.50) for completing the questionnaire.

Measures

In addition to the 40 items that were developed in Studies 5.1 and 5.2, the WLEIS, and the 30 Big Five personality items, we collected data on other variables to test the external validity of this newly developed EI scale. For the student participants, we used HKCEE results as a proxy for mental intelligence. We also included the nine-item life satisfaction measure that was constructed by A. Campbell, Converse, and Rodgers (1976) as an external criterion variable.

For the life insurance agents, we measured two job outcome variables. The agents responded to the four job satisfaction items of the Job Diagnostic Survey (Hackman & Oldham, 1975). The average of these four items was used as an indicator of their job satisfaction level. The sales supervisor provided four indicators of sales performance (namely, number of life insurance contracts, number of insurance contracts other than life insurance, amount of commission earned, and the amount of premium paid by customers) for each agent based on a performance evaluation that took place about one month before this study was conducted. Overall sales performance was measured by a weighted average of these four indicators according to their relative importance as stated by the company. As these indicators were measured differently, they were standardized before the weighted average was calculated. Apart from the Big Five personality dimensions, information on the gender, age, marital status, education level (a proxy for mental intelligence), and job tenure (in terms of years) of the respondents were collected. As the life insurance agents were working for the same company and under the same sales supervisor, we had already controlled for most of the organizational variables (e.g., compensation system and job nature) that might have affected their job performance and satisfaction. However, the working relationship between individual agents and the sales supervisor might still differ across supervisor–subordinate dyads. Since this dyadic relationship could have affected the two outcome variables (e.g., Dansereau, Graen, & Haga, 1975; Graen, Novak, & Sommerkamp, 1982), we measured it using the Leader-Member Exchange measure that was developed by Scandura and Graen (1984) as a final control variable.

Results and analysis

Descriptive statistics, coefficient alphas, and correlations among all measures are shown in Table 5.5. The coefficient alphas of the 40 EI items appeared to be acceptable (α = .83), and the new WEIS had good convergence with the WLEIS (r = .55, p < .01). To further test the suitability of the forced-choice items in measuring the four underlying EI dimensions and the overall EI construct, we conducted two confirmatory factor analyses (CFAs). In each analysis, we created three indicators for each EI dimension by summing three to four items that measured the respective dimension. In the first CFA, a first-order model specifying the relationships among the four dimensions and their respective indicators showed acceptable fit (χ^2 = 179.76, d.f. = 48; goodness-of-fit index [GFI] = .90; standardized root mean residual [SRMR] = .051). On top of this first-order model, we further specified a second-order EI construct with the four EI dimensions as its indicators in the second CFA. The fit appeared to be acceptable as well (χ^2 = 179.97, d.f. = 50; GFI = .90; SRMR = .051).

The average correlation between the new EI scale and the Big Five personality dimensions was .29 and ranged from –.28 to .52. For student participants, EI had a relatively small correlation with the mental intelligence proxy (that is, HKCEE results, r = .07). These results provided cross-validation evidence for Studies 5.1 and 5.2. For the life-insurance-agent participants, EI had a negative correlation with education level (r = –.21). Mayer, Caruso, et al. (2000b) pointed out that EI should be related to age. Thus, the correlation between EI and education was probably confounded by age in this sample because there was a negative correlation between age and education level (r = –.35). This possibility was confirmed when age and education were both regressed on EI. In the regression equation, education was not a significant

Table 5.5 Descriptive statistics, coefficient alphas, and correlations among measures for Study 5.4

	Mean (S.D.)	1	2	3	4	5	6	7	8	9	10	11	12	13	14	16	17
1. NEI	24.1 (3.42)	(.83)															
2. WLEIS	3.45 (0.44)	.55**	(.85)														
3. NEURO	3.81 (0.93)	-.30**	-.46**	(.77)													
4. EXTRA	4.43 (0.98)	.11+	.21**	.02	(.81)												
5. OPEN	3.99 (0.84)	.01	.13*	-.02	.48**	(.70)											
6. AGREE	4.97 (0.85)	.43**	.37**	-.30**	.30**	.15*	(.81)										
7. CONSC	4.63 (0.90)	.40**	.49**	-.26**	.26**	.21**	.50**	(.75)									
8. LS[a]	4.68 (0.92)	.35**	.49**	-.38**	.30**	.11	.22**	.31**	(.92)								
9. HKCEE[a]	2.09 (0.43)	.07	-.17*	.12	-.13	-.07	-.06	.03	-.02	—							
10. Gender[b]	0.51 (0.50)	.17+	.02	.18+	.26**	.11	.27**	.10	—	—	—						
11. Age[b]	4.47 (1.67)	.24*	.18+	-.17+	-.12	-.17+	.06	.17+	—	—	-.08	—					
12. MS[b]	0.59 (0.49)	.09	.12	-.15	-.17+	-.27**	-.06	.10	—	—	-.22*	.67**	—				
13. Edu[b]	3.73 (1.27)	-.21*	-.15	.12	.07	.25*	-.10	-.04	—	—	.07	-.35**	-.22*	—			
14. Tenure[b]	8.18 (7.03)	.25*	.12	-.19+	.04	-.04	.09	.16	—	—	-.04	.49**	.30**	-.26**	—		

15. LMX[b]	3.40 (0.69)	.00	.06	.02	.14	.09	.12	.09	—	—	-.12	-.27**	-.06	.10	-.40**	(.82)	
16. JS[b]	4.01 (0.48)	.31**	.37**	-.15	.23*	.29**	.23*	.24*	—	—	-.01	-.09	-.13	.09	-.03	.29**	(.74)
17. SP[b]	0.00 (0.79)	.31**	.36**	-.14	-.09	-.08	.14	.21*	—	—	.00	.44**	.32**	-.23*	.42**	-.19+	.25**

Notes
Numbers in parentheses are coefficient alphas. For gender, male = 0, female = 1. Age is a multiple-choice format with seven choices. For marital status, single = 0, married = 1. The scale for education level is the same as in Study 5.2. Tenure is in terms of number of years. NEI = the new emotional intelligence (EI) scale consisting of all 40 EI items selected in Studies 5.1 and 5.2; WLEIS = the Wong and Law (2002) self-report EI measure; NEURO = neuroticism; EXTRA = extraversion; OPEN = openness to new experiences; AGREE = agreeableness; CONSC = conscientiousness; LS = life satisfaction; HKCEE = Hong Kong Certificate Education Examination; MS = marital status; Edu = education level; LMX = Leader-Member Exchange scale; JS = job satisfaction; SP = sales performance.

[a]These variables are applicable to the student participants only (n = 158).
[b]These variables are applicable to employee participants only (n = 102).
+p < .10; *p < .05; **p < .01.

Table 5.6 Results of factor analysis for Study 5.4

	Factor 1	Factor 2	Factor 3	Factor 4	Factor 5	Factor 6
NEURO1	.06	−.12	**.75**	−.07	.05	.09
NEURO2	−.12	−.12	**.76**	.14	−.13	.03
NEURO3	.02	.14	**.56**	.06	.20	−.03
NEURO4	.02	.01	**.57**	−.17	−.02	.02
NEURO5	−.04	.18	**.47**	−.07	.16	−.11
NEURO6	−.37	.32	**.32**	−.04	.17	−.12
EXTRA1	−.04	**.61**	.02	−.02	.20	−.04
EXTRA2	.17	**.63**	.08	.04	−.16	.01
EXTRA3	−.15	**.81**	−.03	−.04	−.12	.09
EXTRA4	−.15	**.61**	−.11	−.00	−.14	.25
EXTRA5	.18	**.62**	.13	.02	−.21	.11
EXTRA6	−.40	**.18**	−.14	.18	−.05	.32
OPEN1	−.08	.14	−.06	−.06	.02	**.45**
OPEN2	−.06	.07	−.09	.14	.10	**.64**
OPEN3	−.46	−.16	.12	.15	−.04	**.38**
OPEN4	.15	.01	.14	−.11	−.00	**.47**
OPEN5	.11	.24	.12	.03	.00	**.43**
OPEN6	.00	.06	−.15	.02	.04	**.67**
AGREE1	**.60**	.04	.02	.13	−.14	.04
AGREE2	**.53**	.20	.06	.20	−.22	.02
AGREE3	**.57**	.03	.11	.36	−.12	.07
AGREE4	**.59**	−.11	−.13	.14	−.04	.22
AGREE5	**.46**	.14	−.23	.15	−.04	.03
AGREE6	**.30**	.52	−.21	.06	.09	.15
CONSC1	−.00	−.09	−.04	**.58**	−.13	−.03
CONSC2	−.05	−.02	−.14	**.67**	.03	.06
CONSC3	.16	−.01	.07	**.69**	−.02	−.04
CONSC4	.20	.04	.09	**.50**	.00	−.17
CONSC5	−.19	.08	−.10	**.53**	−.11	.16
CONSC6	.10	.34	−.11	**.32**	.05	.21
NEI-SEA	.22	.10	−.03	.07	**−.68**	−.02
NEI-OEA	−.13	.19	.04	−.01	**−.66**	−.06
NEI-ROE	.23	−.10	−.11	−.07	**−.63**	.06
NEI-UOE	−.07	−.09	−.09	.20	**−.58**	−.12

Eigenvalue	6.79	4.26	2.84	2.04	1.73	1.47
% of variance explained	19.97	12.52	8.34	5.99	5.07	4.31

Notes
NEURO = neuroticism; EXTRA = extraversion; OPEN = openness to new experiences; AGREE = agreeableness; CONSC = conscientiousness (number denotes the specific personality measurement items); NEI-SEA = the 10 new forced-choice emotional intelligence (EI) items on self emotional appraisal; NEI-OEA = the 10 new forced-choice EI items on other's emotional appraisal; NEI-ROE = the 10 new forced-choice EI items on regulation of emotion; NEI-UOE = the 10 new forced-choice EI items on use of emotion.

predictor (β = –.16, n.s.), while age was a marginally significant predictor of EI (β = .18, p < .10).

To test the distinctiveness of the 40 EI items and the Big Five personality dimensions, we used a similar approach to that in Studies 5.1 and 5.2 and calculated scores of the four EI dimensions as indicators of EI (the score for each dimension was the average of 10 items) and conducted a factor analysis with the 30 Big Five personality items. The results are shown in Table 5.6. With a few exceptions among the Big Five items, the corresponding indicators had the highest loadings on their respective factors, and the four EI indicators formed a distinct factor. In fact, the results were even clearer than in Studies 5.1 and 5.2. We therefore conclude that the 40 EI items are distinct from the personality dimensions.`

To test the predictive validity of EI on life satisfaction for the student participants, we conducted a hierarchical regression with life satisfaction as the dependent variable. The Big Five personality dimensions and the proxy for mental intelligence were entered into the equation first. EI was then entered to examine the changes in R^2. The results are shown in Table 5.7. The change in R^2 was .06 (p < .01), which indicated the incremental validity of EI in predicting life satisfaction over and beyond that of personality and mental intelligence. Table 5.7 also shows similar results for the WLEIS.

To test the predictive validity of EI on job outcomes, we conducted a hierarchical regression with sales performance and job satisfaction as dependent variables for the life-insurance-agent participants. Demographics, education level, job tenure, and score on the Leader-Member Exchange measure were entered into the equation first. The Big Five personality dimensions were then entered, followed by EI. The results are shown in Table 5.8. The changes in R^2 after adding the 40 EI items were .04 (p < .05) and .06 (p < .05), respectively, for sales performance and job satisfaction. As shown in Table 5.8, similar results were obtained for the WLEIS.

Table 5.7 Change in the model R^2 for the regression analysis on life satisfaction for the student participants in Study 5.4

	Dependent Variable: Life Satisfaction		
	M_1	M_{2a}	M_{2b}
NEURO	−.34**	−.33**	−.25**
EXTRA	.23**	.23**	.19*
OPEN	−.02	−.01	−.03
AGREE	.05	−.00	.04
CONSC	.22**	.18*	.13
HKCEE	−.05	−.03	−.09
NEI	—	.27**	—
WLEIS	—	—	.32**
R^2	.28**	.34**	.35**
ΔR^2	—	.06**	.08**

Notes
NEURO = neuroticism; EXTRA = extraversion; OPEN = openness to new experiences; AGREE = agreeableness; CONSC = conscientiousness; HKCEE = Hong Kong Certificate Education Examination; NEI = the new forced-choice emotional intelligence measure; WLEIS = the Wong and Law (2002) self-report emotional intelligence measure.

*p < .05; **p < .01.

Table 5.8 Change in the model R^2 for the regression analysis on sales performance and job satisfaction for the life insurance agents in Study 5.4

Independent variables	Dependent Variable: Sales Performance				Dependent Variable: Job Satisfaction			
	M_1	M_2	M_{3a}	M_{3b}	M_1	M_2	M_{3a}	M_{3b}
Gender	.07	.05	.02	.04	−.00	−.03	−.08	−.05
Age	.18	.15	.11	.11	.09	.03	−.02	−.01
MS	.14	.17	.20	.17	−.24⁺	−.17	−.13	−.17
Edu	−.11	−.11	−.09	−.07	.08	.06	.08	.11
Tenure	.31**	.30**	.28*	.31**	.20⁺	.15	.12	.16
LMX	.00	−.02	−.05	−.03	.37**	.31**	.28*	.30**
NEURO	—	.02	.04	.11	—	−.15	−.12	−.04
EXTRA	—	−.11	−.08	−.13	—	.09	.12	.06
OPEN	—	.07	.09	.08	—	.14	.16	.15
AGREE	—	.12	.06	.10	—	.05	−.02	.03

CONSC	—	.03	−.06	−.13	—	.04	−.07	−.14
NEI	—	—	.25*	—	—	—	.32**	—
WLEIS	—	—	—	.35**	—	—	—	.41**
R^2	.30**	.32**	.36**	.39**	.15*	.23*	.29**	.32**
ΔR^2	—	.02	.04*	.07**	—	.08+	.06*	.09**

Notes
MS = marital status; Edu = education level; LMX = Leader-Member Exchange; NEURO = neuroticism; EXTRA = extraversion; OPEN = openness to new experiences; AGREE = agreeableness; CONSC = conscientiousness; NEI = the new forced-choice emotional intelligence measure; WLEIS = the Wong and Law (2002) self-report emotional intelligence measure.

+$p < .10$; *$p < .05$; **$p < .01$.

Discussion

We have developed a short forced-choice EI scale for Chinese respondents in Hong Kong. Adopting the Mayer, Salovey, and Caruso (2000a) definition of EI as a particular set of mental abilities, and using a Likert-type EI measure developed with Chinese respondents in Hong Kong as a starting point, we devised a 40-item forced-choice scale to measure EI. Our results showed that it was possible to develop scenario and ability-paired items to measure EI using a forced-choice format. The results also indicated that the options for each of the 40 newly developed items were of comparable social desirability. Finally, when we used the newly developed WEIS to measure EI, our results showed that EI was distinct from personality and mental intelligence.

This study has both conceptual and practical implications. First, we provide further evidence to suggest that when EI is defined as one's abilities in dealing with emotions, it is distinct from personality traits and mental intelligence as traditionally conceptualized. Given the confusion in the definition and domain of the EI construct in the past, we believe it will be beneficial to EI researchers to adopt this definition of EI in their future work.

In practical terms, although the incremental validity of EI on the criterion variables is not particularly large, we believe that it is high enough to call for more research as well as to arouse the interest of practitioners. There are several reasons to support this claim. First, the incremental variance in life satisfaction that was explained by EI, as shown in Study 5.3, was 6% to 8% for the student sample. This increase in additional variance explained that accounted for life satisfaction is understandable because EI is moderately correlated with the Big Five personality dimensions. In addition, the correlations between life satisfaction and the personality dimensions are quite large. There is limited additional variance left to be accounted for by EI. Second, as EI is a set of abilities, it may be more trainable than dispositional constructs such as personality dimensions. Hence, there may be more room for education practitioners to design effective EI training programs for students.

Third, for sales performance and job satisfaction, the levels of incremental variance explained by EI were around 4% to 9% in Study 5.4. However, EI was already a much better predictor of these two job outcomes than the Big Five personality dimensions and education level (a proxy for mental intelligence). Fourth, the simple correlation between EI and the two criterion variables was .31 (p < .01). As a single predictor of job outcomes for Chinese life insurance agents, this scale already had significant practical utility as a selection instrument (see, e.g., Pearlman, Schmidt, & Hunter, 1980; Schmidt, Hunter, McKenzie, & Muldrow, 1979; Schmidt, Hunter, Pearlman, & Shane, 1979).

Future research could also examine the predictive validity of the WEIS for jobs other than life insurance agent. According to Wong and Law (2002), this validity could be generalized to jobs that require incumbents to present a particular type of emotion. Future research should compare the predictive validity among different jobs or occupations according to this argument.

Although the forced-choice scale developed in this study has acceptable reliability and validity, the results shown in Tables 5.7 and 5.8 indicate that the Wong and Law (2002) Likert-type WLEIS has greater predictive power over the criterion variables. This may indicate that when social desirability or faking is not a major concern, the WLEIS may be a good choice for researchers. However, for practitioners or research projects that need to record individual identity, it may be safest to use both scales to double-check the validity of the Likert-type scale because social desirability and faking may be an important concern. Future research may further compare the two scales or refine the forced-choice scale to see whether it is possible to outperform the Likert-type scale.

As a final note, future research should examine the validity of this EI scale in other cultures. As this scale was developed through Chinese respondents in Hong Kong, we believe that it will be a much better starting point for other Asian cultures than EI scales originating in Western countries. Even if this scale may not be directly applicable to other Asian cultures, the experiences reported in this paper may be useful to Asian EI researchers. They may use a similar methodology to develop EI scales for their societies. Evidence reported in this study clearly demonstrates that it is possible to do so.

Appendix 5.1
The selected 40 forced-choice items

Part I: reactions to various scenarios

For each of the following 20 situations, there are two possible reactions. Please circle the letter of the action (i.e., either A or B) that you would be more likely to take.

Appraisal and expression of emotion in the self
(self emotional appraisal)

1. *When you are very down, you will:*

    a. try to do something to make yourself feel better.
    b. just ignore it because you know your emotion will be back to normal naturally.

2. *When you are upset, you will:*

    a. talk to someone who is close to you about your feeling.
    b. concentrate on something else (e.g., your work, studies, or hobby) so that you can get away from your bad feelings.

3. *Your supervisor assigns a task that is not included in your job responsibility and you do not have any interest in doing it. You will:*

    a. persuade yourself that the task is not that bad and perform the task.
    b. tell your boss that you don't like the task and ask him to find some other suitable person to do the task.

4. *Johnny was working in the Hotline Department, and his job was to handle complaints and answer customer inquiries. However, he did not like his job, and so he found another job in a hotel, serving walk-in customers. He again found that he was sick and tired of handling unreasonable customers. If you were Johnny, you would:*

    a. try to get more training and education in customer service skills.
    b. talk to some experienced people in customer service and seek their advice.

5. *Two managers in your company were hostile and very competitive with each other. You were the head of a department. You were caught in the middle between these two managers because both of them wanted to gain control of your department. This made it difficult for your department to function*

normally because there was a lot of confusion regarding the rules and regulations for your department. You will:

a. pretend that you do not know about the competition between the two managers because politics is always unavoidable. You will let them fight and follow the finalized rules and regulations.
b. try your best to make the rules and regulations clearer so that your department can function normally.

Appraisal and recognition of emotion in others (other's emotional appraisal)

1. *When a friend comes to you because he/she is not happy, you will:*

    a. share his/her feeling.
    b. take him/her to do something he/she likes.

2. *When someone keeps on arguing with you on some unimportant topic, you will:*

    a. not respond to him/her and wait for him/her to stop.
    b. pretend to agree with his/her views and switch the discussion to other topics.

3. *Your friend has a rough relationship with his/her boyfriend/girlfriend because your friend has a bad temper. When your friend talks to you about the rough relationship, you will:*

    a. pretend to agree with him/her that his/her boyfriend/girlfriend is not good enough.
    b. point out that it is your friend's own fault and hope that he/she will improve.

4. *Joyce is the only daughter of her parents. She is very close to her parents and is a very responsible person. Her job performance is excellent, and colleagues like her. Recently her mother had a very serious traffic accident and is in a coma. Although Joyce worries a lot, she does not take time off and tries to do her best at work. If you were Joyce's supervisor, you would:*

    a. let her come to work as usual because she can use her work to distract her from her worries.
    b. assign less work to her so that she can go to the hospital in a more flexible way.

5. *One of your subordinates has just been back at work for a month after giving birth to her first baby. You know that her baby's health condition is not very good. Thus, you found out that this month she had made careless mistakes and took sick leave frequently. She had good performance before the baby was born.*

However, you are certainly not satisfied with her performance in this month. You will:

a. tell her directly that you are not satisfied with her work and discuss with her how she could improve the situation.
b. assign less work to her or transfer her to another position with a lighter workload.

Regulation of emotion in the self (regulation of emotion)

1. *Suppose you get an important award; you will:*

   a. tell everyone and share your happiness with them.
   b. tell only your family and closest friends and celebrate with them.

2. *When you have to do something you don't like, you will:*

   a. try to find some interesting stuff from it.
   b. try to finish it as soon as possible and forget about it.

3. *Your boyfriend/girlfriend is a fan of a particular pop music star. You spent two hours waiting to buy two tickets for this star's concert. You asked him/her to meet you at 7:30 p.m. After one hour he/she had not shown up. You therefore went to the concert by yourself. After the concert, you found your boyfriend/girlfriend. Before you said anything, he/she began scolding you seriously. You will:*

   a. let him/her continue. After he/she finishes, tell him/her that you had already waited for him/her for one hour.
   b. stop him/her immediately. Tell him/her that he/she should consider his/her lateness before scolding others.

4. *Today you go to work as usual. After getting off the Mass Transit Railway (MTR), you find out that you have lost your wallet. Soon after you arrive at the office, your boss complains about your work. When you start to work, your computer is broken. It is clear that today is very unlucky for you, and you are not happy about it. You will:*

   a. not mind and try to find another computer to start your work.
   b. talk to a colleague or friend to release the bad feeling before starting your work.

5. *Your colleague Peter is a very smart person and seems to know a lot. He is able to respond effectively and sensitively to people who are in high positions. Your boss asked you to work with him on a project. Peter has many flashy ideas, but he leaves you to handle all the dirty and donkey tasks. You will:*

   a. discuss this with Peter and insist on sharing your tasks with him.
   b. tell your boss about the situation and see if he/she can offer any advice and/or help.

Use of emotion to facilitate performance (use of emotion)

1. *When you face problems regarding your career or study, you will:*

   a. talk to your friends to seek advice.
   b. handle the problem yourself because everyone should deal with his/her own life.

2. *You have very little chance to get the offer of a job you would like very much. You will:*

   a. still apply for this job and try to prepare well for it.
   b. concentrate your efforts on jobs that you have better chances of getting.

3. *One day, you represent your company to welcome two important investors from Russia. According to Russian custom, people will kiss each other the first time they meet. However, you feel very uncomfortable kissing unknown people, especially those of the same gender as you. You will:*

   a. take the initiative to shake hands with them immediately when they appear to avoid the kissing.
   b. kiss them to show your respect.

4. *One Sunday in summer, you and your boyfriend/girlfriend drove to the beach to enjoy the sunshine. On the way you had a minor accident. The door of your car was damaged, and it would cost some money to repair it. You will:*

   a. drive the car to a familiar mechanic and take the bus to the beach.
   b. go to the beach as planned and fix the car later.

5. *You have an important examination tomorrow, and you are studying hard in your room. Your family is watching a television program which you like very much as well. Since your house is small the noise of the television annoys you. You will:*

   a. ask your family to turn off the television but videotape the program so that you and your family can watch it together tomorrow after your examination.
   b. although a little bit uncomfortable, you put headphones on (to reduce the noise) so that you can concentrate on your studies.

Part II: relative strength of abilities

The following are 20 pairs of abilities. In each pair, please judge which ability is stronger for you. Then circle the letter (i.e., either (a) or (b)) that represents this ability.(Note: You may be strong or weak in both abilities. However, what you need to choose is the relatively stronger one.)

	Ability to:	Ability to:
1	(a) Comprehend the reasons for being happy or unhappy	(b) Learn how to repair a new electric appliance
2	(a) Do mental arithmetic	(b) Control one's emotions
3	(a) Learn how to sing a new song	(b) Concentrate on achieving one's goal
4	(a) Understand others' true feelings by observing their behaviors	(b) Tolerate physical pain when compared to others
5	(a) Comprehend changes in one's emotions	(b) Learn how to dance some new steps
6	(a) Run faster than others	(b) Calm down faster than others when feeling angry
7	(a) Encourage oneself to work hard in unfavorable situations	(b) Learn how to draw or paint
8	(a) Observe details of things	(b) Observe others' emotions
9	(a) Perform better at sport activities than other people	(b) Understand one's own feelings better than other people
10	(a) Use mechanical instruments	(b) Control one's temper
11	(a) Comprehend the rhythm of a song	(b) Set objectives and work hard toward them
12	(a) Understand others' emotions from their behaviors and language	(b) Have better physical endurance than other people
13	(a) Be physically more energetic than others	(b) Understand one's emotions better than others
14	(a) Memorize new phone numbers quickly	(b) Not lose one's temper when angry
15	(a) Motivate oneself to face failure positively	(b) Learn to create an artistic object (e.g., pottery, painting)
16	(a) Comprehend the rationale of complicated problems	(b) Understand others' emotions
17	(a) Evaluate one's own bad emotions	(b) Evaluate others' singing abilities
18	(a) Keep emotionally calm when facing disguised people or situations	(b) Memorize strangers' names
19	(a) Encourage oneself to do one's best	(b) Learn a new sport activity (e.g., soccer)
20	(a) Comprehend others' emotions quickly and accurately	(b) Appreciate the creativity of a movie or a drama

Notes

Appraisal and expression of emotion in the self: Items 1, 5, 9, 13, and 17. Appraisal and recognition of emotions in others: Items 4, 8, 12, 16, and 20. Regulation of emotion in the self: Items 2, 6, 10, 14, and 18. Use of emotion to facilitate performance: Items 3, 7, 11, 15, and 19.

The following are the major contents of the paper in which we gathered further evidence to validate the forced-choice measure.

Wong, C. S., Wong, P. M., & Law, K. S. (2007). Evidence on the practical utility of Wong's emotional intelligence scale in Hong Kong and mainland China. *Asia Pacific Journal of Management*, 24(1), 43–60; these contents are reprinted with permission.

Abstract. Recently, a 40-item forced-choice instrument measuring emotional intelligence (EI) was developed for Chinese respondents in Hong Kong. We collected data in three studies to further test the practical utility of this instrument in Hong Kong and mainland China. The results provided clear evidence for the instrument's practical utility. More research that uses this measure in Asian countries is required.

Purpose of the present studies

Although Wong, Law, and Wong (2004) have provided some preliminary evidence of the validity of Wong's Emotional Intelligence Scale (WEIS) for Chinese respondents in Hong Kong, further evidence is required to test its practical utility in Hong Kong and mainland China. First, Wong and Law (2002) have shown that while emotional intelligence (EI) is related to job outcomes for high emotional labor jobs, the relationship may be much smaller for low emotional labor jobs because emotional labor represents the extent to which the job requires the management of emotions to achieve positive job outcomes (Hochschild, 1983; Morris & Feldman, 1996, 1997). Thus, in high emotional labor jobs, such as flight attendants and bill collectors, EI plays a much more significant role than in low emotional labor jobs, such as assembly line workers. The moderating effect of emotional labor on the EI–job outcome relationship has been confirmed empirically (e.g., Wong & Law, 2002; Wong, Law, & Wong, 2004). To demonstrate the practical utility of WEIS, it is necessary to test whether WEIS is able to capture this differential relationship. It may also be important to see whether WEIS is able to predict job outcomes for high emotional labor jobs that have been identified by human resource practitioners. Practically, confirmatory answers to these two questions would mean that it is possible for practitioners to identify when they can use WEIS to help with human resource decisions.

Second, in practical situations such as personnel selection, job applicants have an incentive to impress recruiters (Law, Mobley, & Wong, 2002). Although Wong, Law, and Wong (2004) examined the social desirability of the choices for each item of WEIS and found no significant differences, they did not test the potential selection error when WEIS scores were used to make selection decisions. This potential error due to respondents' attempts to impress human resource decision makers must be studied before the scale can be applied to practical situations.

Third, the evidence that was provided by Wong, Law, and Wong (2004) was based on Chinese respondents in Hong Kong. There is no evidence that shows the predictive power of WEIS on job outcomes in mainland China. Mainland China has a population of about 1.2 billion, and its rate of economic growth is one of the fastest in the world. Thus, whether WEIS can be used in mainland Chinese samples is an important question for human resource practitioners. As EI is an individual's ability to deal with emotions, this construct should be valid and applicable in different societies. By using self-reports and other EI rating scales, Law, Wong, and Song (2004) have shown that EI is related to job outcomes in a mainland Chinese sample. Thus, it is reasonable to conclude that the relationship between EI and job outcomes should also be valid in mainland China. However, the validity of WEIS as an EI measure has never been tested with mainland Chinese samples. As the first part of WEIS involves items which require respondents to choose their likely reaction in scenarios that are related to emotions, it is unclear whether mainland Chinese will react similarly to Hong Kong Chinese. We believe there should be little difference because both societies are deeply affected by Chinese culture. Although Hong Kong is more commercialized and internationalized, how an individual deals with emotional situations is affected by more basic values in social interactions, such as the norm of reciprocity, saving face, and *guanxi* (i.e., specific relationship in the Chinese context), rather than by the macro business and economic environment. Few differences in these basic values in social interactions have been reported across Chinese societies.

The second part of WEIS requires respondents to evaluate their relative strength in the handling of emotional issues and other types of abilities. Responses to these items may be affected by social desirability with regard to the ability to handle emotional issues. Under the strong influence of Chinese culture, people in both Hong Kong and mainland China should have similar values and desires about the proper handling of emotions. For these reasons, we believe that WEIS should work well for mainland Chinese samples. However, empirical evidence is needed to test the validity of this argument.

The purpose of this study is to provide evidence for the above three issues, which are important for the practical utility of WEIS. Specifically, confirmatory answers to the three issues are needed before we can confidently recommend that human resource practitioners use WEIS in practical situations in Hong Kong and mainland China. We address each of these issues by means of an independent study with its own sources of data. In the following sections, we will report these three studies.

Study 5.5

Purpose

The purpose of this study is to test whether WEIS is able to capture the differential EI–job outcome relationships for high versus low emotional labor jobs that have been identified by human resource practitioners.

Samples

Two samples of hotel employees were investigated. The first sample consisted of 66 housekeepers and 63 restaurant servers (waiters and waitresses) at a five-star hotel in Hong Kong. The two job positions were chosen for three reasons. First, they require different levels of emotional labor, as identified by the human resource manager of the hotel after one of the authors explained to him the concept of emotional labor. In the hotel, the house-keepers were instructed to avoid direct contact with customers, so the emotional labor of the position should be much less than that of restaurant servers, who have frequent contact with customers. Second, the hotel employs a large number of housekeepers and servers and therefore provides a sufficiently large sample size for statistical tests. Third, the hotel uses the same salary level and pay structure for the two positions, which indicates that they are of similar rank and status in the hotel. Hence, the hotel serves as a natural control for the similarity between the incumbents of the two positions.

The second sample consisted of 190 incumbents occupying different job positions at a four-star hotel in Hong Kong. One of the authors discussed the concept of emotional labor with the human resource manager and the human resource officer of the hotel. After the discussion, the manager and the officer were required to evaluate the positions in their hotel and group them into four categories according to the level of emotional labor: "not required," "minimally required," "largely required," and "absolutely required." The four categories were coded from 1 to 4. The senior management of the hotel allowed us to include the following positions, which were classified the same way by both the manager and the officer. From the "not required" to the "absolutely required" emotional labor level, the positions were (a) house-keepers (n = 67), (b) kitchen and security workers (n = 50), (c) front-office workers and restaurant servers (n = 51), and (d) managers and salespeople (n = 32). Hochschild (1983) pointed out that high emotional labor jobs have three characteristics. "First, they require face-to-face or voice-to-voice contact with the public. Second, they require the worker to produce an emotional state in another person. Third, they allow the employer, through training and supervision, to exercise a degree of control over the emotional activities of employees" (p. 147). Brotheridge and Lee (2003) further pointed out that from a job requirement point of view, the emotional labor construct should include the variety, frequency, intensity, and duration of emotional work. As housekeepers are not allowed to meet the customers and their work does not involve deal-ing with people, it is clear that their emotional labor requirement is minimal. Kitchen and security workers have infrequent contact with customers, although they need to co-operate with colleagues to carry out their duties. Although it is limited, they may need to perform some emotional work. Front-office workers, restaurant servers, managers, and salespeople have very frequent contact with customers, and it is clear that the emotional labor requirement is high. However, managers and salespeople have to deal with a much greater variety of internal and external customers. The intensity of emotional work is also higher because their interactions with these customers may involve much more complicated issues, such as the counseling of problem employees, price negotiations, other arrangements, and any activities in response to emergencies. Thus, the classification of the jobs that have been identified appears to be consistent with the characteristics of the emotional labor construct, which indicates that they represent different degrees of emotional labor requirement.

Measures

EI

As our purpose is to investigate the validity and practical utility of WEIS, we used the 40-item WEIS reported by Wong, Law, and Wong (2004).

Emotional labor

For the first sample, a dichotomous variable is used to represent the level of emotional labor. The housekeeper position is coded as 0, while the restaurant server position is coded as 1. For the second sample, a 4-point scale was used that depended on the judgment of the human resource manager and officer. With regard to the level of emotional labor, "not required" is coded as 1, "minimally required" as 2, "largely required" as 3, and "absolutely required" as 4.

Job satisfaction

The participants of both samples responded to the 14 job satisfaction items of the Job Diagnostic Survey (Hackman & Oldham, 1975). The average of these items was used as an indicator of their job satisfaction level. The internal consistency reliabilities (coefficient alpha) for the two samples were .88 and .90.

Organizational commitment

The participants of the first sample also responded to six items measuring their affective commitment to the organization; these items were developed by Meyer, Allen, and Smith (1993). The internal consistency reliability was .91 for this sample.

Job performance

In the second sample, data were collected two weeks after the annual performance interview between the supervisor and the respondents. The four-star hotel uses a forced distribution appraisal system (from 1 to 5) to represent the supervisor's evaluation of the performance level of the employees. The respondents were asked to report their supervisors' evaluation, which they had received two weeks prior, in a multiple-choice questionnaire.

Table 5.9 Descriptive statistics and correlations among measures for sample 1 of Study 5.5

	Mean (S.D.)	EI	JS	OC	NEURO	EXTRA	OPEN	AGREE	CONSC	Age	Edu	MS
1. EI	25.6 (4.17)	1.00										
2. JS	3.12 (.80)	.08	1.00									
3. OC	3.21 (.81)	.14	.67**	1.00								
4. NEURO	3.51 (1.09)	-.19*	-.12	-.19*	1.00							
5. EXTRA	4.33 (1.11)	.16	.02	.23*	.09	1.00						
6. OPEN	3.96 (.98)	-.07	-.07	.02	.01	.39**	1.00					
7. AGREE	5.11 (.90)	.30**	.08	.27**	-.25**	.45**	.23*	1.00				
8. CONSC	5.18 (.95)	.23*	-.04	.15	-.38**	.34**	.30**	.63**	1.00			
9. Age	4.31 (2.14)	.13	.26**	.35**	-.27**	-.13	-.37**	.02	.07	1.00		
10. Edu	2.91 (1.03)	.03	-.15	-.22*	.15	.20*	.24**	.11	.09	-.47**	1.00	
11. MS	1.67 (.55)	.11	.14	.19*	-.25**	-.06	-.22*	.02	.10	.58**	-.33**	1.00
12. Gender	1.42 (.50)	.14	-.20*	-.16	.18	.08	-.07	-.04	-.03	-.07	.07	.14

Notes

n = 129. For age, 1 = 20 or below, 2 = 21–25, 3 = 26–30, 4 = 31–35, 5 = 36–40, 6 = 41–45, 7 = 46–50, 8 = above 50. For marital status, single = 0, married = 1. For gender, 1 = male, 2 = female. EI = Wong's Emotional Intelligence Scale score; JS = job satisfaction; OC = organizational commitment; NEURO = neuroticism; EXTRA = extraversion; OPEN = openness to new experiences; AGREE = agreeableness; CONSC = conscientiousness; Edu = education level; MS = marital status.

*p < .05; **p < .01.

Table 5.10 Descriptive statistics and correlations among measures for sample 2 of Study 5.5

	Mean (S.D.)	EI	EL	JS	JP	NEURO	EXTRA	OPEN	AGREE	CONSC	Age	Edu	MS	Gender
1. EI	26.1 (3.99)	1.00												
2. EL	2.22 (1.07)	.06	1.00											
3. JS	3.32 (.51)	.11	–.08	1.00										
4. JP	3.09 (.73)	.16**	.15*	.19*	1.00									
5. NEURO	3.62 (1.13)	–.15*	–.05	–.33**	–.27**	1.00								
6. EXTRA	4.42 (1.00)	–.07	.06	.04	.08	–.19**	1.00							
7. OPEN	4.02 (.93)	.04	.19**	–.02	.14	–.04	.46**	1.00						
8. AGREE	4.99 (.96)	.15*	–.02	.02	.18*	–.37**	.54**	.21**	1.00					
9. CONSC	5.00 (1.06)	.20**	.06	.04	.21**	–.39**	.46**	.19**	.61**	1.00				
10. Age	3.43 (1.76)	.11	–.26**	.15*	.16*	–.07	–.15*	–.06	–.10	.07	1.00			
11. Edu	3.00 (1.18)	–.04	.48**	–.12	–.02	.04	.16*	.23**	.06	.03	–.43**	1.00		
12. MS	1.45 (.56)	.11	–.20**	.21**	.07	–.08	–.11	–.08	–.04	.02	.61**	–.32**	1.00	
13. Gender	1.44 (.50)	.09	–.14	–.06	.01	.07	.11	–.12	.20**	–.02	.13	–.02	.13	1.00
14. MP	11.1 (4.96)	.08	.45**	.16*	.16*	.00	.05	.24**	–.01	.10	.10	.25**	.05	–.21**

Notes

n = 129. For marital status, single = 1, married = 2. For gender, 1 = male, 2 = female. EI = Wong's Emotional Intelligence Scale score; EL = emotional labor; JS = job satisfaction; JP = job performance; NEURO = neuroticism; EXTRA = extraversion; OPEN = openness to new experiences; AGREE = agreeableness; CONSC = conscientiousness; Edu = education level; MS = marital status; MP = monthly pay (in thousands of Hong Kong dollars).

*p < .05; **p < .01.

Table 5.11 Results of moderated regression for sample 1 of Study 5.5

Independent variables	Dependent Variable: Job Satisfaction		Dependent Variable: Organizational Commitment	
	M_1	M_2	M_1	M_2
(Constant)	3.13**	4.31**	1.73*	2.58**
Gender	−.28⁺	−.26⁺	−.23	−.22
Age	.08⁺	.08⁺	.11*	.11*
Edu	−.04	−.05	−.08	−.09
MS	−.02	−.03	.02	.02
NEURO	−.04	−.03	−.05	−.05
EXTRA	.04	.02	.16*	.15⁺
OPEN	.03	.08	.06	.10
AGREE	.10	.14	.17	.20⁺
CONSC	−.17	−.23*	−.10	−.14
EI	.01	−.03	.01	−.02
Job[a]	.13	−2.67**	.14	−1.8*
EI * job	—	.11**	—	.08*
R^2	.125	.200*	.264**	.300**
ΔR^2	—	.077**	—	.036*

Notes
Edu = education level; MS = marital status; NEURO = neuroticism; EXTRA = extraversion; OPEN = openness to new experiences; AGREE = agreeableness; CONSC = conscientiousness; EI = emotional intelligence.

[a]For job positions, 0 = housekeepers and 1 = servers (waiters and waitresses).
⁺$p < .10$; *$p < .05$; **$p < .01$.

Table 5.12 sub-group correlations between emotional intelligence and job outcomes for Study 5.5

Sample 1 (n = 129)

Job Positions	Sample Size	r (EI, SAT)	r (EI, COM)
1. Housekeepers	66	−.10 (n.s.)	−.02 (n.s.)
2. Servers (waiters/ waitresses)	63	.33 (p < .01)	.33 (p < .01)

Sample 2 (n = 190)

Job Positions	Sample Size	r (EI, SAT)	r (EI, PERF)
1. Housekeepers	67	.04 (n.s.)	−.08 (n.s.)

2. Kitchen and security workers	50	.05 (n.s.)	.08 (n.s.)
3. Front-office workers and waiters/ waitresses	51	.16 (n.s.)	.24 (p < .10)
4. Managers and salespeople	32	.35 (p < .01)	.55 (p < .01)

Table 5.13 Results of moderated regression for sample 2 of Study 5.5

Independent Variables	Dependent Variable: Job Satisfaction		Dependent Variable: Job Performance	
	M_1	M_2	M_1	M_2
(Constant)	4.01**	4.33**	2.31**	3.92**
Age	.01	.01	.10*	.10*
Edu	−.02	−.02	−.05	−.04
MS	.12	.13	−.18	−.17
Gender	−.07	−.07	.04	.02
MP	.00003**	.00003**	.00013	.00011
NEURO	−.17**	−.16**	−.12*	−.09
EXTRA	.03	.03	−.01	.00
OPEN	−.05	−.05	.03	.02
AGREE	−.01	−.01	.05	.05
CONSC	−.08⁺	−.08⁺	.04	.03
EI	.01	−.01	.01	−.05
EL	−.06	−.23	.11	−71⁺
EI * EL	—	.01	—	0.03*
R^2	.233**	.235**	.160*	.187*
ΔR^2	—	.002	—	.027*

Notes
Edu = education level; MS = marital status; MP = monthly pay; NEURO = neuroticism; EXTRA = extraversion; OPEN = openness to new experiences; AGREE = agreeableness; CONSC = conscientiousness; EI = emotional intelligence; EL = emotional labor.

⁺p < .10; *p < .05; **p < .01.

Big Five personality dimensions

We used the McCrae and Costa (1987) adjective scale to measure the Big Five personality dimensions. Davies, Stankov, and Roberts (1998) criticized past EI-related measures for having salient loadings on the Big Five personality dimensions when factor analysis was conducted, and they concluded that EI was an elusive construct. As a result, we controlled for the Big Five personality traits in our analyses to show the incremental validity of WEIS. For the first sample, the internal consistency reliabilities for neuroticism, extraversion, openness to new experiences, agreeableness, and conscientiousness were .84, .85, .78, .80, and .80, respectively. For the second sample, they were .85, .77, .70, .79, and .82.

Demographics and salary level

Age, education level, and marital status were measured by multiple-choice questions. For the second sample, we also asked the respondents to report their monthly salary (in Hong Kong dollars) by responding to an open-ended question.

Results

Descriptive statistics and correlations between all measures for the two samples are shown in Tables 5.9 and 5.10. We used moderated regression to test the moderating effects of emotional labor on the EI–job outcome relationship. In the moderating regression, the demographics, the Big Five personality dimensions, EI, and emotional labor were entered in the first step, while the interaction term between EI and emotional labor was entered in the second step. As shown in Table 5.11, the interaction terms were significant in predicting both job satisfaction and organizational commitment for sample 1. As shown in Table 5.12, the sub-group correlations show that the EI–job satisfaction and EI–organizational commitment correlations are both .33 (p < .01) for the waiters and waitresses, while they are not significant for the housekeepers (r = −.10 and −.02, respectively). Similar results are observed for sample 2 in predicting job performance. We calculated the sub-group correlations to ensure that the correlation between EI and the criterion variables is practically large enough for the jobs with relatively high emotional labor. That is, the correlation between a single predictor and the criterion should be at least at the .20 level (see, e.g., Pearlman, Schmidt, & Hunter, 1980; Schmidt, Hunter, McKenzie, & Muldrow, 1979; Schmidt, Hunter, Pearlman, & Shane, 1979). As shown in Table 5.13, the interaction term for sample 2 was significant in predicting job performance, and the sub-group correlations showed differential correlations between EI and job performance in the predicted direction (r = −.08, .08, .24, and .55, respectively, for housekeepers, kitchen and security workers, front-office workers and restaurant servers, and managers and salespeople). For job satisfaction, although the interaction term was not significant in the moderating regression, the sub-group correlations showed differential correlations in the predicted direction (r = .04, .05, .16, and .35).

Study 5.6

Purpose

In comparison to research settings, respondents may act differently in personnel selection situations in completing WEIS because they may want to impress the recruiter. The purpose of this study is to test the usefulness of WEIS scores when personnel selection decisions have to be made.

Sample, procedure, and measures

One hundred and fifty-three undergraduate students at two universities in Hong Kong were invited to participate in this study for a compensation of HK$100 (about US$12.80). They were asked to complete the first questionnaire, which contained WEIS (i.e., the pretest) questions for research purposes. After completing the first questionnaire, they were instructed to assume that they were applying for a position as a management trainee at a large local bank. The second questionnaire contained a partial description of the position and a statement that informed the respondents that the bank used WEIS (i.e., the posttest; the order and wording of the WEIS items were exactly the same as in the first questionnaire) as a selection instrument. Respondents were told that their job was to try to impress the human resource manager of the bank as much as possible. A human resource manager of the bank would be invited to evaluate their responses and pick the top five candidates. These five candidates would receive a bonus of HK$200 (about US$25.60). To maintain anonymity, the respondents were required to provide only an email address or a mobile phone number on the first page of the posttest WEIS so that the authors could contact them if they received the bonus. All of the 153 students provided contact details, which indicated their willingness to participate.

Results

The mean scores of the pretest and posttest WEIS were 25.60 (standard deviation = 4.99) and 27.61 (standard deviation = 4.93), respectively. In a paired sample t-test, the mean difference was highly significant (t = –5.25, p < .01), which indicates that respondents did react differently during the personnel selection situation compared to the research situation. However, the correlation between the pretest and posttest WEIS scores was quite high (r = .55, p < .01), which indicates that the pretest scores were substantially related to the posttest scores.

To examine the errors that could be introduced during the selection decision as a result of respondents' attempt to impress the recruiter, we conducted two analyses based on common selection practices. In the first analysis, we assumed that WEIS was used as a preliminary scanning instrument to choose candidates for further selection tests, such as interviews. By using the pretest scores of WEIS, 28 candidates with scores higher than one standard deviation above the mean (i.e., over 30) were selected. In the posttest WEIS scores, 47 candidates scored higher than 30. Of the 47 candidates, 21 were from the 28 candidates who were selected from the pretest WEIS scores. Thus, we were able to correctly select 75% (i.e., 21 out of 28) of the candidates for further selection tests when the posttest scores of WEIS were used as a preliminary scanning instrument.

In the second analysis, we assumed that WEIS would be used as a scanning instrument in the final stages of the selection. Thus, we needed to select a very small number of candidates for the final round of consideration. By using the pretest scores of WEIS, the top 11 candidates were identified because they had scores that were higher than one and a half standard deviations above the mean (i.e., scores higher than 32). We did not use two standard deviations above the mean because in so doing only three candidates would have been selected, and this number might have been too small for meaningful comparison. By using the posttest scores of WEIS, the top 19 candidates with scores that were higher than 32 were identified. Of these 19 candidates, 8 of them were from the 11 candidates who were identified by the pretest. Thus, we were able to correctly select 73% (i.e., 8 out of 11) of the candidates when the posttest scores of WEIS were used as a scanning instrument in the final stages of selection.

Study 5.7

Purpose

The purpose of this study is to test the predictive power of WEIS on criterion variables and the usefulness of WEIS when personnel selection decisions have to be made for mainland Chinese samples.

Samples and measures

When one of the authors explained the concept of emotional labor to the head of the nursing department of a large hospital in Beijing who was going to organize a training program, she immediately agreed that the position of nurse was a typical example of a high emotional labor job. Thus, the first sample from mainland China consists of 100 female nurses from various parts of China who participated in the training program held in Beijing. They completed WEIS, and the same Big Five personality and organizational commitment measures as in Study 5.5. For job satisfaction, the four items of the Job Diagnostic Survey (Hackman & Oldham, 1975) that measure the intrinsic job satisfaction were used. We also added one item that asked about their satisfaction with the general job content of nursing. The internal consistency reliabilities for neuroticism, extraversion, openness to new experiences, agreeableness, conscientiousness, organizational commitment, and job satisfaction of this sample were .81, .70, .68,

.83, .77, .86, and .80, respectively. Age, job tenure, and marital status were included as control variables.

The second sample consists of 130 undergraduate students at a large university in mainland China. We conducted this study shortly after the end of the academic year. Basically we used the same procedure as in Study 5.6 and asked participants to complete WEIS twice. The first time, they were told to complete WEIS for research purposes. The second time, they were instructed to assume that they were applying for a job position as a management trainee at a large bank, and their job was to impress the recruiter as much as possible. However, instead of awarding monetary rewards for being among the top five candidates, like their counterparts in Hong Kong, top candidates would receive a reference book. In the first questionnaire, we also asked the participants to report their grade point average in the preceding academic year. In this university, the scale grade point average was a mark that ranged from 0 to 100, with 60 as the passing mark.

Results

For the nurse sample, significant correlations between the WEIS score and both job satisfaction (r = .25, p < .05) and organizational commitment (r = .24, p < .05) were found. Hierarchical regressions were then conducted. Basically, the controlling variables were entered in the first step, and the WEIS score was entered in the second step. The results are shown in Table 5.14. The WEIS score has incremental predictive power on job satisfaction (ΔR^2 = .043, p < .05) and organizational commitment (ΔR^2 = .036, p < .10) for the mainland Chinese nurse sample after controlling for age, job tenure, marital status, and the Big Five personality dimensions.

For the undergraduate student sample, the mean scores of the pretest and posttest WEIS were 25.98 (standard deviation = 4.20) and 27.95 (standard deviation = 4.77), respectively. In a paired sample t-test, this mean difference is highly significant (t = −6.73, p < .01), which indicates that the respondents did react differently during a personnel selection situation than in the research situation. However, the correlation between the pretest and posttest WEIS scores is quite high (r = .73, p < .01), which indicates that the pretest scores are substantially related to the posttest scores.

We conducted the same analyses as in Study 5.6. When WEIS was used as a preliminary scanning instrument to pick candidates, 88% (15 out of 17) of the candidates who were selected by using the pretest scores were also selected by using the posttest scores. When WEIS was used as a scanning instrument in the final stages of selection, 100% (5 out of 5) of the candidates who were selected by using the pretest scores were also selected by using the posttest scores. The mean score of the grade point average was 78.92 (standard deviation = 4.84), and its correlations with the pretest and posttest scores of WEIS were .35 (p < .01) and .24 (p < .01), respectively. Thus, if the grade point average is the criterion variable, the posttest scores of WEIS still have significant

Table 5.14 Results of hierarchical regression for Study 5.7

Dependent Variable Mainland Chinese Nurse Sample

	Job Satisfaction		Organizational Commitment	
	M_1	M_2	M_1	M_2
(Constant)	3.53**	2.40*	3.08**	2.15*
Age	.07	.07	.09	.08
Job tenure	−.01	−.01	−.01	−.01
MS	.16	.12	.14	.11
NEURO	−.21**	−.16*	−.12*	−.09
EXTRA	.26*	.25*	.10	.09
OPEN	−.07	−.04	−.06	−.04
AGREE	−.18	−.17	−.17	−.16
CONSC	.07	.05	.19	.18
EI	—	.04*	—	.03[+]
R^2	.240*	.283*	.163	.199[+]
ΔR^2	—	.043*	—	.036[+]

Notes
MS = marital status; NEURO = neuroticism; EXTRA = extraversion; OPEN = openness to new experiences; AGREE = agreeableness; CONSC = conscientiousness; EI = emotional intelligence.

[+]p < .10; *p < .05; **p < .01.

practical utility as a selection instrument because the predictive validity is at the .20 level.

Discussion

In the last decade, EI has been proposed as a potentially important construct for human resource management. In recent years, the relationships between EI and job outcomes, such as job performance, have been demonstrated with Chinese samples. WEIS, with a forced-choice format, was developed recently with the intention to enhance the applicability of the EI construct in real-life situations. The purpose of this study is to further examine the validity and applicability of this scale in the workplace.

The results of Study 5.5 clearly indicate that WEIS is able to capture the differential EI–job outcome relationships for jobs with different levels of emotional labor that have been identified by human resource practitioners. It appears that WEIS has practical value for jobs with moderate to high levels of emotional labor. The results of Study 5.6 indicate that although the respondents reacted differently during a selection situation than in a research situation, WEIS is still useful in a selection context. In fact, in Study 5.6, we probably created the "worst-case" scenario because we required and encouraged the participants to impress the recruiter as much as possible. They were familiar with the scale because during the selection process they were completing WEIS for the second time. Even in the worst-case scenario, the error rate of not identifying the correct candidates is only about 25%, both for the preliminary screening and for the selection of top candidates for the final round of consideration. Finally, the results of the nurse sample in Study 5.7 indicate that WEIS has similar predictive power on relevant criterion variables for mainland Chinese incumbents of a high emotional labor job as identified by the management practitioner. The results of Study 5.7 also indicate that although mainland Chinese respondents also react differently during a selection process than in a research situation, WEIS is still useful in a selection context.

With the evidence from Wong, Law, and Wong (2004) and this study, we believe that WEIS can be used in practical situations for Hong Kong and mainland Chinese samples. It may be worthwhile for future studies to examine its validity and applicability in other Asian countries.

Note

* As the main purpose of this study is to facilitate EI research in Asia, interested researchers can contact the authors to obtain the scoring key for the following items. For non–profit-making studies, we offer it at no charge.

6 Cultural issues concerning the emotional intelligence construct

At the beginning of the last chapter, I mentioned that I had doubts about the applicability of the Mayer-Salovey-Caruso Emotional Intelligence Test (MSCEIT) in measuring emotional intelligence (EI) across cultures, especially for Chinese respondents. In fact, this was not the only instance that stimulated me to think about cultural issues in studying the EI construct. However, I have to admit that I did not think about this issue at the very beginning. At that time, my major focus was on whether the EI construct was valid and whether it was related to important criterion variables in organizational behavior and human resource management.

The first time I gave serious thought to the cultural issue was in 2003, during the last round of revisions for the *Journal of Applied Psychology* paper. At that time, the editor and reviewers were quite satisfied with our revisions, but one reviewer suddenly raised a concern which he/she said was important. In that paper, we reported results from two student samples, one parent–student dyadic sample, and one employee–colleague–supervisor triadic sample. The reviewer's concern was that the respondents of all four samples were Chinese in either Hong Kong or mainland China. He/she believed our findings might have problems in generalizing to Western samples. He/she said that we should address this cross-cultural limitation. The editor agreed with this comment and indicated that we must be able to satisfy the reviewer's request.

This is not an unusual comment. I have been receiving this type of opinion from time to time in the past 25 years when I have submitted papers to journals in Western countries, especially those in North America. For studies conducted by Asian scholars, it is very normal that the samples studied in our empirical investigations would be Asian people or companies. Even though we had no intention to frame our study as cross-cultural in nature, a lot of Western reviewers would be sensitive to non-Western samples. This is not totally fair because they assume Western samples can be generalized to other cultures but not vice versa.

In the mid-1990s, I wrote to my doctoral thesis supervisor, who was serving as the editor of a mainstream management journal at that time. I asked his view on this issue. He told me that it would be normal for North American editors to take this into account because the majority of the readers of their journals were North American scholars. This situation has gradually changed in the past two decades, but this kind of bias still exists for some North American reviewers. Unfortunately, as far as I know, some Chinese scholars have this mind-set as well, especially those who were trained in Western graduate schools.

Lesson 13: always satisfying the editor and reviewers?

Although I did not agree with the reviewer's comment, I had to respond. At that time I was not very happy, but, looking back, I would like to thank the reviewer because he/she forced me to think about this issue more carefully. This helped me a lot in having a clear position when I investigated different research questions afterward. When we are conducting empirical investigations in social science, it would be normal for us to get samples from only one society. Doubts about the applicability of the results to other societies would be logical and valid. That is, cross-cultural generalizability would always be a valid concern. To fully address this issue, we have to identify conceptually the cultural factors that may affect our findings and empirically replicate the findings in different cultures. As this is not possible for one single study, we need to have a clear position about the issue of cross-cultural generalizability.

There are several ways to position a single study concerning cross-cultural generalizability. First, if our theory or hypotheses were derived from observations of a phenomenon in one single society, we should make it clear that our results may not be generalizable to other societies. This position is a valid one because we have no responsibility for such generalizability because cross-cultural generalizability is not our research question. In my past studies, one line of research investigated how transnational corporations could successfully use local Chinese managers to replace expatriates (e.g., Wong & Law, 1999). This is totally based on the situation in China, and we have no intention to generalize our findings to other societies. This is a valid research question related to the specific situation in mainland China but not necessarily relevant to other countries with different political and economic environments.

The second position is that if we have reasons to believe our findings may not be valid in other cultures, we should address the reasons and state the limitation. Of course, a better way is not to regard culture as an excuse but to go into more detail about the exact impact of culture. I have discussed with many Chinese graduate students in the past 15 years about their thesis topics. Many of them told me that they were very interested in some of the theories or findings in Western countries and wanted to test those theories or findings in China. They thought these would be interesting and worthwhile topics. I think this is normal for students who have first learned about rigorous research and have begun to read the literature. It was a good sign, because they were attracted to the scientific theories and findings reported in the literature. However, it also reflected their inexperience and lack of a good understanding of what a good scientific investigation should be. If we have no reason to suspect that theories and findings originating from one society or setting are not applicable to another setting, there is nothing to justify a replication. The contribution to knowledge will be limited.

My recommendation to the Chinese students was usually that they should examine carefully why they believed the theories and findings might not be applicable to the Chinese setting. This should be conceptualized as concrete cultural differences and conceptual arguments concerning why these cultural differences would make the theories and findings not applicable. After this conceptual work, they should develop modified theories or models that would be more applicable to the Chinese setting. This should be put as testable hypotheses. With these testable hypotheses, empirical studies could be conducted to test whether the original or the modified theories were supported. My research line on career interests mentioned before may serve as a good example. Instead of simply collecting data to test the applicability of Holland's (1985) model in Chinese settings, we carefully examined the situation in Chinese societies and proposed a modified model. Then we collected data to test the original and the modified model as competing theories (Law, Wong, & Leong, 2001; Wong & Wong, 2006). Culture should not be treated as a "slack" variable that can be used to explain a lack of cross-cultural generalizability. Instead, the exact differences among societies should be conceptualized in testable hypotheses.

Lesson 13: Researchers should have a clear idea about the generalizability of their study. This is especially true for cross-cultural generalizability when we have only single-country samples. If we suspect theories and findings are not applicable to a particular setting, we must build up conceptual arguments concerning why they are not applicable.

Lesson 14: have a clear position about cultural issues

When we carefully examined how the reviewer phrased his/her comment, we believed that the reviewer was only asking us to state the possible limitation of cross-cultural generalizability because of our Chinese samples. If we added several sentences acknowledging this limitation, this would be sufficient. However, I did not want to address the comment in this way because it would be too superficial and did not reflect what exactly the situation was about.

Together with the doubts about the MSCEIT items, I gradually had a clearer picture of the cross-cultural issue for the EI construct. Conceptually, we are studying a universal construct that should be relevant to all human beings. The ability to handle emotional issues should be relevant to all cultures. However, the exact behaviors or reactions that are regarded as being emotionally intelligent may differ across cultures. I believed this was a very important point that needed to be clear. Otherwise, the nature of EI and its measurement might be confused, and this would mislead future EI studies. Therefore, instead of simply acknowledging the potential limitation due to our samples, we put in some elaborations and explained this in our letter to the editor and the reviewer. Fortunately, they agreed and allowed us to put the following in the final revision:

> Our second limitation is that all the data in this project were collected in Hong Kong and the PRC [People's Republic of China]. Cross-cultural generalizability of the results may be a concern. We do not know whether EI would vary across different cultures. However, when we go back to the EI literature, we do not find any discussion of EI across cultural boundaries. Our position is that one's ability to understand, regulate, and utilize one's emotions in constructive ways are general human abilities. There is no immediate evidence that the validity of EI, as defined under our four-dimensional view, should vary across culture. While further studies may be needed to verify this position, *we take the general scientific attitude that psychological and management phenomena are considered as universal unless there are theories or evidence showing their cross-cultural variations.*
>
> *While the EI construct may be universal, we agree that behaviors resulting from the EI of an individual may vary across culture.* For example, a non-reactive quiet response by the subordinate when one's boss is making unreasonable demands may reflect high EI among Chinese but probably not among non-Chinese. In this respect, our use of self-report measure of EI may, in fact, be a plus because we asked respondents about their final judgment of the EI of the target person irrespective of the assessment clues or methods they would use. By doing so, we may be able to avoid some cross-cultural differences in expressing emotions or diagnosing emotions because the assessors would be able to use the clues or methods that are appropriate for their specific culture. This issue may have to be considered when behavior- or outcome-oriented tests of EI, such as the MSCEIT, are used across cultural boundaries.

We believed the above two paragraphs were important because they might help future EI researchers in conceptualizing their arguments and developing measurement scales for EI. As a Chinese researcher, I also think this can help Asian scholars to realize that having a single-country sample may not be a key concern if the constructs being investigated are universal.

From time to time, I have heard colleagues and students complaining about the unreasonable requests of reviewers. Some of them believe that they must satisfy all the requests even though the comments may not be reasonable. I think this may not be a good attitude. It is better to treat the dialogue with the editor and reviewers as an intellectual discussion. Although the editor and reviewers have the power to reject our papers, we should not regard ourselves as in an inferior position. The basis of the final decision should be scientific rigor and reasons instead of who has the power to make the decision.

I myself have had a lot of instances when I disagreed with the editors and reviewers. I had some successes as well as failures in debating with them. Some reviewers were really unreasonable. For example, I once got a comment from a reviewer saying that "as authors I expected you do what I asked for instead of arguing with me." To me, this is not reasonable, and I think the reviewer was absolutely wrong about his/her role. I remember that I wrote back politely and said I believed it should be fine for scientists to have different opinions. The paper was rejected at that time, but I did not regret stating my position clearly. I also believed that it was important to uphold this belief.

Lesson 14: Regardless of the results of the review process, we should treat our responses to the editor and reviewers as an intellectual discussion among scientists. If we are too focused on the final acceptance of the paper, we may miss opportunities to make important contributions to knowledge.

Lesson 15: the importance of research grants

As I gave more careful thought to the possible cross-cultural issues involved in studying EI, the first thing I wanted to do was to test whether the MSCEIT could be used with Chinese respondents. In fact, once I learned about the MSCEIT, I began to write grant proposals to study EI in the Chinese setting, and one of the important expenses was to pay the royalties to use the MSCEIT. I also needed the financial resources to translate the MSCEIT into the Chinese language. Writing the grant proposal further forced me to think about the project more carefully.

To apply for a research grant, we needed to have a concrete research question in order to make the project produce a workable output at the end. Therefore, we tried to argue conceptually why EI should be related to job outcomes and come up with a model explaining how general mental abilities (GMA) and EI should each have an independent impact on job performance. We had to study GMA together with EI because at that time there were some arguments in the literature that GMA and EI might interact with each other in affecting job outcomes. We careful reviewed some theoretical models of job performance. Fortunately, it was not too difficult, and we were able to build a simple model linking the impact of GMA and EI on job performance.

We were fortunate to find a connection to collect data from a group of research and development scientists at a large information technology company in China. They had objective performance indicators. To play it safe, we put both the Chinese and English versions of the MSCEIT together so that the scientists could refer to both versions when they responded to the items. The printing cost was quite expensive at that time because we needed to retain the colors of the original English version.

Lesson 15: Applying for research grants is an important exercise. Whenever necessary, we have to apply for financial resources to help us. Of course, it is our responsibility to have comprehensive and workable research ideas in order to come up with the grant proposals.

We found out that MSCEIT scores could not predict job performance and other job outcomes for this Chinese sample. Instead, our self-report EI scale had predictive validity. I was not sure whether I should be happy with our findings or not. On the bad side, it made it difficult for us to rely on the popular MSCEIT for our EI studies in Chinese samples. On the good side, it confirmed my judgment on the cross-cultural issue for EI measurement items.

The following are the major contents of the paper.

Law, K. S., Wong, C. S., Huang, G. H., & Li, X. (2008). The effects of emotional intelligence on job performance and life satisfaction for the research and development scientists in China. Asia Pacific Journal of Management, 25(1), 51–69; these contents are reprinted with permission.

Abstract. Organizational researchers have found evidence for the impact of emotional intelligence (EI) on various organizational outcomes, such as leadership effectiveness, employee job satisfaction, and job performance. However, as an emerging topic, scientifically rigorous study for the validation of the EI construct is still far from satisfactory. To further demonstrate the utility of EI in organizational studies, this study focuses on the incremental validity of EI on job performance beyond that of general mental abilities (GMA), a factor that has long been widely used in personnel selection. We proposed that EI was a significant predictor of job performance over and beyond GMA. Results from a working sample supported our argument. We also compared two measures of EI. Our results showed that a more recently developed self-report EI scale, the Wong and Law Emotional Intelligence Scale (WLEIS), is a better predictor of job performance than the Mayer-Salovey-Caruso Emotional Intelligence Test (MSCEIT) in the Chinese sample under investigation. Implications of the findings are discussed.

Since emotional intelligence (EI) is defined as a set of interpersonally and intrapersonally related human abilities, it should have predictive power on various personal and social outcomes. Both Wong and Law (2002) and Wong, Wong, and Law (2005) argued that *life satisfaction* was one important outcome for people with high EI. The reason is that a person with high EI is able to understand his/her own and others' emotions and draw on these understandings to modify his/her behaviors and attitudes to get positive results. As a result, he/she would be more able to deal with the emotions generated from within and would be generally happier in and more satisfied with his/her life. Wong and Law (2002) and Law, Wong and Song (2004) have found repeated empirical support in multiple samples for this predicted relation. EI would be of interest to organizational researchers only if it can be associated with organizational outcomes, such as employee attitudes, behaviors, and job performance, in addition to life satisfaction. To date, researchers have found that employees' EI is positively related to their job satisfaction and performance (Law, Wong, & Wong, 2004). In addition, a leader's EI was found to affect leadership effectiveness and followers' satisfaction and extra-role behaviors (Rosete & Ciarrochi, 2005; Wong & Law, 2002). Given its great potential and importance, it is regrettable that studies on EI–organizational outcome relations are rare. In the following section, we will discuss the role of EI as a predictor of employees' performance in organizational settings beyond the effect of GMA, the traditional performance predictor.

EI, GMA, and job performance

Organizations are places where individuals are "organized" to work. To the extent that the work requires interaction among individuals, emotions such as excitement, anger, and fear are indispensable in facilitating co-operation. In some workplaces, certain emotions are themselves what the job requires from employees. Typical examples are salespeople, bill collectors, and social workers (e.g., Hochschild, 1983; Pugh, 2001; Sutton, 1991). Employees who are "intelligent" regarding emotions will therefore be more efficient and effective in their interactions with the work environment and their co-workers. This EI–performance link has been proposed in a few previous studies. For example, Lam and Kirby (2002), using a student sample, found that EI contributed to cognitive-based performance. Wong and Law (2002) studied the link in the workplace and found a positive relationship between EI and job performance.

In addition to EI as a general construct, each of the four dimensions of EI may be related to job performance. First, ability in *appraisal and expression of emotion in the self* has been found by psychologists and sociologists to be crucial to an individual's mental and even physical health (Butler et al., 2003; J. S. House, Umberson, & Landis, 1988; Lin, Ye, & Ensel, 1999). Accurate appraisal and expression of one's emotion is necessary for people to develop beneficial interpersonal relationships, to communicate with others about their needs, and thus to fulfill their goals through a higher level of job performance (George, 2000). Second, ability in *appraisal and recognition of emotion in others* enables people to understand others' emotion and respond accordingly by showing appropriate attitudes and behaviors. They would then have a higher chance of being accepted by others and would earn their trust and co-operation more easily. This is crucial for good performance in organizational settings, especially when jobs are highly interdependent with each other, such as when working in teams. Third, individuals with high ability in *regulating emotions* can alter their own emotions so as to lessen any undesired emotional impact on their work environment. Such employees would get out of the sometimes unavoidable negative emotional impact (resulting from, for example, impolite refusals by customers to salespeople, excessive stressful demands by the boss, uncooperative behaviors of peers, etc.) sooner, and therefore their performance would suffer less from the adverse situation. Finally, it is obvious that one's ability to *use one's emotions to facilitate performance* will have a positive impact on one's performance. Individuals with high ability in this dimension are always active in directing the emotions in themselves toward good outcomes. In organizational settings, such employees could cheer themselves up when they know the good mood will help them to complete the job, as well as facilitating a certain emotion if their organizational roles require it.

Although it appears clear that EI may affect job performance, it is important to establish its unique contribution to job performance when compared to other established constructs, especially the traditional intelligence dimensions, such as GMA, which has been shown to be valid predictor of performance. In the personnel psychology literature, research over the last two decades has shown that the variability of performance among workers is very large (Schmidt & Hunter, 1998). Considerable efforts have been put into studying the individual differences that may predict important job outcomes. Although controversies exist, some stable individual differences, such as GMA, have been found to have good general predictive power on performance. GMA, also called general cognitive ability and general intelligence or the *g*-factor, is a well-researched construct for which we have impressive evidence of its capacity to predict important outcomes such as job performance, training success, and career success across jobs, settings, and careers (e.g., Ferris, Witt, & Hochwarter, 2001; O'Reilly & Chatman, 1994; Ree, Earles, & Teachout, 1994). In their review of 85 years of research findings on the validity and utility of selection methods in personnel psychology, Schmidt and Hunter (1998) confirmed that research evidence for the validity of GMA measures for predicting job performance is stronger than for any other method. Other researchers have concluded that *g* is "the single most useful worker attribute for predicting job performance, as a valid predictor in all types of jobs" (Gottfredson, 1986).

This special position of GMA, however, is not free from critics or skeptics. For instance, researchers in psychology and education have criticized the view that what matters for success is intellect alone as a false "IQ-mystique" (e.g., Goleman, 1998). In Goleman's view, given how much emphasis schools and admissions tests put on it, IQ alone "explains surprisingly little of achievement at work or in life" (p. 19). He noted that when IQ test scores were correlated with people's career success, IQ accounts for at most about 25%, and therefore the rest of their job success was left unexplained (p. 19). Other researchers gave an even lower number, stating that GMA accounts for between 10% and 20% of such success, leaving 80% to 90% to be explained by other factors (Gardner, 1993; Mayer & Salovey, 1997). We echo this view and argue that EI would be one possible factor which can provide an incremental contribution in predicting job performance and work success on top of GMA.

There are two related arguments that help explain why EI contributes incremental predictive power on job performance. First, the predictive validity of EI over GMA may be understood from our study of the human mind. Based on early work by Mendelssohn (1755/1971) and a historical review by Hilgard (1980), Mayer and Salovey (1997) pointed out that "since the eighteenth century, psychologists have recognized an influential three-part division of the mind into *cognition* (or thought), *affect* (including emotion), and *motivation* (or conation)" (p. 4). Specifically, "the cognitive sphere includes such functions as human memory, reasoning, judgment, and abstract thought and intelligence is typically used to characterize how well the *cognitive* sphere functions; the *affective* sphere of mental functioning includes the emotions, moods, evaluations, and other feeling states, including fatigue or energy; the last sphere, *motivation*, refers to biological urges or learned goal-seeking behaviors" (p. 4).

The *affective* component of the human mind is clearly related to EI. A person's ability to understand his/her emotions and to regulate his/her emotions would influence his/her affect, moods, and feelings. The *motivation* part of the human mind should be related to the EI dimension of "use of emotion to facilitate performance." People with strong learned goal-seeking behaviors would make use of their emotions to direct their behaviors toward their goals. EI is therefore more related to the affective and motivational sphere of the human, whereas GMA is mainly related to the cognition sphere of the mind. Since all three parts of the human mind are related to human performance, it is logical that both GMA and EI make their own unique contributions to job performance.

Second, a related but somewhat different perspective that supports the unique contribution of EI to performance over and beyond GMA is the theoretical framework of performance. Interestingly, although it is one of the most important dependent variables in management studies, performance has itself been the subject of very little theory building. J. P. Campbell (1990) and J. P. Campbell, McCloy, Oppler, and Sager (1993) highlighted this lack of a common understanding and theory of "performance" and proposed a model that specifies the content of performance, its direct determinants, and its critical dynamic properties. We choose Campbell's job performance model in our discussion of the effects of EI and GMA on performance for two reasons. First, it is the most prominent job performance model in the literature, compared with a few other relevant performance theories (e.g., Hunter, 1983; Pritchard & Roth, 1991). Second, it matches the aforementioned three-part division of the human mind and provides a good theoretical framework with which to study how EI affects job performance.

J. P. Campbell's (1990) model makes clear distinctions among performance components, performance determinants, and the predictors of performance determinants. Performance components are performance dimensions that constitute various parts of the overall job performance. In Campbell's model of performance, eight performance components are identified so that they are "intended to be sufficient to describe the top of the latent hierarchy in all jobs in the *Dictionary of Occupational Titles*" (J. P. Campbell et al., 1993, p. 46). Three major types of individual differences determine the success of each performance component. These individual differences are labeled as the "performance determinants." The three major performance determinants are "declarative knowledge, procedural knowledge and skill, and motivation" (Campbell, 1990, p. 705; Campbell et al., 1993, p. 43). Declarative knowledge (DK) includes knowledge about facts, principles, and goals and self-knowledge, which represents an understanding of a given task's requirements. Procedural knowledge and skill (PKS) includes cognitive skills, psychomotor skills, physical skills, self-management skills, and interpersonal skills. Motivation (MOT) is a combined effect of three choice behaviors: choice to perform, level of effort, and persistence of effort. Campbell posited that each of the eight performance components is a function of the product of the three performance determinants, that is, $PCi =$ $f(DK \times PKS \times MOT)$, where PCi is the ith performance component. Finally, performance predictors are variables that will lead to individual differences in performance determinants. We argue that GMA would be related to DK and PKS, while EI would be related to MOT and part of PKS. Since GMA and EI are responsible for different components of the performance determinants, EI would predict performance over and beyond the contribution of GMA.

GMA would be a reasonable predictor of DK and part of PKS because DK refers mainly to individuals' cognition and understanding of their external worlds in the job environment. GMA could predict PKS because part of PKS consists of cognitive and psychomotor skills that are important components of GMA. On the contrary, EI would be a reasonable predictor of MOT because individuals with high EI are able to regulate their emotions and use their emotions to facilitate their performance. They should then be able to focus their efforts and maintain their motivation level. Furthermore, EI may predict PKS because part of PKS consists of self-management and interpersonal skills, which are highly related to EI.

Our conceptualization of GMA and EI as predictors of Campbell's three performance determinants also matches well with the three-part division of the human mind mentioned above. The relationships are represented diagrammatically in Figure 6.1. First, GMA is closely related to the cognition domain of

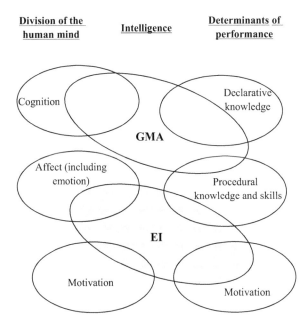

Figure 6.1 The relationship among general mental abilities (GMA)/emotional intelligence (EI), the division of the human mind, and determinants of performance

the human mind, and it is primarily related to DK and part of PKS in the job context. Specifically, individuals with strong cognitive skills or who have high GMA should have a higher chance of mastering DK and some parts of PKS. This, in turn, will have favorable effects on their performance levels. Second, EI is closely related to the affective and motivation domains of the human mind, and it is primarily related to MOT and part of PKS in the job context. Specifically, individuals with high ability in the motivation and affective domains or who have high EI should have a higher chance of mastering the MOT job determinant and some parts of PKS in the job context. This will then result in favorable effects on their job performance levels.

Based on the above discussion, we propose:

> Hypothesis 6.1: EI will have incremental predictive power on job performance over and beyond the effect of GMA.

Measurement: self-report versus ability testing

A considerable part of EI research has centered on the measurement of EI. As Mayer, Caruso, and Salovey (2000b) noted, "The development of theoretical models of emotional intelligence has been paralleled by the development of tests to measure the concept" (p. 320). However, compared with the converging sense on the definition of EI, there is little consensus on its measurement methods (Salovey, Woolery, & Mayer, 2001). Debate on EI in the literature is often caused by the lack of an established measure. For example, Davies, Stankov, and Roberts (1998) concluded that EI was an "elusive" construct because in factor analyses measures of EI-related scales overlapped with the well-established personality factors. However, Salovey et al. (2001) criticized this conclusion as "incredibly premature." Law, Wong, and Song (2004) also disagreed and noted that this conclusion was not justifiable because the EI-related scales under investigation were not developed based on Davies et al.'s adopted four-dimensional definition of EI. Law, Wong, and Song (2004) also successfully demonstrated that when properly defined and measured according to the four-dimensional definition, EI was a distinct and useful construct for psychological and management research.

There are two types of EI measures: task-based tests and self-report scales. Scholars in favor of task-based tests have stated that EI can be assessed most directly by asking a person to solve emotional problems (Mayer, Salovey, et al., 2000a; Salovey et al., 2001). So far, the most prominent measures of this type are the Multifactor Emotional Intelligence Scale (MEIS) and a newer version of this scale, the Mayer-Salovey-Caruso Emotional Intelligence Test (MSCEIT) (Mayer, Caruso, et al., 2000b). Both tests are based on the ability-based EI model (Mayer & Salovey, 1997; Salovey & Mayer, 1990). The MSCEIT has four subscales, each of which includes several subsets. *Perception of Emotion* contains three subsets asking how much a certain kind of emotion is expressed in human faces, landscapes, and abstract designs. *Emotional Facilitation* contains several subscales but centers on the synesthesia subscale, which asks participants to judge the similarity between an emotional feeling, such as love, and other internal experiences, such as temperatures and tastes. *Understanding Emotion* examines how well participants make the right emotional judgments by means of a variety of tasks, such as matching close emotions and reasoning why a certain emotion happens. *Managing Emotion* asks participants to tell the best way to reach certain emotional goals in various situations, such as what the best action is for a sad person who wants to cheer up: "talking to some friends," "seeing a violent movie," "eating a big meal," or "taking a walk alone."

Compared with the limited number of task-based tests, many self-report EI scales have been developed, such as the Emotional Quotient Inventory (EQ-i; Bar-On, 1997) and the Trait-Meta-Mood Scale (TMM; Salovey, Mayer, Goldman, Turvey, & Palfai, 1995). (See Salovey et al., 2001, for an extensive review of available measures.) Usually, self-report measures ask participants' self-judgment on a series of descriptive statements, such as "It is difficult for me to control my anger." Self-report scales can also be applied as other-evaluation scales, that is, asking informants' judgment of the focal person on the self-report scale (Law, Wong, & Song, 2004).

Since EI is argued to be an intelligence facet, direct and objective assessments seem to be better measures than self-evaluation measures. However, unlike traditional general intelligence tests, which have definite correct answers, EI tests have the problem of defining which is the correct choice. Developers of task-based tests argue that there are evolutionary and cultural foundations for the existence of "correct" answers (Mayer, Caruso, et al., 2000b). Three alternatives have been proposed as the criterion: target answer, expert judgment, and group consensus. Positive correlations were found among the three criteria, and the group consensus criterion appeared to be the single best means (Mayer, Caruso, et al., 2000b).

Unfortunately, using norm-referenced criteria may suffer problems in cross-cultural settings. For instance, a non-reactive quiet response by a subordinate to a boss who is making unreasonable demands may be seen as "smart" among Chinese but probably not among Westerners (Law, Wong, & Song, 2004). Moreover, tests developed by Western scholars may not have considered the participants' background in other cultures. For instance, in some MSCEIT items, respondents are asked about the amount of a certain emotion expressed in several faces, but Asian test takers who are not familiar with Western cultures may not be able to "read" the faces correctly. Some MSCEIT questions require a certain quality of education or knowledge in the arts, to make judgments on the expression of, for example, an abstract colorful design. Specific artistic senses may differ across cultures, such as the underlying meanings of various colors. This may make the norm-referenced criteria unreliable or invalid across cultures. While high reliabilities of the MEIS and the MSCEIT have been shown by the developers using American samples (sub- and full-scale internal consistency of around .90; Mayer, Caruso, et al., 2000b), little other empirical evidence, especially outside North America, could be found.

In contrast, while self-report scales may be affected by participants' incorrect self-perception, social desirability, or positive affectivity, they have some comparative advantages. First, they avoid possible assessment clues or methods to get the correct answers because they ask the respondents' judgment directly. Second, they can be used to evaluate others (e.g., Law, Wong, & Song, 2004) so that the self-bias problems can be avoided. Third, self-report measures have been employed for a relatively longer time, and empirical evidence has shown that they can have acceptable reliability and convergent, discriminant, and criterion validity (see, e.g., Law, Wong, & Song, 2004; Wong & Law, 2002). Fourth, feedback about one's ability to handle emotions may be very frequent in social interactions, and thus one's evaluation of this type of ability may be more accurate than other types of abilities such as reasoning and logical deduction. Finally, one attractive feature of such instruments to organizational researchers is that they are usually more practical than the available objective tests because of cost concerns. Based on the above analysis, as we used a sample of Chinese employees from a Chinese company in our empirical study, we predict:

> Hypothesis 6.2: EI as measured by a self-report measure will have comparable predictive power on job performance as a task-based test for Chinese employees.

Method

Sample and procedures

The data used in this study were collected from employees in the research laboratory of a large Chinese computer company in Beijing. The company has more than 12,000 employees, and there are 120 employees in this research laboratory. We sent invitations to all research laboratory employees to participate in the study. All employees were assured that data would be kept confidential and that the study was for research purposes only. Each employee was then contacted in person by one of the authors. Those who were willing to participate completed the Wonderlic test (a well-known test of GMA) within the specific time limitations in the presence of one author. Then the employee was allowed to fill in the rest of the survey questionnaire and return it to this author later. Participation was voluntary; 102 employees agreed to participate in the study and returned their questionnaires, a response rate of 85%. These 102 employees formed the final sample of this study. Among all participants, the mean age was 27; 78% were male, and 70% had earned a graduate degree. The objective performance measure was obtained from the participants' job appraisal records kept in the human resource department of the company.

Variables and measures

Job performance

The company's formal appraisal of employees' performance was used as the measure of job performance. The research laboratory of the company has a formal evaluation system which uses 6 evaluation levels: C, B–, B, B+, A–, and A, from low to high (coded as 1 to 6, respectively). The evaluation is based on the employee's overall job performance, which is directly related to their current and past research outputs. We noticed that the highest level of appraisal, "A," was seldom given, and the percentage who received a "C" in the laboratory was as low as 10% because employees with such a poor evaluation would usually be fired.

EI

Two measures of EI were used. The first measure was the 16-item WLEIS developed by Wong and Law (2002). Coefficient alphas for the EI dimensions of self emotional appraisal, other's emotional appraisal, regulation of emotion, and use of emotion were .82, .81, .87, and .89, respectively. The second measure was the MSCEIT (Mayer, Salovey, & Caruso, 1999), which yields scores on four EI dimensions: perceiving emotions, using emotions, understanding emotions, and managing emotions. It includes 141 items and takes around 30 to 45 minutes to finish. The MSCEIT was scored by the test developer, and no information on test reliability was provided.

GMA

We attempted to control for the effects of GMA on job performance in this study in two ways. First, most participants had very high education levels (70% had graduate degrees) and occupied similar research positions in one company. This company is famous for its research development in China. It has a rigorous selection process based on academic performance and interview results. This, together with the fact that employees were constantly assessed and that only the top performers are retained by the company, leads us to the assumption that its employees are quite homogeneous in their GMA. Second, we control for GMA by directly measuring it with the Wonderlic Personnel Test (Wonderlic Inc., 1999). This GMA test, developed by E.F. Wonderlic in 1937, has been used worldwide for more than 60 years with widely accepted reliability and validity. The mean score of our participants is 37.5. According to the Wonderlic user's manual, the average score for high school graduates is about 18.7, and that for college graduates is around 25.8. The exceptionally high mean Wonderlic score of 37.5 confirmed our argument that GMA was well above average in this sample.

Life satisfaction

This was measured by nine items from the scale developed by A. Campbell, Converse, and Rodgers (1976). The first eight items of this scale are pairs of opposite adjectives (e.g., "interesting" versus "boring," "enjoyable" versus "miserable") with a 7-point Likert-type scale of numbers between them. Participants are requested to circle the number which best describes their feeling toward their lives. The last item is a direct question asking about the level of satisfaction in life, namely, "How satisfied or dissatisfied are you with your life as a whole?" The coefficient alpha of these items was .89 for this sample.

Control variables

We controlled four demographic variables: age, measured by the actual number of years; gender dummy (1 for male, 2 for female); education level (with 1 to 5 indicating degree from low to high: two-year college graduate, four-year university graduate, master, doctoral, and post-doctoral); and job tenure, measured by the number of years that an employee has been in his/her current position in the company.

Results

The means, standard deviations, and correlations among all the variables are presented in Table 6.1. Table 6.1 shows that most of the measures have acceptable reliability estimates. The mean scores on the four MSCEIT dimensions (84.94, 92.45, 82.41, and 77.58 for perceiving emotions, using emotions, understanding emotions, and managing emotions, respectively) of our sample are well below the figures provided by the publisher (mean score = 100). This confirms our argument that task-based EI tests may involve cultural biases when used in another culture. Despite the fact that our participants are highly educated, their scores are relatively low when compared to the norms of Western cultures. The first-order Pearson correlations also provided some preliminary evidence for this argument. Life satisfaction is significantly related to two dimensions of MSCEIT (r = .24 and .31, respectively, for using emotions and managing emotions) and two dimensions of WLEIS (r = .36 and .26, respectively, for regulation of emotion and use of emotion). For job performance, however, it is not related to any of the MSCEIT dimensions but is significantly related to two dimensions of WLEIS (r = .25 and .21, respectively, for other's emotional appraisal and regulation of emotion).

Before testing our hypotheses, we conducted a confirmatory factor analysis (CFA) on the WLEIS scale because the factor structure was known. The key fit indices from the CFA supported the four-factor model (comparative fit index [CFI] = .93; Tucker-Lewis Index [TLI] = .92; root mean square error approximation [RMSEA] = .07). The correlations among the four WLEIS dimensions were all moderate and significant (r ranged from .20 to .33) except one insignificant correlation between the dimensions of other's emotional appraisal and use of emotion (r = .16).

To test the incremental predictive validity of EI as measured by the MSCEIT and the WLEIS, we conducted hierarchical linear regression using job performance and life satisfaction as dependent variables. After entering the four control

Table 6.1 Descriptive statistics, reliability coefficients, and correlations

	Mean	S.D.	1	2	3	4	5	6	7	8	9	10	11	12	13	14
1. Age	27.14	4.00														
2. Gender	1.21	.41	.00													
3. Edu	2.81	.72	.25**	-.02												
4. Tenure	.87	1.24	.47**	-.07	-.11											
5. GMA	37.503	4.99	-.21*	-.01	.04	-.07										
6. M1	84.94	19.20	.06	.21*	-.04	.04	-.08	—								
7. M2	92.45	22.62	-.09	.02	-.00	-.14	-.00	.36**	—							
8. M3	82.41	17.13	-.10	-.10	.04	-.09	.22	.24*	.38**	—						
9. M4	77.58	16.63	-.15	.20	-.14	.02	.17	.31	.22	.12	—					
10. W1	5.46	.88	-.00	.10	.08	.08	-.01	-.05	.12	-.04	.16	(.82)				
11. W2	4.63	1.10	-.06	-.16	.12	-.04	-.04	-.19	-.10	-.09	.06	.33**	(.81)			
12. W3	5.40	1.04	-.22	.11	-.10	-.14	-.05	.08	.17	-.07	.32**	.32**	.29**	(.87)		
13. W4	4.86	.69	-.06	.09	.02	-.03	.10	.24*	.13	-.16	.39**	.20*	.16	.32**	(.89)	
14. LS	5.54	.86	.18	-.15	.10	.09	.01	.18	.24**	-.07	.31**	.10	.07	.36**	.26*	(.89)
15. JP	3.34	.82	.09	.11	.15	.15	-.10	-.15	-.13	-.01	-.05	.15	.25*	.21*	.00	.20

Notes

n = 102. Internal consistency reliability coefficients (alphas) appear on the diagonal. Edu = education level; GMA = general mental abilities; M1 = Mayer-Salovey-Caruso Emotional Intelligence Test (MSCEIT)_ perceiving emotions; M2 = MSCEIT_ using emotions; M3 = MSCEIT_understanding emotions; M4 = MSCEIT_managing emotions; W1 = Wong and Law Emotional Intelligence Scale (WLEIS)_ self emotional appraisal; W2 = WLEIS_other's emotional appraisal; W3 = WLEIS_regulation of emotion; W4 = WLEIS_use of emotion; LS = life satisfaction; JP = job performance.

*p < .05; **p < .01.

Table 6.2 Results of hierarchical multiple regression

Variable	Performance		Life Satisfaction	
	Model 1	Model 2	Model 3	Model 4
Age	.01	.07	−.17	−.13
Gender	.14	.14	.19+	.21
Education	.16	.13	−.04	−.05
Tenure	.05	.06	.06	.07
GMA	−.17	−.06	.01	−.03
MSCEIT				
Perceiving emotions	−.26		.02	
Using emotions	−.16		.32*	
Understanding emotions	.31+		−.47**	
Managing emotions	.15		.23	
WLEIS				
Self emotional appraisal		−.01		−.04
Other's emotional appraisal		.23*		.02
Regulation of emotion		.18		.27*
Use of emotion		−.09		.13
ΔR^2	.05	.10*	.09*	.10*
F change	1.28	2.59*	2.56*	3.00*
Adjusted model R^2	.01	.06	.10	.12

Notes
n = 102. GMA = general mental abilities; MSCEIT = Mayer-Salovey-Caruso Emotional Intelligence Test; WLEIS = Wong and Law Emotional Intelligence Scale.

$^+p < .10$; $^*p < .05$; $^{**}p < .01$.

variables and GMA as the first block, we entered the EI dimensions of each measure in the second step. Results for the regression analyses are shown in Table 6.2. After controlling for all the control variables and GMA, the WLEIS had incremental predictive validity on both job performance ($\Delta R^2 = .10$, p < .05) and life satisfaction ($\Delta R^2 = .10$, p < .05). However, the MSCEIT has incremental predictive validity only on life satisfaction ($\Delta R^2 = .09$, p < .05) and not on job performance ($\Delta R^2 = .05$, p > .05). These results provide support to both hypotheses 6.1 and 6.2.

Discussion

In the past decade and a half, we have observed a rapidly growing interest in EI both in the popular media and among researchers in psychology, sociology, education, and management areas. However, scientifically rigorous studies for the validation of the construct are still far from satisfactory. In comparison to other areas such as education and psychology, up until now there has been a regrettable lack of attention to the EI construct from organizational researchers. Fortunately, a series of studies have shown the construct validity of EI and its potential utility for management studies (e.g., Law, Wong, & Song, 2004; Mayer, Salovey, & Caruso, 2000b; Wong & Law, 2002). As one such effort in this underresearched area, this study contributes to the literature in two aspects. First, it demonstrated the incremental validity of EI on job performance over the effect of GMA. This finding has crucial meaning to organizational research because GMA has long been believed to be the best predictor of job performance. We drew Campbell et al.'s performance component model and did an in-depth analysis to show conceptually how EI and its four dimensions could be contributive to job performance beyond GMA. Second, by focusing on two recently developed EI measures, the task-based test MSCEIT and the self-report scale WLEIS, we discussed and compared these two types of EI measure. Theoretically, EI, as a set of abilities, should be best measured by an objective aptitude test. However, based on our analysis, we expect the WLEIS to be a better predictor for Chinese employees. In this regard, we found evidence for the incremental predictive validity of the WLEIS on job performance but not for the MSCEIT. The relatively low scores on the MSCEIT of our sample may be a demonstration of the potential problems of the application of the MSCEIT in non-Western countries.

Findings from this study have at least three implications. First, it provided evidence for the incremental validity of EI on job performance, which added to our knowledge on the importance of EI in the workplace. As Schmidt and Hunter (1998) said, the incremental validity "translates into incremental utility, that is, into increases in practical value" (p. 266). Personnel psychologists held that when any other personnel measures, such as an integrity test or conscientiousness test, were used, one question must be asked, "How much will each of these measures increase predictive validity for job performance over the .51 that can be obtained by using only GMA?" (Schmidt & Hunter, 1998, p. 266) Result from this study demonstrated that on top of GMA, EI still accounts for about 10% of the overall job performance.

Second, this study further confirmed some recent work (see, e.g., Davies et al., 1998; Wong & Law, 2002) in defining EI as a four-dimensional construct and viewing EI as an overall ability or a set of interrelated abilities. We therefore suggest EI researchers use this definition in future EI research. Third, with a comparison between the task-based and self-report measures of EI, we see that there are pros and cons for both types of measures. The self-report EI measure, when designed properly, may still play an important role in EI research. However, we do not mean to downplay the importance of task-based EI measures. Instead, we believe EI should be best measured by task-based tests provided they can be modified and adjusted across cultures. Further efforts in this direction should be encouraged.

As one of the efforts in this emerging field, we realize several limitations of our study. First, our study was conducted in one company without diverse job types in the sample. This may limit the generalizability of the results. However, we chose this design because it involved fewer confounding factors, so that performance was more comparable. Another advantage is that we have the objectively based overall job performance appraisal from the company, with variations in GMA controlled for this type of job. This may be the reason that, in our study, GMA is not a significant predictor of job performance. Second, although the objective measure of job performance has avoided the problem of common method variance, this is still a problem for life satisfaction. However, the predictive power of EI on these two variables is consistent with previous findings using different sources of information (e.g., Law, Wong, & Song, 2004). Thus, common method variance may not be a serious problem here. Finally, both of the two EI measures we chose were newly developed. While there is some previous evidence for the WLEIS and our results are consistent with them, there is almost no empirical evidence for the MSCEIT for us to compare our findings to. Future research on the reliability, validity, and generalizability of the MSCEIT may be worthwhile.

It is somewhat ironic that given its overwhelming popularity in the mass media, EI seems to be losing its attractiveness as a solid construct in the academic arena. It is encouraging that scholars have accumulated encouraging evidence about the potential contribution to management research when EI is properly defined and measured. With these efforts toward a generally accepted EI construct, future research would have promising chances to investigate its relationship with many other well-established constructs in organizational research.

7 Emotional intelligence and human performance

After conducting the studies reported in the preceding chapters, I was comfortable accepting the conclusion that emotional intelligence (EI) should be related to job outcomes. Although the Mayer-Salovey-Caruso Emotional Intelligence Test (MSCEIT) did not predict the job performance of the scientist sample reported in Chapter 6, a self-report EI measure (i.e., the Wong and Law Emotional Intelligence Scale [WLEIS]) was found to be related to the performance of the Chinese scientists. Together with other samples we had investigated, evidence indicated that EI was related to job performance, in particular for jobs with high emotional labor requirements. Actually, this conclusion is now accepted by most researchers in the management area.

One important issue in studying the effect of EI on performance is its distinctiveness and incremental value over the traditional intelligence concept, i.e., general mental abilities (GMA, or IQ as referred by the popular media). If GMA is highly correlated with EI or EI does not have incremental validity over important criterion variables, it may not be worthwhile to study EI. Although we had come up with a preliminary model which explained the different roles of GMA and EI in human performance, the evidence we gathered had one important limitation. In most of the samples we studied, we used only a proxy measure of GMA in our analyses. For example, we used the university entrance examination results for university student samples and education level for employee samples.

For the Chinese scientist sample, we used a popular and widely accepted GMA test. Unfortunately, the respondents of this sample had an extremely high GMA level because of the entrance requirement of their job. All the respondents had to have excellent academic achievements before they could be hired for the research and development job. With relatively small variance among the respondents, it was difficult to examine the actual incremental predictive power of EI on performance. This was an issue that had been on my mind, and I tried to look for chances to better demonstrate the distinctiveness and incremental validity of EI when compared to GMA.

Lesson 16: the importance of keeping records of research ideas

This research issue had been on my mind for several years. In fact, I kept a file for my investigation on the EI construct and wrote down my ideas whenever they came up. From time to time, I reviewed those ideas and examined whether they were still worthwhile to be kept in my file. This issue had been in my file for several years, and every time I looked at it, I still thought it was worthwhile and tried to imagine how this could be done. One obvious difficulty was that we needed a convincing GMA test. As GMA tests usually involve a time limit, we would need a research setting that would allow us to get the respondents to sit down together while we administered the test. This type of research opportunity might not come up so frequently.

I finally got a chance to design a study to test this research idea. We were allowed to collect data from a university student sample from mainland China because of the connection of a former doctoral student. The strength of this sample was that we could survey the focal students as well as two of their roommates in their dormitory. Also, we could ask the focal student to take a well-established GMA test because the university also welcomed such a record. The weakness of this sample was that it was a student rather than an employee sample.

Considering both the strength and the weakness of the sample, I decided to go ahead with the investigation, but I did not target it as a business management study. I believed it was still very worthwhile because I could focus on different types of human performance instead of job performance only. An obvious type of performance for university students would be their academic results (i.e., grade point average [GPA]). We would have no problem getting this information because of the support from the university and the respondents. According to our performance model, GPA should be more related to GMA and less related to EI.

As we could survey the roommates of the focal students, we could ask for indicators of performance in social interactions. For example, we could ask the extent to which the focal students were liked by their roommates. Liking by roommates should be more related to EI but less related to GMA. Thus, we were able to come up with a research design that could investigate the incremental validity of EI on different types of human performance. We therefore went ahead with collecting data from this research setting.

Lesson 16: Keeping a good record of research ideas and reviewing them from time to time may be a helpful practice. This is especially true for projects that can form a line of research. This can minimize the chance that we will miss an opportunity when it arises.

Lesson 17: another study for a revision?

After collecting and analyzing data from the sample, we came up with a draft paper. We found incremental validity of EI for both academic performance and peer liking over GMA. As expected, GMA had no relationship with peer liking. However, the overall explanatory power of EI and other factors on peer liking was quite small. When we submitted the paper to a journal, the editor and reviewers showed strong concern for this point and questioned whether peer liking was a good indicator of performance in social interactions. They commented that as the impact of EI on performance in social interactions was a core contribution of this paper, they believed we needed another sample to show greater effect if the paper was to be published.

This is a common dilemma that researchers might face during the submission and review process. As it is almost impossible to have perfect data in social science studies, we usually encounter limitations and weaknesses in the results of our empirical studies. A usual reaction from inexperienced researchers is that we can respond to the weakness by collecting another dataset so that we can demonstrate our original expectations more directly. As we get more experience in data collection and analysis, we will gradually notice that every empirical study and dataset has weaknesses. Trying to demonstrate our points with a new dataset will be quite risky and may not work in the way we want.

Thus, when the editor and reviewers ask for another dataset, we need to be very careful because it means a completely new study. Simply repeating the study and hoping that the results will be better may not be a good approach. We have to evaluate carefully why the editor and reviewers are asking for a new dataset. If we promise to get another dataset, we should be prepared that it will not be a simple replication with more measures. We need to design the study in a way that the new dataset will be complementary to the original dataset.

After discussing this with my co-authors at that time, I believed the request of the editor and reviewers was reasonable. The relatively small effect in the original study was due to a lot of factors contributing to peer liking other than EI. In order to show the impact of EI on social performance, we needed to be more focused so that other factors would play a minor role. In other words, we needed stronger controls in the new study in order to show the impact of EI on social performance. To achieve this objective, we decided to create a situation where respondents had to interact with each other. We then measured their evaluation of their partners' social performance in that particular situation. To further simplify the situation, we used a negotiation exercise which involved only two people. Although the situation was simple, the negotiation context would require the participants to utilize various types of social skills such as providing emotional support and managing conflict.

With a rough idea for the design of the new study, I was confident that we could conduct this alternative study that would be complementary to the original study within one year. This could enhance the contribution of our paper if we framed the alternative study as the second study of the paper. We therefore asked for a one-year period to conduct a new study and prepare the revision. The editor agreed to give us a year to revise the paper.

Lesson 17: To deal with weaknesses in an empirical study, it is very tempting to conduct another empirical study. However, in so doing, we must be careful about the value of the new study. It is preferable to have a new study that is complementary to the original study instead of a mere replication with more variables being measured. When a new study is required by the editor and reviewers, we need to review carefully the reasons for such a request and the possibility of a study design that would provide stronger evidence.

Lesson 18: flexibility in the execution of the study

When I asked for a year to revise the paper, I believed that would be more than enough. Because I and my co-authors were teachers in universities, it would not be difficult for us to invite our students to participate in the negotiation exercise. Our plan was to incorporate the study into the courses we were going to teach because negotiation is a topic that needs to be covered in organizational behavior and human resource management courses.

Despite the study's apparent simplicity, we still encountered unexpected difficulties. The first came from our teaching assignments that year. Originally I and my co-authors were supposed to teach several organizational behavior and human resource management classes, and so it would have been easy for us to select some classes for the study. Unfortunately, the number of related undergraduate classes we were assigned to teach that year was smaller than we expected. I was assigned to teach some master's-level classes instead. Although it would be appropriate to conduct the study in the master's-level classes, I did not want to include them because I wanted to be consistent with the sample characteristics of the first study.

To cope with this difficulty, we decided to change our plan of collecting data only in one university. The final sample therefore included classes from two universities. The adjustment we had to make was to use a standardized score for the academic performance because grading standards might not be the same across universities. Fortunately, this should not be a major concern and would not be a threat to our data analysis and conclusions.

The second difficulty was the timing of the teaching assignments. Our original plan was to complete the study in one semester so that we would have plenty of time to analyze the data and draft the revision. Unfortunately, it turned out that we could complete the data collection only after two semesters if we wanted a large enough sample size. We made some adjustments in our work schedule to accommodate this change.

The third unexpected issue was that we made a careless mistake in one class. In turning in the write-ups for the study, student participants in one class did not put down their student identification number on the first set of their responses used to calculate their GMA. As we could not match the GMA with other variables, we could not use data from this class. Fortunately, the sample size from the other three classes was over 100, which was sufficient to conduct the analyses we needed. As the results were consistent with our expectations, we did not need to collect more data and could write up the revision.

Lesson 18: In executing a study, we have to be flexible because unexpected issues will come up. It is always nice to have contingency plan during the data collection period.

In preparing the revision, we discussed why the first study found a smaller effect of EI on peer liking than expected. Then we presented the sample, procedure, and results of the second study. The editor and reviewers were satisfied with our revision and asked for only minor amendments before the paper was formally accepted.

The following are the major contents of the paper.

Song, L. J., Huang, G. H., Peng, K. Z., Law, K. S., Wong, C. S., & Chen, Z. (2010). Differential effects of general mental ability and emotional intelligence on academic performance and social interactions. *Intelligence*, **38**, 137–143; these contents are reprinted with permission.

Abstract. This study considers the debate about whether emotional intelligence (EI) has incremental validity over and above traditional intelligence dimensions. We propose that EI and general mental abilities (GMA) differ in predicting academic performance and the quality of social interactions among college students. Using two college student samples, we find support for the notion that EI and GMA each have a unique power to predict academic performance and that GMA is the stronger predictor. However, the results also show that EI, but not GMA, is related to the quality of social interactions with peers. The theoretical contributions and implications of the study and some recommendations for future studies are discussed.

Over the past two decades, the construct of emotional intelligence (EI) has received much research attention, but it has also been one of the most controversial concepts in both the lay and academic fields of psychology and management (Mayer, Salovey, & Caruso, 2000b). The debate on EI has focused on its nature and validity as a psychological construct, and one of the most contentious issues is whether it should be classified as one of the facets of "intelligence" (e.g., Mayer, Caruso, & Salovey, 2000a; Roberts, Zeidner, & Matthews, 2001). If EI is "intelligence" in nature, then the next crucial question is whether it has incremental validity over and above traditional intelligence dimensions.

In this study, we have sought to provide some answers to the second question because there is limited empirical evidence reported in the literature. By adopting the widely accepted definition of EI as "the ability to perceive accurately, appraise, and express emotion; the ability to access and/or generate feelings when they facilitate thought; the ability to understand emotion and emotional knowledge; and the ability to regulate emotions to promote emotional and intellectual growth" (Mayer & Salovey, 1997, p. 10), we test whether EI has incremental validity over general mental abilities (GMA) in predicting academic performance and the quality of social interactions of students over and beyond GMA.

We organize this paper as follows. We begin with a discussion of the theoretical reasons for the differences between EI and GMA in predicting the academic performance of students and the quality of their social interactions, and then we develop some hypotheses. We then describe two studies that we conducted to test the hypotheses on the incremental predictive validity of EI. Finally, we discuss the contributions and limitations of the study as a whole.

EI, GMA, academic performance, and social interactions

GMA, which is also known as general cognitive ability, general intelligence, or the *g*-factor, is a well-researched construct with impressive supporting evidence for its capacity to predict important outcomes such as job performance and career success across jobs, settings, and careers (e.g., Ferris, Witt, & Hochwarter, 2001; O'Reilly & Chatman, 1994). In their review of 85 years of research findings on the validity of selection methods in personnel psychology, Schmidt and Hunter (1998) confirmed that the evidence of the validity of GMA measures in predicting job performance is stronger than for any other method. Other researchers have concluded that *g* is "the single most useful worker attribute for predicting job performance, as a valid predictor in all types of jobs" (Gottfredson, 1986, p. 380). As *g* is closely related to learning abilities, there is also relatively strong evidence of its predictive power on students' academic performance (e.g., Petrides, Frederickson, & Furnham, 2004).

Although it is clear that GMA is a valid and important predictor of human performance, we echo the recent view that there remains a large amount of variance in performance that can only be explained by other factors (e.g., Gardner, 1993; Mayer & Salovey, 1997). EI is a possible factor that may make an incremental contribution in predicting performance over and above GMA. First of all, most human performance models argue that in addition to analytic and reasoning abilities and specific knowledge, abilities that are related to social interactions are also important determinants of performance (e.g., J. P. Campbell, 1990; J. P. Campbell, McCloy, Oppler, & Sager, 1993). However, GMA predicts job performance across jobs and settings primarily by predicting learning and the acquisition of job knowledge, rather than by predicting the quality of social interactions (Kuncel, Hezlett, & Ones, 2004; Schmidt & Hunter, 1993; Schmidt, Hunter, & Outerbridge, 1986).

Second, there is evidence that different components and mechanisms of the brain may be involved in cognitive abilities and emotional abilities related to social interactions (Hilgard, 1980; Mayer & Salovey, 1997). Neuroscientists are gradually discovering the biological and physiological details of human emotions. For example, the amygdala, which is a primitive system in the brain, has been found to act as an emotional sentinel, without which humans are unable to gauge the emotional significance of events (Ekman & Davidson, 1994). This indicates that specific brain systems have evolved to handle emotionally significant stimuli. For the students to perform well academically, they need both cognitive abilities, such as language and reasoning, and emotional abilities, such as the ability to stay calm before and during examinations. Thus, both GMA and EI should have unique effects on academic performance. In this study, our focus is on the effect of EI, and we therefore propose the following hypothesis.

Hypothesis 7.1: EI has an incremental power to predict academic performance above and beyond the effect of GMA.

Furthermore, as EI is more closely related to social interactions, we expect it to have a much greater effect than GMA on the part of student performance that is related to social interactions. There is some preliminary evidence in the literature to support this argument. For example, Lopes, Salovey, Côté, and Beers (2005) found that the ability to regulate emotions, as measured by a test of EI, was able to explain the quality of individuals' social interactions with their peers and that the explanatory power of EI was above and beyond that of the Big Five personality traits and verbal and fluid intelligence. However, Lopes et al. used only one facet of EI, emotional regulation abilities, and did not investigate overall EI. In a school setting, one of the most important types of social interaction among students is that which occurs with their peers, which leads us to hypothesize the following:

Hypothesis 7.2: EI has an incremental power to predict the quality of the social interactions of students with their peers above and beyond the effect of GMA.

Study 7.1

Sample and procedure

Through the student counseling office, we approached 506 freshman and sophomore undergraduate students residing in the dormitory of a large university in Shanghai, China. The students voluntarily participated in a test that measured their GMA and afterward completed a questionnaire measuring the Big Five personality dimensions and demographic variables. After completing the questionnaire, the student participants were asked to take two questionnaires to two of their roommates. One of the roommates was asked to evaluate the degree to which they liked the focal student participant, and the other was asked to evaluate the EI of the student participant. The two roommates were asked to complete the questionnaires and send them back to the researchers directly. All participants were assured of the confidentiality of their responses. As some of the roommates did not return their questionnaires, the final sample size was 222. The mean age of the participants was 21, and 53% were male. We obtained details of the participants' academic performance from the university three months after the survey.

Variables and measures

EI

The 16-item Wong and Law Emotional Intelligence Scale (WLEIS; Wong & Law, 2002) was used by one set of roommates to evaluate the EI level of the focal student participants.

GMA

We measured GMA using the English version of the Wonderlic Personnel Test (Wonderlic Inc., 1999). This test has been used worldwide for more than 60 years and has widely accepted reliability and validity (Geisinger, 2001; Pesta & Poznanski, 2008). According to the Wonderlic user's manual, the average score for high school graduates is about 18.7 and that for college graduates is around 25.8. The mean score of our sample was 20.6 with a standard deviation of 6.6.

Academic performance

The formal GPA of the students was used to represent their academic performance. In the university from which the sample was taken, a scale of 0 to 100 was used to represent the students' overall academic performance.

Peer liking

In this study, we used peer liking as an indicator of the quality of the social interaction of the participants. We asked each selected peer about the extent to which they liked the focal student. This was measured by the four-item Liking for Subordinates Scale developed by Wayne and Ferris (1990). We adopted a systematic translation and back-translation procedure (Brislin, 1970) for this scale. We then adjusted the wording of the items so that they could be used for students' ratings of their liking for a peer. A sample item was "I like this roommate very much." The ratings were given on a 7-point Likert-type scale. The coefficient alpha for the sample was .92.

Personality traits

There is evidence suggesting that EI is related to but distinct from the Big Five personality traits (Law, Wong, & Song, 2004). We therefore controlled for the Big Five traits of personality, as measured by the 80-item adjective scale developed by McCrae and Costa (1987). The coefficient alphas of the five dimensions (neuroticism, extraversion, openness, agreeableness, and conscientiousness) in this study ranged from .87 to .92. Law, Wong, and Song (2004) used this scale in the Chinese context.

Demographic variables

We controlled for three demographic variables: age, gender, and the hometown of the students. Age was measured by the actual number of years of age. We controlled age because it may influence the GMA and EI level, according to the developmental criterion of intelligence (Mayer, Caruso, et al., 2000a). Gender was treated as a dummy variable (1 for male, 2 for female). The hometown variable indicated whether or not the participants came from the Shanghai area (0 for students from Shanghai, 1 for students from other areas). This may be an important variable because of the university admissions policy in China, in which a greater quota of university places is apportioned to students from the local area.

Results

The descriptive statistics, correlations, and coefficient alphas are shown in Table 7.1. The results show that most of the measures had acceptable reliability estimates. The EI scores did not correlate strongly with the Big Five personality traits, suggesting that, unlike other measures of EI, the WLEIS is only weakly related to personality. The relationships between GMA and EI and the outcome variables were as expected.

To test the incremental effect of EI over GMA on the two dependent variables, we ran two hierarchical regressions. In the first and second steps of these regressions, we added the demographic variables and the Big Five personality dimensions, respectively. In the next step, we added GMA, and then we added the EI scores in the final step. The results are shown in Table 7.2. GMA has a significant effect on academic performance ($\beta = .27$, $p < .01$) but no effect on peer-rated liking ($\beta = .01$, n.s.). EI has an incremental power to predict academic

Table 7.1 Descriptive statistics, reliability coefficients, and correlations for Study 7.1

	Mean	S.D.	1	2	3	4	5	6	7	8	9	10	11	12
1. Age	21.30	1.00	—											
2. Gender (1 = male)	1.47	.50	-.10*	—										
3. Local (0 = local)	.47	.50	.06	.20**	—									
4. NEURO	3.32	.93	-.08	.03	.03	(.87)								
5. OPEN	4.75	.96	.02	-.04	-.06	-.21**	(.87)							
6. EXTRA	4.47	.91	-.06	.09	-.08	.04	.44**	(.88)						
7. AGREE	5.30	.73	.01	.13*	-.13*	-.34**	.39**	.37**	(.89)					
8. CONSC	5.38	.78	.07	.04	-.12*	-.43**	.30**	.14**	.57**	(.92)				
9. GMA	20.63	6.55	-.12	.27**	.16*	.03	-.07	-.05	-.05	.01				
10. WLEIS	3.52	.61	-.01	.00	.01	-.15*	.03	-.09	.04	.13*	.14*	(.89)		
11. GPA	78.47	5.69	-.34**	.40**	.08	.06	-.13*	-.03	.08	.18**	.41**	.22**	—	
12. Peer liking	3.86	.88	-.07	.05	.02	.09	-.03	-.01	.07	-.06	.03	.12*	.14**	(.92)

Notes

n = 222. The internal consistency reliability coefficients (alphas) appear on the diagonal. NEURO = neuroticism; OPEN = openness; EXTRA = extraversion; AGREE= agreeableness; CONSC = conscientiousness; GMA = general mental abilities; WLEIS = Wong and Law Emotional Intelligence Scale; GPA = grade point average.

*p < .05; **p < .01.

Table 7.2 Results of the hierarchical multiple regression for Study 7.1

Independent Variables	DV = GPA		DV = Liking	
	Model 1	Model 2	Model 1	Model 2
Age	−.29**	−.29**	−.05	−.05
Gender	.28**	.29**	.01	.02
Local	.02	.02	.02	.02
NEURO	.11	.13*	.11	.13
OPEN	−.13*	−.14*	−.02	−.02
EXTRA	−.05	−.03	−.07	−.06
AGREE	.01	.01	.20*	.21*
CONSC	.28**	.26**	−.11	−.12
GMA	.27**	.25**	.02	−.01
WLEIS		.17**		.15*
ΔR^2	.07**	.03**	.00	.02*
F change	23.83**	9.66**	.06	4.56*
R^2	.40**	.43**	.04	.06
Adjusted model R^2	.38**	.40**	.00	.01

Notes
n = 222. ΔR^2 of Model 1 is compared with the model in which GMA is not included as an independent variable. The coefficients reported are beta values. DV = dependent variable; NEURO = neuroticism; OPEN = openness; EXTRA = extraversion; AGREE= agreeableness; CONSC = conscientiousness; GMA = general mental abilities; WLEIS = Wong and Law Emotional Intelligence Scale.

*$p < .05$; **$p < .01$.

performance after controlling for GMA and several other variables ($\beta = .17$, $\Delta R^2 = .03$, $p < .01$). Hypothesis 7.1 is thus supported. EI also has an effect on peer liking after controlling for GMA and several other variables ($\beta = .15$, $\Delta R^2 = .02$, $p < .05$). Hypothesis 7.2 is thus supported.

Supplementary analyses showed that GMA has some power to predict academic performance after controlling for EI. That is, GMA explains some of the variance in academic performance that cannot be explained by EI. This strengthens the argument that GMA and EI make unique contributions in explaining academic performance.

Study 7.2

Purpose

In Study 7.1, we used peer liking as the indicator of the quality of social interactions. However, as our participants had been dormitory mates for almost a year, factors other than EI may have strongly influenced their peer-liking ratings. The small amount of variance in peer liking explained by EI in Study 7.1 may be an indicator of this problem, and thus the evidence from Study 7.1 in support of hypothesis 7.2

is quite weak and may not be convincing. To create a stronger test of hypothesis 7.2, it appears necessary to have better control over other factors affecting the quality of social interactions between the student participants, and it was with this purpose in mind that we designed Study 7.2. In Study 7.2, we randomly paired college students who were not familiar with each other to perform a task in a negotiation context, reasoning that the quality of the social interaction would be well reflected in the partner's evaluation after the interactive negotiation task.

Sample and procedure

We invited business students from two major universities in China, 35 from Beijing and 89 from Hong Kong, to participate in the study. All of the students were taking a human resource management course. Among the participants, 60.5% were female. The study involved the following steps. First, we administered the Eysenck IQ test (Eysenck, 1994), which took 30 minutes. Second, the participants completed a questionnaire that evaluated their EI, positive affectivity, and personality, which took about 20 minutes. Third, the students were randomly assigned into pairs. Fourth, they spent 10 minutes reading the description of the negotiation task, which was modified from the Ugli orange exercise (Hall, Bowen, Lewicki, & Hall, 1975). In the exercise, the students had to convince their opponents to give up bidding for the Ugli orange, which was in limited supply, because they needed the oranges themselves to save thousands of lives. However, the truth was that one of the students in the pair needed the juice, whereas the other needed the rind. If they were able to discover this, then they could cooperate rather than compete. If they could not discover this, then they were obliged to go on bidding, and only one of them obtained the oranges. Fifth, the students carried out the negotiation task for 20 minutes. Sixth, after the negotiation task, the students completed a two-page evaluation of the negotiation results and of their perception of their negotiation partner. Finally, we held a debriefing session for the students.

Variables and measures

EI

The 16-item WLEIS was used by each participant to evaluate their own EI level. The coefficient alphas for the four dimensions and the total scale were .87, .78, .70, .90, and .81, respectively.

GMA

We measured the GMA of the students using the English version of the Eysenck IQ Test (Eysenck, 1994). This test provides culture-fair items that do not require much previous knowledge or a specific cultural background (Eysenck, 1994, 2006).

Academic performance

The students' grades for the human resource management course were used to indicate their academic performance, and they were collected after the end of the semester in which the study was conducted. As the students were from three classes at two universities, we calculated the standardized Z-scores to represent their academic performance.

Quality of social interactions

Interpersonal competence is a concept that is often subsumed in functional adaptation (Cohen, 2003), and we thus used it as an indicator of the quality of social interactions. According to Semple et al. (1999), interpersonal competence refers to "the individual's ability or capacity to solve life problems and to achieve effective human interactions" (p. 127). Buhrmester, Furman, Wittenberg, and Reis (1988) came up with an Interpersonal Competence Questionnaire and identified five domains of interpersonal competence that include initiation of social interaction, negative assertion, disclosure, emotional support, and conflict management. Among these domains, emotional support and conflict management are the most relevant to assessing interpersonal competence in dealing with the conflicts and emotions involved in negotiation. The items on both of these scales are appropriate for ratings by others. A sample item in the emotional support scale is "Being able to show genuine empathetic concern even when a companion's problem is uninteresting to you." A sample item in the conflict management scale is "Being able to work through a specific problem with a companion without resorting to global accusations." We adopted a systematic translation and back-translation procedure (Brislin, 1970) to render the scales appropriate for use in a Chinese context.

Control variables

We controlled for personality traits, positive affectivity, and success in negotiation. The Big Five personality traits were measured using the same 80-item scale as in Study 7.1. The coefficient alphas of the five dimensions in Study 7.2 ranged from .83 to .92. Positive affectivity was measured by the 10-item scale of Watson and Clark (1988), and it achieved a coefficient alpha of .79 for the sample. We included this as a control variable, because students may give different evaluations of their negotiation opponents simply because they differ in mood. As for success in negotiation, the negotiation materials were designed in such a way that the two parties were not actually in conflict. Thus, the success of the negotiation was reflected by whether the pair of students reached this "no-conflict" situation. We coded success in finding out that there was no real conflict as 1 and not being able to detect that as 0. This needs to be controlled because the students may have evaluated their opponents more favorably when the end result was good. We also tried to control for age and gender but found no significant differences in the results and conclusions. For simplicity's sake, we do not include these control variables in reporting the results.

Results

The descriptive statistics and correlations are presented in Table 7.3. The results show that EI was positively related to academic performance (course grade;

Table 7.3 Descriptive statistics, reliability coefficients, and correlations for Study 7.2

	Mean	S.D.	1	2	3	4	5	6	7	8	9	10	11	12
1. NEURO	3.65	.88	(.83)											
2. OPEN	4.40	.99	-.20*	(.89)										
3. EXTRA	4.31	.88	-.04	.41**	(.86)									
4. AGREE	4.88	.71	-.47**	.25**	.23**	(.87)								
5. CONSC	4.84	.82	-.48**	.15+	.16+	.42**	(.92)							
6. Positive affectivity	3.37	.56	-.28**	.26**	.38**	.12	.42**	(.79)						
7. Result of negotiation	.51	.50	.02	-.02	-.05	-.06	.06	.09	1.00					
8. GMA	16.96	4.63	-.03	.18*	.02	-.02	.11	.24**	.00	1.00				
9. WLEIS	3.58	.46	-.45**	.40**	.16+	.29**	.55**	.39***	-.01	.15+	(.81)			
10. Z-score: course grade	.00	.99	-.19*	.00	-.01	.09	.31**	.28**	.02	.22*	.31**	1.00		
11. Emotional support	3.70	.49	-.11	.10	.26**	.04	.13	.16+	.15	.11	.22*	-.00	(.85)	
12. Conflict management	3.71	.52	-.10	.07	.15+	.05	.24**	.11	.20*	.11	.26**	.02	.72**	(.86)

Notes

n ranges from 118 to 124. The internal consistency reliability coefficients (alphas) appear on the diagonal. NEURO = neuroticism; OPEN = openness; EXTRA = extraversion; AGREE = agreeableness; CONSC = conscientiousness; GMA = general mental abilities; WLEIS = Wong and Law Emotional Intelligence Scale.

+p < .10; *p < .05; **p < .01.

$r = .31, p < .01$), and it was significantly correlated with the partner's evaluation of social interactions, including interpersonal support and conflict management ($r = .22, p < .05$, and $r = .26, p < .01$, respectively). These results are consistent with our predictions.

We used hierarchical regression analysis to test our hypotheses, and we present the results in Table 7.4. We entered the Big Five personality traits and GMA as control variables in the first block. We then entered EI in the second block. Model 2 shows that EI has an incremental power to predict academic performance after controlling for GMA and several other variables ($\beta = .24, \Delta R^2 = .03, p < .05$). Hypothesis 7.1 is thus supported. Model 4 shows that EI is a marginally significant predictor of emotional support after controlling for GMA and several other variables ($\beta = .23, \Delta R^2 = .03, p < .10$). Model 6 shows that

Table 7.4 Results of the hierarchical multiple regression for Study 7.2

Independent Variables	DV = Z-score: Course Grade		DV = Emotional Support		DV = Conflict Management	
	Model 1	Model2	Model 3	Model 4	Model5	Model6
NEURO	−.08	−.03	−.12	−.08	−.04	.00
OPEN	−.08	−.15	−.04	−.11	−.02	−.09
EXTRA	−.02	−.01	.30**	.32**	.18	.20⁺
AGREE	−.03	−.02	−.08	−.08	−.09	−.08
CONSC	.28**	.17	.06	−.03	.25*	.16
Positive affectivity			−.03	−.06	−.10	−.13
GMA	.20*	.19*	.11	.10	.10	.10
Negotiation result			.16⁺	.17⁺	.20*	.21*
WLEIS		.24*		.23⁺		.24*
ΔR²	.14**	.03*	.12⁺	.03⁺	.13⁺	.03*
F change	3.07**	4.56*	1.78⁺	3.64⁺	1.90⁺	4.06*
R²	.14**	.17**	.12⁺	.15*	.13⁺	.16*
Adjusted model R²	.10**	.12**	.05⁺	.08*	.06⁺	.09*

Notes
n = 124. The coefficients reported are beta values. DV = dependent variable; NEURO = neuroticism; OPEN = openness; EXTRA = extraversion; AGREE = agreeableness; CONSC = conscientiousness; GMA = general mental abilities; WLEIS = Wong and Law Emotional Intelligence Scale.

⁺p < .10; *p < .05; **p < .01.

EI has an incremental power to predict conflict management after controlling for GMA and several other variables (β = .24, ΔR^2 = .03, p < .05). Hypothesis 7.2 is thus also supported.

Discussion

Over the past decade or so, we have observed a rapidly growing interest in EI both in the popular media and among researchers in various areas. However, the validity of EI as a psychological construct is still far from established. There is limited evidence concerning its incremental contribution over and above traditional cognitive intelligence in explaining human performance. In this study, we attempt to provide some evidence for the incremental contribution of EI in predicting students' academic and social performance. Our findings show that EI has a unique power to predict the academic performance of students and the quality of their social interactions with peers, after controlling for GMA and personality traits.

Despite its contribution of providing empirical evidence about the incremental validity of EI, this study has three limitations that should be noted and overcome in future research. First, in Study 7.1, we found very small effects for all of the independent variables on peer liking. Although Study 7.2 provides stronger support for the effect of EI on the quality of social interactions, its conclusions may not be generalizable to other social situations because we created a nego-tiation task for students who were not familiar with each other. Future research could attempt to investigate additional indicators of the quality of social interac-tions in a variety of social situations to overcome this problem.

Second, our samples are composed of university students, whose GMA and probably EI may be higher than those of the overall student population, which includes high school students who cannot get into universities. This range restriction may have lowered the correlations and subsequent effects of GMA and EI on the dependent variables. When this is applied to other student samples, such as primary and secondary students, the effects of GMA and EI may even be larger, and it may be worthwhile for future research to investigate this possibility.

Third, the samples used in the two studies were composed of Chinese college students. Although there is no evidence to show that the EI construct and its effects are culturally bound, it may be worthwhile for future research to use more diverse samples to strengthen the generalizability of our findings. For example, the question of whether EI will become more or less important if the interacting partner is from another culture is an interesting topic for future study.

To conclude, we have found support that EI has a unique power to predict the academic performance of college students and the quality of their social interactions with peers. We call for further validation of the construct, particularly the differing effects of EI and other traditional intelligence dimensions as pro-posed in this study.

8   Emotional intelligence training

After gathering evidence about the validity of emotional intelligence (EI) that made me feel more comfortable studying the construct further, I began to think about other possible implications of EI. One obvious question is whether the level of EI can be raised by training. This is also very relevant to the area of human resource management. On top of selecting people with adequate abilities, a common approach in human resource management is to train the employees so that they can develop the necessary abilities. To me, this is a very logical question to answer. If EI is trainable, it has greater value to my area of expertise.

It is difficult to enhance general mental abilities (GMA) by training. This is our general understanding about this traditional intelligence dimension. Although the trainability of GMA may be debatable, it is quite clear that we do not have good training programs to enhance the GMA level of adults.

EI may be different from GMA in its trainability. EI represents how well we handle issues related to emotions. From my own experience, I believe my ability to handle emotions has gradually been improving since I was a teenager. Two factors are important. The first factor is the introspection teaching by Confucius. As a native Chinese, I was educated through informal means to review my own mistakes and to try not to commit those mistakes again ever since I was a child. This is regarded as what a wise person should do. Negative emotions are not comfortable. We usually would regret it if we did not handle them adequately. Through reviewing our regrets and mistakes, we could learn how to handle them better in the future.

The second important factor is the chance to learn. We will gain little if we lack chances to handle issues related to emotions. Life experiences provide such chances. I believe my improving ability to handle issues related to emotions is probably due to the fact that I need to face emotional situations from time to time. Another type of chances is the observation of other people. If they handle emotions nicely, we can learn from them. If they do not handle emotions adequately, we can also remind ourselves not to commit similar mistakes. Thus, if we can incorporate these types of life experiences into a training program, conceptually EI should be trainable. I therefore believe it is worthwhile to gather evidence to show that EI is trainable.

Lesson 19: exchanging ideas with colleagues

Although I believe EI should be trainable, I have doubts about the traditional way of conducting research on training. Usually, we need to use experiments to show the effectiveness of a training program. Specifically, we need two groups of participants. The best way is to randomly assign participants to the two groups. If random assignment is not possible, we need to provide good evidence that the two groups are comparable. Then one group (usually referred to as the experimental group) will go through the training program, and the other group (usually referred to as the control group) will not receive training. Both before and after the training, all participants are assessed for the attitude or ability that the training program is targeted to enhance. If the control group shows no improvement while the training group shows improvement in the intended attitude or ability, then we can conclude that the training program is effective.

I was not sure whether the above research design was suitable to show the trainability of EI at that time. This was because I had little idea about the contents of an effective EI training program. As EI was a popular concept, some EI training programs were offered by consultants both for employees in business organizations and for students in primary and secondary schools. Although my review was not comprehensive, I tried my best to gather information about the contents of some of these training programs. I found out that most of them were about explanation of the EI construct and awareness of emotions. Most of the evidence for the training's effectiveness was simply the satisfaction of the participants with the training programs after they had attended them. Thus, I did not find rigorously designed EI training programs and convincing evidence of the effectiveness of those training programs.

On top of lacking evidence for training effectiveness, I had doubts about the possibility of training EI in a short period of time such as a one- or two-day workshop. My own experiences indicated to me that introspection based on a lot of situations involving emotional issues had gradually improved my ability to behave adequately in similar situations. This could not happen in a short period of time. Thus, my speculation was that an effective EI training program would involve the presentation of many real-life experiences, practice in role-playing exercises, detailed analyses of different situations from different perspectives, and so forth. Without a reasonable training program, it may not be very appropriate to use the traditional research design to show the effectiveness of an EI training program.

Another important issue was that we did not have a very convincing EI measure at that time. Without a widely accepted EI measure, a research design that depended on the comparison of EI scores might not provide good evidence of the effectiveness of EI training programs. Instead of designing an EI training program, I believed it would be more appropriate to study whether EI was trainable first.

Lesson 19: Although there may be some forms of good research design for some types of research questions, we need to keep a critical mind to see whether they are appropriate to the specific situation we are facing. Some conditions may need to be met before we can apply the established research design.

Lesson 20: exchanges of research ideas at conferences

That was the situation I faced in the year of 2002. I believed it was not the appropriate time to design an EI training program and study its effectiveness. Instead, we had to show that EI was trainable first. I searched the literature and tried to get more ideas about how this could be done. I came across the discussion on the effects of "nature" versus "nurture," which was exactly what I needed. That is, on top of genetic reasons, do life experiences and other conditions have an impact on an individual's EI level? This should be the first research question related to EI training.

Although I had some preliminary thoughts and searched the literature to get more ideas about EI training, it was not the most important study that I wanted to conduct at that time. I was still busy getting more evidence to show the validity of the EI construct and to develop the forced-choice scale.

In December 2002, I presented my work on the development of the forced-choice EI scale at the Asia Academy of Management conference in Bangkok, Thailand. After talking about the evidence on the forced-choice scale, I mentioned that there were many research questions related to the EI construct that could be explored in the future. One such question was the trainability of EI. After the session ended, one participant told me that he was very interested in the idea. He was a faculty member working for a university in Singapore at that time. We talked about this idea for about 45 minutes, and I told him everything I knew, including my preliminary idea for the study design. I was very happy to see someone who was so interested in my work, but I did not perceive that we had come up with a very concrete plan for moving forward. I simply thought this was an excellent exchange between two scientists who were both interested in a particular research topic.

To my surprise, half a year later I received an email from this Singaporean professor. He told me that based on our discussion in Bangkok he had collected data from an undergraduate student sample in Singapore. He sent me the data and asked me how we should analyze the data and proceed. I felt happy but also guilty because I had not done anything yet, while he had moved so fast. I believed I should make equal contributions, and so I told him that it would be better if we could have data from both Singapore and Hong Kong. I immediately collected data from a student sample in Hong Kong and combined the two subsamples. The results supported our idea, but the effect size was quite small.

The collaboration with this Singaporean colleague reinforced for me the importance of presenting ideas at conferences and on other possible occasions. When I was a doctoral student, my professor told me that it would be a good idea to present a paper at a conference before submitting it to a journal. We could get feedback and insights from the people who were interested in listening to our presentation. Unfortunately, some faculty and graduate students nowadays do not realize the important function of academic conferences. They regard attending conferences as a tourist trip. Some of them are even absent from their own presentations. This is certainly not ethical. In fact, discussing research ideas at conferences with people who are interested in related topics is one of the enjoyable activities for scientists.

Lesson 20: Attending conferences and discussion with colleagues who are interested in related topics should be regarded as a kind of enjoyment for scientists. We never know how it will end up helping our research work.

Lesson 21: working as a team

With the data from both the Singaporean and Hong Kong undergraduate students, I discovered that the proxy variables for the effect of nurture could explain only a very small portion of the variance in EI after controlling for the effect of nature. This forced me to think about other important proxy variables for the effect of nurture. I was invited to Taiwan by a long-term friend to help with the oral examinations of her graduate students. As usual, we talked about our research projects. She was interested in the idea of EI trainability as well. We therefore had a more thorough discussion and came up with an important proxy of life experiences that may stimulate the development of EI. When people are in their 20s, most of them are facing a lot of choices, such as going to graduate school, choosing their future career, preparing for marriage, and so on. If we can show that age has an impact on EI, it is definitely an effect of nurture rather than nature. We came up with a concrete plan to collect data from the graduate students at her university.

The results of the graduate student sample showed a much greater explanatory power for the effects of nurture on EI. I think this experience reinforces the importance of discussing our research ideas with colleagues so that we can expand our horizons in doing research. To me, being able to make friends and collaborate with them on research projects are major bonuses in my career.

We framed the graduate student sample as the second study in the paper and submitted it to the 2004 Asia Academy of Management conference. Fortunately, it was accepted for presentation (Wong, Foo, Wang, & Wong, 2004). We presented the paper in Shanghai and revised the paper according to the feedback we received. As the samples of the paper were undergraduate and graduate students, we submitted the paper to a psychology rather than a management journal. Unfortunately, it was rejected after one round of revision.

We examined carefully the reasons for rejection. My interpretation was that the reviewers might have perceived our work as going too far from the existing literature. Of course, skepticism about the EI construct was also an important reason. We therefore searched for journals that might be more receptive to this piece of work, and we found a journal specializing in studies of intelligence.

We submitted the paper to this journal, and after three rounds of revision, the paper was accepted. Interestingly, a critical comment from one of the reviewers was that EI might not be an appropriate topic for the journal as it was not a well-established concept of intelligence. In order to respond to this comment, I searched through the papers published in the journal. Fortunately, I found about five papers published in the previous five years that were related to EI. The reviewer and editor were convinced that EI was a relevant topic for the journal.

The experience of the preparation of this paper may remind us that we need to be flexible in executing the research idea, collecting data, and choosing a publication outlet. I was particularly thankful to my Singaporean and Taiwanese collaborators. I was very much pushed by them to think and work hard to make the idea workable. I had a strong sense of responsibility to make the final product a publishable output because of them. Both of them did not talk about authorship. They simply wanted to test the idea and see whether the data supported our initial expectation. They respected me as the project leader and let me make the decisions although they would provide comments and opinions as far as possible. They never insisted on their views as long as they knew I had already considered them. This made the process smooth and our collaboration a very happy process. I wish every scientist could have such experiences.

Lesson 21: When we are working as a team on a research project, it is essential to respect the project leader and allow him/her to make the decisions. Other team members should try their best to provide comments but not insist on their opinions when the leader has already considered the comments.

The following are the major contents of the paper.

Wong, C. S., Foo, M. D., Wang, C. W., & Wong, P. M. (2007). The feasibility of training and development of EI: An exploratory study in Singapore, Hong Kong and Taiwan. *Intelligence*, 35, 141–150; these contents are reprinted with permission.

Abstract. The existing literature on emotional intelligence (EI) has concentrated on demonstrating the effects of EI on either mental health or job outcomes such as job attitudes and performance. There is relatively little discussion concerning how EI, as a set of interrelated abilities related to handling emotions, is developed. Understanding how EI develops may be a significant first step for organizations to develop effective EI training programs. As an exploratory effort, we borrowed the basic argument from theories in human development to argue that life experiences affect EI development. Based on samples of university students from Singapore and Hong Kong, whether one of the parents was a full-time parent was a significant predictor of the students' EI. This finding was cross-validated with a sample of graduate students in Taiwan. Furthermore, age as a proxy for life experiences for this graduate student sample was found to be a significant predictor of EI. Implications for EI research and training are discussed.

Understanding whether emotional intelligence (EI) can be learned may be a significant foundation for EI training activities and programs. As an exploratory effort, we attempted to demonstrate that apart from personality traits and parents' EI, parents' devotion to their child and some life experiences may affect EI development. In the following paragraphs, we develop specific hypotheses on the development of EI and test these hypotheses in Study 8.1 with university students in Singapore and Hong Kong. Study 8.2, based on a sample of graduate students in Taiwan, was designed to cross-validate the findings in Study 8.1 and to further explore the potential influences of life experiences in EI development. Finally, implications for future EI research are discussed.

Training and development of EI

The clarification of EI as a set of interrelated abilities instead of dispositional traits in the literature (e.g., Mayer, Caruso, & Salovey, 2000a; Wong & Law, 2002) has important implications for training and development. If EI is a set of non-ability dispositions and traits, then it may not be possible to develop or enhance it through training activities and programs. This is especially true for the training of adults. As a set of abilities, there is a possibility that EI may be developed or enhanced by training programs. If EI is solely an inherent talent that has little to do with one's life or developmental experiences, then it may be difficult to design effective EI training programs. However, if EI is not solely an inherent talent but is also related to some types of life and developmental experiences, then we may design effective training programs for EI. A basic issue in human development is whether nature or nurture is more important in the development of personal abilities (e.g., Masten & Coatsworth, 1998). If nature is important in determining an individual's EI, training activities may not be effective. For instance, although general mental abilities (GMA) predict job performance and are the common factor behind a set of abilities such as language and reasoning, nature is generally believed to be more important than nurture in determining a person's GMA. Thus, it is quite difficult to improve GMA through the use of training programs.

On the contrary, if nurture, i.e., the human experiences resulting from interactions with the physical and social worlds, is important in determining a person's EI, training programs that organize these experiences in a systematic manner may be effective. In evaluating the competencies being developed in master of business administration programs, some studies found that these programs could develop competencies that are closely related to EI, such as relationship management and interpersonal abilities (e.g., Boyatzis, Stubbs, & Taylor, 2002; Goleman, Boyatzis, & McKee, 2002). Unfortunately, these studies provided only indirect evidence that EI may be developed through education programs because EI was not measured according to the four ability-based dimensions. Similarly, although many companies are offering EI training activities, little scientific evidence has been provided to show their effectiveness. It is difficult to evaluate the validity of these activities because very little is known about how an individual develops abilities in handling emotions.

Purpose and hypotheses of this study

Compared to GMA, EI is a relatively new construct, and our knowledge about it is quite limited. Thus, it may not be appropriate or possible for us to examine the exact effect of heritability versus environmentality on EI. Instead, we attempt to make a small step in this direction. That is, we try to provide evidence to show the possibility that some "non-nature" experiences may be important for the development of EI. If EI can be enhanced through developmental experiences, then it is worthwhile for researchers to study various potential nurture factors and to continue their search for effective EI training activities.

Although the main objective of this study is to examine whether nurture affects EI, two hypotheses on potential nature effects are provided so that nurture effects over and above these potential nature effects can be examined. Undoubtedly, an important factor of nature affecting one's EI level is one's parents' EI level. The parents' EI level may also affect the experiences that a person goes through in developing abilities to handle emotions. For instance, according to social learning theory (Bandura, 1977), high-EI parents may handle their emotions in a more appropriate manner, and thus their children may develop EI by observing and learning from such role models. Therefore, we hypothesize:

> Hypothesis 8.1: A person's EI level is positively related to one's parents' EI level.

Apart from parents' EI, the non-ability dispositional traits may largely reflect the nature factors that affect a person's EI development. The Big Five personality dimensions are non-ability dispositional traits that have received a lot of research attention (e.g., Barrick & Mount, 1991; McCrae & Costa, 1987). Conceptually, several Big Five personality dimensions should be closely related to EI (Saklofske, Austin, & Minski, 2002). For instance, neuroticism is a general tendency to over-react to negative stimuli from the environment; a person with strong neurotic characteristics could have difficulty in developing abilities to handle emotions appropriately. Agreeableness is a general tendency to be co-operative and to accommodate others' opinions and comments. Thus, a person strong in agreeableness could find it easier to develop abilities to understand others' emotions and to regulate their own emotions. Finally, conscientiousness is a general tendency to react carefully to stimuli from the environment, such as by paying attention to details and being patient. Thus, a person high in conscientiousness could find it easier to regulate his/her own emotions and to use these emotions to facilitate performance. Therefore, we hypothesize:

> Hypothesis 8.2: A person's personality traits are related to one's EI level.

Both one's parents' EI and one's personality may reflect largely the nature factors in EI development. If nurture factors are also important, the specific experiences that a person encounters may have a significant impact on EI development. As an exploratory effect, this study examines parent–child experiences as an objective indicator of nurture effects. The parent–child relationship is one of the most important factors constituting the child's social environment, and the reciprocal interactions between the child and the social environment have an enduring impact on the child's development (e.g., Bronfenbremer & Evans, 2000). For example, a friendly child is likely to evoke positive reactions from parents, and these reactions may reinforce the child to be friendly. If either the mother or father, or both of them, is a full-time parent as the child is growing up, it is likely that this child will have more experiences interacting with them. While not suggesting that parents who are working full-time do not provide emotional support to their children, we argue that a child who has a full-time parent has more chances to experience emotionally related issues with the parent and thus to learn to handle his/her emotions more appropriately. Furthermore, Polanyi (1962) argued that some types of knowledge and skills cannot be specified in detail. These knowledge types, often referred to as tacit knowledge, may be learned by modeling after others (Choo, 1998, p. 117). Children can gain knowledge of practical skills through life experiences and by guidance from parents and other adults (Sternberg et al., 2001). EI is a type of tacit knowledge which may not be specified in detail, and children may need to implicitly learn from their parents' actions. Having a full-time parent might provide more such opportunities for children to model after their parents and thereby develop EI skills. Therefore, we hypothesize:

> Hypothesis 8.3: A person's EI level is positively related to having a mother or father who is a full-time parent when he/she is growing up.

Study 8.1

Sample and procedure

The sample came from universities in Singapore (164 students) and Hong Kong (126 students). All participants are full-time students, and 31% are male. The students were briefed on the purpose of the study before they were given two questionnaires. One was for them to complete, and they were asked to give the other to one of their parents to complete. Parents were advised to put their completed questionnaires in the envelopes attached to the surveys if they did not want their children to have access to their responses. All invited students and parents returned their questionnaires.

Measures

EI

Both the parents and the students completed Wong's Emotional Intelligence Scale (WEIS), an EI measure developed for Chinese respondents (Wong, Law, & Wong, 2004).

Personality traits

We used the McCrae and Costa (1987) adjective scale to measure the Big Five personality dimensions. For this sample, the internal consistency reliabilities for neuroticism, extraversion, openness to new experiences, agreeableness, and conscientiousness were .80, .82, .67, .81, and .79, respectively.

Full-time parent

In the parent questionnaire, respondents were asked to indicate whether one or both of them were full-time parents during the period when the student was growing up. "Yes" to this item was coded as 1, while "No" was coded as 0.

Control variables

Four variables that could affect students' EI were controlled. First, the student's gender was coded with a dummy variable (female = 0, male = 1). EI could affect males and females differently. For example, Brackett, Mayer, and Warner (2004) found that EI was related to negative behaviors for college-age males but not for college-age females. Second, parent respondents were required to report their family income in an open-ended question. As the income levels were different between Singapore and Hong Kong, this variable was standardized for respondents from each society before they were pooled together to form the final sample. Third, the students' academic achievement was measured by a proxy variable. Some evidence suggests that EI is positively related to intelligence (Schulte, Ree, & Carretta, 2004). The proxy variable was their scores on the university entrance examination; students were asked to report this result in the questionnaire. This variable was standardized for respondents from each society because different scales were used for the two societies. Fourth, a dummy variable, "REGION," was used to capture the potential effect of different societies. Singapore was coded as 1, and Hong Kong as 0.

Results

Descriptive statistics and correlations among all measures are shown in Table 8.1. Female students had a marginally higher EI score than their male counterparts (mean score difference = 1.1, t = 1.94, p < .10). As shown in Table 8.1, EI was significantly correlated with some personality dimensions (for neuroticism, agreeableness, and conscientiousness, r = −.22, p < .01, r = .32, p < .01, and r = .27, p < .01, respectively), their parents' EI (r = .26, p < .01), and full-time parent status (r = .12, p < .05). Thus, hypotheses 8.1 to 8.3 received some initial support. A hierarchical regression was used to test the three hypotheses. In step 1, the control variables were entered in the equation. In step 2, the parent's EI level was entered. In step 3, the Big Five personality dimensions were entered, while in the final step the variable full-time parent was entered. The results in Table 8.2 show that parents' EI was significantly related to the

Table 8.1 Descriptive statistics and correlations among measures for Study 8.1

	Mean (S.D.)	1	2	3	4	5	6	7	8	9	10	11
1. Student's EI	25.2 (4.59)	(.73)										
2. Parent's EI	25.8 (4.64)	.26**	(.70)									
3. Full-time	.49 (.51)	.12*	.12*	—								
4. Income	.00 (1.00)	-.04	.16**	.19**	—							
5. Gender	.31 (.47)	-.11	-.17**	-.12*	-.03	—						
6. Exam	.00 (1.00)	.03	-.06	.09	.01	-.02	—					
7. NEURO	3.93 (.98)	-.22**	-.06	-.07	.02	-.24**	-.06	(.80)				
8. EXTRA	4.65 (1.03)	.04	.08	.05	.01	-.09	-.01	-.04	(.82)			
9. OPEN	4.39 (.94)	-.09	.07	.06	.09	-.02	-.12*	-.11	.44**	(.67)		
10. AGREE	5.04 (.84)	.32**	.06	.08	-.09	-.11	.06	-.27**	.18**	.02	(.81)	
11. CONSC	4.57 (.98)	.27**	.01	-.04	-.05	-.03	.09	-.29**	.24**	.15*	.36**	(.79)
12. Region	.57 (.50)	.15*	.14	.17**	.00	-.04	.00	-.04	.31**	.33**	.10	.09

Notes

n ranges from 258 to 290. Reliability figures are in parentheses. EI = emotional intelligence; NEURO = neuroticism; EXTRA = extraversion; OPEN = openness; AGREE = agreeableness; CONSC = conscientiousness.

$*p < .05$; $**p < .01$.

Table 8.2 Regression analysis for Study 8.1

Independent Variables	Dependent Variable: Student's EI			
	M_1	M_2	M_3	M_4
Income	−.04	.00	−.03	−.06
Gender	−.10	−.11	−.07	−.06
Exam	.04	−.05	−.02	−.04
Region	.13*	.16*	.13*	.11
Parent's EI			.24**	.23*
NEURO		−.15*	−.13*	−.12
EXTRA		.00	−.00	−.00
OPEN		−.19**	−.18**	−.18**
AGREE		.23**	.22**	.21**
CONSC		.13	.14*	.15*
Full-time parent				.13*
R^2	.033	.101**	.239**	.254**
ΔR^2		.068**	.138**	.015**

Notes
N = 250. EI = emotional intelligence; NEURO = neuroticism; EXTRA = extraversion; OPEN = openness; AGREE = agreeableness; CONSC = conscientiousness.

*p < .05; **p < .01.

students' EI (ΔR^2 = .068, p < .01) after controlling for the control variables. Thus, hypothesis 8.1 was supported. Supporting hypothesis 8.2, the Big Five personality dimensions were significantly related to students' EI (ΔR^2 = .138, p < .01) after accounting for the control variables and parents' EI. Supporting hypothesis 8.3, having at least one full-time parent had significant effects on students' EI (ΔR^2 = .015, p < .05) after accounting for the control variables, parents' EI, and the Big Five personality dimensions. The beta-weights for parents' EI and full-time parent status were .23 (p < .01) and .13 (p < .05), respectively.

Study 8.2

Purpose of Study 8.2

Although the results in Study 8.1 supported our hypotheses, the incremental amount of variance in EI explained by the full-time parent variable was small and the R^2 change was only 1.5%. Stronger evidence may be needed for the potential effects of life experiences on EI development before beginning to search for specific experiences and activities that can be incorporated into EI training programs. Study 8.2 used participants in their 20s to test the relationship of age and major (in addition to having had a full-time parent) with the participants' EI level. Past studies have found mixed effects of age on EI. While Hemmati, Mills, and Kroner (2004) found no relationship between age and EI, Kafetsios (2004) found a positive relationship between these factors. The average age of participants in these studies was 37 years (S.D. 11.7) and 38.7 years (S.D. 13.5), respectively, while all participants in Study 8.2 were in their 20s. If specific life experiences are important for EI development, university graduates may go through some of the most significant experiences in their 20s that shape their abilities to handle emotions. They have to consider making career choices, starting careers, being treated as independent and mature adults, probably having serious love affairs, and getting married. As a proxy of experiences, age for people in their 20s should be positively related to their EI level. Thus, we hypothesize:

Hypothesis 8.4: For people in their 20s, age is positively related to the EI level.

Educational experiences may be different among people owing to the specific subject content. For example, students majoring in the arts and social sciences may be exposed to more human and emotional issues than their counterparts majoring in the natural sciences or engineering. It is also possible that students high in EI may be more likely to choose subjects in arts and social sciences, and the subject contents may further reinforce their learning of EI. Thus, we hypothesize:

Hypothesis 8.5: People majoring in the arts and social sciences have higher EI levels than people majoring in the natural sciences and engineering.

Sample and procedure

The sample was 152 graduate students at a university in Taiwan. All participants were full-time students, and 45% were male. We followed the same procedures as in Study 8.1. In addition to completing a questionnaire, participants also gave the parent questionnaire to one of their parents. Participants received NT$300 (about US$10) when both questionnaires were returned.

Measures

The measures of EI, the Big Five personality dimensions, and the control variables used in Study 8.1 were also used in this study. The internal consistency reliabilities of the EI measure for the parent and student sample were .80 and .75, respectively. The internal consistency reliabilities for neuroticism, extraversion, openness to new experiences, agreeableness, and conscientiousness were .80, .81, .78, .80, and .71, respectively. The graduate students reported their ages (open-ended question), which ranged from 22 to 29 years, with a mean of 23.2 (S.D. 1.54). A multiple-choice question was used to ask the major of their graduate programs. A dummy variable was created to represent this (1 = arts and social sciences, 0 = natural sciences and engineering).

Results

Descriptive statistics and correlations among all measures are shown in Table 8.3. As shown in Table 8.3, EI was significantly correlated to some personality

Table 8.3 Descriptive statistics and correlations among measures for Study 8.2

	Mean (S.D.)	1	2	3	4	5	6	7	8	9	10	11	12	13
1. Student EI	25.5 (4.35)	(.71)												
2. Parent's EI	26.2 (4.45)	.23**	(.68)											
3. Full-time	.56 (.50)	.16*	-.01	—										
4. Age	23.2 (1.54)	.23	-.02	-.09	—									
5. Major	.85 (.36)	.08	.09	-.09	.09	—								
6. Income	70.2 (31.5)	-.09	.01	.00	-.00	.04	—							
7. Gender	.45 (.50)	-.05	-.12	-.15	.02	-.24**	-.09	—						
8. Exam	364.9 (74.0)	-.06	-.02	.03	.10	.07	-.12	.08	—					
9. NEURO	3.84 (1.02)	-.28**	-.01	-.06	-.09	.21**	.04	-.22**	-.00	(.80)				
10. EXTRA	4.56 (.93)	.22**	.09	.14	-.06	.00	.15	-.08	-.20*	-.19*	(.81)			
11. OPEN	4.70 (.96)	.14	.12	.09	-.02	.00	.06	.06	-.03	-.25**	.47**	(.78)		
12. AGREE	5.16 (.80)	.21**	.06	-.04	-.12	-.04	.10	-.05	-.22**	-.37**	.45**	.30**	(.80)	
13. CONSC	4.78 (.86)	.23**	.10	.02	.02	-.14	.09	.02	-.10	-.35**	.31**	.42**	.30**	(.71)

Notes

n ranges from 147 to 152. Reliability figures are in parentheses. EI = emotional intelligence; NEURO = neuroticism; EXTRA = extraversion; OPEN = openness; AGREE = agreeableness; CONSC = conscientiousness.

*p < .05; **p < .01.

Table 8.4 Regression analysis for Study 8.2

Independent Variables	Dependent Variable: Student's EI			
	M_1	M_2	M_3	M_4
Income	−.10	−.13	−.12	−.14
Gender	−.07	−.10	−.08	.02
Exam	−.07	−.04	−.03	−.06
Parent's EI		.22**	.20*	.20**
NEURO			−.23*	−.18*
EXTRA			.14	.13
OPEN			−.01	−.05
AGREE			.03	.13
CONSC			.08	.09
Parent's EI			.20*	.20**
Full-time parent				.21*
Age				.26**
Major				.13
R^2	.016	.065**	.178**	.278**
ΔR^2		.049**	.113*	.100**

Notes
N = 141. EI = emotional intelligence; NEURO = neuroticism; EXTRA = extraversion; OPEN = openness; AGREE = agreeableness; CONSC = conscientiousness.

*p < .05; **p < .01.

dimensions (neuroticism: r = −.28, p < .01; extraversion: r = .22, p < .01; agreeableness: r = .21, p < .01; and conscientiousness: r = .23, p < .01), parents' EI (r = .23, p < .01), and full-time parent status (r = .16, p < .05). The results of the hierarchical regression are shown in Table 8.4; they show that the parent's EI was significantly related to the student's EI (ΔR^2 = .048, p < .01). Thus, hypothesis 8.1 was supported. Supporting hypothesis 8.2, the Big Five personality dimensions were significantly related to students' EI (ΔR^2 = .113, p < .01). Finally, the three proxy variables of life experiences provided a significant explanation of students' EI (ΔR^2 = .100, p < .01). The beta-weights for full-time parent, age, and major of graduate program were .21 (p < .05), .26 (p < .01), and .13 (n.s.), respectively, in the last regression equation. Thus, hypotheses 8.3 and 8.4 were supported, while hypothesis 8.5 was not.

Discussion

Discussion of findings

In the last decade, EI has been proposed to be a potentially important construct for human resource management. After clarifying its definition and domains as a set of interrelated abilities related to handling emotions, EI has been shown to have significant impacts on a person's mental health and job outcomes. However, very little is known about how EI is developed, and it is unclear whether EI can be improved or enhanced through training activities and programs. This study attempts to provide some initial evidence to show that EI may be learned through some types of life experiences.

The results of this study indicated that a large amount of variance in EI was left unexplained after controlling for the parent's EI and the Big Five personality dimensions, which should have reflected largely the effects of nature on EI. For the nurture effects, having a full-time parent was found to be positively related to the university students' EI. These results were cross-validated with a second sample of graduate students in Taiwan. Age, another indicator of the nurture effects of experience for people in their 20s, was also found to be significantly related to the graduate students' EI. It appears that there are potentially large nurture effects that enhance one's EI level. It is therefore worthwhile for researchers to identify other experiences that may lead to the development of EI and to use these experiences to design effective EI training programs.

Limitations of the study

This study should be viewed as a first step toward examining nurture effects on EI development, and several limitations should be noted. First, this study measured the EI level of only one parent. Future research could measure the EI level of both parents. However, even if the other parent accounts for a similar amount of variance in the students' EI as was found in this study (i.e., 6.8% and 4.8%), a large amount of variance cannot be accounted for by the parents' EI level. Thus, it appears that apart from biological givens from the parents, our conclusion that EI can be learned through life experiences will not be invalidated even if both parents' EI levels are taken into consideration.

The second limitation is that we examined only three objective indicators of the potential effects of life experiences and found significant effects for two of them (i.e., whether one of the parents is a full-time parent and age of the graduate students in their 20s). Further, this study examines EI development in adults, but mechanisms for EI change in children could be different. Future research can investigate the effects of other life experiences and life stages on EI development. For example, researchers may interview high-EI individuals to identify their life experiences and examine whether these experiences can be acquired in a training environment.

The third limitation is that we did not find significant effects of the major of study on EI. However, it is premature to conclude that educational experiences are not related to EI learning. We measured only the major of the graduate program rather than the details of the educational experiences, and most of the respondents in this study were in social science fields. Only 22 (14.9%) of the respondents were majoring in the natural sciences or in engineering, and this might limit the predictive power of this variable. The beta-weight and p-value of this variable were .13 and .104, respectively, which just failed to reach a marginally significant level. It is therefore worthwhile for future studies to further examine the potential effects of educational experiences on EI level.

Conclusion

Despite these limitations, there are theoretical and empirical implications of this study. Theoretically, future research can develop conceptual frameworks to identify potential antecedents of EI. Specifically, theories related to human development may be of particular relevance. For example, the ecological systems theory of child development (e.g., Bronfenbrenner & Evans, 2000) specifying the important components of the social environment can be modified and applied to the development of EI.

Practically, antecedents identified by the conceptual framework could be used to guide the design of EI training activities and programs. Furthermore, existing EI training activities and programs should be rigorously evaluated. For example, the particular experiences introduced by the training activities should be examined to see whether they are related to one's abilities in handling emotions as specified by the four EI domains. In addition, the effectiveness of EI training programs should be studied according to commonly accepted experimental designs. For example, designs with control groups and comparison between pretest and posttest EI levels should be used to test training effectiveness.

9 Emotional intelligence and leadership

As reported in Chapter 2, an important breakthrough at the beginning of our journey on emotional intelligence (EI) research was the *Leadership Quarterly* paper. In that paper, the last sample provided direct evidence showing the effect of leaders' EI on subordinates' job outcomes. I regarded this evidence as preliminary and did not feel very comfortable with evidence from a single sample. I still looked for opportunities to gather more evidence to show the relationship between managers' EI and ordinary employees' job outcomes.

After making the EI concept popular in late 1990s, writers in the popular media also advocated that good leaders needed to be emotionally intelligent. This idea was also published in *Harvard Business Review* articles. When I read those reports, I believed we were facing a similar situation as for the EI construct. That is, we did not have sufficient scientifically rigorous evidence showing the importance of EI in leadership, but this idea was already accepted by the popular media. This further motivated me to try to gather more rigorous empirical evidence to show the impact of managers' EI on subordinates' job outcomes.

Lesson 22: flexible and workable research design

My original thought was to study work teams. That is, I could try to demonstrate the relationship between team leaders' EI and team members' job outcomes. As we already knew that the team members' EI could affect their job outcomes, we needed to include both the team members' EI and the leaders' EI in our analysis. A study showing the effect of the EI of both supervisor and subordinate could be quite interesting. However, if we collected data from teams, cross-level independent variables would be involved because, for each team, there is only one leader but under him/her there will be more than one subordinate. The data would be nested. For this type of data, Hierarchical Linear Modeling (HLM) is the appropriate analytical technique, but at that time this method had not yet been introduced into the management area, and I had no idea how to handle this type of data appropriately. In the supervisor–subordinate dyadic sample I got for the *Leadership Quarterly* paper, I asked each supervisor to evaluate only one subordinate to avoid this problem.

If I continued to ask each supervisor to evaluate only one subordinate to avoid the nested-data problem, I would simply be conducting a replication study. The evidence provided might be limited. I therefore tried to come up with alternative research designs and to demonstrate the impact of EI in leadership. One possible alternative was to conduct an experiment in which we randomly assigned subordinates to work under leaders with different levels of EI and observed their differences in job outcomes. The disadvantage of this research design was that we would need to create quite artificial job duties and work environments. Whether the findings in such an artificial work environment could be generalized to real-life organizations might be highly questionable.

Another possible way was to investigate the average EI level of managers in an organization, not the impact of an individual manager's EI. If organizations with managers with higher EI levels also had employees with higher levels of job outcomes, then we could demonstrate the importance of having high EI managers for organizations. To conduct this type of study, the unit of analysis would be organizations instead of individual employees or teams. It would be difficult to find a large number of organizations which would allow us to survey a sufficient number of managers and employees. Also, the structure of these organizations would need to be simple enough so that the number of layers of middle management would be small. The perfect situation would be that there was only one level of middle management.

I had given some thought to other alternatives, but each of them had disadvantages and difficulties. I thus waited for opportunities to execute at least one alternative. Fortunately, I got the opportunity in the year 2004 when a quasi-government agency in Hong Kong asked me to help them to conduct a survey on school teachers in Hong Kong. I immediately recognized that primary and secondary schools might be good targets because they essentially had only one layer of middle management. There were more than 1,200 schools in Hong Kong, and the size of each school was not very large. The structure of schools was simple. A typical school had a top manager (i.e., the principal) and a layer of middle managers (senior teachers working in administrative positions or as subject panel heads). Suddenly, it appeared that my research idea might be workable.

Lesson 22: When we have a research question, there may be alternative research designs to provide evidence to answer the question. We should be flexible so that we will not miss opportunities to execute a workable design.

Lesson 23: selling points of the study

When I discussed the project in more detail with the government agency, I found that there were several limitations. First, we could only conduct a mail survey. I decided to focus on job satisfaction as data on this attitudinal job outcome could be collected through a self-report questionnaire. Second, the government agency intended to survey only six teachers from each school, and we could not increase the number. I therefore asked them to request the school to distribute questionnaires to both senior teachers who played the role of middle managers and front-line teachers.

With the practical limitations in data collection, I had to evaluate whether a reasonable research paper could be produced. I tried to think about the possible "selling points" of the research paper. Even though we could survey only a few teachers from one school, the final sample size could be quite large. From past records, at least one-third of the schools would respond to questionnaire surveys conducted by this government agency. In other words, we could have data from at least 400 schools. If six teachers from each school responded to the survey, the sample size would be 2,400 or more. Not too many studies have a sample of this size, and so this would definitely be an attractive point.

As we were studying teachers, I read some of the related studies in the education literature. I discovered that there was some discussion about EI in this body of literature, but the attention was not from the management perspective. Instead, most of the concern about EI in the education literature was about the importance of EI for students and how students could be educated to develop a higher EI level. I also discussed my observations with some secondary school teachers. They told me that in business management it was reasonable that we were concerned about job performance. However, for them, if EI was related to students' life satisfaction or to teachers' job satisfaction, then EI would be a very worthwhile construct to be investigated. I therefore believed that the topic itself, i.e., the relationship between teachers' EI and their job satisfaction, would be a good selling point within the education literature.

Lesson 23: During the planning stage of a research study, it may be helpful to visualize the final research paper and its selling points. We should be confident that the final paper should make some contribution to the relevant literature. If we cannot convince ourselves, it is better to think again before we collect data.

Lesson 24: fit the journal's format of writing

When I read selected papers in the education literature, I realized that the format and style were a little bit different from management papers. In the management literature, conceptual and empirical papers are quite different. For empirical papers, the format of reporting is quite standardized. However, in the education papers I read, I discovered that most of the empirical papers would include more qualitative arguments and evidence. I thought I might need to strengthen this part in the final research paper.

I added one more study to show that EI should be relevant to the job of primary and secondary school teachers. While it was clear that the job of teacher should have a high emotional labor requirement, we had no evidence showing that the EI of middle managers of schools was a relevant factor for their jobs. I thus asked 107 front-line teachers who participated in an in-service training course to answer a simple question. I asked them to list the attributes that were important for middle managers of schools. Using independent analysts, we could show whether the attributes were related to EI or not. Fortunately, the results supported my expectation that a significant number of the attributes listed by front-line teachers were related to EI. I framed this qualitative study as the first study of the paper and the large sample survey as the second study.

It took about half a year to execute the survey and input all the data. We needed about three months to prepare the practical report for the government agency. Then we drafted the research paper and submitted it to the 2006 Asia Academy of Management conference in Tokyo, Japan. Fortunately, the paper was accepted for presentation and got valuable comments (Wong, Wong, & Peng, 2006). We further revised the paper and tried to submit it to journals in the education field. After several rounds of revision, the paper was accepted and published (Wong, Wong, & Peng, 2010).

Lesson 24: In planning a research project as well as drafting a paper, it may be necessary to take into account the tradition of a particular field and their journals' preferences with regard to content as well as reporting format and style.

This project provides further evidence for the role of leaders' EI in the workplace. Although it provides cross-validation evidence for the study in the *Leadership Quarterly* paper, I think it is not sufficient, and I hope future research can use other research designs and samples from other industries to show the role of EI in leadership. To me, the two samples may be regarded as a little bit better than preliminary evidence. That is, I am comfortable saying that EI plays a role in managerial jobs, but the details of this role need to be further investigated. I would not make my conclusion as strong as those stated in the popular media.

The following are the major contents of the paper.

Wong, C. S., Wong, P. M., & Peng, K. Z. (2010). Effect of middle-level leader and teacher emotional intelligence on school teachers' job satisfaction: The case of Hong Kong. *Educational Management, Administration and Leadership*, 38(1), 59–70; these contents are reprinted with permission.

Abstract. Despite the emerging consensus on the definition of emotional intelligence (EI) and its importance in business organizations, relatively little empirical evidence has been reported in the education literature. We conducted two studies to investigate the impact of middle-level leader and teacher EI on teachers' job outcomes. In Study 9.1, 107 teachers were asked to list the attributes of successful middle-level leaders in their schools. In Study 9.2, 3,866 school teachers and middle-level leaders were surveyed on their EI and job satisfaction level. The results provide support concerning the impact of teacher and middle-level leader EI on school teachers' job satisfaction. Implications are discussed.

Proponents of emotional intelligence (EI) argue that both leader and subordinate EI should have a positive impact on job outcomes such as performance and satisfaction (e.g., Goleman, 1995; Goleman, Boyatzis, & McKee, 2002).

Research conducted in business organizations has provided empirical evidence for these claims (e.g., Law, Wong, & Song, 2004; Wong & Law, 2002). Although education researchers also argue that school leader and teacher EI will have a positive impact on school operations and teachers' job outcomes (e.g., Bloom, 2004; Elias, Harriett, & Hussey, 2003; Marlow & Inman, 2002), there is relatively little empirical evidence supporting this claim.

The main purpose of this study is to empirically investigate the potential effects of school leader and teacher EI on teachers' job satisfaction. Specifically, we concentrate on the middle-level leaders of schools (i.e., senior teachers responsible for administrative duties) because they should have frequent interactions with front-line teachers. In the following paragraphs, we state our research questions explicitly and report two empirical studies providing evidence to address these questions. Finally, implications for future EI research in the education setting are discussed.

In this study, we concentrate on the potential impact of school leader EI on teachers' job satisfaction. Locke (1969) defined job satisfaction as "the pleasurable emotional state resulting from the appraisal of one's job as achieving or facilitating one's job values" (p. 316). This definition is commonly used by other researchers in both business and education settings (Ho, 2003; Hoy & Miskel, 1991; Ma & MacMillan, 1999; McCormick & Ilgen, 1980; Weiss & Cropanzano, 1996; K. F. Wu & Watkins, 1996). According to Crossman and Harris (2006), the factors affecting job satisfaction can be broadly categorized as environmental, psychological, or demographic. The most significant positive environmental factors are those related to the working environment and the nature of the job (Corwin, 2001; Scott & Dinham, 2003). For example, recognition, support, and respect from colleagues and superiors can cultivate a feeling of job satisfaction (Dinham & Scott, 1998; Evans, 1998; Voluntary Service Organization, 2000). For psychological factors, there are many studies investigating the potential influence of personality (e.g., O'Brien, 1983; Spector & O'Connell, 1994) on job satisfaction. Finally, the effects of demographic factors such as age and gender on job satisfaction have also been investigated in the literature (e.g., Brush, Moch, & Pooyan 1987; Chaplain, 1995; Clark, Oswald, & Warr, 1996; Hickson & Oshagbemi, 1999; National Union of Teachers, 2001; Spector, 1997). However, relatively few studies have been conducted to investigate how leaders' abilities, attitudes, and behaviors may affect teachers' job satisfaction in schools.

Research setting, questions, and strategy

This study attempts to test the potential impact of leaders' EI on teachers' job satisfaction in schools. Conceptually, having more understanding, sensitive, considerate, and comforting leaders should help teachers to have a more pleasurable emotional state resulting from the appraisal of their jobs and the school environment. Thus, school leaders' EI should be positively related to front-line teachers' job satisfaction. However, empirical evidence concerning this relationship is quite limited. The present study therefore attempts to address research questions that are related to this relationship, using Hong Kong as the research setting.

In Hong Kong, while primary and secondary schools vary slightly in structure, size, and curriculum, a typical school usually consists of around 1,000 students, 40 to 60 teachers, and 10 to 15 non-teaching staff members and a few temporary teaching assistants on a monthly or yearly basis. About 10 to 15 senior teachers will take up administrative duties and assume leading roles in their respective areas. For example, the disciplinary master will lead a team of teachers to handle disciplinary issues and incidents; the chairperson of a subject panel (e.g., English language, mathematics, and chemistry panels) will lead a team of teachers teaching the same subject to handle issues related to that particular subject. These senior teachers serve as the middle-level leaders to help the principal run the school. They have direct and frequent contact with ordinary front-line teachers.

Despite the potential importance of the middle-level leaders in the school operations, most of the discussion of school leadership in the literature concentrates on school principals (Daresh, 2002; L. J. Matthews & Crow, 2003). Because the empirical evidence on school middle-level leader and teacher EI is limited, our purpose is to collect evidence to answer the following research questions:

1. Is teacher EI related to their job outcomes such as job satisfaction? Wong, Wong, and Law (2005) collected data on 89 teachers from two secondary schools and found that the correlation between their EI and job satisfaction was at the .30 level. Is this finding generalizable to all Hong Kong teachers?
2. Leaders with high EI are more empathic and sensitive to subordinates' feelings and concerns. Conceptually, it is reasonable to deduce that this may have a positive impact on subordinates' job outcomes. However, proponents of this argument have concentrated on the leaders' point of view. From the subordinates' point of view, do they actually think that supervisors' EI is valuable? Will Hong Kong school teachers perceive middle-level leaders with high EI as being an important asset to the school operations?
3. Empirically, Wong and Law (2002) found that supervisor EI had positive effects on subordinate job satisfaction and organizational citizenship behavior in a sample of 146 supervisor–subordinate dyads of middle-level government officials. Is this also true for Hong Kong school teachers and their middle-level leaders?

To answer the above questions, we conducted two studies. In Study 9.1, we asked 107 school teachers about the attributes of successful middle-level leaders (i.e., senior teachers with official leading roles in the administration of the school). In Study 9.2, we surveyed teachers of all 496 secondary and 712 primary schools in Hong Kong to investigate the impact of teacher and middle-level leader EI on teachers' job satisfaction.

Study 9.1

Participants and procedure

One hundred and seven Hong Kong school teachers enrolled in an in-service training course were invited to participate in this study. These teachers were relatively junior, did not occupy administrative positions, and came from different secondary and primary schools. They were briefed with the definition of "middle-level leaders" of their schools. Specifically, middle-level leaders refers to senior teachers who take up formal administrative positions such as disciplinary master and chair of subject panels. Once the participants were clear about this definition, they were asked to write down 5 to 10 attributes they considered most important for successful middle-level school leaders.

Two research assistants who are familiar with the definition of EI were invited to independently evaluate the write-up of these teachers. They used the following scale to evaluate each write-up: (1) the score is 0 if none of the attributes is related to EI; (2) the score is 1 if some of the attributes are related to EI (e.g., good communication skills, good interpersonal skills, and ability to handle stress); and (3) the score is 2 if some of the attributes are actually within the domains of EI (e.g., empathetic, sensitive to teachers' feelings and emotions, and able to control their own emotions).

Results

As we directly asked teachers to list the attributes of successful middle-level leaders in order to minimize the possibility of framing their thoughts, we rely on the judgment of the two raters concerning the write-ups of the teachers. The inter-rater reliability is thus critical before we can proceed to interpret our findings. The correlation between the evaluation of the two raters was .69 (p < .01), indicating acceptable agreement among them. We therefore proceeded to take the average of the ratings from the two raters. The mean is 0.80 with a standard deviation of .55. Table 9.1 reports the percentages of various

Table 9.1 Frequencies of ratings in Study 9.1

Ratings of the Two Raters	Number	%
1. At least one of the raters scored as 0	44	41.12
2. Both raters scored as 1	50	46.73
3. One rater scored as 1 and the other rater as 2	4	3.74
4. Both raters scored as 2	9	8.41
Total	107	100.00

Note
A rating of 0 means the attributes listed were not related to emotional intelligence at all; a rating of 1 means some of the attributes were related to emotional intelligence; a rating of 2 means that one or more dimensions of emotional intelligence were mentioned.

combinations of evaluation. As shown in Table 9.1, the number of write-ups that received a score of 0 from at least one of the raters (i.e., none of the attributes mentioned was related to EI) is 44 (41.12%). For the remaining 63 (58.88%) write-ups, both raters agreed that some of the attributes reported are related to EI. Thus, it appears that the majority of teachers believe that the EI of middle-level school leaders is important for their success.

Study 9.2

Participants and procedure

With the endorsement of the Hong Kong Teachers' Center, a quasi-government agency, we sent packages with a cover letter, stamped reply envelope, and six copies of a questionnaire to all 496 secondary and 712 primary schools in Hong Kong. In each package, a cover letter addressed to the principal explained that the purpose of the survey was to collect information about teachers' characteristics and opinions. Principals were asked to choose six of their teachers and distribute questionnaires to them, preferably including both senior teachers occupying administrative positions and ordinary front-line teachers. To ensure confidentiality, principals were instructed to inform the participating teachers that no one would have access to the completed questionnaires except the researchers. The principal would not look at the completed questionnaires. A big stamped reply envelope was provided to each school, and after all the teachers had put their questionnaires into the envelope, these completed questionnaires were sent directly back to the center.

Six hundred and sixty-four (259 secondary and 405 primary) schools responded to our request, representing a response rate of 55%. A total of 3,866 completed and usable questionnaires were returned. About two-thirds (68.3%) of the respondents were female teachers. More than two-thirds (71.0%) were ordinary front-line teachers, while the rest (29.0%) held administrative positions (e.g., disciplinary master or subject panel chair). Four hundred and thirty-seven schools had both types of respondents (i.e., teachers holding administrative positions and ordinary teachers).

Measures

EI was measured using the 16-item scale developed by Wong and Law (2002), with a 5-point Likert-type response format. For this sample of 3,866 respondents, the internal consistency reliability (coefficient alpha) was .92, with a mean and standard deviation of 3.55 and .43, respectively. Job satisfaction was measured by the four items of the Job Diagnostic Survey (Hackman & Oldham, 1975), with a 5-point Likert-type response format. We also added one item that asked about respondents' overall satisfaction with their job. The internal consistency reliability of these five items was .89, with a mean and standard deviation of 3.52 and .61, respectively.

Results

For the 3,866 teachers, the correlation between their EI and their job satisfaction scores was .30 (p < .01). For the 437 schools with both types of respondents (i.e., teachers holding administrative positions and ordinary front-line teachers), we calculated the average EI and job satisfaction score of the two types of respondents for each school. Descriptive statistics and correlations among the average EI and job satisfaction scores are shown in Table 9.2. Middle-level leaders' average EI is significantly related to the average of ordinary front-line teachers' job satisfaction (r = .21, p < .01).

We conducted two sets of hierarchical regression analyses to examine the potential impact of middle-level leaders' EI on ordinary teachers' job satisfaction level. The results are shown in Table 9.3. In the first set (Model 1a and 1b), middle-level leaders' EI has a significant impact on ordinary front-line teachers' job satisfaction (β = .18, p < .01) after controlling for ordinary front-line

Table 9.2 Descriptive statistics and correlations among variables for Study 9.2

	Mean (S.D.)	1. AEI	2. AJS	3. EI	4. JS
1. AEI	3.76 (.25)	1.00			
2. AJS	3.51 (.41)	.38**	1.00		
3. EI	3.75 (.36)	.12*	–.00	1.00	
4. JS	3.52 (.46)	.21**	.20**	.26**	1.00

Notes
n = 437. AEI = average emotional intelligence of teachers holding administrative positions; AJS = average job satisfaction of teachers holding administrative positions; EI = average emotional intelligence of ordinary teachers; JS = average job satisfaction of ordinary teachers.

*p < .05; **p < .01.

Table 9.3 Results of hierarchical regression analyses for Study 9.2

	Model 1a	Model 1b	Model 2a	Model 2b
1. EI	.26**	.24**	.26**	.24**
2. AJS	—	—	.20**	.15**
3. AEI	—	.18**	—	.12*
R^2	.065**	.099**	.107**	.119**
ΔR^2	—	.032**	—	.012*

Notes
n = 437. Numbers reported are standardized beta coefficients. Dependent variable is the average job satisfaction of ordinary teachers. EI = average emotional intelligence of ordinary teachers; AJS = average job satisfaction of teachers holding administrative positions; AEI = average emotional intelligence of teachers holding administrative positions.

*p < .05; **p < .01.

teachers' EI level. One may argue that middle-level leaders' job satisfaction may be related to ordinary front-line teachers' job satisfaction because of factors such as a common organizational climate or support within the same school. As the middle-level leaders' job satisfaction will also be affected by these organizational factors, we controlled both middle-level leaders' job satisfaction and ordinary front-line teachers' EI level in the second set of analyses (Model 2a and 2b). Middle-level leaders' EI still has a significant impact on ordinary front-line teachers' job satisfaction ($\beta = .12$, $p < .05$).

Discussion

EI is becoming an important topic in psychological, management, and education research. The results of this study indicate that the findings in business organizations may also be valid in the school setting. School teachers in Hong Kong believe that middle-level leaders' EI will be important for their success, and a survey of a large sample of teachers also indicates that teacher and middle-level leader EI levels are positively related to teachers' job satisfaction.

Before we discuss the implications of this study, three limitations should be noted. First, as an exploratory effort, we directly asked teachers to list the attributes of successful middle-level leaders in order to minimize the possibility of framing their thoughts in Study 9.1. Thus, we rely on the judgment of the two raters concerning the write-ups of the teachers. Although the inter-rater agreement appears to be acceptable, future research may attempt to provide more concrete guidance to participants. In so doing, more details concerning the importance of middle-level leader EI may be discovered. For example, teachers may be asked to provide behavioral examples of successful versus unsuccessful middle-level leaders. From these examples, researchers may draw more concrete conclusions about the roles of leaders' EI in affecting their success.

Second, in order to have a large and representative sample of Hong Kong schools and teachers in Study 9.2, we have to use self-report measures of EI and job satisfaction rather than EI tests and more objective job outcomes such as job performance. Future research may attempt to use more objective EI tests and investigate the relationship between EI and job outcomes other than job satisfaction.

Third, in studying the relationship between leaders' EI and followers' job outcomes, it may be preferable to use leader–follower dyadic observation. However, this may not be suitable in our research setting. In a typical Hong Kong school, each front-line teacher will need to teach more than one subject and take up different administrative duties. As they do not have an "immediate" leader, we have to investigate the middle-level leaders and the front-line teachers as two groups and examine the relationship between the average EI of the middle-level leaders and the average job satisfaction of the front-line teachers. If possible, future research may investigate an education setting that can offer clear leader–follower dyads to cross-validate our findings from Study 9.2.

Despite these three limitations, there are both conceptual and practical impli-cations of this study. Conceptually, this study supports the basic idea that the teaching profession requires both teachers and school leaders to have a high level of ability to handle their emotions. Practically, this may imply that in selecting, training, and developing teachers and school leaders, EI should be one of the important concerns. Up to now, it is rare to find teacher training institutions that have EI as one of their screening criteria. Although EI may be mentioned in some in-service training programs, we seldom see a systematic design based on the rigorous ability-based definition of EI. It is even rarer to find scientifically rigorous evidence concerning any improvements in EI for participants who completed those training programs. With the evidence provided by this study, it may be worthwhile for educational researchers to spend more efforts on designing better training programs to improve the EI of teachers and school leaders.

10 Alternative conceptualizations of emotional labor

As reported in Chapters 3 and 4, I used the concept of emotional labor to predict the differential impact of emotional intelligence (EI) on different types of jobs. I mentioned that there are two alternative conceptualizations of emotional labor. Traditionally, it has been studied as coping strategies that job incumbents adopt in order to perform emotionally demanding duties. Deep acting refers to the incumbents actually having the emotion appropriate for the situation, while surface acting means the incumbents only pretend to have the emotion. The major finding according to this conceptualization in the literature is that incumbents who frequently use surface acting to cope with their job duties will have a higher chance of emotional exhaustion, which is a critical component of burnout. The reason is that although surface acting may help the job incumbents to perform their job duties, they would experience dissonance between their true and expressed emotions.

I adopt the other conceptualization of emotional labor in studying EI. I regard emotional labor as a particular type of job requirements related to emotions. That is, it can be defined as the extent to which the job incumbent is required to present certain types of emotions in order to perform the job adequately. Although not the same, the two definitions of emotional labor are both valid and useful for our understanding of some phenomena in the workplace. However, we need to make sure which definition we are using in our studies, especially when we are discussing the relationships between emotional labor and other variables.

I learned of the emotional labor concept in the same year I first encountered the EI concept, i.e., in 1996 when I had my first sabbatical leave in Taichung. I served as an external examiner for the graduation thesis of a master's student. Her thesis was about emotional labor. When I discussed her thesis with her, I found that the usual conceptualization of emotional labor as coping strategy was fine but that the original proponent of the concept had focused more on the nature of the job duties (Hochschild, 1983). This was why the original writing on the concept had listed examples of jobs with high versus low emotional labor requirements. This stimulated my original thought that if emotional labor represented a particular type of job demands, EI should be the required ability to deal with the demands. Thus, I chose the job requirement definition in my early conceptualization although I also recognized the concepts of deep acting and surface acting. I thought it would be nice to further study the relationship among EI, the emotional demands of the job, and the coping strategies. However, this idea was not a high priority at that time.

Lesson 25: avoid data mining

The chance to work on this idea came almost 10 years later. In 2005, a master's student from mainland China applied to the doctoral program of the Chinese University of Hong Kong. As her master's thesis was about EI and emotional labor, I was assigned to be her supervisor. Interestingly, the master's thesis was mostly based on our papers published in 2002 and 2004. There were some extensions; the most important one was about the relationship between emotional labor and emotional exhaustion. This relationship was tested with a relatively large sample using measures of emotional demands, EI, surface acting, deep acting, and emotional exhaustion.

The master's thesis was framed mainly as an extension in the Chinese setting, and it was written in Chinese. The key contribution was related to the dependent variable of emotional exhaustion. The conceptual framework was the job demands-resources model (Demerouti, Bakker, Nachreiner, & Schaufeli, 2001), which argued that job demands (e.g., emotional demands) and job resources (e.g., supervisor support) were contributing factors to burnout. The master's thesis argued that on top of emotional demands and supervisor support, EI could reduce the extent of burnout because EI could be regarded as a type of personal resources.

To me, this was a chance to study my original idea of investigating the two different conceptualizations of emotional labor. Unlike most studies, in which I have some concrete conceptual arguments and research questions before collecting data, this was a different situation. That is, the data were already available. In some research areas which depend mostly on secondary data, this may be a normal situation. However, in my research area, most of the research projects are based on primary data. It is not a common practice for us to try to develop conceptual arguments after the data are available.

In Chapter 1, we discussed briefly the nature of science and scientific investigations. The key is to propose and test theories in terms of relationships among variables. Thus, the best procedure is that we should have the conceptual arguments before data collection. If we have the data on hand and try to work backward to deduce the relationship among the variables, it would be dangerous because we might make up unreasonable stories to fit the sample's specific data. We call this data mining. Data mining is suitable only for extremely large samples, and the purpose is not to uncover and test causal relationships. Rather, the sole purpose is to make predictions but not offer explanations. For example, in the marketing area, a company may examine which type of customers would have the highest chance of buying their products. Why customers with a particular profile have a higher chance of buying is not their major concern. Instead, as long as customers with such a profile would buy more from the company, the conclusions from the data analyses are useful.

This is certainly not the case for scientific research that wants to explain why variables are related. Thus, data mining is not an acceptable approach in theory building and testing. However, the reality is that sometimes we have the data before we have concrete conceptual arguments. Does this mean that we should never use existing data? The answer is certainly no. I think the most important principle is that we have to ignore the data when we develop the conceptual arguments and hypotheses. That is, we should forget about the data and come up with the conceptual arguments before we use the data to test our expectations regarding the phenomena. Whether we already have the data should not affect our conceptual development. In fact, we can even look for existing datasets that are available instead of collecting new data if existing datasets can already test our conceptual arguments.

Lesson 25: In scientific investigations for the purpose of theory building and testing, data mining is dangerous. If datasets are already available, we should ignore the data in developing our conceptual arguments and expectations about the relationships among variables.

Lesson 26: framing of a paper

Realizing the danger of data mining, we did not look at the data and instead tried to build conceptual arguments concerning the role of emotional labor when we defined it based on the two alternative conceptualizations. I carefully studied the job demands-resources model and found that the concept of emotional demands was in fact very close to my definition of emotional labor. It means the extent to which the job duties impose demands on the job incumbents that are related to emotions. Thus, this model argues that emotional demands are related to burnout, and this should be a very reasonable expectation regarding what actually happens in the workplace.

The concept of job resources under the job demands-resources model is more abstract. Basically, it means anything that can help the incumbents to cope with emotional demands to reduce the chance of burnout. One common type of resources reported in the literature is supervisor support. That is, if we have a supportive supervisor, the chance that we would experience burnout because of high job demands would be reduced. This again is a very reasonable expectation. However, the original idea of the model is that job resources serve as buffers that help reduce the impact of job demands on burnout. In other words, job resources serve as a moderator of the job demands–burnout relationship.

I found that the idea of job resources being a moderator was not very consistent in the literature. Some studies found that resources had a direct effect on burnout, and the moderator argument did not receive statistically significant evidence. Despite this inconsistent finding reported in the literature, I like the original moderating idea, and I think it should reflect the real-life situation. Therefore, I decided to work on this idea with the student and tried to come up with an explanation of the inconsistent findings. In so doing, I believed we could make both conceptual and empirical contributions to the literature.

After careful discussion, we came up with a straightforward explanation by utilizing the concepts of deep acting and surface acting. Basically, emotional demands were objective requirements and would induce the job incumbents to react. Incumbents could use either deep acting or surface acting to fulfill the job requirements. When they used deep acting, the chance of burnout would be minimal. However, if they used surface acting, the chance of burnout would increase. Thus, coping strategies such as deep acting and surface acting should be the mediators that were ignored in the job demands-resources model.

Furthermore, EI could enhance the relationship between emotional demands and deep acting while reducing the relationship between emotional demands and surface acting. The reason was that high-EI people could internalize the necessary emotions more easily, and so they could use deep acting as their coping strategy. Supervisor support could moderate the relationships between coping strategies and burnout. The reason was that supervisors could reinforce incumbents using deep acting and comfort incumbents using surface acting. This in turn would reduce the chance of burnout.

Through the above conceptual development, we were able to develop a model that linked up emotional demands, coping strategies, resources, and burnout to represent the principles underlying the reality. All the variables involved could be found in the data reported in the master's thesis, so there was no need to collect data from another sample. More important, we believed that if we could test our conceptual arguments for the extended model with both mediators and moderators, we could resolve the inconsistent findings reported in the literature. A research paper on this topic should be able to make some contributions and be worthwhile for publishing.

Lesson 26: Framing a paper in such a way that it can make contributions to the literature should be done before data analyses are conducted. Regardless of whether the data would support the proposed arguments or not, it is essential to be confident that the framing represents some advancement in our knowledge.

Lesson 27: new statistical techniques

Although we were confident that the conceptual arguments would be meaningful, the model involved both mediators and moderators. At that time, statistical techniques that could test this type of model were not well established. In the past, we had to test each mediator and moderator separately. This might not be ideal, but we had to use this analytical approach when better alternatives were not available. Fortunately, when we completed our conceptual arguments, some discussion began to appear in the literature concerning how to test this type of complicated model. These models were labeled as either mediated moderation or moderated mediation.

We therefore searched the literature that discussed mediated moderation or moderated mediation models. It took us several months to learn the arguments for these types of models and, more important, the ways these models could be tested using statistical techniques. At that time, one of the proposed techniques was to use the logic of regression. Some other techniques were being developed, but we were not very clear on how they would emerge. We used the traditional approach (i.e., analyze the relationships separately) and the newly proposed regression approach to analyze the data. Most of our expectations were supported, and so we wrote up the paper.

Lesson 27: There are always advances in research methodology such as statistical techniques and relevant computer software. We have to keep track of the state-of-the-art methods to know whether they may be applicable to our research projects.

After we finished the draft of the paper, we submitted it to a journal, but the paper was rejected. My interpretation was that the editor and reviewers were not ready for the complicated model and its statistical analyses. We submitted the paper to another journal. After two rounds of revision, mostly about further elaboration on the model and the data analysis method, we got the paper accepted for publication.

Interestingly, during our submission process, the mediated moderation and moderated mediation models were becoming more and more popular. Some people even believed that we must come up with such models to impress editors and reviewers. I disagree with such conclusions because our model should represent the real phenomenon. If the phenomenon is not so complicated, then we should not make our model a complicated one. I wish most of the editors and reviewers could keep a clear mind on this issue. At any rate, more standardized statistical techniques have been developed to test these models. It is no longer the regression approach. The more widely accepted method involves a statistical technique called bootstrapping, and new statistical software has been developed.

The following are the major contents of the paper.

Peng, K. Z., Wong, C. S., & Che, H. S. (2010). The missing link between emotional demands and exhaustion. *Journal of Managerial Psychology*, 25(7), 777–798; these contents are reprinted with permission.

Abstract. The negative impact of job demands on strain has been proposed and tested extensively since the 1970s. However, the exact mechanism underlying this relationship has not been clearly specified in the literature. To identify that missing link, this study develops a specific model with mediated moderation to explain the relationship between emotional demands and exhaustion. Emotional intelligence is hypothesized to be a moderator between emotional demands and coping strategies, while supervisor support is hypothesized as a moderator between coping strategies and exhaustion. The results from a large sample (n = 418) of life insurance agents provide preliminary support for this mediated moderation model. The theoretical and practical implications are discussed here.

Most human resource researchers and practitioners agree that the well-being of employees should be one of the major concerns of management. Researchers have made suggestions about how to minimize the negative impact of job demands on employee outcomes. The job-demands-control model argues that it is the combination of high job demands and low control that leads to high levels of employee strain (Karasek, 1979). The job-demands-control-support model (DCS; Karasek & Theorell, 1990) adds social support to the model as a buffer against the negative impact of job demands on strain. The more recent job demands-resources model (JD-R; Bakker, Demerouti, & Euwema, 2005; Bakker, Demerouti, & Verbeke, 2004; Demerouti, Bakker, Nachreiner, & Schaufeli, 2001) uses an expanded concept of "job resources" to represent control, support, and other possible factors that can help employees to handle job demands as the buffer against the negative impact of job demands.

One of the fundamental arguments of these models is that although job demands have a negative impact on employee well-being, that impact can be reduced if employees have the appropriate resources to deal with those demands. In statistical terms, job demands and resources have an interaction effect on employees' well-being. Unfortunately, the proposed interaction effect has received limited empirical support in past studies (e.g., de Lange, Taris, Kompier, Houtman, & Bonger, 2003; Wall, Jackson, Mullarkey, & Parker, 1996). This indicates that the moderators of employee well-being may be more complicated than expected.

Aside from job resources, researchers have investigated the importance of coping strategies for employee well-being (e.g., Daniels, 1999; Daniels & Harris, 2005; Ito & Brotheridge, 2003; Latack, Kinicki, & Prussia, 1995). For example, Daniels and Harris (2005) argue that employees adopt coping behaviors to reduce the negative impact of job demands and avoid burnout. According to the framework of the DCS and JD-R models, such coping behavior involves the execution or elicitation of resources embedded in the work environment (de Jonge & Dormann, 2002). Thus, the incorporation of coping strategies into the DCS and JD-R framework may better explain the exact relationship among job demands, job resources, and employee well-being. Specifically, as coping strategies are induced by job demands and their adoption may affect well-being, they can be conceptualized as a mediator of the moderating effects proposed by the DCS and JD-R models. This may be the missing link that explains the inconsistent results of past studies and the possibly complicated moderating effects of job demands and job resources on employee well-being.

The purpose of this study is to specify that missing link by focusing on employee reactions to emotional demands – a specific type of job demand – by applying the coping-strategy argument. We chose emotional demands as our focus because strategies to cope with this type of demand have been extensively investigated in the emotional labor literature (e.g., Grandey, 2000; Gross, 1998a; Hochschild, 1983). In the literature, deep acting and surface acting are identified as the two main types of coping strategies adopted in response to emotional demands. Following this classification of coping strategies, we propose the model shown in Figure 10.1. In brief, we argue that in response to emotional demands,

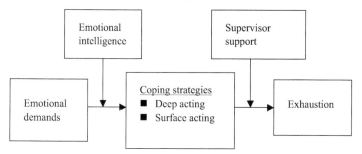

Figure 10.1 Proposed link between emotional demands and exhaustion

employees use coping strategies such as deep and surface acting, which in turn affect their level of exhaustion. Furthermore, the choice of coping strategies and their effects on exhaustion depend on job resources, such as emotional intelligence and supervisor support. In the following paragraphs, we introduce the components of our proposed model and develop some specific hypotheses. An empirical study of a sample of insurance agents conducted to test the hypotheses of the model is then reported. Finally, we discuss the implications of the study and offer some conclusions.

Proposed model describing the effect of emotional demands on exhaustion

Emotional demands have received increased research attention with the growing dominance of the service sector. To perform a service job adequately, employees may be required to present particular types of emotion that differ from their true feelings. Faced with these emotional demands, employees must react through the "management of feeling to create a publicly observable facial and bodily display" (Hochschild, 1983, p. 7). For example, a flight attendant may be very unhappy but must still present a friendly attitude and demonstrate a willingness to serve. Conversely, a debt collector may be very happy but still needs to present a tough expression. Managing emotions to perform a job adequately is referred to as "emotional labor." The rules behind the presentation of emotions required by an organization or job are called the "display rules" (Ekman & Friesen, 1975; Goffman, 1959; Hochschild, 1983). Expression according to the display rules that contradicts genuinely felt emotions can result in emotional dissonance and can negatively affect employee well-being (Hochschild, 1983; Kinman, 2009).

In the emotional labor literature, the possible coping reactions of employees to the emotional demands of their jobs are classified as either surface acting or deep acting (Grandey, 2000; Gross, 1998a, 1998b). Surface acting emphasizes the management of observable expressions, whereas deep acting emphasizes the management of true feelings. When using surface acting, employees present the required emotions without aligning these emotions with their true inner feelings. They thus experience alienation from their true emotions, which results in a high level of strain. When using deep acting, employees consciously modify their feelings to express the desired emotion, thereby avoiding the alienation from their true emotions and reducing the strain. Empirical evidence has demonstrated that these two emotional labor strategies have different relationships with employee burnout (e.g., Brotheridge & Grandey, 2002; Grandey, 2003; Gross & John, 2003; Totterdell & Holman, 2003).

There are three components of burnout: exhaustion, depersonalization, and reduced personal accomplishment. We concentrate our discussions on the exhaustion component, because exhaustion is usually regarded as the core component of burnout and the cause of the other two components (Leiter & Maslach, 1988; Maslach, 1982; Maslach, Schaufeli, & Leiter, 2001). According to Schaufeli, Maslach, and Marek (1993), exhaustion is an action whereby one distances oneself emotionally and cognitively from one's work. It is related to psychosomatic complaints, depression, and other long-term effects of stress (Maslach et al., 2001; Schaufeli & Enzmann, 1998).

Emotional demands are found to be related to exhaustion across various occupations (Brotheridge & Grandey, 2002). In a laboratory study, emotional demands to inhibit emotions from being expressed were found to be the cause of strong physiological effort (Gross & Levenson, 1997). In the emotional labor literature, emotional demands are argued to be inherently stressful (Hochschild, 1983), and empirical studies have found that emotional labor is related to exhaustion (Abraham, 1998; Brotheridge & Lee, 1998; Hochschild, 1983; Morris & Feldman, 1997). The impact of emotional demands on exhaustion is also consistent with the basic argument of the DCS and JD-R models. We thus hypothesize:

Hypothesis 10.1: Emotional demands are positively related to exhaustion.

As deep acting and surface acting are coping strategies to deal with the emotional demands of a job, these types of behavior are likely to be induced by emotional demands. Thus, when employees have to deal with more emotional demands in their job, they are more likely to adopt coping behavior involving one strategy or the other. We thus hypothesize:

Hypothesis 10.2a: Emotional demands are positively related to deep acting.

Hypothesis 10.2b: Emotional demands are positively related to surface acting.

As discussed, deep acting can reduce alienation from one's true inner emotions, but surface acting cannot do so (Brotheridge & Lee, 1998; Hochschild,

1983). Both the emotional labor literature (Abraham, 1998; Hochschild, 1983; Morris & Feldman, 1997) and the emotional regulation theory (Gross, 1998b) argue that the alienation from true inner emotions is the main cause of exhaustion. According to this line of thought, surface acting results in the alienation from feelings and greater exhaustion. This relationship has received consistent support in empirical studies (e.g., Brotheridge & Grandey, 2002; Grandey, 2003). In contrast, deep acting may help to reduce emotional arousal, thereby reducing exhaustion (Grandey, 2000, based on the findings of Gross, 1998a). This is because reducing emotional arousal helps employees feel more positive about their work situation. Through deep acting, employees recognize the genuine needs of clients and the contribution they make when they act according to the display rules required by the organization. Brotheridge and Grandey (2002) found that deep acting also helps to reduce the other dimensions of burnout. Grandey (2003) suggested that whereas surface acting causes stress, deep acting does not, but there is little direct evidence in the literature on the negative effect of deep acting on stress or burnout suggested by Grandey (2000). The limited empirical support notwithstanding, it seems reasonable that if deep acting is related to exhaustion, then the relationship should be negative rather than positive. We thus hypothesize:

Hypothesis 10.3a: Surface acting is positively related to exhaustion.

Hypothesis 10.3b: Deep acting is negatively related to exhaustion.

As coping strategies are induced by emotional demands and are targeted at reducing exhaustion, they mediate the effect of emotional demands on exhaustion. Grandey's (2000) theoretical model of emotional labor proposes this mediating effect conceptually. Empirical support has been found in past studies to show that employees engage in coping strategies to reduce job demands that lead to stressful feelings (e.g., Daniels, 1999; Daniels & Harris, 2005; Ito & Brotheridge, 2003; Latack et al., 1995). We thus hypothesize:

Hypothesis 10.4: The relationship between emotional demands and exhaustion is mediated by deep and surface acting.

As deep acting can reduce exhaustion, why do some employees still use surface acting to handle emotional demands? According to the DCS and JD-R models, employees must possess the necessary control, support, and other resources to deal with job demands appropriately. In the case of emotional demands, employees must be able to understand the emotions of their customers or clients, regulate their own emotions, and use their emotions to maximize their performance. In other words, employees need a high level of emotional intelligence, which is a set of abilities to deal with one's own emotions and those of others (Law, Wong, & Song, 2004; Mayer & Salovey, 1997; Van Rooy & Viswesvaran, 2004; Wong & Law, 2002), to be able to perform deep acting. There is ample evidence to show that people with a high level of emotional intelligence are happier and more successful in their careers (Carmeli, 2003; Carmeli, Yitzhak-Halevy, & Weisberg, 2009; Dulewicz & Higgs, 2000), as they have the ability to effectively deal with emotions in the workplace. Thus, employees who have a higher level of emotional intelligence may be more capable of engaging in deep acting to get the job done, whereas employees with a low level of emotional intelligence are more likely to engage in surface acting. We thus hypothesize:

> Hypothesis 10.5a: Emotional intelligence moderates the relationship between emotional demands and deep acting. Specifically, the higher the level of emotional intelligence, the stronger the relationship.

> Hypothesis 10.5b: Emotional intelligence moderates the relationship between emotional demands and surface acting. Specifically, the higher the level of emotional intelligence, the weaker the relationship.

As discussed earlier, employees may be more positive in their attitude toward their work if they are able to perform deep acting to handle their job demands. These positive feelings may be further reinforced if their work environment provides recognition and encouragement of their deep acting efforts and accomplishments. The negative feelings caused by surface acting may also be moderated by the work environment. An important factor in the work environment is the emotional support of supervisors. Both the DCS and JD-R models identify supervisor support as an important resource that can help employees to deal with exhaustion in the workplace (Carver, Schein, & Weintraub, 1989; Constable & Russell, 1986; Gilbreath & Benson, 2004; Goolsby, 1992; Maslach & Pines, 1977; Pennebaker, 1990; Pines & Aronson, 1988; Russell, Altmaier, & Van Velzen, 1987). Clearly, if supervisors can provide recognition and help reinforce the value of employees' deep acting efforts, then the effect of deep acting on exhaustion may be further enhanced.

In contrast to the situation with deep acting, employees may have negative and unpleasant feelings after engaging in surface acting as a result of the alienation from their true emotion. However, this feeling may not lead to exhaustion if their work environment provides comfort and helps them to realize that their contribution to the organization is valued. By sharing stressful events with other employees and recognizing employee surface acting efforts, supervisors can provide emotional support that may prevent an employee's negative feelings from growing into exhaustion. Adequate supervisor support may then reduce the negative impact of surface acting on exhaustion. We thus hypothesize:

> Hypothesis 10.6a: Supervisor support moderates the relationship between deep acting and exhaustion. Specifically, the higher the level of supervisor support, the stronger the relationship.

Hypothesis 10.6b: Supervisor support moderates the relationship between surface acting and exhaustion. Specifically, the higher the level of supervisor support, the weaker the relationship.

In summary, we hypothesize a model of the relationship between emotional demands and exhaustion with mediated moderation effects (Muller, Judd, & Yzerbyt, 2005), as shown in Figure 10.1. The two types of coping strategies are the mediators in the model, and emotional intelligence and supervisor support are the moderators of the mediated relationships.

Methods

Sample and context

The sample in this study consists of 418 insurance salespersons from the two largest insurance companies in a medium-sized city in western China. A top-level manager in each company distributed the questionnaires to salespersons in the company during one of their daily meetings. A total of 500 questionnaires with a cover letter were distributed. The cover letter explained to the employees that their participation would be voluntary and anonymous and that the information collected would be used only for research purposes. Four hundred and eighteen completed questionnaires were returned, representing a response rate of 83.6%. Only front-line insurance salespersons were chosen, because these positions have strong emotional demands (Hochschild, 1983). The sample was demographically diverse: 73.2% were female, 81.3% were unmarried, and 57.4% had a college education or above. Further, 45.5% were aged 31–40, 26.9% were aged 41 or above, and 27.3% were aged 21 or below. In terms of job tenure, 24.9% had held their job for less than 1 year, 34.9% for 1–5 years, 33% for 6–10 years, and 7.3% for 21 years or more.

The two insurance organizations are similar. Both are state owned, with similar management structures, compensation systems, and marketing strategies. The insurance salespersons in both companies perform similar tasks, such as meeting with their supervisor and other colleagues in the morning and engaging in close personal interaction with customers. Although each salesperson works independently, both the salespersons and their supervisors receive commissions for successful sales. Thus, supervisors are willing to provide support to their subordinates. As the two organizations are the biggest in their region, they have a large customer base. The salespersons do make cold calls, but referrals and incoming clients constitute important sources of new business.

Measures

Emotional demands

We adopted the emotional demands scale for Chinese respondents developed by C. Y. Wu (2003) based on scales published in Western countries. The scale consists of 18 items that are statements of the emotional demands of performing various job duties. The respondents were asked to evaluate the frequency of and effort required for each item on a 6-point response scale. For example, respondents were asked to evaluate the frequency of the following statement: "To perform my job, I have to speak nicely so that others will feel happy." After reporting the frequency on the 6-point scale (1 = seldom, 6 = always), they were then asked to evaluate how much effort they made with regards to the corresponding item on another 6-point scale (1 = minimal, 6 = maximal). The average of all the frequency and effort items represents the level of emotional demands of a job.

Deep acting and surface acting

We adopted the scale of Grandey (2003) to measure this construct, which consists of six items for deep acting and five items for surface acting. Back-translation was used to develop a Chinese version of the scale. Respondents were asked to evaluate how often the situation described in each statement occurred in their daily work on a 6-point response scale (1 = never, 6 = always). An example of a deep acting item is "When I serve my clients, I feel and express true happiness." An example surface acting item is "I pretend to be in a good mood, even though my true feelings are not the same."

Emotional intelligence

Wong's Emotional Intelligence Scale (WEIS), which is an ability-based scale of emotional intelligence developed for Chinese respondents (Wong, Law, & Wong, 2004), was used to measure this construct.

Supervisor support

The 5-item scale for supervisor support was selected from the social support scale developed by Zhao (1995). The respondents were asked to evaluate each item on a 6-point scale (1 = never, 6 = always). An example item is "In performing my job, my supervisor provides me with help and support."

Exhaustion

Exhaustion was measured by five items on a 6-point scale (1 = never, 6 = always) taken from the Maslach Burnout Inventory-General Survey (Schaufeli, Leiter, Maslach, & Jackson, 1996). The Chinese version of these items was adopted from the work of Li and Shi (2003). An example item is "I feel exhausted after a whole day at work."

Control variables

Demographic variables, including gender, education, and job tenure, were measured by multiple-choice items.

Analytical strategies

Three sets of analyses were conducted. First, we used Harman's single-factor method (Podsakoff, Mackenzie, Lee, & Podsakoff, 2003) to test for common method bias. Confirmatory factor analysis (CFA) was then conducted to compare the fitness of the one-factor model with that of the five-factor model. These analyses also helped to determine the appropriateness of the measures used in the study.

   Second, the correlations were calculated, and tests of the proposed mediators and moderators were conducted using the common procedures of regression analyses. As the two moderators of emotional intelligence and supervisor support may exert their moderating effect in different positions, before and/or after coping, the regression analysis tested their hypothesized positions. Their moderating effects in the position not hypothesized were also tested to further validate that our results were not due to chance.

   Third, the method of testing mediated moderation models proposed by Muller et al. (2005) was applied. In this method, only one moderator and one mediator are included. We followed this procedure by specifying one moderator and one mediator each time. It is possible to use structural equation modeling to test the proposed model. However, six interaction terms and their reliability estimates would be involved, and although researchers have proposed various ways to calculate interaction terms, there is no consensus on the exact calculation method that should be adopted (e.g., Ping, 1995, 1996). As the final results of structural equation modeling are sensitive to these calculations, the traditional analytical tools of correlation and regression appeared to be more appropriate to test our hypotheses.

Results

The means, standard deviations, reliabilities (coefficient alphas), and correlations of the variables are presented in Table 10.1. All of the reliability coefficients are above the .70 level. As expected, emotional demands are positively related to exhaustion ($r = .21$, $p < .01$), supporting hypothesis 10.1. Emotional demands are not correlated with deep acting ($r = -.01$, n.s.) but are significantly related to surface acting ($r = .14$, $p < .01$), which supports hypothesis 10.2b but not hypothesis 10.2a. Surface acting is positively correlated with exhaustion ($r = .26$, $p < .01$), whereas deep acting has a negative relationship with exhaustion ($r = -.17$, $p < .01$), supporting hypotheses 10.3a and 10.3b.

   In the evaluation of the appropriateness of the measures used, the CFA results indicate that the fit of the six-factor measurement model (i.e., emotional demands,

Table 10.1 Descriptive statistics and correlations among measures

	Mean	S.D.	1	2	3	4	5	6	7	8
1. Exhaustion	3.35	1.01	(.77)							
2. Emotional demands	3.55	0.70	.21**	(.86)						
3. Emotional intelligence	22.52	8.74	-.32**	-.08	(.77)					
4. Supervisor support	3.54	1.16	-.20**	-.07	.25**	(.82)				
5. Deep acting	4.70	0.66	-.17**	-.01	.18**	.14**	(.87)			
6. Surface acting	3.00	0.89	.26**	.14**	-.04	.03	.04	(.86)		
7. Gender	0.73	0.44	.03	-.06	.12*	.04	.07	-.03	—	
8. Education	1.65	0.61	-.10*	-.04	.03	-.12*	.07	-.06	-.16**	—
9. Tenure	2.26	1.00	.20**	-.04	-.02	-.23**	-.11*	-.06	.04	-.01

Notes

n = 418. The numbers in parentheses are the coefficient alphas. For gender, male = 0, female = 1. For education, secondary school level = 1, post-secondary diploma = 2, bachelor's degree = 3, graduate degree = 4. For tenure, 1 = less than 1 year, 2 = 1–5 years, 3 = 6–10 years, 4 = more than 10 years.

*p < .05; **p < .01.

deep acting, surface acting, emotional intelligence, supervisor support, and exhaustion) is reasonable (χ^2 = 736.59, d.f. = 335; root mean square error approximation [RMSEA] = .053; Tucker-Lewis Index [TLI] = .92; incremental fit index [IFI] = .93; comparative fit index [CFI] = .93), whereas the one-factor model is not acceptable (χ^2 = 3420.45, d.f. = 350; RMSEA = .16; TLI = .43; IFI = .47; CFI = .47).

Table 10.2a reports moderated regression analyses testing hypotheses 10.5a and 10.5b. In predicting deep acting, the interaction term between emotional demands and emotional intelligence is significant (β = .10, p < .05), providing preliminary support for hypothesis 10.5a. Similarly, the interaction term is also significant (β = .16, p < .01) in predicting surface acting, providing preliminary support for hypothesis 10.5b. To determine the direction of the interaction, we followed the procedure of Aiken and West (1991) to plot the interactions. The results are shown in Figures 10.2a and 10.2b. The direction in Figure 10.2a is consistent with hypothesis 10.5a that employees with a high level of emotional intelligence will adopt deep acting to cope with increased emotional demands. The plot of surface acting in Figure 10.2b shows the direction to be opposite to that specified by hypothesis 10.5b. That is, employees with a high level of emotional intelligence use more rather than less surface acting to cope with increased emotional demands. Finally, to further validate that these findings are not due to chance, the non-hypothesized interaction terms between emotional demands and supervisor support were tested, and the results are reported in Table 10.2b. As expected, these interaction terms are not significant.

Table 10.2 Moderated regression testing the link between emotional demands and coping strategies

(a) Interaction between Emotional Demands and Emotional Intelligence

Independent Variables	*DV: Deep Acting*		*DV: Surface Acting*	
	Model 1	*Model 2*	*Model 1*	*Model 2*
1. Gender	.07	.07	−.02	−.02
2. Education	.07	.08+	−.06	−.04
3. Tenure	−.11*	−.11*	−.05	−.06
4. Emotional demands (ED)	.01	.03	.13**	.16**
5. Emotional intelligence (EI)	.16**	.17**	−.04	−.03
6. Interaction (ED * EI)		.10*		.16**
R	.22**	.24**	.17*	.23*
R^2	.05**	.06**	.03*	.05**
F value	4.27**		2.30*	
d.f.	5		5	
Change in R^2	—	.01*	—	.02**
Change in F value	—	4.14*	—	9.99*
Change in d.f.	—	1	—	1

(b) Interaction between Emotional Demands and Supervisor Support

Independent Variables	DV: Deep Acting		DV: Surface Acting	
	Model 1	Model 2	Model 1	Model 2
1. Gender	.09	.09+	−.03	−.02
2. Education	.10	.09+	−.06	−.06
3. Tenure	−.08	−.08	−.05	−.04
4. Emotional demands (ED)	.01	.01	.14**	.14**
5. Supervisor support (SS)	.12*	.13*	.01	.01
6. Interaction (ED * SS)		.04		.03
R	.19*	.20*	.162+	.164+
R^2	.038*	.04*	.026+	.027+
F value	3.22*		2.20+	
d.f.	5		5	
Change in R^2	—	.002	—	.001
Change in F value	—	.77	—	.30
Change in d.f.	—	1	—	1

Notes
n = 418; DV = dependent variable.

+p <. 10; *p < .05; **p < .01.

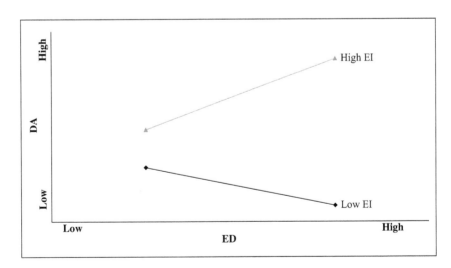

Figure 10.2a Interaction plot of the moderating effect of emotional intelligence (EI) on the relationship between emotional demands (ED) and deep acting (DA)

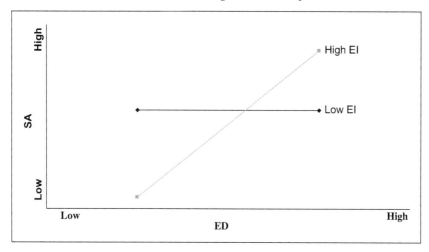

Figure 10.2b Interaction plot of the moderating effect of emotional intelligence (EI) on the relationship between emotional demands (ED) and surface acting (SA)

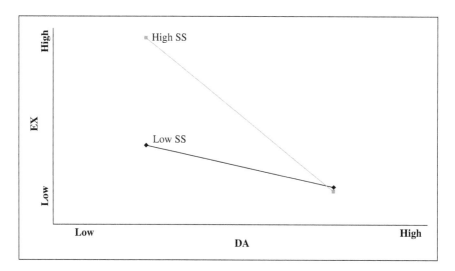

Figure 10.2c Interaction plot of the moderating effect of supervisor support (SS) on the relationship between deep acting (DA) and exhaustion (EX)

Table 10.3a reports the moderated regression analyses testing hypotheses 10.6a and 10.6b. In predicting exhaustion, the interaction term between deep acting and supervisor support is significant (β = .13, p < .01), providing preliminary support for hypothesis 10.6a. We again followed the procedure of Aiken and West (1991) to plot the direction of interaction. The results are shown in Figure 10.2c.

Table 10.3 Moderated Regression testing the link between coping strategies and exhaustion

(a) Interaction between Emotional Intelligence and Coping Strategies

Independent Variables	DV: Exhaustion		Independent Variables	DV: Exhaustion	
	Model 1	Model 2		Model 1	Model 2
1. Gender	.05	.05	1. Gender	.05	.05
2. Education	−.07	−.07	2. Education	−.06	−.06
3. Tenure	.19**	.19**	3. Tenure	.21**	.21**
4. Emotional intelligence (EI)	−.30**	−.30**	4. Emotional intelligence (EI)	−.30**	−.31**
5. Deep acting (DA)	−.09*	−.09*	5. Surface acting (SA)	.26**	.26**
6. Interaction (EI * DA)		−.02	6. Interaction (EI * SA)		−.05
R	.393**	.394	R	.462**	.464
R²	.155**	.155**	R²	.213**	.215**
F value	15**		F value	22.26**	
d.f.	5		d.f.	5	
Change in R²	—	.000	Change in R²	—	.002
Change in F value	—	.19	Change in F value	—	1.05
Change in d.f.	—	1	Change in d.f.	—	1

(b) Interaction between Supervisor Support and Coping Strategies

Independent Variables	DV: Exhaustion		Independent Variables	DV: Exhaustion	
	Model 1	Model 2		Model 1	Model 2
1. Gender	.02	.03	1. Gender	.02	.02
2. Education	−.10*	−.10*	2. Education	−.10*	−.09*
3. Tenure	.15**	.16**	3. Tenure	18**	.18**
4. Supervisor support (SS)	−.12**	−.14**	4. Supervisor support (SS)	−.17**	−.17**
5. Deep acting (DA)	−.16**	−.15**	5. Surface acting (SA)	.27**	.28**
6. Interaction (SS * DA)		.13**	6. Interaction (SS * SA)		−.06
R	.30**	.33**	R	.388**	.392**

R²	.09**	.106**	R²		.150**	.154**
F value	8.16**		F value		14.51**	
d.f.	5		d.f.		5	
Change in R²	—	.016**	Change in R²		—	.003
Change in F value	—	7.09**	Change in F value		—	1.56
Change in d.f.	—	1	Change in d.f.		—	1

Notes
n = 418. DV = dependent variable.
⁺p < .10; *p < .05; **p < .01.

The direction is consistent with hypothesis 10.6a, in that the effect of deep acting on exhaustion is much greater for employees with strong supervisor support. However, the interaction term between surface acting and supervisor support is not significant ($\beta = -.06$, n.s.), and thus hypothesis 10.6b is not supported. To further validate that this finding is not due to chance, the non-hypothesized interaction terms between (1) emotional intelligence and deep acting and (2) emotional intelligence and surface acting were also tested. The results are reported in Table 10.3b. As expected, these interaction terms are not significant.

Table 10.4 reports the results of testing hypothesis 10.4 on the mediating effect of coping strategies on the relationship between emotional demands and exhaustion. After entering the coping strategies and the hypothesized interaction terms, the beta term of emotional demands drops from .21 (p < .01) to .17 (p < .01), and the explanatory power for exhaustion increases from 10% to 28%. Furthermore, most of the hypothesized mediating terms are significant.

Although these results are consistent with the prediction of hypothesis 10.4, they give only an overall picture of the mediation process, because we added all of the proposed effects between emotional demands and exhaustion into the regression. This complication does not allow us to use traditional significance tests such as the Sobel test (1982) on the mediating effect. We thus conducted an independent Sobel test for deep acting and surface acting. In addition, our model proposes that emotional demands and emotional intelligence will have interaction effects on the mediators of deep and surface acting. We thus conducted a Sobel test for the mediation of both the main effect and the interaction effects (i.e., the interaction between emotional demands and emotional intelligence). The results indicate that the main effect of emotional demands on exhaustion is mediated not by deep acting (Sobel Statistic = −0.50, n.s.) but by surface acting (Sobel Statistic = 2.87, p < .01). However, deep acting and surface together mediate the interaction effect of emotional demands and emotional intelligence on exhaustion (Sobel Statistics = −1.67, p < .10, and 2.81, p < .01, respectively). Thus, hypothesis 10.4 is supported.

To further investigate the proposed mediated moderation model, we followed the procedure suggested by Muller et al. (2005), designed to test this kind of

Table 10.4 Results for the test of the mediating effect on exhaustion

Independent Variables	Direct Effect Model	Mediation Model
1. Gender	.02	.07+
2. Education	-.08+	-.04
3. Tenure	.21**	.19**
4. Emotional demands (ED)	.21**	.17**
Effects of the Mediation Process:		
5. Emotional intelligence (EI)	—	-.27**
6. Supervisor support (SS)	—	-.06
7. Deep acting (DA)	—	-.13**
8. Surface acting (SA)	—	.24**
9. Interaction (ED * EI)	—	.07+
10. Interaction (DA * SS)	—	.12**
11. Interaction (SA * SS)	—	-.11*
R	.308**	.529**
R^2	.10**	.28**
F value	10.76**	—
d.f.	4	—
Change in R^2	—	.18**
Change in F value	—	14.85**
Change in d.f.	—	7

Notes
n = 418. The dependent variable is exhaustion.
$^+p < .10$; $^*p < .05$; $^{**}p < .01$.

relationship. As the example provided by Muller et al. involves only one mediator and one moderator, we also conducted our analysis using one mediator and one moderator at a time, meaning that four models were tested in total. According to Muller et al., three regression analyses must be conducted for each model. The mediated moderation hypothesis is then supported if the three designated beta terms (shown in bold and italics in the tables) of these three regression analyses are significant. Table 10.5a reports the results from testing the mediated moderation involving deep acting (mediator) and emotional intelligence (moderator). As all three designated beta terms are significant, the model with both the mediator and moderator is supported. Table 10.5b reports the results testing the mediated moderation involving surface acting (mediator) and emotional intelligence (moderator). Again, as all three designated beta terms are significant, the model with both mediation and moderation is supported.

Table 10.6a reports the results of the testing of the model involving deep acting (mediator) and supervisor support (moderator). Table 10.6b reports the

Table 10.5 Test of mediated moderation using Muller, Judd, and Yzerbyt's (2005) method for emotional intelligence

(a) Mediated Moderation of Emotional Intelligence and Deep Acting

Independent Variables	DV: Exhaustion	DV: Deep Acting	DV: Exhaustion
1. Gender	.05	.07	.06
2. Education	−.06	.08+	−.05
3. Tenure	.20**	−.11*	.19**
4. Emotional demands (ED)	.21**	.025	.22**
5. Emotional intelligence (EI)	−.30**	.16**	−.28**
6. Deep acting (DA)	—	—	(−.11*)
7. Interaction (ED * EI)	(.10*)	(.10*)	.10*
8. Interaction (EI * DA)	—	—	−.04
R	.44**	.24**	.45**
R^2	.19**	.06**	.20**
F value	16.27**	4.27	13.02**
d.f.	6	6	8

(b) Mediated Moderation of Emotional Intelligence and Surface Acting

Independent Variables	DV: Exhaustion	DV: Surface Acting	DV: Exhaustion
1. Gender	.05	−.02	.06
2. Education	−.06	−.04	−.05
3. Tenure	.20**	−.06	.21**
4. Emotional demands (ED)	.21**	.16**	.18**
5. Emotional intelligence (EI)	−.30**	−.03	−.30**
6. Surface acting (SA)	—	—	(.22**)
7. Interaction (ED * EI)	(.10*)	(.16**)	.07
8. Interaction (EI * SA)	—	—	−.07+
R	.44**	.23**	.50**
R^2	.19**	.05**	.25**
F value	16.27**	3.62**	16.72**
d.f.	6	6	8

Notes

n = 418. The beta coefficients in parentheses are the conditions supporting the proposed mediated moderation according to Muller et al.'s method. DV = dependent variable.

$^+p < .10$; $^*p < .05$; $^{**}p < .01$.

Table 10.6. Test of mediated moderation using Muller, Judd, and Yzerbyt's (2005) method for supervisor support

(a) Mediated Moderation of Supervisor Support and Deep Acting

Independent Variables	DV: Exhaustion	DV: Deep Acting	DV: Exhaustion
1. Gender	.03	.09+	.04
2. Education	−.10*	.09+	−.09+
3. Tenure	.18**	−.08	.18**
4. Emotional demands (ED)	.20**	*(.01)*	.20**
5. Supervisor support (SS)	−.15**	.13*	−.12*
6. Deep acting (DA)	—	—	−.15**
7. Interaction (ED * SS)	*(.08)*	.04	.07
8. Interaction (SS * DA)	—	—	*(.12*)*
R	.35**	.20*	.388**
R^2	.12**	.04*	.15**
F value	9.47**	2.81*	8.94**
d.f.	6	6	8

(b) Mediated Moderation of Supervisor Support and Surface Acting

Independent Variables	DV: Exhaustion	DV: Surface Acting	DV: Exhaustion
1. Gender	.03	−.02	.03
2. Education	−.10*	−.06	−.09+
3. Tenure	.18**	−.04	.20**
4. Emotional demands (ED)	.20**	*(.14**)*	.17**
5. Supervisor support (SS)	−.15**	.01	−.15*
6. Surface acting (SA)	—	—	.26**
7. Interaction (ED * SS)	*(.08)*	.03	.09+
8. Interaction (SS * SA)	—	—	*(−.08+)*
R	.35**	.16+	.43**
R^2	.12**	.03+	.19**
F value	9.47**	1.88+	11.76**
d.f.	6	6	8

Notes
n = 418. The beta coefficients in parentheses are the conditions supporting the proposed mediated moderation according to Muller et al.'s method. DV = dependent variable.

+p < .10; *p < .05; **p < .01.

results of the testing of the mediated moderation model involving surface acting (mediator) and supervisor support (moderator). In both sets of analyses, not all three designated beta terms are significant, and thus the mediated moderation is not supported.

Discussion

According to the DCS and JD-R models, the negative effects of job demands on employee strain are moderated by control and support resources. However, the exact mechanism of this moderating effect has not been investigated in detail. Recent studies on coping strategies have shed some light on this missing link. Building on this work, we developed a mediated moderation model that incorporates the finding that the moderation of emotional intelligence and supervisor support is mediated by the two basic coping strategies of surface acting and deep acting. By including this missing link between emotional demands and exhaustion, the controversial empirical results of the moderation proposed by the JD-R and DCS models can be resolved.

We then tested this mediated moderation model and found that it is preliminarily supported by the results. Our main findings can be summarized as follows. First, the mediating role of the two coping strategies in the link between emotional demands and exhaustion is supported. Second, strong support is found for the moderating effect of emotional intelligence on the relationship between emotional demands and exhaustion. The moderating effect occurs between emotional demands and the two coping strategies. Third, partial support is found for the moderating effect of supervisor support on the relationship between emotional demands and exhaustion. The moderating effect is on the relationship between deep acting and exhaustion. However, the evidence for the moderation of supervisor support is relatively weak.

There is also an unexpected finding. Following the arguments in the literature (e.g., Gross, 1998a), we argue that employees with a high level of emotional intelligence engage in more deep acting and less surface acting when emotional demands increase. However, our results show that employees with a high level of emotional intelligence also engage in more surface acting when emotional demands increase. This may indicate that surface acting is not as easy as might first be thought. To perform surface acting, employees need to identify emotional cues, to adjust to perform the "right" emotions, and to control their true emotions even when they are not consistent with those displayed. In this regard, perhaps emotional intelligence is also important for the performance of surface acting. This unexpected result may provide new insight for researchers and management practitioners. Rather than viewing surface acting as negative, perhaps we should appreciate employees who put effort into displaying the required behavior even when it is not consistent with their inner feelings. This finding also reinforces the importance of emotional intelligence and confirms that it is a vital resource to help employees perform emotionally demanding tasks, regardless of the strategy adopted to do so.

Taken as a whole, the proposed mediated moderation model is supported by our empirical findings. The study contributes to the literature on the DCS and JD-R models, in that the proposed model helps to explain the inconsistent support for the buffering effect of job resources on job demands in previous studies. Future research could adopt this perspective to further examine the relationships among job demands, coping strategies, job resources, and employee outcomes. This study also contributes to the literature on emotional intelligence, as it provides clear evidence of its vital role in helping employees to handle emotionally demanding tasks.

Implications and future research

Our investigation has at least two important implications. First, our results may offer a means of further refining the DCS and JD-R models by illustrating the necessity of incorporating the role of coping strategies into the model to gain a more comprehensive understanding of how employees respond to job demands. Furthermore, to achieve a more exact elucidation of the relationship between job demands and employee strain, it may be beneficial to discuss different types of job demands rather than regarding them *en masse*. In so doing, the exact types of relevant control, support, and resources can be better identified. For example, emotional intelligence is probably an important personal resource in coping with emotional demands, but it may not be so relevant for physically demanding job duties. Future research could therefore study the mechanism of other types of job demands. Other job demands frequently mentioned by researchers using the DCS and JD-R models are heavy workloads and work pressure. It is pertinent to ask how employees react when they face these job demands, and how different types of resources may affect those reactions. For instance, employees who are given autonomy (another job resource suggested by the DCS and JD-R models) in their job may change procedures and concentrate on higher-priority tasks, whereas those without autonomy may simply extend their working hours and thus run a greater risk of becoming exhausted. If this is the case, then autonomy may have a positive buffering effect. These are interesting questions that merit future research to further enrich the DCS and JD-R models.

Second, our results indicate that surface acting and deep acting are not correlated. This may be very important, because the two strategies are usually conceptualized as "either–or" alternatives in the emotional labor literature. However, at least for insurance salespersons, our results indicate that this is an over-simplified conceptualization. For example, insurance salespersons may choose a third alternative of not following the display rules and not engaging in any acting at all. This may be particularly relevant in jobs such as insurance sales, in which it is difficult for the management to supervise or monitor the interactions between employees and clients. Furthermore, when an insurance salesperson has established a very good relationship with a particular client, it is likely that they will come to interact as good friends and be honest with each other. At this stage, the no-acting alternative may be the most appropriate. Future research could thus investigate alternatives other than surface and deep acting in response to emotional demands. However, these possible alternatives notwithstanding, our findings clearly show that employees who adopt deep acting rather than surface acting reduce the possibility of burnout. A recent study found that dispositional factors such as personality are more related to surface acting than to deep acting (Dicfcndorff, Croyle, & Gosserand, 2005), indicating that deep acting is probably a type of skill that can be developed and trained by organizations. Hence, future research could also investigate how organizations could train their employees to use deep acting in response to emotional job demands.

Limitations

Before we conclude, four limitations of this study must be noted. First, as an initial effort to suggest a reasonable extension to the DCS and JD-R models, we only examined one type of job demand (emotional demands), two types of coping behaviors (deep and surface acting), and two possible moderators (emotional intelligence and supervisor support). Future research could explore different types of job demands, job controls, and resources to further refine and enrich the explanatory power of the model.

Second, owing to the nature of the constructs, we were obliged to rely mostly on employees to provide the information, which may have resulted in the inflation of the relationships among the constructs as a result of common method variance. However, as the key hypotheses of the study involve indirect and moderating effects, our conclusion should be less subject to common method bias. The CFA results and the insignificant correlations for several key variables (emotional intelligence and surface acting, surface acting and supervisor support, and deep acting and surface acting) also indicate that the extent of common method variance is minimal. Nevertheless, future research should use multiple indicators of different constructs, such as others' ratings of emotional intelligence (Law, Wong, & Song, 2004), and an objective indicator of burnout, such as physiological symptoms of stress, to avoid common method variance.

Third, our sample consists of Chinese respondents who were salespersons in the insurance industry. It is thus possible that our findings may not be generalizable to employees in other cultures. However, as pointed out by Law, Wong, and Song (2004), emotional intelligence should be an ability that can be generalized across cultures. Insurance agents are usually not under close and bureaucratic supervision, and this is also true of the two organizations under investigation. Thus, although our respondents worked for state-owned companies in China, we believe that the context is comparable to that of workers in other organizations. However, it would certainly be worthwhile to conduct further research in other industries and cultures to cross-validate our findings.

Finally, we used cross-sectional data to test our model. The mediation effects are tested using the procedures of Baron and Kenny (1986). As the causal directions are assumed rather than tested for this type of design, we are cautious in making causal inferences about the mediation proposed in reporting our results (Stone-Romero & Rosopa, 2008). Although we followed the literature in assuming that emotional demands induce coping strategies, it is possible that coping strategies may also affect employees' perceptions of the level of emotional demands. Employees who can easily adopt deep acting may feel that their jobs are less emotionally demanding. Thus, emotional demands and coping strategies may be reciprocally related. Similarly, coping strategies and exhaustion may be reciprocally related in that employees who feel exhausted may not be able to engage in deep or surface acting. Future research should use an experimental or longitudinal design to test these possible causal directions (Stone-Romero & Rosopa, 2008).

Conclusion

Despite these limitations, the findings of this study provide preliminary support for the proposed mediated moderation model in which emotional intelligence moderates the relationship between emotional demands and coping strategies, although the moderation of supervisor support on the relationship between coping strategy and exhaustion received only partial support. These findings have both theoretical and empirical implications. Theoretically, they suggest a means by which the DCS and JD-R models can be further refined and extended to give a better understanding of the relationship between job demands and employee strain. Practically, our results demonstrate the importance of emotional intelligence and the use of deep acting in preventing exhaustion among employees. They also indicate that supervisor support is especially important to buffer employees who engage in surface acting from exhaustion. It may thus be beneficial for practitioners to provide effective training in deep acting and supervisor support to enhance employee well-being, which would improve employee job performance and long-term vocational health.

11 Summary and review

In 2010, a meta-analysis on emotional intelligence (EI) was published in the *Journal of Applied Psychology* (Joseph & Newman, 2010). Meta-analysis means a quantitative way to summarize the findings of past studies in order to come up with an overall estimate concerning the relationship between two variables. The major concern of EI meta-analysis is the relationship between EI and job outcomes. The conclusion of this meta-analytic paper is that EI is related to job outcomes, especially for jobs with high emotional labor requirement. In fact, this conclusion had been confirmed in some other meta-analytic publications.

This meta-analytic study, however, makes me feel very uncomfortable because of its conceptualization of the EI construct. It proposes a cascading model in which EI has three dimensions, namely, emotion perception, emotion understanding, and emotion regulation. These dimensions are regarded as separate constructs that are causally related. Emotion perception (i.e., the ability to perceive emotions accurately) is the cause of emotion understanding (the ability to understand one's own emotions). Emotion understanding is in turn the cause of emotion regulation (i.e., the ability to regulate one's emotions). Emotion regulation is then the cause of job outcomes.

I feel uncomfortable using the cascading model to conceptualize EI because if the model is true, then there is no need to have the EI construct at all. We should study the three constructs directly, and there is no need to label them under the umbrella of EI. Also, as the most important cause of job outcomes is emotion regulation, we should concentrate our efforts on studying how people can improve their abilities in regulating their emotions. Thus, accepting the cascading model as the true representation of the reality actually means that we should forget about the EI construct.

Lesson 28: challenges from contradictory information

I am not saying that the cascading model must be wrong. However, it is clearly contradictory to the proposal of an EI construct which means the overall abilities to handle issues or problems related to emotions. As Joseph and Newman had presented results based on their cascading assumption, I re-analyzed their data with the alternative conceptualization that an overall EI construct was formed from the dimensions. I found out that this alternative conceptualization actually had a better predictive power on job outcomes. I therefore drafted a short note and submitted it to the journal as a response to Joseph and Newman's paper.

Unfortunately, but somehow as expected, the short note was rejected. The main reason was that there was little "incremental contribution" of the note. The editor and reviewers did not agree that this was an important issue. While we were wondering how we could publish this idea, the editors of a book invited us to write a review on the EI literature, especially that with implications for Chinese researchers. I believed it would be a good time to summarize my thoughts about this line of research, and so I agreed to contribute a chapter. I searched for the studies reported in both Chinese and English and summarized my thoughts on the EI construct, including the above idea on the cascading model; EI measures; and its relationships with other variables.

I think this book chapter, which was rigorously reviewed by the two editors, should be a good summary and concluding chapter for this book as well. As my final lesson from my EI research experiences, I think we should be prepared for ideas in the field that are contradictory to our work. We should welcome those ideas and try to be objective in evaluating them. They may provide good insights and opportunities for us to develop new research projects.

Lesson 28: There are always challenges and new advances in the research area we are interested in. Some of the new information may be contradictory to what we believe. This may be a good opportunity for us to further advance our knowledge.

The following are the major contents of the paper.

Wong, C. S., & Peng, K. Z. (2012). Chinese emotional intelligence. In X. Huang and Michael H. Bond (Eds.), *Handbook of Chinese organizational behavior: Integrating theory, research and practice*, **pp. 87–102. Cheltenham, UK: Edward Elgar, MPG Books Group; these contents are reprinted with permission.**

Introduction

The concept of emotional intelligence (EI) was first proposed in the year 1990 and became a popular concept in the media after the publication of Goleman's (1995) best-selling trade book. In the scientific arena, the number of academic publications on EI is extensive, even though it was subjected to strong criticism in its first 10 years. We searched the PsycINFO database for journal articles using the key words "emotional intelligence" every three years since 1990. As shown in Table 11.1, only 13 articles had been published as of 1999. However, since 1999 the number of journal publications on this topic has increased tremendously – 1,240 articles have been published between 1999 and 2010.

Table 11.1 Number of publications with "emotional intelligence" as key words in PsycINFO since 1990

	1990–1992	1993–1995	1996–1998	1999–2001	2002–2004	2005–2007	2008–2010
All publication types	2	4	17	133	398	695	870
Journal papers	2	2	9	71	241	411	517

The trend is clear: more and more researchers are investigating the EI concept. It appears that EI researchers have overcome their initial skepticism, and the EI concept is now widely accepted by academic journal editors and reviewers. However, we believe that some fundamental issues about the validity of the EI concept remain unresolved. As there have already been quite a number of qualitative reviews (e.g., G. Huang, Law, & Wong, 2006; Murphy, 2006; Walter, Cole, & Humphrey, 2011) and quantitative reviews (e.g., Joseph & Newman, 2010; O'Boyle, Humphrey, Pollack, Hawver, & Story, 2010; Van Rooy & Viswesvaran, 2004) of the EI literature, we will attempt to concentrate our efforts in this review on some of the still-unresolved issues and hope to provide insights for future EI researchers, especially Chinese EI researchers.

We organize our discussion using the following structure: first, we will briefly review the history of EI research since the construct was proposed in 1990; second, we will discuss cross-cultural issues and the role of Chinese EI researchers; third, we will explore the deficiency in EI measures, a critical issue in EI research, especially when the various measures are used despite various cultures of origins; fourth, we will introduce the most recent conceptualization of EI and discuss why the fundamental issue about the validity of EI as a scientific construct is still unresolved; and, finally, we conclude this review by summarizing some directions for future EI research, especially in Chinese societies.

A brief history of research on EI since 1990

Although education, psychology, and management scholars have long recognized the important role of social and interpersonal skills, it was not until 1990 that the concept of EI was proposed. The term "emotional intelligence" originally appeared in two academic journal articles published that year (Mayer, Dipaolo, & Salovey, 1990; Salovey & Mayer, 1990) and is rooted in the historically earlier concept of social intelligence. EI was proposed for exploring "multiple intelligences," as an alternative to the traditional concept of general mental abilities (GMA; Gardner, 1993). It is unfortunate that while searching for a non-GMA concept of ability, early proponents of the EI concept did not clearly specify its domain based on the traditional definition of intelligence. Later, researchers and practitioners gradually included other non-ability dimensions, such as motivation and personality, as part of EI (e.g., Bar-On, 1997; Goleman, 1995, 1998).

This imprecision and inconsistency created serious confusion as to the definition of EI, limiting its use as a scientifically rigorous construct. Some critics even questioned the validity of the EI construct, claiming that it might be just another example in the game of "reinventing the wheel" by relabeling an established set of constructs in the well-researched area of emotions, motivation, and personality (e.g., Ciarrochi, Chan, & Caputi, 2000; G. Matthews, Zeidner, & Roberts, 2002). Davies, Stankov, and Roberts (1998) demonstrated empirically that measures of EI developed before 1998 cannot form a distinct factor in factor analysis when combined with the well-established Big Five personality measures.

In response, two lines of effort were initiated to clarify the definition of the EI construct. The first one was to distinguish the differences between "trait EI" and "ability EI." For example, Petrides and Furnham (2000a, 2000b, 2001) defined trait EI (or emotional self-efficacy) as a constellation of behavioral dispositions and self-perceptions concerning one's ability to recognize, process, and utilize emotion-laden information. It pertains to the realm of personality and is measured by self-report questionnaires. In contrast, ability EI (or cognitive-emotional ability) refers to the actual ability to recognize, process, and utilize emotion-laden information; therefore, it must be measured by performance tests.

The second line of effort concentrates on the ability conceptualization of EI. The aim is to investigate the validity of EI as a facet of intelligence when it is defined as the ability to handle emotional issues. This line of effort does not assume that actual ability must be measured by performance tests. Instead, it focuses on the ability definition of EI and considers whether the items used in its measurement are based on and responsive to this definition. To date, studies that take this ability view of EI have accumulated convincing evidence that EI meets the standard for an "intelligence" (e.g., Côté & Miners, 2006; Law, Wong, & Song, 2004; Wong, Foo, Wang, & Wong, 2007).

Specifically, EI is qualified as a facet of intelligence according to the three criteria that are highlighted by Mayer, Caruso, et al. (2000a). There are conceptual, correlational, and developmental criteria. The conceptual criterion requires that EI reflects mental abilities for dealing with emotions instead of preferred ways of behaving. That is, intelligence refers to ability rather than personality. Gardner (1993) defined intelligence as "the *ability* to solve problems, or to fashion products, that are valued in one or more cultural or community settings" (p. 7, italics added). The definition by Mayer, Salovey, and their co-authors (2000b, 2002) meets this requirement. Following this ability-based definition, researchers demonstrated that EI is distinct from personality dimensions. It has predictive validity on job-related outcomes, such as job satisfaction and performance, beyond that of the Big Five personality measures, even for a self-report EI measure that was developed according to this ability view (e.g., Law, Wong, & Song, 2004; Wong & Law, 2002).

The second criterion is the correlational criterion. If EI were an intelligence construct, then it "should represent a set of correlated abilities that are similar to, but distinct from, mental abilities" (Mayer, Caruso, et al., 2000a, p. 270). In other words, if EI is to be regarded as an intelligence construct, then it should correlate with other intelligence constructs such as GMA. These correlations cannot be too high (discriminant validity), nor can they be too low (convergent validity). Empirical evidence in the literature has shown that the dimensions of EI are moderately correlated among themselves but only mildly correlated with GMA (Côté & Miners, 2006; Mayer, Salovey, et al., 2000b; Wong & Law, 2002), just like other intelligence constructs. The empirical evidence greatly encourages the researchers in this school.

The third argument of Mayer, Caruso, et al. (2000a) is that intelligence should be developmental in its nature. The verbal ability of a person, for example, should increase as one becomes older while using one's native language. For Chinese samples, Wong, Wong, and Law (2005) found that EI is positively correlated with age among incumbents of six different job types. Wong, Foo, et al. (2007) further demonstrated that EI is positively related to proxy variables of family and life experiences. Mayer, Salovey, et al. (2000b) also showed with a series of studies that EI increases with age and experience, which qualifies it as an ability rather than a personality trait.

With these efforts and progress in the development of various EI measures after 1998 (e.g., Mayer, Salovey, & Caruso, 1999; Wong & Law, 2002), at least three EI research findings have received convincing support, not only for Western respondents, but also in Chinese samples. First, EI has been shown to be related to leaders' behaviors and the effectiveness of their leadership (e.g., Tang, Yin, & Nelson, 2010; Wong & Law, 2002). Second, EI is related to various job-related outcomes over and above the contributions of GMA and personality. Examples of job outcomes that are related to EI include satisfaction and performance (e.g., Law, Wong, & Song, 2004; Wong et al., 2005), well-being, work stress, burnout and coping strategies (e.g., Chang & Chang, 2010; F. Y. Cheung & Tang, 2009; X. Huang, Chan, Lam, & Nan, 2010; K. Z. Peng, Wong, & Che, 2010), and organizational commitment (e.g., W. Wu, Liu, Song, & Liu, 2006). Third, in education EI has been shown to be related to students' attitudes and behaviors (e.g., Chan, 2007, 2008b; Siu, 2009; Song et al., 2010; Wong, Wong, & Chau, 2001) and the job outcomes of school teachers (e.g., Chan, 2006, 2008a; Wong, Wong, & Peng, 2010).

Besides examining the reviews reported in the English literature, we also searched for EI studies published in Chinese in journals in both mainland China and Taiwan. Specifically, we searched for EI studies published from 1990 to 2010 in the major journals listed in the education, psychology, and management areas of the mainland Chinese National Science Foundation and three major journals in Taiwan. We found 50 Chinese papers in these journals that are related to the EI construct; all of them used Chinese samples. Most of the papers published before 2004 discussed the EI construct and studies reported in the English literature (e.g., Z. Peng, Lin, Zhang, & Che, 2004; Zhang, 1999).

More recent studies have concentrated on testing the factor structure and psychometric properties of various EI measures reported in the English literature when translated and administered to Chinese respondents (e.g., Y. Huang, Lu, Wang, & Shi, 2008; Wang & Lo, 2008) or assessed the relationships between EI and outcome variables similar to those in studies reported in the English literature, such as students' attitudes and behaviors (Y. Liu & Zou, 2010) or employees' job attitudes and performance (e.g. M. T. Chen, Lee, & Huang, 2007; Chu & Kao, 2005; Yu & Yuan, 2008). It appears that the issues investigated and results reported in papers published in the Chinese language are in line with the English EI literature.

Cross-cultural issues and the role of Chinese EI researchers

As reviewed in the last section, there are many EI studies using Chinese samples, and their results are consistent with the mainstream EI literature. In fact, some are pioneers in several research directions. For example, Wong and associates were the first group to empirically show that EI is related to important job outcomes (Law, Wong, & Song, 2004; Wong & Law, 2002) and report on the feasibility of EI training (Wong, Foo, et al., 2007). They also proposed that the relationship between EI and job outcomes should depend on the extent to which the job requires incumbents to present prescribed emotions, e.g., customer service workers. This moderation has received empirical support (e.g., Wong & Law, 2002; Wong et al., 2005) and is widely accepted by EI researchers (Joseph & Newman, 2010). However, to date we have not seen many cross-cultural issues being explored in the literature. This may due to the relatively universal nature of the EI construct (see also Yik, 2010), despite the fact that Chinese emotional expression differs from that of other cultural groups (Bond, 1993; S. Wong, Bond, & Rodriguez Mosquera, 2008).

As EI is the ability to handle emotion-related issues, it is common to all human beings. As with any other great civilizations in human history, Chinese culture provides many teachings concerning the importance of considering both emotion and reason, counseling that is unwise to let either emotion or reason alone guide our lives. Without emotion, human beings lack the passion and persistence that lead to great achievement. Without reason, human beings are unable to plan and execute great achievements. Thus, it is not surprising that the EI construct and its nomological network may be universally applicable to all societies. Law, Wong, and Song (2004) put it in the following way:

> We do not know whether EI varies across different cultures. However, when we go back to the EI literature, we do not find any discussion of EI across cultural boundaries. Our position is that one's abilities to understand, regulate, and use one's emotions in constructive ways are general human abilities. There is no immediate evidence that the validity of EI, as defined under our four-dimensional view, should vary across cultures. Whereas further

studies may be needed to verify this position, we take the general scientific attitude that psychological and management phenomena are considered as universal unless there are theories or evidence showing their cross-cultural variations.

(p. 495)

However, taking this position does not mean that there are no cross-cultural issues in EI research. The biggest issue may be its measurement or the manifestation of EI in different social contexts. While the EI construct may be universal to all human societies, the behaviors that differentiate the level of EI among people may differ among cultures. Law, Wong, and Song (2004) argued, "Although the EI construct may be universal, we agree that behaviors resulting from the EI of an individual may vary across cultures. For example, a nonreactive quiet response by the subordinate when one's boss is making unreasonable demands may reflect high EI among Chinese workers, but probably not among non-Chinese workers" (p. 495).

Thus, the cultural norms and expectations surrounding emotional expression must be considered when assessing the EI level of an individual. In fact, there is some preliminary evidence showing that the most well-known EI measure developed in North America based on judgment of appropriate behaviors (the Mayer-Salovey-Caruso Emotional Intelligence Test [MSCEIT]; Mayer et al., 1999) may not be valid for Chinese respondents (Law, Wong, Huang, & Li, 2008). Thus, developing EI measures that are valid for a specific culture or for comparison across cultures may be an important research direction.

Until now we have assumed that EI measures were valid for all Chinese respondents. As China is a vast country, there are many differences among different regional cultures, in which different cultures of minority people are embedded. The mean score for a scale specifically developed for Chinese respondents (Wong's Emotional Intelligence Scale [WEIS]; Wong, Law, & Song, 2004, Wong, Wong, et al., 2007) was much lower for respondents in an inland province (K. Z. Peng et al., 2010) than for those in more developed areas of China (e.g., Wong, Wong, et al., 2007), although the EI scores were related to important job outcomes, as expected. As the WEIS is composed of forced-choice items and each item has only two options, it is not very meaningful to examine the measurement invariance across samples. However, given the fact that the psychometric properties and predictive validity are acceptable among various Chinese samples, we believe the scale is valid. The difference in mean scores may reflect different stages of social and economic development, as well as other factors that future research may further investigate.

Deficiencies in EI measures

One of the fundamental issues vexing EI researchers is the lack of a convincing way to measure individual levels of EI. The EI literature describes three basic problems concerning EI measurement: first, as EI is a particular type of ability, using self-report methods to measure EI may lack face validity, especially compared with the performance tests widely used to measure GMA. Practically, using self-report EI measures in research involving other self-report measures may easily fall into the problem of common method variance (Lindebaum & Cartwright, 2010). Some researchers even confuse the definition of EI with its measurement method. They argue that if EI is measured by a subjective evaluation method, such as self-report or other ratings (i.e., the EI level of the focal person is evaluated by other people who are familiar with the focal person), then it must not be truly measuring EI as defined under the ability model (e.g., Petrides & Furnham, 2000a, 2000b, 2001). The rationale is that, for GMA, there is evidence that self-report scores produce correlations with GMA tests that are only in the .20 range. This is why they created the concepts of trait EI versus ability EI and argued that researchers are investigating a trait instead of ability when EI is measured by self-report.

We disagree with this position. EI is not the same as GMA. Depending on the nature of the ability under investigation, a self-report or other rating may be reliable and valid. For example, if we ask people to evaluate their eyesight or their running speed, the answers should be reliable and valid. Whether one can evaluate one's own ability to handle emotion-related issues accurately may be an empirical question that has not yet been addressed. Furthermore, when asked to evaluate another person with whom one is very familiar, perhaps an accurate judgment can be made because self-evaluation bias does not exist when others provide the rating of the target. We must handle emotions frequently in our daily lives, and we receive feedback concerning how well we do so. Thus, we should have ample opportunity to understand how well we or those close to us do at handling emotional issues. However, this is an empirical question that requires evidence to provide a definitive answer. Thus, while self-report or other rating methods appear to be inferior to performance tests and lack convincing face validity, it is too early to conclude that the only valid way to measure ability is by tests similar to those for GMA assessment.

Second, although performance tests have high face validity, it is difficult to construct performance tests of EI that are comparable to GMA tests. Unlike problems in language, mathematics, or reasoning, it is almost impossible to create an emotion-related problem with only one correct answer. Even for measures like the MSCEIT, which claims to be an EI performance test, the "correct" answer may be debatable, especially across different cultures. For example, one MSCEIT item is a photo of a person, and respondents are required to determine the emotions experienced by the person from that person's facial expression. Answers indicating a high EI level are derived using expert judgment or a norm-referenced method.

Neither method is convincing because the judgment of experts or the majority of respondents may not be the best answer. WEIS, a forced-choice scale developed for Chinese respondents, attempts to avoid this problem by using a criterion-based validation method. That is, items are selected only if they are related to criterion variables that are conceptually correlated with EI (e.g., life satisfaction). The social desirability of the choices and the possibility of faking were carefully checked during its development and cross-validation (Wong, Wong, & Song, 2004; Wong, Wong, et al., 2007). For example, one of the WEIS items is "When you are very down, you will: (a) try to do something to make yourself feel better, or (b) just ignore it because you know your emotion will return to normal naturally." This item is selected because respondents choosing (a) and (b) differ significantly in their responses to criterion variables as well. However, using such a criterion-validation method makes it difficult to interpret why one choice indicates high EI while the other does not. In the above item, it is not easy to explain why the choice of (a) or (b) represents a higher EI level on the part of the respondents. The difficulty in identifying correct answers for scales like the MSCEIT and WEIS indicates that they are not true performance tests for EI. In fact, we doubt whether EI tests comparable to GMA tests can be developed, because it is not clear how the "correct" answers for the test items can be identified objectively.

Third, although we should not be too pessimistic about self-report or other-rated EI measures, and there is some evidence concerning their measurement invariance across cultures (Whitman, Van Rooy, Viswesvaran, & Kraus, 2009), their validity is subject to skepticism. To demonstrate the validity of such EI measures, we require a good criterion of the true EI level of respondents, but this is still missing in the EI literature. The best we can obtain is probably the multi-trait multi-method (MTMM) approach used by Law, Wong, and Song (2004). Using both self-report and other ratings of EI in MTMM analysis, Law, Wong, and Song (2004) reported discriminant, convergent, and predictive validities of their EI measures. However, validity evidence resulting from such a method can only demonstrate consistency among raters, and such ratings are able to predict some criterion outcome. Whether the construct measured is truly EI (i.e., the ability to handle emotional issues) is still debatable because it could be a particular trait or attitude that received consistent responses from the various raters. Evidence from MTMM may be convincing for many abstract psychological constructs, and, as discussed before, others' ratings may validly measure EI. However, if EI is truly an objective human ability, a definitive measure should be a true performance test rather than a subjective assessment by oneself or others.

Alternatively, an EI test score should be able to show a strong relationship with objective physiological responses. In recent years, an increasing number of studies have used brain-imaging techniques to study emotions (e.g., DeYoung, Shamosh, Green, Braver, & Gray, 2009; Koenigs, Barbey, Postle, & Grafman, 2009), and it is almost certain that some brain regions, such as the amygdala, play critical roles in human emotions (Goleman, 1995). However, few brain-imaging study designs have been based on the conceptualization of the EI construct directly.

The work of Bar-On, Tranel, Denburg, and Bechara (2003) may be one of the few exceptions. They compared 12 patients who had focal, stable lesions in brain structures believed to be important for EI with 11 patients who had lesions in brain structures not related to EI. The EI scores of the two patient groups differed significantly, as measured by a self-report scale and a decision-making exercise. This study provides preliminary evidence for a possible relationship between a self-report EI measure and physiological structures. However, the sample size in this study was small, and the EI measure contained both ability and non-ability items. Thus, it is difficult to draw definitive conclusions because differences in the self-report ratings may have been the result of factors other than brain structure differences. For example, the self-perceptions of the two groups of patients may have differed because of weaknesses in brain structures rather than a lower ability to handle emotional issues.

Brain-imaging studies have demonstrated that, even for similar tasks, coordination among different parts of the brain is necessary to carry out the tasks (e.g., Fehr, Code, & Herrmann, 2007; Friedrich & Friederici, 2009). As EI refers to the ability to process emotion-related information and the subsequent judgment concerning how to respond appropriately, it inevitably involves the coordination of different brain regions. That is, regions involving emotional arousal and those involving cognitive abilities related to rational judgment are both needed to respond adequately. For example, everyone feels fear when confronted with a snake-like structure (i.e., automatic emotional arousal). In such conditions, people with high EI may calm down in a relatively short period and thus be able to arrive at an accurate assessment more easily and handle their emotions more appropriately. On the contrary, people with low EI may not be able to manage their emotions and make an accurate assessment because they are greatly influenced by their emotions. Furthermore, if the negative emotions exist for a longer period because they are not good at regulating and managing emotions, negative effects on physical and/or psychological health will result. This suggests the potential for EI researchers to design appropriate studies to investigate how brain activity differs when people need to handle emotional situations.

The nature of EI as a multidimensional construct

A more fundamental issue is the question of EI as a scientifically rigorous construct. In the past 20 years, researchers have come to agree that EI is multidimensional. Although the exact dimensions are not the same among researchers, the differences are minimal. For example, Mayer, Salovey, et al. (2000a) used emotion perception, emotion understanding, emotion facilitation, and emotion regulation as the four dimensions of the EI construct, but some researchers also include the ability to understand others' emotions as one of the dimensions (e.g., Wong & Law, 2002).

Despite this important progress in explicating the domains of the EI construct, we believe that two important issues in the EI literature still contain confusing messages. The first is that the term "EI" should have precluded its usage as a trait. The two words, "emotional" and "intelligence," indicate a set of abilities related to handling emotions; therefore, we disagree with terms such as trait EI.

Our position is that if EI is a facet of intelligence, then the term "trait" should not be used. Accordingly, we believe that EI researchers should make it clear that the so-called trait model and mixed model of EI are incorrect. Further, researchers who adopt these models should not label their construct as EI.

More important, EI is questioned as a scientifically rigorous construct because, before its proposal, numerous rigorously researched emotion-related constructs already existed, such as empathy (e.g., Mahsud, Yukl, & Prussia, 2010; Taylor, Kluemper, & Mossholder, 2010) and emotion regulation (e.g., Gross, 1998a, 1998b). What are the differences between EI and these constructs? If EI is merely a total set of these emotion-related constructs, why shouldn't we just conceptualize and theorize about these constructs independently? To make EI a rigorous construct, EI should be a higher-level construct built on these constructs. In other words, these constructs are similar to the separate dimensions of a multidimensional EI construct (Law, Wong, & Mobley, 1998; Wong, Law, & Huang, 2008).

The most appealing way forward may be to define the EI construct in straightforward and clear terms: as the ability to handle emotional issues (Wong & Law, 2002). In our daily experience, we are aware that people differ in this ability. What makes the EI conceptualization complicated is that many situations involve emotional issues, and the ability to handle oneself in an emotionally effective way can manifest itself in numerous ways. For example, in some situations, understanding other's emotions (empathy) helps us handle these situations effectively. However, in other situations, our ability to regulate our emotions may be critical; in many cases, we need a combination of these abilities. A single construct that can generalize across these situations would constitute a parsimonious and powerful conceptualization to describe emotion-related abilities. Although it is questionable whether a single construct can completely describe this ability, it nevertheless creates a challenging and appealing task for scientists.

Unfortunately, EI researchers do not appear to completely understand the importance of this fundamental issue regarding EI as a possible multidimensional construct. For example, Joseph and Newman (2010) conducted a meta-analysis on the EI construct and conceptualized EI as a cascading model in which the three dimensions (emotion perception, emotion understanding, and emotion regulation) are related in a sequential manner, affecting job performance. Figure 11.1 represents the core of their model. In the full model, cognitive ability and conscientiousness are also hypothesized to have direct effects on job performance. Using structural equation modeling to analyze the meta-analytic correlation matrix, these researchers concluded that the model is supported because emotion regulation completely mediated the effects of emotion perception and emotion understanding on job performance (Joseph & Newman, 2010, p. 65).

Although we agree that the cascading model may represent a possible conceptualization of the EI concept, it has a clear disadvantage. The EI dimensions are regarded as distinct but related constructs. However, under this conceptualization, an overall EI construct does not exist. EI becomes merely a label for

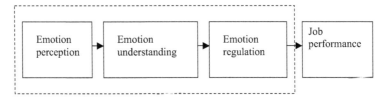

Figure 11.1 Joseph and Newman's (2010) conceptualization of emotional intelligence

related constructs rather than a scientific construct in and of itself. Wong, Law, et al. (2008) refer to this as a "pseudo-multidimensional construct" and conclude that the label provides limited utility in either theory building or empirical investigation.

Chinese EI researchers have offered an alternative conceptualization of an overall EI construct as a person's ability to handle emotional issues. Wong and Law (2002) describe it as follows:

> However, as EI is a multidimensional construct, one final issue is the estimation of the overall EI construct from its dimensions. Law, Wong, and Mobley (1998) pointed out that there are three types of multidimensional constructs, namely: profile, aggregate, and latent. . . . As the EI construct represents interrelated sets (dimensions) of abilities, it fits mostly the latent type. That is, the EI construct exists at a deeper level than its dimensions, and the dimensions should be interrelated because they are manifestations of the EI construct. This definition is also comparable to the traditional intelligence construct, which is defined as the common factor behind various sets (dimensions) of abilities in verbal comprehension, word fluency, space, number, memory, and reasoning.
>
> (p. 260)

Thus, EI can be a latent multidimensional construct (Law et al., 1998). Figure 11.2 illustrates the nature of this type of construct. For the sake of simplicity, Figure 11.2 assumes that there are only three dimensions underlying the EI construct. Figure 11.2a shows that the overall EI construct is a true multidimensional construct, which is the common source of its dimensions. Figure 11.2b shows the EI construct from a variance-partitioning perspective (Law et al., 1998), in which only the common variance among the dimensions ($C_{1, 2, 3}$) is the true variance for the EI construct. None of the other variances that are either unique to one dimension (U_1, U_2, and U_3) or shared by two dimensions (C_{12}, C_{13}, and C_{23}) are part of the EI construct. If the EI construct can be conceptualized in this way, then the common variance behind all, instead of only some, of its dimensions must be extracted to investigate its relationship with other constructs (Edwards, 2001). For example, if dimension 3 in Figure 11.2b is

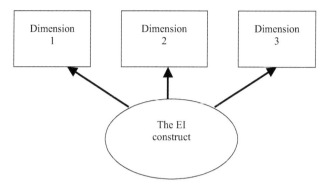

Figure 11.2a Relationship between the emotional intelligence (EI) construct and its dimensions under the alternative conceptualization

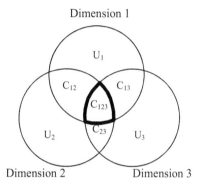

Figure 11.2b The variance of the true emotional intelligence construct under the alternative conceptualization

U = unique; C = common.

not included in the analysis, C_{12} will be regarded as part of the true variance of the multidimensional construct. This may lead to incorrect conclusions about the relationship between the multidimensional construct and other constructs.

Joseph and Newman (2010) used Mayer and Salovey's (1997) definition of ability-based EI in their analyses but included only three of their four dimensions, namely, emotion perception, emotion understanding, and emotion regulation. The dimension of emotion facilitation and other dimensions that may be captured by EI measures other than the MSCEIT (Mayer, Salovey, Caruso, & Sitarenios, 2003) were not included in their analysis. As this is an extremely important issue for the validity of an overall EI construct, we attempted to test the feasibility of Wong and Law's (2002) alternative conceptualization of the EI construct.

We included all possible dimensions and examined the relationship between the common variance behind these dimensions and other criterion variables. We tested the possibility of such an alternative latent EI construct using the same dataset as Joseph and Newman (2010, p. 63). Specifically, we specified a latent EI construct as the common factor behind all of its dimensions and the other EI measures reported in their meta-analytic results, and we used factor analysis to calculate its correlations with cognitive abilities, the Big Five personality measures, and job performance. We then used regression analysis to determine whether our EI construct predicts job performance better than emotion regulation does. Under the cascading model, emotion regulation is a better predictor of job performance than any of the other EI dimensions. If the latent EI construct model is an inferior conceptualization than the cascading model, its predictive power on job performance should be smaller than that of emotion regulation. If it is not a feasible conceptualization, it may have no predictive power on job performance at all.

Table 11.2 shows the results of our analyses. Similar to the conclusions of Joseph and Newman (2010, p. 70), we found that emotion regulation is related to job performance, positively for high emotional labor jobs and negatively for low emotional labor jobs, after controlling for the Big Five personality dimensions and cognitive abilities. However, the latent EI construct shows a similar pattern of relationships, with stronger results in terms of a larger incremental R^2. This additional analysis thus shows that, compared with the results when EI is conceptualized as a sequence of cascading dimensions, it is more feasible to conceptualize EI as a latent multidimensional construct.

It is encouraging that this simple re-analysis shows that EI can be conceptualized as a latent multidimensional construct and operationalized as the common variance among abilities related to handling emotions. This is similar to the traditional conceptualization of intelligence, GMA. Otherwise, it may be unnecessary to use EI as a label for the distinct but causally linked constructs that are related to abilities in handling emotions. If EI is merely a label rather than a construct, it has little role in scientific investigation, suggesting that we should concentrate on its dimensions, such as empathy and emotion regulation, instead of EI itself.

While this simple analysis is meaningful, the results are preliminary because of some important limitations. First, even for meta-analyses, few studies have investigated the relationship between EI and job performance. The sample sizes identified in Joseph and Newman's meta-analysis are only 220 (high emotional labor jobs) and 223 (low emotional labor jobs). Second, the relatively small incremental R^2 (i.e., the predictive power of EI over and above that provided by the Big Five personality dimensions and cognitive abilities) may be due to the fact that we still do not have very good measures of EI. The relatively small correlations among different EI measures suggest room for improvement in the accuracy of measurement scales. Third, it may be important to accumulate more evidence regarding the relationship between EI and job performance.

Table 11.2 Results of regression analyses on job performance using Joseph and Newman's (2010) data

	High Emotional Labor (n = 220)			Low Emotional Labor (n = 223)			Total (n = 562)		
Cognitive ability	.374**	.351**	.312**	.409**	.428**	.462**	.456**	.446**	.448**
Conscientiousness	.214**	.197**	.159*	.256**	.269**	.297**	.226*	.219**	.219**
Emotional stability	-.012	-.018	-.034	.030	.036	.044	.001	.002	-.002
Agreeableness	.021	-.020	-.031	.035	.067	.074	-.002	-.019	-.008
Extraversion	.079	.059	.038	.090	.106	.118	.088	.080*	.083
Openness	.017	.003	-.016	-.059	-.047	-.035	-.042	.048	-.046
Emotion regulation	—	.171*	—	—	-.139*	—	—	.073	—
Emotional intelligence (latent construct)	—	—	.246*	—	—	-.207*	—	—	.034
ΔR²	—	.024*	.042*	—	.017*	.032*	—	.004	.001
R²	.191**	.215**	.233**	.241**	.258**	.273**	.254**	.258**	.255

*p < .05; **p < .01.

With few studies reporting on this relationship, it is difficult to conduct meaningful meta-analyses that allow us to draw stronger conclusions. However, it shows that there is still an opportunity for Chinese EI researchers to conceptualize and test the validity of a single EI construct that may be powerful in describing human abilities for handling emotion-related issues. Skill in handling these emotionally charged issues could be especially important in Chinese culture (Bond, 1993), and a metric for assessing EI enables the conducting of cross-cultural studies to assess the truth of this claim.

Conclusion

In the foregoing discussion, we have signaled some important research directions for EI researchers, especially for researchers of Chinese populations. In short, they include examining potential differences in manifestations of EI across countries or Chinese provinces, deficiencies in existing EI measures that may be explored by brain-imaging techniques, and the nature of EI as a multidimensional construct.

These areas clearly need much more research, but they are by no means exhaustive. For example, some Chinese EI researchers are pioneers in providing preliminary but important evidence showing that EI should be trainable (Wong, Foo, et al., 2007). However, to date, few well-designed studies have evaluated the contents and effectiveness of such training. To the best of our knowledge, Nelis, Quoidbach, Mikolajczak, and Hansenne (2009) have reported the only study on training for higher levels of EI using a rigorous training design with before-and-after measures and control groups.

Once the construct and its measurement are better defined, it will be important to explore the validity of the EI concept in organizational settings, especially whether it adds predictive power to other established measures for predicting organizational effectiveness, like the Big Five personality dimensions, both Western and Chinese in provenance (see M. Cheung, Fan, & Yao, 2012). What is the effect of high EI among individuals in the process of teambuilding (see Ng, Lee, & Cardova, 2012), ostracism (Xu & Huang, 2012), building harmonious relationships (see W. Liu & Friedman, 2012; Lun, 2012), and balancing work–family conflicts? How is EI perceived by others – what are the behavioral manifestations used to characterize someone as high in restraint and emotional stability, basic characteristics that are preferred in Chinese culture (Yik & Bond, 1993), assuming that the term "restraint" is used to describe persons with high EI? Finally, if the conceptualization of a latent EI construct is valid, it may open up another line of research concerning possible EI dimensions that may vary across cultures, such as the concept of emotional ambivalence (S. X. Chen, Cheung, Bond, & Leung, 2005). From both the theory side of how people can improve their EI and the empirical side concerning effective training programs, EI researchers have many issues to investigate. In conclusion, we believe that many EI issues should be investigated, and we expect Chinese EI researchers will continue to contribute to this meaningful body of knowledge

Appendix
What's next?

In the past few years, I have still been thinking about research projects on the emotional intelligence (EI) construct. There are at least three things I want to do, but that have not been very successful up to now. The first thing is to build up a scientific theory of EI. All of the studies we had conducted were basically around the construct of EI. We are not able to build up a theory yet. Drawing from the overall perspective of human resource management, we made the argument that EI would interact with emotional labor in affecting job outcomes. This is just an application of an overall perspective but not a sophisticated theory. As discussed briefly in Chapter 1, a theory should include at least some basic assumptions about the phenomena we encounter (e.g., human nature), constructs and their relationships, the rationale behind the relationships, and boundary conditions for the relationships.

The closest we get is the discussion about the performance model based on various functions of the human mind, that is, in the study on Chinese scientists reported in Chapter 6. In fact, we got a best-paper award from the *Asia Pacific Journal of Management* for that year mainly because of the proposal of such a model. However, we did not test the model directly, and I myself would not regard the model as a sophisticated theory. For example, we discuss only performance as the dependent variable. This may be too narrow regarding the role of EI in the workplace. We may need much more work in order to build up a theory of EI.

This weakness of working on a construct instead of theory may be common in my area of study. When I was a doctoral student in the late 1980s, I remember that the focus of my major courses was more on various theories (e.g., learning and motivation, job design, and decision making) than individual constructs. However, studies reported in mainstream journals since the 1980s have usually been around a particular construct. Many new constructs have been proposed and studied, but relatively few theories have been developed. I believed that when we had sufficient knowledge about a construct, we should be able to develop a theory to help explain phenomena of a broader scope. I wish this would happen for the EI construct in the future.

The second thing I attempted to do is to study EI from the physiological perspective. My idea is that as EI involves brain activities, the most convincing evidence is to observe the brain activities when people are dealing with emotional issues or problems. Brain-imaging techniques may provide the opportunity to study EI from this physiological perspective. Thus, we can design experimental materials that can stimulate people's emotions and force them to face and handle emotional issues. Brain activities during the process of handling emotional issues can then be observed.

Unfortunately, after visiting some of the brain-imaging facilities and reading more about this technique, I found that it was not as sophisticated as I had imagined. While brain imaging could examine brain activities, it was still difficult to observe the reaction of the brain for a relatively long period of time. Usually, it would work best if we tried to spot the brain reaction at a particular point in time, but not the whole process. Despite this limitation, I wrote up a research proposal and tried to obtain research money to work on brain-imaging projects. Research grants were necessary because it would be very costly to use brain-imaging machines.

The reviewers of the grant proposal had extreme opinions in opposite directions. In Hong Kong, reviewers used a 5-point scale to evaluate our grant proposal (1 means absolutely not suitable to be funded, while 5 means a project definitely should be funded). If the average score of a proposal was less than or equal to 4, it would not have a chance to be discussed by the panel making the final decision. The score of my proposal was 3 because reviewers gave it either a 5 or a 1. I am not sure if I should proceed further with this idea because I will retire within a few years. Perhaps it is better to let future scholars to work on it, especially when brain-imaging techniques become more advanced and not so costly. However, it may be an important step to uncover how human beings actually deal with emotional issues.

The third type of projects I wanted to do is how we could actually apply our understanding of the EI construct to help practitioners better utilize their human resources. One logical step is to help them select applicants with higher EI for jobs that have high emotional labor requirements. Existing measurements of EI may not be very suitable for various reasons such as cross-cultural generalizability, relatively high cost, and the ease with which job applicants can fake their responses. Human resource practitioners may also be skeptical about using a paper-and-pencil test to assess this type of construct.

Several years ago, my co-author and I came up with an idea that perhaps we could develop some job-specific EI interview questions. An interview is the most common selection tool that human resource practitioners are familiar with. If we could develop questions based on specific job contents and differentiate applicants' EI level based on their answers, there would be a high chance that practitioners would adopt this selection mechanism.

The dilemma of going in this direction is that it would be a study on a particular technology rather than developing and testing scientific theories. As explained in previous chapters, the original purpose of scientific research is to develop and test scientific theories. To develop interview questions and a scoring mechanism for them for a particular job is basically a project that comes up with a specific technology. In the past 20 years, the academic discipline of management has been emphasizing the conceptual contribution of research papers. That is, our work should contribute to the advancement of conceptual arguments and theories. This viewpoint is accepted by many journal editors and reviewers. A research paper focusing on the development of a particular technique for a particular job would have great difficulty getting published in academic journals.

Despite this dilemma, we went ahead with conducting the project. One reason was that my co-author in Taiwan needed to supervise master's students. Many master's students did not have the intention to continue their studies and pursue an academic career. It would be more suitable to train some of them in the technology rather than on the theoretical side. The research project of developing specific interview questions and the rating mechanism would be suitable. We therefore completed some studies in this line and wrote a paper based on two master's theses. The training of the students was completed smoothly, but, as expected, we encountered great difficulties in trying to publish our work. The paper was rejected by three journals after one round of revision each.

Although we framed our study as trying to bridge the EI concept and the more practical emotional competency (EC) concept, we were able to persuade only one reviewer in each journal about the value of the paper. The editors and other reviewers had strong opinions about the limited conceptual contribution of our work. As this was the majority view, we were not successful in publishing our work on demonstrating how to develop interview questions to assess the EI level of customer service officers at a telecommunication company in Taiwan.

As a final record of my journey in studying the EI construct up to now, I attach the paper as the appendix in this book. In the future, if our field becomes more receptive to this type of technological instead of theoretical contributions, I hope we can see more projects on the application side of the EI construct.

Title: Assessing job applicants' emotional competency in interviews

Authors: Ching-Wen Wang, Kelly Z. Peng, Chi-Sum Wong, Ya-Jing Gua, and Hsin-Chieh Hsieh

Abstract. There is confusion between the concepts of emotional intelligence (EI) and emotional competency (EC) in the literature. Following the classification of Ashkanasy and Daus (2005), we define EI as a set of interrelated abilities, while EC refers to employees' behaviors that lead to high performance in a particular emotional job context. The present study attempts to bridge the theoretical foundation of EI with the practical concern of selecting people with the appropriate EC for a particular job by designing interview questions based on specific job contexts. Using the customer service officer as example, we find that answers to carefully designed questions are related to the job applicant's EI, and the EC score assessed by interview questions can predict incumbent job performance and turnover intention. Implications are discussed.

Emotional intelligence (EI) has recently emerged as an important topic for management researchers and consultants because it is believed to be related to human performance in various job contexts. After some confusion and debates in its initial stage, academic researchers seem to have come to a consensus that EI should be defined as a set of interrelated abilities including (1) perception of emotion (in self and others), (2) assimilation of emotion to facilitate thoughts, (3) understanding of emotion, and (4) management and regulation of emotion in self and others (e.g., Mayer, Salovey, & Caruso, 2002, 2004, 2008; Wong & Law, 2002). As abilities to handle emotional issues, EI will affect how people perform when they face situations that involve human emotions or interactions. For example, an employee with high EI should be able to remain calm and polite when an angry customer is complaining in a rude manner. Thus, for jobs that need employees to exhibit appropriate behaviors in emotional job contexts, employee EI level should have a positive effect on both job attitudes and performance. This conclusion is confirmed in different meta-analytic studies (Joseph & Newman, 2010; O'Boyle, Humphrey, Pollack, Hawver, & Story, 2010; Van Rooy & Viswesvaran, 2004).

Although the effect of EI on job attitudes and performance for jobs involving emotional job contexts is clear (e.g., Wong & Law, 2002; Wong, Wong, & Law, 2005), there are at least two important issues that need to be addressed before this relationship can be applied by human resource practitioners in selection, placement, or other human resource decisions. The first issue is the confusion in the definition of EI and the measurement methods in the literature (Ashkanasy & Daus, 2005), and its difficulties in being applied to human resources practices. The second issue is that, as a particular type of intellectual ability, while EI can certainly affect people's behaviors across different situations, its effect on specific job contexts may be vague. Thus, human resource practitioners may still need to find a way to predict people's behaviors in specific emotional job contexts although we know that the concept of EI may be helpful (Meisler & Vigoda-Gadot, 2013).

The purpose of this study is to address the above two issues so that we can bridge the theoretical foundation of the EI concept with the practical concern of human resource decisions. In the following paragraphs, we will first review the EI concept and its measurement methods as reported in the literature. Following Ashkanasy and Daus's (2005) classification, we then redefine emotional competency (EC) as people's behaviors in specific emotional job contexts. While this is related to EI, it should be more predictive of people's job attitudes and performance for a particular job context. We then propose the use of a structured interview to assess applicants' EC for particular jobs. Using a customer service officer (CSO) as an example, we designed a three-stage validation study. In the first stage, interview questions that may help assess applicant EC for this particular job are designed. We then compare the hiring decisions using EI measures versus selection interviews based on the questions developed in the first stage. Finally, we examine the relationship between interview question answers and EI measures in a student sample and the predictive validity of those answers on job performance and turnover intention in an employee sample. The implications of our findings are then discussed.

Definition, domains, and measures of EI

The notion of EI originally appeared in two 1990 academic journal articles (Mayer, Dipaolo, & Salovey, 1990; Salovey & Mayer, 1990). These early proponents of the concept defined EI as a set of interrelated human abilities used to deal with emotional issues. However, later researchers and practitioners gradually included other non-ability dimensions such as motivation and personality (e.g., Bar-On, 1997; Goleman, 1998), which has created serious confusion concerning its definition. On the other hand, because EI measures developed before 1998 are unable to form a distinct factor when factor analyzed with the well-established Big Five personality measures, the validity of the EI construct has been seriously questioned (Davies, Stankov, & Roberts, 1998).

In response, two related lines of effort have been initiated. The first distinguishes between "trait EI" and "ability EI." For example, Petrides and Furnham (2000a, 2000b, 2001) argued that trait EI (or emotional self-efficacy) refers to a constellation of behavioral dispositions and self-perceptions concerning one's ability to recognize, process, and utilize emotion-laden information, which pertains to personality. On the contrary, ability EI (or cognitive-emotional ability) refers to one's actual ability to recognize, process, and utilize emotion-laden information, as a kind of intelligence.

The second line of effort is to classify three streams of research based on various conceptual domains and measurements of EI (Ashkanasy & Daus, 2005). Stream 1 researchers define EI as a set of interrelated abilities and use the MSCEIT (Mayer-Salovey-Caruso Emotional Intelligence Test; Mayer, Salovey, & Caruso, 2002), which is an ability-based measure with correct answers. Stream 2 researchers adopt a similar definition of the EI concept as above but use self- or peer-report measures with correct answers (e.g., Law, Wong, & Song, 2004; Wong & Law, 2002; Schutte et al., 1998). Stream 3 researchers expand the domains of the EI concept and include a mixture of personality and behavioral preferences items in their measurement scales, such as Goleman's Emotional Competency Index (ECI; Sala, 2002) and the Emotional Quotient Inventory (EQ-i; Bar-On, 1997). Researchers have labeled this stream as the "mixed model of EI." The term "emotional intelligence" should refer to people's intellectual abilities instead of personality or behavioral preferences. Thus, trait EI or the mixed model of EI should not be labeled as EI, which created much confusion in the EI literature.

From a rigorous scientific point of view, the mixed model proposed by Stream 3 researchers is not an independent and distinct construct. It is a mixture of ability, personality, and behavioral preferences. Although it also has predictive validity on job attitudes and performance (Joseph & Newman, 2010; O'Boyle et al., 2010), there are at least three weaknesses in applying this model and using the EQ-i or ECI in making selection or other human resource decisions for specific job positions. First, we are not sure about the underlying reason for its predictive validity. If its relationship with job outcomes is only because of personality, then it has added nothing new to our knowledge because the relationship between personality and job outcomes is well known.

Second, the measures of the mixed model are not targeted toward a specific job context. The effects of employee intellectual ability, personality, and behavioral preferences on job outcomes may vary across specific job contexts. For example, the personality trait of agreeableness in general may be related to attitudes and performance in serving customers. However, if the specific job context requires the incumbent to uphold regulations, such as a police officer practicing law enforcement, the general trait of agreeableness may not lead to better job outcomes.

Third, the ECI and EQ-i consist of self-report items asking the respondents to evaluate their abilities, personality, and behavioral preferences using a Likert-type format. We have no objection to using this format for self-assessment, training and development, or purely research purposes. However, if the respondents know that their answers may affect their chance of getting a job, a better placement, or even a promotion, they may fake their answers, and they are perfectly capable of doing so under this reporting format. Law, Mobley, and Wong (2002) found that university graduates in Hong Kong would fake their answers even for self-report bio-data items when they were in a selection context. Wong, Wong, and Law (2007) demonstrated that even for forced-choice items, respondents would change their answers when they were told that they would receive a prize if an experienced recruiter selected them as the suitable candidates for further consideration in the recruitment process. Thus, if the respondents have an incentive to fake their answers, they will certainly say that they are good at understanding and regulating their own emotions.

Although the first two streams of EI research present a much more convincing definition and domain of the EI concept, they also share some of the shortcomings of the third stream if being applied to practical human resource decisions. First, as a general type of intellectual ability, EI's effect on job attitudes and performance may vary across specific job contexts. It is difficult for practitioners to assess the strength of the predictive validity of the EI concept in their specific situation. Second, although the self-report measures developed by Stream 2 researchers have been shown to be distinct from personality constructs (e.g., Law, Wong, & Song, 2004; Wong & Law, 2002), they may be subject to the same risk of faking by respondents who want to affect the decision makers via their responses. For example, it is quite impossible for a job applicant to respond negatively to statements such as "I can control my emotions." To avoid self-bias, rating by others may be a viable alternative. However, it may be very difficult for human resource practitioners to find relevant others to provide honest comments on the EI of the focal person.

Third, there is clear empirical evidence that the MSCEIT used by Stream 1 researchers is able to capture a distinct construct that is different from personality (e.g., Ashkanasy & Daus, 2005; Brackett & Mayer, 2003; Iliescu, Ilie, Ispas, & Ion, 2013). The items of the MSCEIT that have a correct answer are more persuasive than self-evaluation items for measuring intellectual abilities, and respondents may not be able to fake their answers even if they want to. However, some of its items use the "rating-the-extent-of" scales (i.e., test takers rate the appropriateness, strength, or extent of each alternative, rather than selecting the correct option). MacCann and Roberts (2008) found that this response format would affect the final test scores, and this is why they attempted to develop alternative EI measures that are free from this response-format effect. Although there are reports on the reliability and validity of the MSCEIT (e.g., Mayer, Salovey, & Caruso, 2002, 2004, 2008), it is quite inconvenient for practitioners to check the reliability and validity of the measure based on their own sample because the scoring mechanism is not readily accessible. Finally, there is some preliminary evidence showing that the MSCEIT may not be universally applicable across cultures (e.g., Law, Wong, Huang, & Li, 2008). This is not very surprising as its scoring rubric is based on the consensus of expert or population-representative samples (MacCann & Roberts, 2008).

In short, while EI research has clearly laid down the theoretical foundation for the definition and domain of the EI concept as a particular type of intellectual ability and its potential effects on job attitudes and job performance, two issues have to be addressed before its utility in practice can be materialized. The first is to adapt the concept to specific emotional job contexts, and the second is to develop measurement methods to help practitioners make human resource decisions. To address these issues, we apply EC to address the two issues and then use a structured interview as its assessment method.

Proposed definition of EC and its assessment method

We totally agree with Ashkanasy and Daus' (2005, p. 443) comments on Stream 3 EI research: "Our point here is to say to practitioners and researchers who wish to use and to further develop these measures and concepts, 'Go ahead, by all means, but please do not confuse them with emotional intelligence.'" In this respect, we acknowledge that Goleman (1998, 1999) prefers to use the term "emotional competency" in his consulting applications (i.e., as in the ECI). However, defining EC as personality, motivations, and behavioral preferences is still too general to make the concept applicable to specific job contexts. Its overlap with personality and motivation will also fail to make it an independent concept. Goleman and a colleague (Boyatzis & Goleman, 2002) have redefined EC as "a set of actual behaviors," distinct from general intelligence, that involve a person's interaction with self and others in successfully resolving environmental challenges.

To distinguish this EC concept from EI, Boyatzis (2009) and a colleague (Boyatzis & Sala, 2004) further point out that EC describes the actual use of EI behaviors that lead to superior performance, which means that EC constitutes EI in action and is the last side of the overall content domain of EI. Therefore, it is clear that EC is a set of actual emotional behaviors to recognize and manage the emotions of self and others to get superior performance in a specific context (Seal & Andrews-Brown, 2010). Thus, a counselor who is able to actively listen to the client and exhibit an empathic and willing-to-help attitude is high on EC for this particular job context; a bill collector who is able to stay firm in requiring the debtor to repay the debt on time and present an non-empathic attitude is high on EC for this particular job context. Some job positions may require the incumbent to exhibit high EC for multiple tasks. For example, a manager who is able to patiently encourage some subordinates who lack self-confidence and also able to force some subordinates who are over-confident to follow the rules and procedures strictly has high EC for the managerial job context. These examples indicate that EC may not be transferrable to all other job contexts. All other things being equal, an excellent counselor may have low EC to perform the bill collector job, while an outstanding bill collector may perform poorly in a counseling job.

Why will people vary in their EC level in a particular situation? Besides the important role of EI (Seal, Sass, Bailey, & Liao-Torth, 2009), personality, motivation, general behavioral preferences, and even professional training are all possible reasons. However, their effects may vary depending on the exact situation. For example, EI, agreeableness, and the tendency to be friendly may be more strongly related to EC in the context of counseling than in the context of bill collecting. People can also be trained to engage in appropriate behaviors in specific situations. For examples, bank tellers can be trained to smile and greet the customers who show up at their counters in a prescribed way; bill collectors can be trained to ignore the explanations of the debtor and to look impatient by just repeating their demands again and again. Thus, it is quite clear that EC is job specific.

While EI predicts EC (Seal et al., 2009), EC should be more predictive of job attitudes and performance because it represents a set of actual behaviors that are appropriate to the specific emotional job context. Researchers have developed differential behavioral models of EC concerning different jobs, including retail jobs (Giardini & Frese, 2006), sales jobs (Vij, Sharma, & Sharma, 2010), managerial jobs (Bailesteanu & Burz, 2011), and nursing jobs (Yiu, Mak, Ho, & Chui, 2010). Although they have developed differential sets of EC behaviors for each specific job, translating the EC models into practices is necessary for particular practitioners. In the current study, we also would like to follow this practice through using a structured interview to capture the specific actual behaviors of EC as the process of developing a structured interview is the process of identifying behaviors. In the next section, we review the literature on structured interviews, the types of questions, and the process that can be used to develop the specific set of actual behaviors. Then we will report our three-stage validation of assessing EC for the job position of CSO.

Structured interviews and common types of questions

One message of the selection interview literature is clear: interview validity can be greatly improved when the interview is structured and the questions are relevant to the nature of the job. The predictive validity of an unstructured interview is close to zero; it has no predictive power on important job attitudes and performance. According to Campion, Pursell, and Brown (1988), a typical structured interview should include six steps: (1) develop questions based on job analysis, (2) ask the same questions of each candidate, (3) anchor the rating scales for scoring answers with examples and illustrations, (4) have an interview panel record and rate answers, (5) consistently administer the process to all candidates, and (6) give special attention to job-relatedness, fairness, and documentation in accordance with testing guidelines. It is very appropriate to use structured interviews in human resource selection and recruitment. First, studies have shown that interview performance is related to some components of EI, such as empathy and self-regulation of mood (e.g., Fox & Spector, 2000). Second, in comparison with other selection methods, such as developing specific role-playing exercises in an assessment center, interviews are a much more common and less costly selection practice (Johnson, Wilding, & Robson, 2014). Our proposal involves only a more careful design of the interview questions and their scoring mechanism based on our EI and EC knowledge. Third, the literature on structured interviews provides well-established recommendations concerning how the structured-interview questions can be developed for specific job positions.

The two types of questions most commonly used in structured interviews (Campion, Palmer, & Campion, 1997) are the situational interview (SI; Latham, Saari, Pursell, & Campion, 1980) and patterned behavior description interview (PBDI; Janz, 1982) questions. SI questions are based on goal-setting theory (Locke, 1968), which argues that human intention (i.e., goals) is the prerequisite for actual behavior (Latham & Skarlicki, 1995). Hence, SI questions attempt to capture how people intend to behave in a particular situation. To render these questions job related, Latham et al. (1980) suggest that the situation be developed through the critical incident technique (Flanagan, 1954) because critical incidents are actual situations that incumbents have to deal with in their jobs with specific behaviors.

PBDI questions are based on the assumption of behavioral consistency. In other words, past behavior is a good predictor of future behavior (Janz, 1982). Hence, by asking job applicants how they handled actual situations in the past, recruiters can predict how they will handle similar situations in the future (Pulakos & Schmitt, 1995). As for SI questions, the critical incident technique is recommended to develop situations similar to those encountered by job applicants in the past. To make sure that job applicants are referring to the intended experiences, interviewers usually probe more deeply into their responses (Klehe & Latham, 2005).

Thus, both SI and PBDI questions may be able to assess respondent EC levels for the specific job contexts, identified by the specific set of behaviors in the critical incidents. As stated above, EI should be an important factor behind EC in specific job contexts, and EC should contribute directly to job attitudes and performance with actual behaviors.

To assess EC, recruiters may use critical incidents of a particular job position that involves emotional issues to create SI and PBDI questions. The key is to follow the advice and procedures of Campion et al. (1988) to develop interview questions. To demonstrate this possibility, we conducted our validation study in three stages, which are described in the following sections.

Stage 1: development of interview questions

We chose the position of CSO in a large Taiwanese telecommunications company to develop SI and PBDI questions to assess the EC of this particular job. The major duty of a CSO is to handle customer inquiries and complaints through face-to-face and telephone conversations, and the key requirement is to maintain good customer relationships. Because of its customer service nature, this is a high emotional labor job (Hochschild, 1983), and EI is therefore likely to be very important (Joseph & Newman, 2010; Wong & Law, 2002).

Undergraduate seniors are recruited every year for this position. We interviewed the company's customer service department head, the person responsible for the recruitment and selection of applicants. We asked her to provide examples of critical incidents that CSOs face frequently in their jobs and to give us the actual interview questions used in selection interviews. We chose seven critical incidents that create emotional contexts. Based on each incident, we developed one SI and one PBDI question. As EI should have an important effect on job attitudes and performance for this particular job position, we developed anchor descriptions that should indicate high versus low EI levels according to the EI definition and domains of Stream 1 and 2 studies, as classified by Ashkanasy and Daus (2005).

We followed Klehe and Latham's (2005) format and generated descriptions for the anchors of 1, 3, and 5 on a 5-point Likert-type scale. Two EI experts, who had published at least one journal paper in the past two years on the topic of EI, were asked to independently rate the suitability of the 14 questions and the anchors in evaluating the EI level of respondents on a 4-point scale ranging from "very unsuitable" to "very suitable." The 10 questions with the highest ratings were selected for subsequent stages. The following paragraphs provide examples of the chosen critical incident, SI question, PBDI question, and evaluation anchors.

Critical incident

CSOs need to answer calls from customers. Sometimes these customers are in a bad mood. To express their frustration and dissatisfaction, these customers will verbally attack the CSO using very rude language. After handling these calls, some CSOs feel the need to get away from their desks for a short break. After calming down, they will go back to work and handle the next call normally.

SI question

Suppose a customer calls the complaints hotline and uses very rude language in expressing his/her dissatisfaction with the company's services. Your emotions are negatively affected. How would you handle this situation to ensure that you can answer the next call normally?

PBDI question

Please recall a real-life situation in which your emotions were negatively affected because a family member, teacher, friend, or customer scolded you harshly. You needed to calm down and return your emotions to a normal state in a short period of time to be able to handle something important. Can you describe the situation? What did you do? What were the final results?

Anchors for scoring

Three behavioral anchors are provided on the 5-point scale:

1. Anchor for 5: I would consider the situation from the frustrated customer's point of view. By using empathy, I can understand the customer's emotions, thereby ridding myself of the negative emotions brought on by the customer's rudeness and being able to get back to work normally.
2. Anchor for 3: Because of the unhappy feelings resulting from the exchange with the customer, I would try to be alone for a short while. Alternatively, I might talk to someone about the bad experience. Once I had managed to get rid of my unhappy feelings, I would be able to return to work normally.
3. Anchor for 1: Although I would feel negative emotions after being scolded by the customer, I would try to ignore or suppress these emotions and continue working.

Interview questions that do not involve an emotional context

From the actual interview questions used by the head of the company's CSO department, we identified four questions that do not involve emotional context, as follows.

1. Please give us three reasons for why we should hire you.
2. How much do you know about the position of CSO? Please describe as much as you can.

3. Is there any specialized training or experience from your studies and student life that will help you in the position of CSO?
4. To perform the duties of a CSO, you also need computer skills. Can you tell us what kind of computer skills you have?

These four questions primarily concern applicants' general characteristics, their understanding of the position, and their technical skills. We used them as the interview questions for the control group in stage 3. As there was no behavioral anchor for these four questions, the following rating anchors were used: 1 = very unsuitable for the job, 2 = unsuitable for the job, 3 = not sure, 4 = suitable for the job, and 5 = very suitable for the job.

Stage 2: hiring decisions based on EI measures and EC scores from interviews

The major purpose of this study is to examine the possibility of assessing job applicant EC in selection interviews based on our understanding that EI should be important for the job position. If the two decisions do not converge at all, then the selection interviews may have failed to assess the job applicant EC levels for this job. Therefore, we conducted selection interviews using the questions developed in stage 1 to examine whether the decisions made by interviewers would be similar to those based on EI measures.

Sample and procedure

One hundred undergraduate seniors at a large Taiwan university were invited to participate in the study. They completed two EI measures which were developed based on the definition and domains of Stream 1 and 2 studies. They also responded to an application form with items related to their backgrounds. From the scores of these two EI measures, we randomly selected 10 students from above and 10 students from below the mean of both scales. These students were told that their backgrounds were judged to be suitable for the position of CSO, and they were further invited to participate in a face-to-face interview. They were encouraged to try their best in the interview so that they could better equip themselves for other job interviews. In each interview, the interviewers asked two SI questions and two PBDI questions. The four questions were randomly selected from the 10 questions developed in stage 1, and the interviewers were instructed to complete the interview within 20 minutes.

Measures

EI SCALES

Participants completed two EI scales developed from Chinese respondents with evidence of reliability and validity in multiple Chinese samples. The first was the 16-item Wong and Law Emotional Intelligence Scale (WLEIS; Law, Wong, & Song, 2004; Wong & Law, 2002). The second was the 40-item forced-choice

Wong's Emotional Intelligence Scale (WEIS; Wong, Law, & Wong, 2004; Wong, Wong, & Law, 2007).

An experienced human resource practitioner and a doctoral student in management, who did not know the 20 interviewees, served as interviewers. They were briefed with information about the CSO position. After the briefing, a discussion session was held to make sure they were familiar with the EI concept, the 10 questions, and evaluation anchors. Right after each participant interview, the interviewers were asked to provide scores for each question. After all interviews were completed, they made a hiring decision based on their scores and a short discussion. They were asked to provide a consensus decision for each interviewee.

To assess the inter-rater agreement on the answer scores, we added up the scores for the two SI questions for each interviewer and came up with a total SI score for each interviewee. The same procedure was also carried out for the two PBDI questions. The correlations between the two interviewers' total SI and PBDI scores were .52 ($p < .01$) and .77 ($p < .01$), respectively, which indicates good agreement between the two interviewers. We then averaged the two interviewers' SI and PBDI scores to examine their correlations with the two EI measures. The correlations between the SI questions and the interviewees' WEIS and WLEIS were both .41 ($p < .05$) and .41 ($p < .05$). For the PBDI questions, they were .52 ($p < .01$) and .49 ($p < .01$), respectively. Hence, the interview scores appear to be related to the scores on the two EI measures.

The final hiring decisions made jointly by the two interviewers were 80% consistent with the classification of high- versus low-EI groups according to the two EI measures. The results are shown in Table A.1. The $\chi 2$ statistic (7.20, $p < .01$) indicated that the decisions were significantly associated with the original EI classification.

Stage 3: answers to interview questions, EI measures, and job outcomes

Stage 2 provided evidence that decisions made based on carefully designed interview questions could be similar to those based on EI measures for this job position in which EI should be an important concern. However, during interviews, interviewers can probe into questions and observe information not provided by interviewee answers, such as that gleaned from tone, gesture, and facial expression. In addition, as we could not conduct a large number of interviews owing to interviewer fatigue, we chose only 10 high-EI and 10 low-EI interviewees; we therefore needed more evidence to show that the questions developed

Table A.1 Hiring decisions in Stage 2

Hiring Decisions	High-EI Interviewees(n = 10)	Low-EI Interviewees(n = 10)
Hired	8 (80%)	2 (20%)
Not hired	2 (20%)	8 (80%)
χ^2	7.20** (d.f. = 1)	

Notes
EI = emotional intelligence.

*p < .05; **p < .01.

in stage 1 are in fact related to EI measures. To qualify these interview questions as a selection instrument, we also needed evidence that they are related to important job attitudes and performance. In stage 3, respondents answered the questions in written format using a computer-assisted environment. If the markers' evaluation was related to EI measures and job outcomes, then this would provide stronger evidence for the validity of the questions developed in stage 1.

Samples and procedure

We employed a student and incumbent sample in this stage. The student sample was used to investigate the relationship between EI measures and markers' evaluations of each type of interview question. The incumbent sample was used to examine the relationship between markers' evaluations of interview answers and two important job outcomes, namely, turnover intention and job performance. For the student sample, we invited 186 undergraduate seniors (81 males and 105 females) from two Taiwanese universities to participate. These students were instructed to complete the two EI measures, then provided with some information about the CSO job and asked to play the role as if they were applying for the position. When the students were ready, they were asked to type their answers to the questions provided on the computers within 20 minutes.

Student participants were randomly assigned one of the three sets of computer-assisted questions developed in stage 1. The first set consisted of the five SI questions, and the second set included the five PBDI questions. The four non–EI-related questions used by the company were included in the third set. As our sample size was not very large, the chance of being assigned the last set of questions was only half that of the other two sets, creating a control group with the purpose of providing a basis of comparison for the other two groups. The final sample sizes for the SI, PBDI, and control groups were 73, 72, and 38, respectively.

We obtained help from the company for the job incumbent sample. During one week's office hours, 87 CSOs were invited to a conference room equipped with personal computers. We assured them that the study's sole purpose was research and that individual responses would not be provided to company management. On a voluntary basis, all 87 CSOs agreed to participate. They were asked to respond to three SI and three PBDI questions developed in stage 1. The six questions were projected on a large screen one by one. They typed their answers in a Word document using personal computers and saved the documents under their names, with a maximum of four minutes to answer each question. After completing the questions, they were also asked to respond to three items on turnover intention and three items on their sex, age, and tenure. The information was all emailed to one of the authors. The annual job performance data of these CSOs were obtained from the company three months after they participated in the study.

Measures

EI SCALES FOR THE STUDENT SAMPLE

Student participants completed the WLEIS and WEIS scales.

SCORING OF THE STUDENT ANSWERS

Three Taiwanese master of business administration students who did not know about the design of this study were invited to be markers. They were briefed on the EI concept and provided with the three sets of questions and the evaluation anchors developed in stage 1. Each marker was responsible for marking two-thirds of the student participants, covering all three experimental conditions and using the evaluation anchors. In so doing, each student participant's answers were marked by two markers, and the agreement was calculated. The average of the scores provided by the two markers was used as the final mark for the student participants.

SCORING OF THE INCUMBENT ANSWERS

Four company supervisors were invited to evaluate the incumbent participants' answers to the six SI and PBDI questions. These supervisors did not know the identities of the incumbent participants; instead, they were briefed about the definition and domains of EI and were asked to compare the incumbent participants' written answers with the evaluation anchors developed in stage 1 to decide on answer marks. Two raters were assigned to mark the 44 CSOs' answers, and the other two raters marked the other 43 CSOs' responses.

TURNOVER INTENTION OF THE INCUMBENTS

Turnover intention was measured by the four-item scale developed by Chatman (1991). A sample item is "To what extent have you thought seriously about changing organizations since beginning work here?" with a 5-point Likert-type scale, and the coefficient alpha for this sample was .70.

JOB PERFORMANCE OF THE INCUMBENTS

Annual job performance data were obtained from the company records at the end of the year – about three months after the incumbent participants responded to the interview questions and turnover intention items. When we interviewed the department head at stage 1, she told us that the company attempts to evaluate CSOs according to objective indicators instead of supervisors' subjective judgments. Three components make up the job performance ratings of the CSOs: punctuality and attendance; the quantity of work, which basically amounts to the total number of customers served; and the quality of work, which is rated by supervisors but largely determined by the number and nature of customer complaints and compliments. The supervisors compile the scores for the three components every three months, and an annual total score is calculated as the formal yearly performance rating. The highest score is 100.

ANALYSIS AND RESULTS

For the student sample, the inter-rater correlations for the marks of the SI and PBDI question groups were both .41 (p < .01). Markers appeared to reach reasonable agreement on their judgment for the SI and PBDI questions, but they did not show significant agreement on their marks (r = –.11, n.s.) for the control group. We conducted an analysis of variance (ANOVA) to examine whether student participants in the three experimental conditions differed in their WEIS and WLEIS scores (see Table A.2). The differences are not statistically significant, which indicates that the random assignment was successful.

The relationship between the EI measures and the markers' SI and PBDI question scores are shown in Table A.3. The final mark of the PBDI questions is significantly related to WEIS, whereas that of the SI is significantly related to both WEIS and WLEIS.

As for the incumbent sample, the inter-rater correlations for the two pairs of raters were .63 (p < .01) and .51 (p < .01), indicating substantial agreement

Table A.2 EI Scores of student participants in Stage 3

EI Measures	SI Group (n = 73)	PBDI Group (n = 72)	Control Group (n = 38)	ANOVAF-Statistics
1. WEIS	Mean = 27.08 (S.D. = 3.41)	Mean = 26.18 (S.D. = 3.83)	Mean = 27.75 (S.D. = 3.83)	2.051
2. WLEIS	Mean = 3.61 (S.D. = 0.44)	Mean = 3.62 (S.D. = 0.42)	Mean = 3.60 (S.D. = 0.37)	0.027

Notes
EI = emotional intelligence; SI = situational interview; PBDI = patterned behavior description interview; WEIS = Wong's Emotional Intelligence Scale; WLEIS = Wong and Law Emotional Intelligence Scale.

*p < .05; **p < .01.

Table A.3 Criterion-related validity in Stage 3

EI Measures	SI Group (n = 73)	PBDI Group (n = 72)	Control Group (n = 38)
1. WEIS	r = .11	r = .26*	r = .01
2. WLEIS	r = .28*	r = .27*	r = .17

Notes
EI = emotional intelligence; SI = situational interview; PBDI = patterned behavior description interview; WEIS = Wong's Emotional Intelligence Scale; WLEIS = Wong and Law Emotional Intelligence Scale.

*p < .05; **p < .01.

Table A.4 Descriptive statistics and correlations among variables for the incumbent participants in Stage 3

	Mean	S.D.	1	2	3	4	5	6
1. Sex	0.88	0.38	1.00					
2. Age	31.69	6.44	.26*	1.00				
3. Tenure	3.74	0.75	.04	.29*	1.00			
4. EC-interview scores	3.88	0.59	.21	.18	.05	1.00		
5. Turnover intention	2.59	0.63	−.05	−.05	.10	−.33**	1.00	
6. Job performance	82.04	9.03	−.02	−.38**	.01	.47**	−.22	1.00

Notes
n = 87. For sex, female = 0, male = 1. EC = emotional competency.

*p < .05; **p < .01.

between raters. Hence, we used the average marks of the two raters to represent the final scores of the incumbent participants. The descriptive statistics and correlations are shown in Table A.4. As expected, the interview answer scores are significantly related to turnover intention and the company record of job performance. To further examine this predictive validity, we conducted regression analyses on turnover intention and company record of job performance by first entering sex, age, and tenure as control variables. Even after controlling for these three variables, the interview answer scores still showed significant effects on job performance and turnover intention.

Discussion

This study contributes to the literature on EI and EC in three ways. First, from our study, it appears clear that both EI and EC are important concepts and have their unique roles in the area of human resource management. While EI helps us to conceptualize a type of basic ability, its application to specific job positions is relatively limited when compared to EC. EC is a set of behaviors needed to perform well in specific emotional contexts so that employee performance will be more predictable by EC in the workplace.

Second, there is a clear relationship between EI and EC. EI is the foundation for EC, while EC describes the actual use of EI behaviors that lead to superior performance. In other words, EC constitutes EI in action and is the last side of the overall content domain of EI. Our current study also supports these assertions. Future research in the field should consider both concepts instead of debating which one is more relevant and valid.

Third, we showed that EC could be measured with a structured interview. Both SI and PBDI questions seem valid in predicting job incumbents' turnover intention and company record of job performance. As a single predictor, the validity coefficient is already large enough to justify using it as a selection instrument (e.g., Pearlman, Schmidt, & Hunter, 1980; Schmidt, Hunter, McKenzie, & Muldrow, 1979). Interview scores evaluated by interviewers using the face-to-face format also appear to be highly correlated with results using EI measures reported in the literature. Unfortunately, we were not able to conduct a study similar to stage 3 because the supervisors were familiar with the job incumbents, and conducting too many interviews might have tired them. However, all of the evidence gathered for this study indicates that if face-to-face interviews are conducted with both SI and PBDI questions, then supervisors should be able to select candidates with a lower turnover intention who can be expected to exhibit good performance in the future.

In a practical sense, it should be noted that for each specific job, the same procedure to develop the interview questions and the rating forms can be studied and validated. The written answers may be used for preliminary screening when a large number of applicants have to be evaluated. Future research may examine the possibility of developing a computer-aided marking system for large numbers of applicants. Face-to-face interviews may be conducted in the second stage with a limited number of applicants who have high scores on their SI and PBDI answers. The results from the student sample in stage 3 indicate that although either SI or PBDI questions alone are related to EI measures, their relationship is relatively weak. When both SI and PBDI questions were used in the face-to-face interview and the incumbent sample, the validity appeared to be much higher. Hence, practitioners should consider incorporating both SI and PBDI questions if they are going to assess applicant EC in the selection process for job positions in which EI is an important concern.

Some limitations of this study should be noted before closing. First, although we investigated only one job position, we are confident that similar validity can be found for other positions in which EI is an important concern. Whether our findings are generalizable to other job positions should be investigated further in future research. Our study has demonstrated how this can be done by utilizing our EI knowledge in developing questions from critical incidents and anchors for evaluation. This should be valuable for human resource practitioners.

Second, we used students instead of a true job applicant sample. Therefore, some of them may not have been interested in the CSO position, which may have led to random error in their interview responses. Future research may use actual job applicants to cross-validate our results.

Third, the size of our sample of job incumbents in stage 3 was only 87. Although relatively small in a statistical sense, this number is quite large for a single job position in one company. Future research may consider studying positions from a job family to allow a larger-scale study that can provide stronger evidence for the generalizability of the findings.

Fourth, our interview questions assess behavioral intentions and past behaviors in specific emotional contexts. It is our judgment from EI knowledge that guides us to develop interview questions and the scoring anchors. Our results support this initial judgment that EI is related to EC for this job position. However, we have little idea concerning how other factors such as personality, behavioral preferences, and training and development experiences will affect this specific EC. Future research may investigate this issue.

Fifth, it may be argued that the supervisors' evaluations of the employee answers to interview questions in the incumbent sample were affected by their job knowledge. In the most extreme case, supervisors may have been evaluating employee performance instead of employees' answers. Although we cannot rule out this possibility completely, we do not believe this alone can account for the observed correlation for three reasons. First, the behaviorally anchored evaluation form provided clear instructions for the supervisors to rate employees accordingly. Supervisors were asked to compare the written answers with the behavior anchors tightly. There was very little room for the supervisors to relate the written answers to their job knowledge or performance standards. Second, company performance records are based on objective indicators (such as punctuality and attendance). Finally, if the ratings on employees' answers reflected only the supervisors' performance judgment, then they would have been unlikely to have a significant relationship with employees' turnover intention.

Despite these limitations, we believe the evidence found in this study is sufficient to justify the value of using computer-assisted and face-to-face interviews to assess job applicants' EC for job positions where EI is an important concern. More research in this direction would be worthwhile, and it is hoped that organizations will eventually benefit by investing in the design of appropriate interview questions for job positions that require employees to perform in emotional job contexts.

References

Abraham, R. (1998). Emotional dissonance in organizations: Antecedents, consequences, and moderators. *Genetic, Social, and General Psychology Monographs,* 124(2), 229–246.

Abraham, R. (1999). Emotional intelligence in organizations: A conceptualization. *Genetic, Social, and General Psychology Monographs,* 125(2), 209–224.

Adelmann, P. K. (1989). *Emotional labor and employee well-being.* Unpublished doctoral dissertation, the University of Michigan.

Aiken, L. S., and West, S. G. (1991). *Multiple regression: Testing and interpreting interactions.* London: Sage.

Andrews, F. M. and Robinson, J. P. (1991). Measures of subjective well-being. In J. P. Robinson, P. R. Shaver, and L. S. Wrightsman (Eds.), *Measures of personality and social psychological attitudes,* pp. 61–114. San Diego: Academic Press.

Ashkanasy, N. M., and Daus, C. S. (2005). Rumors of the death of emotional intelligence in organizational behavior are vastly exaggerated. *Journal of Organizational Behavior,* 26, 441–452.

Ashkanasy, N. M., and Hooper, G. (1999). *Perceiving and managing emotion in the workplace: A research agenda based on neurophysiology.* Paper presented at the Third Australian Industrial and Organizational Psychology Conference, Brisbane, Australia, June 24–25.

Atwater, L., and Yammarino, F. (1992). Does self–other agreement on leadership perceptions moderate the validity of leadership and performance predictions? *Personnel Psychology,* 45(1), 141–164.

Bagby, R. M., Taylor, G. J., and Parker, J. D. (1994). The twenty item Toronto Alexithymia Scale: II. Convergent, discriminant, and concurrent validity. *Journal of Psychosomatic Research,* 38, 33–40.

Bagozzi, R. P., and Yi, Y. (1990). Assessing method variance in multitrait-multimethod matrices: The case of self-reported affect and perceptions at work. *Journal of Applied Psychology,* 75(5), 547–560.

Bailesteanu, G., and Burz, R. (2011). Leader's emotional potential evaluation. In *Managerial Challenges of the Contemporary Society Proceedings,* pp. 8–11. Clujnapoca: Babes Bolai University.

Bakker, A. B., Demerouti, E., and Euwema, M. C. (2005). Job resources buffer the impact of job demands on burnout. Journal of Occupational Health Psychology, 10(2), 170–180.

Bakker, A. B., Demerouti, E., and Verbeke, W. (2004). Using the Job Demands-Resources model to predict burnout and performance. Human Resource Management, 43, 83–104.

Bandura, A. (1977). *Social learning theory*. Englewood Cliffs, NJ: Prentice-Hall.

Bar-On, R. (1997). *Bar-On Emotional Quotient Inventory: Technical manual*. Toronto: Multi-Health Systems.

Bar-On, R. (2000). Emotional and social intelligence: Insights from the Emotional Quotient Inventory. In R. Bar-On and J.D.A. Parker (Eds.), *Handbook of emotional intelligence*, pp. 363–388. New York: Jossey-Bass.

Bar-On, R., and Parker, J.D.A. (1997). Introduction. In R. Bar-On and J.D.A. Parker (Eds.), *Handbook of emotional intelligence*, pp. xi–xv. New York: Jossey-Bass.

Bar-On, R., Tranel, D., Denburg, N.L., and Bechara, A. (2003). Exploring the neurological substrate of emotional and social intelligence. *Brain*, 126, 1790–1800.

Baron, R.M., and Kenny, D.A. (1986). The moderator–mediator variable distinction in social psychological research: Conceptual, strategic, and statistical considerations. Journal of Personality and Social Psychology, 51, 1173–1182.

Barrick, H.J., and Mount, M.K. (1991). The big-five personality dimensions and job performance: A meta-analysis. *Personnel Psychology*, 44, 1–26.

Bass, B.M. (1990). *Handbook of leadership: A survey of theory and research*. New York: Free Press.

Becker, T.E., Billings, R.S., Eveleth, D.M., and Gilbert, N.L. (1996). Foci and bases for employee commitment: Implications for job performance. *Academy of Management Journal*, 39(2), 464–482.

Bentler, P.M. (1990). Comparative fit indexes in structural models. *Psychological Bulletin*, 107, 238–246.

Blau, P.M. (1964). *Exchange and power in social life*. New York: John Wiley.

Bloom, G.S. (2004). Emotionally intelligent principals: Addressing the affective demands of newcomers through one-on-one coaching. *School Administrator*, 61, 14–18.

Boal, K.B., and Hooijberg, R. (2000). Strategic leadership research: Moving on. *Leadership Quarterly Yearly Review of Leadership*, 11(4), 515–550.

Boal, K.B., and Whitehead, C.J. (1992). A critique and extension of the stratified systems theory perspective. In R.L. Phillips and J.G. Hunt (Eds.), *Strategic leadership: A multiorganizational-level perspective*, pp. 237–255. Westport, CT: Quorum.

Bond, M.H. (1993). Emotions and their expression in Chinese culture. *Journal of Nonverbal Behavior*, 17, 245–262.

Borgen, F.H. (1986). New approaches to the assessment of interest. In W.B. Walsh and S.H. Osipow (Eds.), *Advances in vocational psychology, Vol. 1: The assessment of interests*. Hillsdale, NJ: Erlbaum.

Bower, G.H. (1981). Mood and memory. *American Psychologist*, 36, 129–148.

Boyatzis, R.E. (2009). Competencies as a behavioral approach to emotional intelligence. *Journal of Management Development*, 28(9), 749–770.

Boyatzis, R.E., and Goleman, D. (2002). *The Emotional Competency Inventory (ECI)*. Boston: Hay Group.

Boyatzis, R.E., and Sala, F. (2004). Assessing emotional intelligence competencies. In G. Gehr (Ed.), *The measurement of emotional intelligence*, pp. 147–180. New York: Nova Science.

Boyatzis, R.E., Stubbs, E.C., and Taylor, S.N. (2002). Learning cognitive and emotional intelligence competencies through graduate management education. *Academy of Management Learning and Education*, 1(2), 150–162.

Brackett, M. A., and Mayer, J. D. (2003). Convergent, discriminant, and increment validity of competing measures of emotional intelligence. *Personality and Social Psychology Bulletin*, 29, 1147–1158.

Brackett, M., Mayer, J., and Warner, R. (2004). Emotional intelligence and its relation to everyday behavior. *Personality and Individual Differences*, 36(6), 1387–1402.

Brislin, R. (1970). Back-translation for cross-cultural research. *Journal of Applied Psychology*, 1, 185–216.

Brislin, R. W. (1980). Translation and content analysis of oral and written material. In H. C. Triandis and J. W. Berry (Eds.), *Handbook of cross-cultural psychology, Vol. 2: Methodology*, pp. 349–444. Boston: Allyn & Bacon.

Bronfenbremer, U., and Evans, G. W. (2000). Developmental science in the 21st century: Emerging theoretical models, research designs, and empirical findings. *Social Development*, 9(1), 115–125.

Brotheridge, C. M., and Grandey, A. A. (2002). Emotional labor and burnout: Comparing two perspectives of "people work." *Journal of Vocational Behavior*, 60, 17–39.

Brotheridge, C. M., and Lee, R. (1998). *On the dimensionality of emotional labor: Development and validation of an emotional labor scale.* Paper presented at the First Conference on Emotions in Organizational Life, San Diego, CA, August.

Brotheridge, C. M., and Lee, R. T. (2003). Development and validation of emotional labor scale. *Journal of Occupational and Organizational Psychology*, 76, 365–379.

Brown, D., and Brooks, L. (1990). *Career choice and development*, 2nd ed. San Francisco: Jossey-Bass.

Brush, D. H., Moch, M. K., and Pooyan, A. (1987). Individual demographic differences and job satisfaction. *Journal of Occupational Behaviour*, 8(1), 139–155.

Buhrmester, D., Furman, W., Wittenberg, M., and Reis, H. (1988). Five domains of interpersonal competence in peer relationships. *Journal of Personality and Social Psychology*, 55, 991–1008.

Butler, E. A., Egloff, B., Wilhelm, F. W., Smith, N. C., Erickson, E. A., and Gross, J. J. (2003). The social consequences of expressive suppression. *Emotion*, 3, 48–67.

Cammann, C., Fichman, M., Jenkins, D., and Klesh, J. (1979). *The Michigan Organizational Assessment Questionnaire.* Unpublished manuscript, University of Michigan, Ann Arbor, Michigan.

Campbell, A., Converse, P. E., and Rodgers, W. L. (1976). *The quality of American life: Perceptions, evaluation and satisfaction.* New York: Russell Sage.

Campbell, D. T., and Fiske, D. W. (1959). Convergent and discriminant validation by the multitrait-multimethod matrix. *Psychological Bulletin*, 56(2), 81–105.

Campbell, J. P. (1990). Modeling the performance prediction problem in industrial and organizational psychology. In M. D. Dunnette and L. M. Hough (Eds.), *Handbook of industrial and organizational psychology*, 2nd ed., Vol. 1, pp. 687–732. Palo Alto, CA: Consulting Psychologists Press.

Campbell, J. P., McCloy, R. A., Oppler, S. H., and Sager, C. E. (1993). A theory of performance. In N. Schmitt, W. C. Borman, and Associates (Eds.), *Personnel selection in organizations*, pp. 35–70. New York: Jossey-Bass.

Campion, M. A. (1988). Interdisciplinary approaches to job design: A constructive replication with extensions. *Journal of Applied Psychology*, 73(3), 467–481.

Campion, M.A., Palmer, E., and Campion, J.E. (1997). A review of structure in the selection interview. *Personnel Psychology*, 50, 655–702.

Campion, M.A., Pursell, E.D., and Brown, B.K. (1988). Structured interviewing: Raising the psychometric properties of the employment interview. *Personnel Psychology*, 41, 25–42.

Carmeli, A. (2003). The relationship between emotional intelligence and work attitudes, behavior and outcomes: An examination among senior managers. *Journal of Managerial Psychology*, 18(8), 788–813.

Carmeli, A., Yitzhak-Halevy, M., and Weisberg, J. (2009). The relationship between emotional intelligence and psychological wellbeing. *Journal of Managerial Psychology*, 24(1), 66–78.

Carson, K.D., and Carson, P.P. (1998). Career commitment, competencies, and citizenship. *Journal of Career Assessment*, 6(2), 195–208.

Carson, K.D., Carson, P., and Philips, J.S. (1997). *The ABCs of collaborative change*. Chicago: American Library Association.

Carver, C.S., Schein, M.F., and Weintraub, J.K. (1989). Assessing coping strategies: A theoretically based approach. Journal of Personality and Social Psychology, 56(2), 267–283.

Chan, D.W. (2005). Self-perceived creativity, family hardiness, and emotional intelligence of Chinese gifted students in Hong Kong. *Journal of Secondary Gifted Education*, 16(2–3), 47–56.

Chan, D.W. (2006). Emotional intelligence and components of burnout among Chinese secondary school teachers in Hong Kong. *Teaching and Teacher Education*, 22(8), 1042–1054.

Chan, D.W. (2007). Leadership competencies among Chinese gifted students in Hong Kong: The connection with emotional intelligence and successful intelligence. *Roeper Review: A Journal on Gifted Education*, 29(3), 183–189.

Chan, D.W. (2008a). Emotional intelligence, self-efficacy, and coping among Chinese prospective and in-service teachers in Hong Kong. *Educational Psychology*, 28(4), 397–408.

Chan, D.W. (2008b). Giftedness of Chinese students in Hong Kong: Perspectives from different conceptions of intelligences. *Gifted Child Quarterly*, 52(1), 40–54.

Chang, C.P., and Chang, F.J. (2010). Relationships among traditional Chinese personality traits, work stress, and emotional intelligence in workers in the semiconductor industry in Taiwan. *Quality and Quantity: International Journal of Methodology*, 44(4), 733–748.

Chaplain, R.F. (1995). Stress and job satisfaction: A study of English primary school teachers. *Educational Psychology*, 15(4), 473–489.

Chatman, J.A. (1991). Matching people and organizations: Selection and socialization in public accounting firms. *Administrative Science Quarterly*, 36, 459–484.

Chen, M.T., Lee, H.M., and Huang, H.S. (2007). The relationship among practical intelligence, emotional intelligence and professional performance of Taiwanese elementary school teachers. *Bulletin of Educational Psychology*, 29(2), 295–316. (In Chinese)

Chen, S.X., Cheung, M.C., Bond, M.H., and Leung, J.P. (2005). Decomposing the construct of ambivalence over emotional expression in a Chinese cultural context. *European Journal of Personality*, 19, 185–204.

Chen, Z.Y. (1997). *Loyalty to supervisor, organizational commitment and employee outcomes: A Chinese case*. Unpublished doctoral thesis, the Hong Kong University of Science and Technology, Hong Kong.

Cheung, F.Y., and Tang, C.S. (2009). The influence of emotional intelligence and affectivity on emotional labor strategies at work. *Journal of Individual Differences*, 30(2), 75–86.

Cheung, M., Fan, W., and Yao, J. (2012). Chinese personality and vocational behavior. In M. Bond and X. Huang (Eds.), *Handbook of Chinese organizational behavior: Integrating theory, research and practice*, pp. 359–379. Cheltenham, UK: Edward Elgar.

Choo, C.W. (1998). *The knowing organization: How organizations use information to construct meaning, create knowledge, and make decisions*. New York: Oxford University Press.

Chu, L.C., and Kao, H.R.S. (2005). The moderation of mediation experience and emotional intelligence on the relationship between perceived stress and negative mental health. *Chinese Journal of Psychology*, 47(2), 157–179. (In Chinese)

Ciarrochi, J.V., Chan, A.Y.C., and Caputi, P. (2000). A critical evaluation of the emotional intelligence construct. *Personality and Individual Differences*, 28(3), 539–561.

Ciarrochi, J.V., and Scott, G. (2006). The link between emotional competence and well-being: A longitudinal study. *British Journal of Guidance and Counselling*, 34(2), 231–243.

Clark, A., Oswald, A., and Warr, P. (1996). Is job satisfaction U-shaped in age? *Journal of Occupational and Organizational Psychology*, 69, 57–81.

Cohen, C.I. (2003). *Schizophrenia into later life: Treatment, research and policy*. Washington, DC: APA Publishing.

Constable, J.F., and Russell, D.W. (1986). The effect of social support and the work environment upon burnout among nurses. *Journal of Human Stress*, 12(1), 20–26.

Cooper, R.K. (1996/1997). *EQ map interpretation guide*. San Francisco, CA: ATT and Essi Systems.

Corwin, J. (2001). The importance of teacher morale in combating teacher shortage. *Baylor Business Review*, 19(1), 18–21.

Costa, P.T., and McCrae, R.R. (1985). *The NEO Personality Inventory Manual*. Odessa, FL: Psychological Assessment Resources.

Côté, S., and Miners, C.T.H. (2006). Emotional intelligence, cognitive intelligence, and job performance. *Administrative Science Quarterly*, 51, 1–26.

Crawford, M. (2007). Rationality and emotion in primary school leadership: An exploration of key themes. *Educational Review*, 59(1), 87–98.

Crossman, A., and Harris, P. (2006). Job satisfaction of secondary school teachers. *Educational Management, Administration and Leadership*, 34(1), 29–46.

Daniels, K. (1999). Coping and the job demands–control–support model: An exploratory study. International Journal of Stress Management, 6(2), 125–144.

Daniels, K., and Harris, C. (2005). A daily diary study of coping in the context of the job demands–control–support model. Journal of Vocational Behavior, 66, 219–237.

Dansereau, F., Alutto, J.A., Nachman, S.A., Al-Kelabi, S.A., Yammarino, F.J., Newman, J., Naughton, T.J., Lee, S., Markham, S.E., Dumas, M., Kim, K., and Keller, T. (1995). Individualized leadership: A new multiple-level approach. *Leadership Quarterly*, 6(3), 413–450.

Dansereau, F., Graen, G.B., and Haga, W. (1975). A vertical dyad linkage approach to leadership in formal organizations. *Organizational Behavior and Human Performance*, 13, 46–78.

Daresh, J.C. (2002). *What it means to be a principal: Your guide to leadership.* Thousand Oaks, CA: Corwin.

Davies, M., Stankov, L., and Roberts, R.D. (1998). Emotional intelligence: In search of an elusive construct. *Journal of Personality and Social Psychology*, 75, 989–1015.

Day, D.V. (2000). Leadership development: A review in context. *Leadership Quarterly Yearly Review of Leadership*, 11(4), 581–614.

de Jonge, J., and Dormann, C. (2002). The DISC model: Demand-induced strain compensation mechanisms in job stress. In M.F. Dollard, A.H. Winefield, and H.R. Winefield (Eds.), *Occupational stress in the service professions*, pp. 43–74. Washington, DC: Taylor & Francis.

de Lange, A.H., Taris, T.W., Kompier, M.A.J., Houtman, I.L.D., and Bonger, P.M. (2003). The very best of the millennium: Longitudinal research and the demand-control-(support) model. *Journal of Occupational Health Psychology*, 8(4), 282–305.

Demerouti, E., Bakker, A.B., Nachreiner, F., and Schaufeli, W.B. (2001). The job demands–resources model of burnout. *Journal of Applied Psychology*, 86, 499–512.

DeYoung, C.G., Shamosh, N.A., Green, A.E., Braver, T.S., and Gray, J.R. (2009). Intellect as distinct from openness: Differences revealed by fMRI of working memory. *Journal of Personality and Social Psychology*, 97, 883–892.

Diefendorff, J.M., Croyle, M.H., and Gosserand, R.H. (2005). The dimensionality and antecedents of emotional labor strategies. Journal of Vocational Behavior, 6, 339–357.

Dinham, S., and Scott, C. (1998). A three domain model of teacher and school executive satisfaction. *Journal of Educational Administration*, 38(4), 379–396.

Dulewicz, V., and Higgs, M. (2000). Emotional intelligence, a review and evaluation study. *Journal of Managerial Psychology*, 15(4), 341–372.

Edwards, J.R. (2001). Multidimensional constructs in organizational behavior research: An integrative analytical framework. *Organizational Research Methods*, 4(2), 144–192.

Ekman, P., and Davidson, R.J. (Eds.). (1994). *The nature of emotion: Fundamental questions.* New York: Oxford University Press.

Ekman, P., and Friesen, W.V. (1975). Unmasking the face. Englewood Cliffs, NJ: Prentice-Hall.

Elias, M.J., Harriett, A., and Hussey, C.S. (Eds.). (2003). *EQ + IQ = best leadership practices for caring and successful schools.* Thousand Oaks, CA: Corwin.

Evans, L. (1998). *Teacher morale, job satisfaction and motivation.* London: Paul Chapman.

Eysenck, H.J. (1964). *Know your own IQ.* Harmondsworth, UK: Penguin.

Eysenck, H.J. (1990). *Check your own IQ,* 2nd ed. Harmondsworth, UK: Penguin.

Eysenck, H.J. (1994). *Test your IQ.* Toronto: Penguin Books.

Eysenck, H.J. (2006). *The structure and measurement of intelligence.* New Brunswick, NJ: Transaction.

Farh, L.J., and Cheng, B.X. (1997). Modesty bias in self-ratings in Taiwan: Impact of item working, modesty value, and self-esteem. *Chinese Journal of Psychology*, 39(2), 103–118.

Fehr, T., Code, C., and Herrmann, M. (2007). Common brain regions underlying different arithmetic operations as revealed by conjunct fMRI-BOLD activation. *Brain Research*, 1172, 93–102.

Ferris, G.R., Witt, L.A., and Hochwarter, W.A. (2001). Interaction of social skill and the general mental ability on job performance and salary. *Journal of Applied Psychology*, 86(6), 1075–1082.

Fineman, S. (Ed.). (1993). *Emotion in organizations*. London: Sage.

Fineman, S. (Ed.). (2000). *Emotions in organizations*, 2nd ed. London: Sage.

Fischer, K.W., Shaver, P.R., and Carnochan, P. (1990). How emotions develop and how they organize development. *Cognition and Emotion*, 4, 81–127.

Fisher, B.M., and Edwards, J.E. (1988). Consideration and initiating structure and their relationships with leader effectiveness: A meta-analysis. *Proceedings of the Academy of Management*, August, 201–205.

Flanagan, J.C. (1954). The critical incident technique. Psychological Bulletin, 51(4), 327–358.

Foo, M.D., Elfenbein, H., Tan, H.H., and Aik, V.C. (2004). Emotional intelligence and negotiation: The tension between creating and claiming value. International Journal of Conflict Management, 15, 411–429.

Forgas, J.P. (1995). Mood and judgment: The affect infusion model (AIM). *Psychological Bulletin*, 117, 39–66.

Fox, S., and Spector, P.E. (2000). Relations of emotional intelligence, practical intelligence, general intelligence, and trait affectivity with interview outcomes: It's not all just "G." *Journal of Organizational Behavior*, 21, 203–220.

Fried, Y., and Ferris, G.R. (1987). The validity of the job characteristics model: A review and meta-analysis. *Personnel Psychology*, 40, 287–322.

Friedman, H.S., Prince, L.M., Riggio, R.E., and Dimatteo, M.R. (1980). Understanding and assessing nonverbal expressiveness: The Affective Communication Test. *Journal of Personality and Social Psychology*, 39, 333–351.

Friedrich, R., and Friederici, A.D. (2009). Mathematical logic in the human brain: Syntax. *PLoS ONE*, 4, 1–7.

Frijda, N.H. (1986). *The emotions*. New York: Cambridge University Press.

Gardner, H. (1983). *Frames of mind: The theory of multiple intelligences*. New York: Basic Books.

Gardner, H. (1993). *Multiple intelligences: The theory in practice*. New York: Basic Books.

Geisinger, K. (2001). Review of the Wonderlic Personnel Test and scholastic level exam. In B.S. Plake and J.C. Impara (Eds.), *The fourteenth mental measurements yearbook* (pp. 1360–1363). Lincoln, NE: Buros Institute of Mental Measurements.

George, J.M. (2000). Emotions and leadership: The role of emotional intelligence. *Human Relations*, 53(8), 1027–1055.

George, J.M., and Bettenhausen, K. (1990). Understanding prosaic behavior, sales performance, and turnover: A group-level analysis in a service context. *Journal of Applied Psychology*, 75, 698–709.

Giardini, A., and Frese, M. (2006). Rescuing the negative effects of emotion work in service occupation: Emotional competency as a psychological resource. *Journal of Occupational Health Psychology*, 11(1), 63–75.

Gilbreath, B., and Benson, P.G. (2004). The contribution of supervisor behaviour to employee psychological wellbeing. *Work and Stress*, 18(3), 255–266.

Giles, C., and Hargreaves, A. (2006). The sustainability of innovative schools as learning organizations and professional learning communities during standardized reform. *Education Administration Quarterly*, 42(1), 124–156.

Goffman, E. (1959). Presentation of self in everyday life. New York: Overlook.

Goleman, D. (1995). *Emotional intelligence*. New York: Bantam Books.

Goleman, D. (1997). Foreword. In R. Bar-On and J.D.A. Parker (Eds.), *Handbook of emotional intelligence*, pp. vii–viii. New York: Jossey-Bass.

Goleman, D. (1998). *Working with emotional intelligence*. New York: Bantam Books.

Goleman, D. (1999). Emotional competence. *Executive Excellence*, 16(4), 19.

Goleman, D., Boyatzis, R., and McKee, A. (2002). *Primal leadership: Realizing the power of emotional intelligence*. Boston: Harvard Business School Press.

Goolsby, J.R. (1992). A theory of role stress in boundary spanning positions of marketing organizations. Journal of the Academy of Marketing Science, 20(2), 155–164.

Gottfredson, L.S. (1986). Societal consequences of the g factor in employment. *Journal of Vocational Behavior*, 29, 379–410.

Graen, G.B., Novak, M., and Sommerkamp, P. (1982). The effects of leader–member exchange and job design on productivity and satisfaction: Testing a dual attachment model. *Organizational Behavior and Human Performance*, 30, 109–131.

Grandey, A.A. (2000). Emotion regulation in the workplace: A new way to conceptualize emotional labor. *Journal of Occupational Health Psychology*, 5(1), 95–110.

Grandey, A.A. (2003). When the "show must go on": Surface acting and deep acting as determinants of emotional exhaustion and peer-rated service delivery. Academy of Management Journal, 46, 86–96.

Gross, J.J. (1998a). Antecedent- and response-focused emotion regulation: Divergent consequences for experience, expression, and physiology. *Journal of Personality and Social Psychology*, 74(1), 224–237.

Gross, J.J. (1998b). The emerging field of emotion regulation: An integrated review. *Review of General Psychology*, 2(3), 271–299.

Gross, J.J. (2002). Emotion regulation: Affective, cognitive, and social consequences. *Psychophysiology*, 39, 281–291.

Gross, J.J., and John, O.P. (2003). Individual differences in two emotion regulation processes: Implications for affect, relationships, and well-being. *Journal of Personality and Social Psychology*, 85, 348–362.

Gross, J., and Levenson, R. (1997). Hiding feelings: The acute effects of inhibiting negative and positive emotions. Journal of Abnormal Psychology, 106(1), 95–103.

Hackman, J.R., and Oldham, G.R. (1975). Development of the Job Diagnostic Survey. *Journal of Applied Psychology*, 60(2), 159–170.

Hackman, J.R., and Oldham, G.R. (1980). *Work redesign*. Reading, MA: Addison-Wesley.

Hale, G.A. (1984). *Summaries of studies involving the Test of English as a Foreign Language 1963–1982*. Princeton, NJ: Educational Testing Service.

Hall, D.T., Bowen, D.D., Lewicki, R.J., and Hall, F.S. (1975). *Experiences in management and organizational behavior*. Chicago: St. Clair.

Hemmati, T., Mills, J., and Kroner, D.G. (2004). The validity of the Bar-On Emotional Intelligence Quotient in an offender population. *Personality and Individual Differences*, 37(4), 695–706.

Hickson, C., and Oshagbemi, T. (1999). The effect of age on the satisfaction of academics with teaching and research. *International Journal of Social Economics*, 26(4), 537–544.

Hilgard, E. R. (1980). The trilogy of mind: Cognition, affection, and conation. *Journal of the History of the Behavioral Sciences*, 16, 107–117.

Ho, C. L. (2003). *Job satisfaction in teachers: Its latest construct, predictors and measurement*. Unpublished doctoral dissertation, the Chinese University of Hong Kong.

Ho, C. L., and Au, W. T. (2006). Teaching satisfaction scale: Measuring job satisfaction of teachers. *Educational and Psychological Measurement*, 66(1), 172–185.

Hochschild, A. R. (1983). *The managed heart*. Berkeley: University of California Press.

Hofstede, G. (1991). *Cultures and organizations: Software of the mind*. London: McGraw-Hill.

Holland, J. L. (1959). A theory of vocational choice. *Journal of Counseling Psychology*, 6, 35–45.

Holland, J. L. (1985). *Making vocational choices: A theory of vocational personalities and work environments*, 2nd ed. Englewood Cliffs, NJ: Prentice Hall.

Hollander, E. P. (1980). Leadership and social exchange processes. In K. Gergen, M. S. Greenberg, and R. H. Wills (Eds.), *Social exchange: Advances in theory and research*, pp. 103–118. New York: Winston-John Wiley.

Hooijberg, R., Hunt, J. G., and Dodge, G. E. (1997). Leadership complexity and development of the leaderplex model. *Journal of Management*, 23(3), 375–408.

House, J. S., Umberson, D., and Landis, K. R. (1988). Structures and processes of social support. *Annual Review of Sociology*, 14, 293–318.

House, R. J., and Aditya, R. N. (1997). The social scientific study of leadership: Quo vadis? *Journal of Management*, 23(3), 409–473.

Hoy, W. K., and Miskel, C. (1991). *Educational administration: Theory, research and practice*, 4th ed. New York: McGraw-Hill.

Huang, G., Law, K. S., and Wong, C. S. (2006). Emotional intelligence: A critical review. In L. V. Wesley (Ed.), *Intelligence: New research*, pp. 95–113. New York: Nova Science.

Huang, X., Chan, S. C. H., Lam, W., and Nan, X. (2010). The joint effect of leader-member exchange and emotional intelligence on burnout in call centers in China. *International Journal of Human Resource Management*, 21(7), 1124–1144.

Huang, Y., Lu, A., Wang, L., and Shi, J. (2008). Validation of the emotional intelligence. *Acta Scientiarum Naturalium Universitatis Pekinensis*, 44(6), 970–976. (In Chinese)

Hui, C., Law, K. S., and Chen, Z. X. (1999). A structural equation model of effects of negative affectivity, leader-member exchange, and perceived mobility on in-role and extra-role performance: A Chinese case. *Organizational Behavior and Human Decision Processes*, 77(1), 3–21.

Hunter, J. E. (1983). A casual analysis of cognitive ability, job knowledge, and job performance. *Journal of Vocational Behavior*, 29, 340–362.

Iliescu, D., Ilie, A., Ispas, D., and Ion, A. (2013). Examining the psychometric properties of the Mayer-Salovey-Caruso Emotional Intelligence Test: Findings from an eastern European culture. *European Journal of Psychological Assessment*, 29(2), 121–128.

Ito, J. K., and Brotheridge, C. M. (2003). Resources, coping strategies, and emotional exhaustion: A conservation of resources perspective. Journal of Vocational Behavior, 63, 490–509.

Izard, C. E. (1992). Basic emotions, relations among emotions, and emotion–cognition relations. *Psychological Review*, 99, 561–565.

Izard, C. E. (1993). Four systems for emotion activation: Cognitive and noncognitive processes. *Psychological Review*, 100, 68–90.

Jacobs, T. O. (1970). *Leadership and exchange in formal organizations*. Alexandria, VA: Human Resources Research Organization.

James, C., and Vince, R. (2001). Developing the leadership capability of headteachers. *Educational Management and Administration*, 29(3), 307–317.

James, L. R., Demaree, R. G., and Wolf, G. (1984). Estimating within-group inter-rater reliability with and without response bias. *Journal of Applied Psychology*, 69(1), 85–98.

Janz, T. (1982). Initial comparisons of patterned behavior description interviews versus unstructured interviews. *Journal of Applied Psychology*, 67(5), 577–580.

Johnson, G., Wilding, P., and Robson, A. (2014). Can outsourcing recruitment deliver satisfaction? A hiring manager perspective. *Personnel Review*, 43(2), 303–326.

Jöreskog, K. G., and Sörbom, D. (1993). *LISREL 8: Structural equation modeling with the SIMPLIS command language*. Chicago: Scientific Software International.

Joseph, D. L., and Newman, D. A. (2010). Emotional intelligence: An integrative meta-analysis and cascading. *Journal of Applied Psychology*, 95, 54–78.

Kafetsios, K. (2004). Attachment and emotional intelligence abilities across the life course. *Personality and Individual Differences*, 37(1), 129–145.

Karasek, R. A. (1979). Job demands, job decision latitude, and mental strain: Implications for job redesign. Administrative Science Quarterly, 24(2), 285–308.

Karasek, R., and Theorell, T. (1990). Healthy work: Stress, productivity, and the reconstruction of working life. New York: Basic Books.

Kaufhold, J. A., and Johnson, L. R. (2005). The analysis of the emotional intelligence skills and potential problem areas of elementary educators. *Education*, 125(4), 615–626.

Kidd, J. M. (1998). Emotion: An absent presence in career theory. *Journal of Vocational Behavior*, 52, 275–288.

Kinman, G. (2009). Emotional labour and strain in "front-line" service employees: Does mode of delivery matter? *Journal of Managerial Psychology*, 24(2), 118–135.

Klehe, U. C., and Latham, G. P. (2005). The predictive and incremental validity of the situational and patterned behavior description interviews for teamplaying behavior. *International Journal of Selection and Assessment*, 13, 108–115.

Koenigs, M., Barbey, A. K., Postle, B. R., and Grafman, J. (2009). Superior parietal cortex is critical for the manipulation of information in working memory. *Journal of Neuroscience*, 29, 14980–14986.

Kuhn, T. S. (1970). *The structure of scientific revolutions*. Chicago: University of Chicago Press.

Kuncel, N. R., Hezlett, S. A., and Ones, D. S. (2004). Academic performance, career potential, creativity, and job performance: Can one construct predict them all? *Journal of Personality and Social Psychology*, 86, 148–161.

Lam, L. T., and Kirby, S. L. (2002). Is emotional intelligence an advantage? An exploration of the impact of emotional and general intelligence on individual performance. *Journal of Social Psychology*, 142(1), 133–143.

Landy, F. J., Shankster, L. J., and Kohler, S. S. (1994). Personnel selection and placement. *Annual Review of Psychology*, 45, 261–296.

Latack, J. C., Kinicki, A. J., and Prussi, G. E. (1995). An integrative process model of coping with job loss. Academy of Management Review, 20, 311–342.

Latham, G. P., Saari, P. P., Pursell, M. A., and Campion, M. A. (1980). The situational interview. *Journal of Applied Psychology*, 65, 422–427.

Latham, G. P., and Skarlicki, D. P. (1995). Criterion-related validity of the situational and patterned behavior description interviews with organizational citizenship behavior. *Human Performance*, 8, 67–80.

Law, K. S., Mobley, W. H., and Wong, C. S. (2002). Impression management and faking in biodata scores among Chinese job seekers. *Asia Pacific Journal of Management*, 19, 541–556.

Law, K. S., Song, L. J., and Wong, C. S. (2002). *Emotional intelligence as an intelligence facet: Construct validation and its predictive power of job outcomes.* Paper presented at the Academy of Management Meeting, Denver, CO, August 12–14.

Law, K. S., Wong, C. S., Huang, E. G., and Li, X. (2004). *Beyond general mental abilities: Incremental validity of emotional intelligence on job performance.* Paper presented at the Academy of Management Meeting, New Orleans, LA, August 8–11.

Law, K. S., Wong, C. S., Huang, G. H., and Li, X. (2008). The effects of emotional intelligence on job performance and life satisfaction for the research and development scientists in China. *Asia Pacific Journal of Management*, 25(1), 51–69.

Law, K. S., Wong, C. S., and Leong, F. (2001). The cultural validity of Holland's model and its implications on human resource management: The case of Hong Kong. *International Journal of Human Resource Management*, 12(3), 1–13.

Law, K. S., Wong, C. S., and Mobley, W. H. (1998). Toward a taxonomy of multidimensional constructs. *Academy of Management Review*, 23(4), 741–755.

Law, K. S., Wong, C. S., and Song, L. J. (2004). The construct validity of emotional intelligence and its potential utility for management studies. *Journal of Applied Psychology*, 89, 483–496.

Leiter, M. P., and Maslach, C. (1988). The impact of interpersonal environment on burnout and organizational commitment. *Journal of Organizational Behavior*, 9, 297–308.

Li, C., and Shi, K. (2003). The influence of distributive justice and procedural justice on job burnout. *Acta Psychologica Sinica*, 35, 677–684. (In Chinese)

Lin, N., Ye, X., and Ensel, W. M. (1999). Social support and depressed mood: A structural analysis. *Journal of Health and Social Behavior*, 40, 344–359.

Lindebaum, D., and Cartwright, S. (2010). A critical examination of the relationship between emotional intelligence and transformational leadership. *Journal of Management Studies*, 47(7), 1317–1342.

Liu, W., and Friedman, R. (2012). Managing conflicts in Chinese organizations. In M. Bond and X. Huang (Eds.), *Handbook of Chinese organizational behavior: Integrating theory, research and practice*, pp. 272–288. Cheltenham, UK: Edward Elgar.

Liu, Y., and Zou, H. (2010). Adolescents' emotional intelligence and its relation to social adjustment. *Journal of Beijing Normal University*, 217, 65–71. (In Chinese)

Locke, E.A. (1968). Toward a theory of task motivation and incentives. *Organizational Behavior and Human Performance*, 3, 157–189.

Locke, E. (1969). What is job satisfaction? *Organizational Behaviour and Human Performance*, 4, 309–336.

Loher, B.T., Noe, R.A., Moeller, N.L., and Fitzgerald, M.P. (1985). A meta-analysis of the relation of job characteristics to job satisfaction. *Journal of Applied Psychology*, 70, 280–289.

Lopes, P.N., Salovey, P., Côté, S., and Beers, M. (2005). Emotion regulation ability and the quality of social interaction. *Emotion*, 5, 113 118.

Lun, V.M. (2012). Harmonizing conflicting views about harmony in Chinese culture. In M. Bond and X. Huang (Eds.), *Handbook of Chinese organizational behavior: Integrating theory, research and practice*, pp. 467–479. Cheltenham, UK: Edward Elgar.

Ma, X., and MacMillan, R.B. (1999). Influences of workplace conditions on teachers' job satisfaction. *Journal of Educational Research*, 93, 39–47.

MacCann, C., and Roberts, R.D. (2008). New paradigms for assessing emotional intelligence: Theory and data. *Emotion*, 8(4), 540–551.

Mahsud, R., Yukl, G., and Prussia, G. (2010). Leader empathy, ethical leadership, and relations-oriented behaviors as antecedents of leader–member-exchange quality. *Journal of Managerial Psychology*, 25(6), 561–577.

Marlow, L., and Inman, D. (2002). *Pro-social literacy: Are educators being prepared to teach social and emotional competence?* Paper presented at the 92nd Annual Meeting of the National Council of Teachers of English, Atlanta, GA, November 21–24.

Marsh, H.W., and Hocevar, D. (1983). Confirmatory factor analysis of multitrait-multimethod matrices. *Journal of Educational Measurement*, 20(3), 231–248.

Martinez-Pons, M. (1997). The relation of emotional intelligence with selected areas of personal functioning. *Imagination, Cognition and Personality*, 17(1), 3–13.

Maslach, C. (1982). Burnout: The cost of caring. Englewood Cliffs, NJ: Prentice Hall.

Maslach, C., and Pines, A. (1977). The burn-out syndrome in the day care setting. Child Care Quarterly, 6, 100–113.

Maslach, C., Schaufeli, W.B., and Leiter, M.P. (2001). Job burnout. Annual Review of Psychology, 52, 397–422.

Masten, A.S., and Coatsworth, J.D. (1998). The development of competence in favourable and unfavourable environment: Lessons from research on successful children. *American Psychologist*, 53(2), 205–220.

Mathieu, J.E., and Farr, J.L. (1991). Further evidence for the discriminant validity of measures of organizational commitment, job involvement, and job satisfaction. *Journal of Applied Psychology*, 76, 127–133.

Mathieu, J.E., Hofmann, D.A., and Farr, J.L. (1993). Job perception–job satisfaction relations: An empirical comparison of three competing theories. *Organizational Behavior and Human Decision Processes*, 56, 370–387.

Matthews, G., Zeidner, M., and Roberts, R.D. (2002). *Emotional intelligence: Science and myth*. Cambridge, MA: MIT Press.

Matthews, L.J., and Crow, G.M. (2003). *Being and becoming a principal: The conceptions for contemporary principals and assistants*. Boston: Pearson Education.

Mayer, J.D., Caruso, D.R., and Salovey, P. (2000a). Emotional intelligence meets traditional standards for an intelligence. *Intelligence*, 27, 267–298.

Mayer, J.D., Caruso, D.R., and Salovey, P. (2000b). Selecting a measure of emotional intelligence: The case for ability testing. In R. Bar-On and J.D.A. Parker (Eds.), *Handbook of emotional intelligence*, pp. 320–342. New York: Jossey-Bass.

Mayer, J.D., Dipaolo, M.T., and Salovey, P. (1990). Perceiving affective content in ambiguous visual stimuli: A component of emotional intelligence. *Journal of Personality Assessment*, 54, 772–781.

Mayer, J.D., and Salovey, P. (1993). The intelligence of emotional intelligence. *Intelligence*, 17, 433–442.

Mayer, J.D., and Salovey, P. (1997). What is emotional intelligence? In P. Salovey and D. Sluyter (Eds.), *Emotional development and emotional intelligence: Educational implications*, pp. 3–34. New York: Basic Books.

Mayer, J.D., Salovey, P., and Caruso, D. (1997). *Emotional IQ test. CD-ROM version*. Richard Viard (producer). Needham, MA: Virtual Entertainment.

Mayer, J.D., Salovey, P., and Caruso, D.R. (1999). *Instruction manual for the MSCEIT: Meyer-Salovey-Caruso Emotional Intelligence Test*. Toronto: Multi-Health Systems.

Mayer, J.D., Salovey, P., and Caruso, D. (2000a). Emotional intelligence as zeitgeist, as personality, and as a mental ability. In R. Bar-On and J.D.A. Parker (Eds.), *The handbook of emotional intelligence: Theory, development, assessment, and application at home, school and in the workplace*, pp. 92–117. San Francisco: Jossey-Bass.

Mayer, J.D., Salovey, P., and Caruso, D. (2000b). Models of emotional intelligence. In R. Sternberg (Ed.), *Handbook of intelligence*, pp. 396–420. Cambridge: Cambridge University Press.

Mayer, J.D., Salovey, P., and Caruso, D.R. (2002). *Mayer-Salovey-Caruso Emotional Intelligence Test: User's manual*. Toronto: Multi-Health Systems.

Mayer, J.D., Salovey, P., and Caruso, D.R. (2004). Emotional intelligence: Theory, findings and implications. *Psychological Inquiry*, 15(3), 197–215.

Mayer, J.D., Salovey, P., and Caruso, D.R. (2008). Emotional intelligence: New ability or eclectic traits? *American Psychologist*, 63(6), 503–507.

Mayer, J.D., Salovey, P., Caruso, D.R., and Sitarenios, G. (2003). Measuring emotional intelligence with the MSCEIT V2.0. *Emotion*, 3, 97–105.

McCormick, E.J., and Ilgen, D.R. (1980). *Industrial psychology*, 7th ed. Englewood Cliffs, NJ: Prentice Hall.

McCrae, R.R. (2000). Emotional intelligence from the perspective of the five-factor model of personality. In R. Bar-On and J.D.A. Parker (Eds.), *The handbook of emotional intelligence: Theory, development, assessment, and applications in home, school, and in the workplace*, pp. 263–276. San Francisco: Jossey-Bass.

McCrae, R.R., and Costa, P.T., Jr. (1987). Validation of the five-factor model of personality across instruments and observers. *Journal of Personality and Social Psychology*, 52(1), 81–90.

Mehrabian, A., and Epstein, N. (1970). A measure of emotional empathy. *Journal of Personality*, 40, 525–543.

Meisler, P., and Vigoda-Gadot, E. (2013). Perceived organizational politics, emotional intelligence and work outcomes: Empirical exploration of direct and indirect effects. *Personnel Review*, 43(1), 116–135.

Mendelssohn, M. (1755/1971). *Moses Mendelssohn: Gesammelte Schriften. Jubiläumsausgabe*. Vol. 1, *Schriften zur Philosophie and Ästhetik*. Stuttgart: Friedrich Frommann Verlag (Gunther Holzboog). (Original work published in 1755).

Meyer, J.P., Allen, N.J., and Smith, C.A. (1993). Commitment to organizations and occupations: Extensions and test of a three-component conceptualization. *Journal of Applied Psychology*, 78(4), 538–555.

Morris, J.A., and Feldman, D.C. (1996). The dimensions, antecedents, and consequences of emotional labor. *Academy of Management Review*, 21(4), 986–1010.

Morris, J.A., and Feldman, D.C. (1997). Managing emotions in the workplace. *Journal of Managerial Issues*, 9(3), 257–274.

Muller, D., Judd, C.M., and Yzerbyt, V.Y. (2005). When moderation is mediated and mediation is moderated. Journal of Personality and Social Psychology, 89(6), 852–863.

Mumford, M.D., Zaccaro, S.J., Harding, F.D., Jacobs, T.O., and Fleishman, E.A. (2000). Leadership skills for a changing world: Solving complex social problems. *Leadership Quarterly*, 11(1), 11–35.

Murphy, K.R. (2006). *A critique of emotional intelligence: What are the problems and how can they be fixed?* Mahwah, NJ: Lawrence Erlbaum.

National Union of Teachers. (2001). *Who's leaving? And why? Teachers reasons for leaving the profession.* London: National Union of Teachers.

Nelis, D., Quoidbach, J., Mikolajczak, M., and Hansenne, M. (2009). Increasing emotional intelligence: (How) is it possible? *Personality and Individual Differences*, 47, 36–41.

Ng, I., Lee, Y., and Cardova, P. (2012). Building teams in Chinese organizations. In M. Bond and X. Huang (Eds.), *Handbook of Chinese organizational behavior: Integrating theory, research and practice*, pp. 237–257. Cheltenham, UK: Edward Elgar.

O'Boyle, E.H., Jr., Humphrey, R.H., Pollack, J.M., Hawver, T.H., and Story, P.A. (2010). The relation between emotional intelligence and job performance: A meta-analysis. *Journal of Organizational Behavior*, 32, 788–818.

O'Brien, G.E. (1983). Locus of control and retirement. In H.M. Lefcourt (Ed.), *Research in locus of control*, Vol. 3, pp. 7–72. New York: Academic Press.

O'Reilly, C.A., III, and Chatman, J.A. (1994). Working smarter and harder: A longitudinal study of managerial success. *Administrative Science Quarterly*, 39, 603–627.

Ortony, A., Clore, G.L., and Collins, A. (1988). *The cognitive structure of emotions.* New York: Cambridge University Press.

Paulhus, D.L., Lysy, D.C., and Yik, M.S.M. (1998). Self-report measures of intelligence: Are they useful as proxy IQ tests? *Journal of Personality*, 66, 525–554.

Pearlin, L., and Schooler, C. (1978). The structure of coping. *Journal of Health and Social Behavior*, 19, 2–21.

Pearlman, K., Schmidt, F.L., and Hunter, J.E. (1980). Validity generalization results for tests used to predict job proficiency and training success in clerical occupations. *Journal of Applied Psychology*, 65, 373–406.

Pellitteri, J. (1999). *The relationships between emotional intelligence, cognitive reasoning, and defense mechanisms.* Unpublished doctoral dissertation, New York University.

Peng, K.Z., Wong, C.S., and Che, H.S. (2010). The missing link between emotional demands and exhaustion. *Journal of Managerial Psychology*, 25(7), 777–798.

Peng, Z., Lin, X., Zhang, J., and Che, H. (2004). The ability model of emotional intelligence. *Advances in Psychological Sciences*, 12(6), 817–823. (In Chinese)

Pennebaker, J. (1990). Opening up: The healing power of confiding in others. New York: Morrow.

Pesta, B. J., and Poznanski, P. J. (2008). Black–white differences on IQ and grades: The mediating role of elementary cognitive tasks. *Intelligence*, 36, 323–329.

Petrides, K. V., Frederickson, N., and Furnham, A. (2004). The role of trait emotional intelligence in academic performance and deviant behavior at school. *Personality and Individual Differences*, 36, 277–293.

Petrides, K. V., and Furnham, A. (2000a). Gender differences in measured and self-estimated trait emotional intelligence. *Sex Roles*, 42, 449–461.

Petrides, K. V., and Furnham, A. (2000b). On the dimensional structure of emotional intelligence. *Personality and Individual Differences*, 29, 313–320.

Petrides, K. V., and Furnham, A. (2001). Trait emotional intelligence: Psychometric investigation with reference to established trait taxonomies. *European Journal of Personality*, 15, 425–448.

Pines, A., and Aronson, E. (1988). Career burnout: Causes and cures. New York: Free Press.

Ping, R. (1995). A parsimonious estimating technique for interaction and quadratic latent variables. *Journal of Marketing Research*, 32, 336–347.

Ping, R. (1996). Latent variable interaction and quadratic effect estimation: A two-step technique using structural equation analysis. *Psychological Bulletin*, 119, 166–175.

Podsakoff, P. M., MacKenzie, S. B., Lee, J. Y., and Podsakoff, N. P. (2003). Common method biases in behavioral research: A critical review of the literature and recommended remedies. Journal of Applied Psychology, 88, 879–903.

Podsakoff, P. M., MacKenzie, S. B. Morrman, R. H., and Fetter, R. (1990). Transformational leader behaviors and their effects on followers' trust in leader, satisfaction, and organizational citizenship behaviors. *Leadership Quarterly*, 1, 107–142.

Polanyi, M. (1962). *Personal knowledge: Towards a post-critical philosophy*. New York: Harper Torchbooks.

Pritchard, R. D., and Roth, P. G. (1991). Accounting for nonlinear utility functions in composite measures of utility and performance. *Organizational Behavior and Human Decision Processes*, 50, 341–359.

Pugh, S. D. (2001). Service with a smile: Emotional contagion in the service encounter. *Academy of Management Journal*, 44(5), 1018–1027.

Pulakos, E. D., and Schmitt, N. (1995). Experience-based and situational interview questions: Studies of validity. *Personnel Psychology*, 48, 289–308.

Rafaeli, A., and Sutton, R. I. (1987). Expression of emotion as part of the work role. *Academy of Management Review*, 12, 23–37.

Ree, M. J., Earles, J. A., and Teachout, M. S. (1994). Predicting job performance: Not much more than *g*. *Journal of Applied Psychology*, 79(4), 518–524.

Roberts, R. D., Zeidner, M., and Matthews, G. (2001). Does emotional intelligence meet traditional standards for an intelligence? Some new data and conclusions. *Emotion*, 1, 196–231.

Roger, D., and Najairan, B. (1989). The construction and validation of a new scale for measuring emotion control. *Personality and Individual Differences*, 10, 845–853.

Roseman, I. J., Dhawan, N., Rettek, S. I., and Naidu, R. K. (1995). Cultural differences and cross-cultural similarities in appraisals and emotional responses. *Journal of Cross-Cultural Psychology*, 26(1), 23–48.

Rosete, D., and Ciarrochi, J. 2005. Emotional intelligence and its relationship to workplace performance outcomes of leadership effectiveness. *Leadership and Organization Development Journal*, 26(5), 388–399.

Russell, D.W., Altmaier, E., and Van Velzen, D. (1987). Job-related stress, social support, and burnout among classroom teachers. Journal of Applied Psychology, 72, 269–274.

Saklofske, D.H., Austin, E.J., and Minski, P.S. (2002). Factor structure and validity of a trait emotional intelligence measure. *Personality and Individual Differences*, 34(4), 707–721.

Sala, F. (2002). *Emotional Competence Inventory: Technical manual*. Philadelphia, PA: McClelland Center for Research, Hay Group.

Salovey, P., Hsee, C.K., and Mayer, J.D. (1993). Emotional intelligence and the self-regulation of affect. In D.M. Wegner and J.W. Pennebaker (Eds.), *Handbook of mental control*, pp. 258–277. Englewood Cliffs, NJ: Prentice-Hall.

Salovey, P., and Mayer, J.D. (1990). Emotional intelligence. *Imagination, Cognition and Personality*, 9, 185–211.

Salovey, P., Mayer, J.D., Caruso, D., and Lopes, P.N. (2003). Measuring emotional intelligence as a set of abilities with the Mayer-Salovey-Caruso Emotional Intelligence Test. In S.J. Lopez and C.R. Snyder (Eds.), *Positive psychological assessment: A handbook of models and measures*, pp. 251–265. Washington, DC: American Psychological Association.

Salovey, P., Mayer, J.D., Goldman, S.L., Turvey, C., and Palfai, T. (1995). Emotional attention, clarity and repair: Exploring emotional intelligence using the Trait Meta-Mood Scale. In J.W. Pennebaker (Ed.), *Emotion, disclosure, and health*, pp. 125–154. Washington, DC: American Psychological Association.

Salovey, P., Woolery, A., and Mayer, J.D. (2001). Emotional intelligence: Conceptualization and measurement. In G.J.O. Fletcher and M.S. Clark (Eds.), *Blackwell handbook of social psychology: Interpersonal processes*, pp. 279–307. Malden, MA: Blackwell.

Scandura, T.A., and Graen, G.B. (1984). Moderating effects of initial leader–member exchange status on the effects of a leader–membership intervention. *Journal of Applied Psychology*, 69, 428–436.

Schaufeli, W.B., and Enzmann, D. (1998). The burnout companion to study and practice. London: Taylor & Francis.

Schaufeli, W.B., Leiter, M.P., Maslach, C., and Jackson, S.E. (1996). The Maslach Burnout Inventory – general survey. In C. Maslach, S.E. Jackson, and M.P. Leiter (Eds.), Maslach Burnout Inventory, 3rd ed., pp. 19–26. Palo Alto, CA: Consulting Psychologists Press.

Schaufeli, W.B., Maslach, C., and Marek, T. (1993). The future of burnout. In W.B. Schaufeli, C. Maslach, and T. Marek (Eds.), Professional burnout: Recent developments in theory and research, pp. 253–260. Washington, DC: Taylor & Francis.

Schmidt, F.L., and Hunter, J.E. (1993). Tacit knowledge, practical intelligence, general mental ability and job knowledge. *Current Directions in Psychological Science*, 2, 8–9.

Schmidt, F.L., and Hunter, J.E. (1998). The validity and utility of selection methods in personnel psychology: Practical and theoretical implications of 85 years of research findings. *Psychological Bulletin*, 124, 262–274.

Schmidt, F.L., Hunter, J.E., McKenzie, R., and Muldrow, T. (1979). The impact of valid selection procedures on workforce productivity. *Journal of Applied Psychology*, 64, 609–626.

Schmidt, F.L., Hunter, J.E., and Outerbridge, A.N. (1986). Impact of job experience and ability on job knowledge, work sample performance, and supervisory ratings of job performance. *Journal of Applied Psychology*, 71, 432–439.

Schmidt, F.L., Hunter, J.E., Pearlman, K., and Shane, G.S. (1979). Further tests of the Schmidt–Hunter Bayesian validity generalization procedure. *Personnel Psychology*, 32, 257–281.

Schulte, M.J., Ree, M.J., and Carretta, T.R. (2004). Emotional intelligence: Not much more than g. *Personality and Individual Differences*, 37(5), 1059–1068.

Schutte, N.S., Malouff, J.M., Bobik, C., Coston, T.D., Greeson, C., Jedlicka, C., Rhodes, E., and Wendorf, G. (2001). Emotional intelligence and interpersonal relations. *Journal of Social Psychology*, 141(4), 523–536.

Schutte, N.S., Malouff, J.M., Hall, L.E., Haggerty, D.T., Cooper, J.T., Charles, J., Golen, C.J., and Dornleim, L. (1998). Development and validation of a measure of emotional intelligence. *Personality and Individual Differences*, 25, 167–177.

Scott, C., and Dinham, S. (2003). The development of scales to measure teacher and school occupational satisfaction. *Journal of Educational Administration*, 41(1), 74–86.

Seal, C.R., and Andrews-Brown, A. (2010). An integrative model of emotional intelligence: Emotional ability as a moderator of the mediated relationship of emotional quotient and emotional competence. *Organization Management Journal*, 7, 143–152.

Seal, C.R., Sass, M.D., Bailey, J.R., and Liao-Torth, M. (2009). Integrating the emotional intelligence construct: The relationship between emotional ability and emotional competence. *Organization Management Journal*, 9, 204–214.

Semple, S.J., Patterson, T.L., Shaw, W.S., Grant, I., Moscona, S., and Jeste, D.V. (1999). Self-perceived interpersonal competence in older schizophrenia patients: The role of patient characteristics and psychosocial factors. *Acta Psychiatrica Scandinavica*, 100, 126–135.

Shapiro, L.E. (1997). *How to raise a child with a high EQ: A parent's guide to emotional intelligence*. New York: Harper Collins.

Siu, A.F.Y. (2009). Trait emotional intelligence and its relationships with problem behavior in Hong Kong adolescents. *Personality and Individual Differences*, 47(6), 553–557.

Sobel, M.E. (1982). Asymptotic confidence intervals for indirect effects in structural equation models. Sociological Methodology, 13, 290–312.

Song, L.J., Huang, G.H., Peng, K.Z., Law, K.S., Wong, C.S., and Chen, Z. (2010). Differential effects of general mental ability and emotional intelligence on academic performance and social interactions. *Intelligence*, 38, 137–143.

Sosik, J.J., and Megerian, L.E. (1999). Understanding leader emotional intelligence and performance: The role of self–other agreement on transformational leadership perceptions. *Group and Organization Management*, 24(3), 367–390.

Spearman, C. (1904). "General intelligence," objectively determined and measured. *American Journal of Psychology*, 15, 201–293.

Spearman, C. (1927). *The abilities of man*. New York: Macmillan.

Spector, P. E. (1997). *Job satisfaction: Application, assessment, causes and consequences.* London: Sage.

Spector, P. E., and O'Connell, B. J. (1994). The contribution of personality traits, negative affectivity, locus of control and type A to the subsequent reports of job stressors and job strains. *Journal of Occupational and Organizational Psychology*, 67, 1–11.

Sternberg, R. J. (1985). *Beyond IQ: A triarchic theory of human intelligence.* Cambridge: Cambridge University Press.

Sternberg, R. J. (1997). Managerial intelligence: Why IQ isn't enough. *Journal of Management*, 23(3), 475–493.

Sternberg, R. J., Nokes, C., Geissler, P. W., Prince, R., Okatcha, F., and Bundy, D. A. (2001). The relationship between academic and practical intelligence: A case study in Kenya. *Intelligence*, 29, 401–418.

Stone-Romero, E. F., and Rosopa, R. J. (2008). The relative validity of inferences about mediation as a function of research design characteristics. Organizational Research Methods, 11, 326–352.

Stough, C., and Palmer, B. R. (2002). *The development of a workplace measure of emotional intelligence – the Swinburne University Emotional Intelligence Test (SUEIT).* Paper presented at the Third Conference on Emotions and Organisational Life, Gold Coast, Queensland, Australia, July.

Sutton, R. I. (1991). Maintaining norms about expressed emotions: The case of bill collectors. *Administrative Science Quarterly*, 36, 245–268.

Sutton, R. I., and Rafaeli, A. (1988). Untangling the relationship between displayed emotions and organizational sales: The case of convenience stores. *Academy of Management Journal*, 31, 461–487.

Tang, H.W.V., Yin, M. S., and Nelson, D. B. (2010). The relationship between emotional intelligence and leadership practices: A cross-cultural study of academic leaders in Taiwan and the USA. *Journal of Managerial Psychology*, 25(8), 899–926.

Taylor, S. G., Kluemper, D. H., and Mossholder, K. W. (2010). Linking personality to interpersonal citizenship behaviour: The mediating effect of empathy. *Journal of Occupational and Organizational Psychology*, 83(4), 815–834.

Thorndike, E. L. (1920). Intelligence and its uses. *Harper's Magazine*, 140, 227–235.

Totterdell, P., and Holman, D. (2003). Emotion regulation in customer service roles: Testing a model of emotional labor. Journal of Occupational Health Psychology, 8, 55–73.

Tucker, L. R., and Lewis, C. (1973). The reliability coefficient for maximum likelihood factor analysis. *Psychometrika*, 28, 1–10.

Turner, B. A. (1986). Sociological aspects of organizational symbolism. *Organizational Studies*, 7, 101–115.

Van Maanen, J., and Kunda, G. (1989). "Real feelings": Emotional expression and organizational culture. *Research in Organizational Behavior*, 11, 43–103.

Van Rooy, D. L., and Viswesvaran, C. (2004). Emotional intelligence: A meta-analytic investigation of predictive validity and nomological net. *Journal of Vocational Behavior*, 65, 71–95.

Van Scotter, J. R., and Motowidlo, S. J. (1996). Interpersonal facilitation and job dedication as separate facets of contextual performance. *Journal of Applied Psychology*, 81, 525–531.

Vij, S., Sharma, R., and Sharma, M.K. (2010). A study of identifying the emotional competence of Indian salespeople. *IUP Journal of Marketing Management*, 9(3), 24–40.

Voluntary Service Organization. (2000). *The meaning of work*. Available at: www.vso.org.uk/media/report htm.

Wall, T.D., Jackson, P.R., Mullarkey, S., and Parker, S.K.T. (1996). The demands–control model of job strain: A more specific test. Journal of Occupational and Organizational Psychology, 69, 153–166.

Walter, F., Cole, M.S., and Humphrey, R.H. (2011). Emotional intelligence: Sine qua non of leadership or folderol? *Academy of Management Perspectives*, 25(1), 45–59.

Wang, C.K., and Lo, K.Y. (2008). Cognitive representation of emotional intelligence: Similarity and difference between gender and cohorts. *Research in Applied Psychology*, 39, 215–251. (In Chinese)

Warwick, J., and Nettlebeck, T. (2004). Emotional intelligence is …? *Personality and Individual Differences*, 37(5), 1091–1100.

Watson, D., and Clark, L.A. (1988). Development and validation of brief measures of positive and negative affect: The PANAS scales. *Journal of Personality and Social Psychology*, 54(6), 1063–1070.

Wayne, S.J., and Ferris, G.R. (1990). Influence tactics, affect, and exchange quality in supervisor–subordinate interactions: A laboratory experiment and field study. *Journal of Applied Psychology*, 75, 487–499.

Weisinger, H. (1998). *Emotional intelligence at work: The untapped edge for success*. San Francisco, CA: Jossey-Bass.

Weiss, H.M., and Cropanzano, R. (1996). Affective events theory: A theoretical discussion of the structure, causes, and consequences of affective experiences at work. *Research in Organizational Behaviour*, 18, 1–74.

Wharton, A.S. (1993). The affective consequences of service work. *Work and Occupations*, 20(2), 205–232.

Wharton, A.S., and Erickson, R.J. (1995). The consequences of caring: Exploring the links between women's job and family emotion work. *Sociological Quarterly*, 36(2), 273–296.

Whitman, D.S., Van Rooy, D.L., Viswesvaran, C., and Kraus, E. (2009). Testing the second-order factor structure and measurement equivalence of the Wong and Law Emotional Intelligence Scale across gender and ethnicity. *Educational and Psychological Measurement*, 69(6), 1059–1074.

Wilding, J., Valentine, E., Marshall, P., and Cook, S. (1999). Memory, IQ and examination performance. *Educational Psychology*, 19(2), 117–132.

Williams, L.J. (1988). *Affective and nonaffective components of job satisfaction and organizational commitment as determinants of organizational citizenship and in-role behaviors*. Unpublished doctoral dissertation, Indiana University, Bloomington.

Williams, L.J., and Brown, B.K. (1994). Method variance in organizational behavior and human resources research: Effects on correlations, path coefficients, and hypothesis testing. *Organizational Behavior and Human Decision Processes*, 57(2), 185–206.

Wonderlic Inc. 1999. *Wonderlic personnel test and scholastic level exam user's manual*.

Wong, C.S. (1997). The effects of organizational commitment and job satisfaction on turnover: The case of Hong Kong. In *Proceedings of the Eighth International*

Conference on Comparative Management, pp. 134–140. National Sun Yat-Sen University, Kaohsiung, Taiwan, May 25–27.

Wong, C. S., and Campion, M. A. (1991). Development and test of a task level model of motivational job design. *Journal of Applied Psychology*, 76(6), 825–837.

Wong, C. S., Cheung, M.F.Y., and Peng, K. Z. (2012.) Reliability of general mental ability and emotional intelligence tests of Chinese respondents. *Nanjing Business Review*, 9(2), 116–126. (In Chinese)

Wong, C. S., Foo, M. D., Wang, C.W., and Wong, P.M. (2004). *The feasibility of training and development of EI: An exploratory study in Singapore, Hong Kong and Taiwan*. Paper presented at the Fourth Asia Academy of Management Conference, Shanghai, China, December 16–18.

Wong, C. S., Foo, M. D., Wang, C.W., and Wong, P.M. (2007). The feasibility of training and development of EI: An exploratory study in Singapore, Hong Kong and Taiwan. *Intelligence*, 35, 141–150.

Wong, C. S., and Law, K. S. (1999). Managing localization of human resources in the PRC: A practical model. *Journal of World Business*, 34(1), 26–40.

Wong, C. S., and Law, K. S. (2000). *The effect of emotional intelligence on job outcomes: An exploratory study*. Paper presented at the Academy of Management Meeting, Toronto, Canada, August 7–9.

Wong, C. S., Law, K. S., and Huang, G. H. (2008). On the importance of conducting construct-level analysis of multidimensional constructs in theory development and testing. *Journal of Management*, 34(4), 744–764.

Wong, C. S., Law, K. S., and Wong, P. M. (2004). Development and validation of a forced choice emotional intelligence measure for Chinese respondents in Hong Kong. *Asia Pacific Journal of Management*, 21(4), 535–559.

Wong, C. S., and Peng, K. Z. (2012). Chinese emotional intelligence. In X. Huang and M. H. Bond (Eds.), *Handbook of Chinese organizational behavior: Integrating theory, research and practice*, pp. 87–102. Cheltenham, UK: Edward Elgar.

Wong, C. S., and Wong, P. M. (2006). Validation of the Wong's career interest assessment questionnaire and the revised Holland's hexagonal model of occupational interests in four Chinese societies. *Journal of Career Development*, 32(4), 378–393.

Wong, C. S., Wong, P. M., and Chau, S. L. (2001). Emotional intelligence, students' attitudes towards life and attainment of education goals: An exploratory study in Hong Kong. *New Horizons in Education*, 44, 1–11.

Wong, C. S., Wong, P. M., and Law, K. S. (2002). *The interaction effect of emotional intelligence and emotional labor on job satisfaction: A test of Holland's classification of occupations in Hong Kong*. Paper presented at the Third International Conference on Emotions and Organizational Life, Gold Coast, Australia (Bond University), July 15–16.

Wong, C. S., Wong, P. M., and Law, K. S. (2005). The interaction effect of emotional intelligence and emotional labor on job satisfaction: A test of Holland's classification of occupations. In C.E.J. Härtel, W. J. Zerbe, and N.M. Ashkanasy (Eds.), *Emotions in organizational behavior*, pp. 235–250. Mahwah, NJ: Lawrence Erlbaum.

Wong, C. S., Wong, P. M., and Law, K. S. (2007). Evidence on the practical utility of Wong's Emotional Intelligence Scale in Hong Kong and mainland China. *Asia Pacific Journal of Management*, 24(1), 43–60.

Wong, C. S., Wong, P. M., and Peng, K. Z. (2006). *Effect of middle-level leader and teacher emotional intelligence on school teachers' job satisfaction: The case of Hong*

Kong. Paper presented at the fifth Asia Academy of Management Conference, Tokyo, Japan, December 19–21.

Wong, C.S., Wong, P.M., and Peng, K.Z. (2010). Effect of middle-level leader and teacher emotional intelligence on school teachers' job satisfaction: The case of Hong Kong. *Educational Management, Administration and Leadership,* 38(1), 59–70.

Wong, S., Bond, M.H., and Rodriguez Mosquera, P.M. (2008). The influence of cultural value orientations on self-reported emotional expression across cultures. *Journal of Cross-Cultural Psychology,* 39, 224–229.

Wu, C.Y. (2003). *Emotional labor in work: Conceptual development, related constructs and psychological process.* Unpublished doctoral dissertation, National Taiwan University. (In Chinese)

Wu, K.F., and Walkins, D. (1996). A Hong Kong study of the Job Description Index. *Psychologia,* 37, 89–94.

Wu, W., Liu, Y., Song, L.J., and Liu, J. (2006). Effects of organizational leadership on employee commitment: The moderating role of emotional intelligence. *Journal of Psychology in Chinese Societies,* 7(2), 283–306.

Xu, E., and Huang, X. (2012). Ostracism, Chinese style. In M. Bond and X. Huang (Eds.), *Handbook of Chinese organizational behavior: Integrating theory, research and practice,* pp. 258–271. Cheltenham, UK: Edward Elgar.

Yik, M.S.M. (2010). How unique is Chinese emotion? In M.H. Bond (Ed.), *The Oxford handbook of Chinese psychology,* pp. 205–220. New York: Oxford University Press.

Yik, M.S.M., and Bond, M.H. (1993). Exploring the dimensions of Chinese person perception with indigenous and imported constructs: Creating a culturally balanced scale. *International Journal of Psychology,* 28, 75–95.

Yiu, J.W., Mak, W.W.S., Ho, W.S., and Chui, Y.Y. (2010). Effectiveness of a knowledge-contact program in improving nursing students' attitudes and emotional competence in serving people living with HIV/AIDS. *Social Science and Medicine,* 7(1), 38–44.

Yu, Q., and Yuan, D. (2008). The impact of the emotional intelligence of employees and their managers on the job performance of the employees. *Acta Psychologica Sinica,* 40(1), 74–83. (In Chinese)

Zaccaro, S.J., Mumford, M.D., Connelly, M.S., Marks, M.A., and Gilbert, J.A. (2000). Assessment of leader problem-solving capabilities. *Leadership Quarterly,* 11(1), 37–64.

Zavalia, A. (1965). Development of the forced-choice rating scale technique. *Psychological Bulletin,* 63(2), 117–124.

Zhang, W. (1999). Is EQ the key to success? *Nankai Business Review,* 4, 27–45. (In Chinese)

Zhao, M.Y. (1995). *The work stress, social support and emotional exhaustion of the front-line supervisors of agricultural association.* Unpublished master's thesis, National Taiwan Normal University. (In Chinese)

Index

Note: Italicized page numbers indicate a figure on the corresponding page. Page numbers in bold indicate a table on the corresponding page.

For Product Safety Concerns and Information please contact our EU
representative GPSR@taylorandfrancis.com
Taylor & Francis Verlag GmbH, Kaufingerstraße 24, 80331 München, Germany

www.ingramcontent.com/pod-product-compliance
Ingram Content Group UK Ltd.
Pitfield, Milton Keynes, MK11 3LW, UK
UKHW021014180425
457613UK00020B/945

* 9 7 8 0 3 6 7 3 5 0 3 8 3 *